THE
JAMES BROWN
READER

THE JAMES BROWN READER

50 Years of Writing About THE GODFATHER OF SOUL

EDITED BY
NELSON GEORGE
AND ALAN LEEDS

 A PLUME BOOK

PLUME
Published by the Penguin Group
Penguin Group (USA) Inc., 375 Hudson Street, New York, New York 10014, U.S.A. •
Penguin Group (Canada), 90 Eglinton Avenue East, Suite 700, Toronto, Ontario, Canada
M4P 2Y3 (a division of Pearson Penguin Canada Inc.) • Penguin Books Ltd, 80 Strand,
London WC2R 0RL, England • Penguin Ireland, 25 St Stephen's Green, Dublin 2, Ireland
(a division of Penguin Books Ltd) • Penguin Group (Australia), 250 Camberwell Road,
Camberwell, Victoria 3124, Australia (a division of Pearson Australia Group Pty Ltd) •
Penguin Books India Pvt Ltd, 11 Community Centre, Panchsheel Park, New Delhi – 110 017,
India • Penguin Group (NZ), 67 Apollo Drive, Rosedale, North Shore 0632, New Zealand
(a division of Pearson New Zealand Ltd) • Penguin Books (South Africa) (Pty) Ltd, 24
Sturdee Avenue, Rosebank, Johannesburg 2196, South Africa

Penguin Books Ltd, Registered Offices: 80 Strand, London WC2R 0RL, England

First published by Plume, a member of Penguin Group (USA) Inc.

First printing, May 2008
10 9 8 7 6 5 4 3 2 1

Copyright © Nelson George and Alan Leeds, 2008
All rights reserved

Photographs courtesy of Alan Leeds's archive.

Pages 315–316 constitute an extension to this copyright page.

℗ REGISTERED TRADEMARK — MARCA REGISTRADA

CIP data is available.
ISBN 978-0-452-28946-8

Printed in the United States of America
Set in Electra
Designed by Eve L. Kirch

Contents

PART II: 1970s

PART III: 1980s

PART IV: 1990s

PART V: 2000-2007

Acknowledgments

A special thank you to Nicole Nelch, for without her hard work, dedication, and perseverance this book would not exist.

Time Line

by Alan Leeds

1933

May 3: James Joseph Brown Jr. born to James Joseph and Susan Brown in Barnwell, South Carolina.

1937

James's parents split up, leaving the youngster in his father's custody. He is primarily raised by an aunt in nearby Augusta, Georgia.

1949

Convicted of breaking and entering, James Brown is imprisoned at the Alto Reform School near Toccoa, Georgia.

1952

June 14: Brown is paroled and settles in Toccoa, Georgia, where he works as a janitor and sings with pal Bobby Byrd's Gospel Starlighters.

1953

The Gospel Starlighters form the Avons, a companion group to perform secular music. Brown marries Velma Warren of Toccoa.

1955

The Avons are renamed the Famous Flames and move to Macon, Georgia, after Little Richard recommends them to his manager Clint Brantley.

November: The Flames record a demo of their song "Please, Please, Please" at a Macon radio station.

1956

January: Record producer Ralph Bass signs the Famous Flames to Federal Records, a subsidiary of King Records in Cincinnati, Ohio.

March: "Please, Please, Please" becomes a national R & B hit and the Flames begin touring the Southeast, often appearing on bills with the likes of Ray Charles, B. B. King, Guitar Slim, The "5" Royales, and Hank Ballard and the Midnighters.

December: The Flames sign with Ben Bart's Universal Attractions, a major New York talent agency.

1957

March: Unable to duplicate the success of their first record, the group goes home. By October, Brown has resumed performing with a new set of Famous Flames.

1958

September 18: Faced with being dropped by Federal Records, Brown records "Try Me" in New York, and the record becomes his first No. 1 disc.

October: On the strength of "Try Me," road bookings increase and Brown picks up a full-time combo led by saxophonist J. C. Davis.

1959

April 24: Brown, his band, and a third group of Flames make their debut at Harlem's Apollo Theater in support of Little Willie John.

October: Frustrated that King Records has no interest in recording his band, Brown cuts "(Do the) Mashed Potatoes" under the name of drummer Nat Kendrick for Dade Records in Miami. The disc becomes a surprise hit and King has a rapid change of heart.

1960

February: Brown spends a couple of weeks as part of an all-star tour that includes Fats Domino, Jerry Lee Lewis, Hank Ballard, and B. B. King.

December 2: Brown opens his first Apollo Theater engagement as a headliner.

1961

February 9: A marathon recording session produces three hits, "Lost Someone," "Night Train," and "Shout and Shimmy."

March: A press release announces James Brown's debut as an organist and band leader on his spring tour of Texas and California.

October 19: Brown and the Flames make their national television debut on Dick Clark's popular *American Bandstand*.

1962

October 24: Brown records his show at the Apollo Theater.

1963

March: "Prisoner of Love" becomes Brown's first Top 20 single on the pop charts.

May: James Brown Live at the Apollo is released and spends a year near the top of both the pop and R & B charts. Brown's tour itinerary skyrockets from the "chitlin' circuit" to concert halls and college bookings.

August: Brown signs an agreement to produce protégés Bobby Byrd and Anna King for Smash Records of Chicago. Smash expresses interest in acquiring Brown as an artist when his King contract expires.

September: Brown headlines the Biggest Show of Stars, thirty days of one-nighters with a cast that included Marvin Gaye, Martha and the Vandellas, and the Drifters.

October 4: Brown encounters creative differences with King Records while recording "Oh Baby Don't You Weep" in Cincinnati. He vows to cut ties with the label.

1964

March: Brown forms the Fair Deal Record Corporation to produce *Showtime*, an album he then leased to Smash Records. King Records claims Brown violated their agreement and begins legal action.

April 2–5: Brown makes his first "downtown" New York appearance at the Paramount Theater for pop radio's WMCA Easter show that costarred the Four Seasons.

July: Brown continues recording for Smash Records while his contractual status is in limbo. The single with "Out of Sight" and "Maybe the Last Time" is a two-sided hit. In October, a New York District Court grants King an injunction prohibiting Smash from distributing any further James Brown recordings. Brown refuses to record for King.

October 28: James and the Flames film *The T.A.M.I. Show,* an all-star pop music extravaganza featuring the Rolling Stones, the Beach Boys, Marvin Gaye, the Supremes, Smokey Robinson and the Miracles, Gerry and the Pacemakers, Jan and Dean, and Chuck Berry. The film is rushed into theatrical release in December.

November 5: The James Brown Show breaks the Apollo Theater house record.

December: James and the Flames make a cameo appearance in the Frankie Avalon teen film *Ski Party,* introducing a new song, "I Got You (I Feel Good)." Due to the ongoing legal battle between Smash and King, the song is unavailable on record.

1965

February: Brown schedules an impromptu, all-night recording session while on tour in Charlotte, North Carolina. He holds on to the tape of "Papa's Got a Brand New Bag," unsure what label will release it.

June: After a year without a new record, Brown reluctantly agrees to give "Papa's Got a Brand New Bag" to King Records. The revolutionary record becomes one of 1965's biggest hits, holding the No. 1 position on the R & B charts for a staggering eight weeks and reaching No. 8 on the elusive pop charts.

August: Suddenly in demand by teen-aimed TV shows, Brown tapes guest appearances on *Shindig, Where the Action Is, Shivaree,* and *The Lloyd Thaxton Show.*

October: King releases "I Got You (I Feel Good)." The record bolts to No. 3 on the pop charts and tops the R & B charts for six weeks.

November 4: Brown breaks his own house record at the Apollo Theater in New York.

1966

March 10–17: Brown takes his show to Paris and the UK for the first time. London's influential *Ready, Steady, Go!* devotes an entire TV program to Brown. The Paris show is filmed and telecast throughout France.

March 19: Brown's debut at New York's Madison Square Garden draws 14,000 fans.

April: Brown leases a sleek six-passenger Lear Jet with which to navigate his hectic schedule of concerts, TV appearances, recording dates, and business obligations.

"It's a Man's Man's Man's World" is released and quickly becomes Brown's third No. 1 R & B record and his third Top 10 pop single.

May 1: Brown, the Flames, and his entire band perform a ten-minute medley on CBS TV's prime-time *Ed Sullivan Show*.

May: Brown is presented with a lifetime membership by the NAACP.

June 25: Brown breaks from his tour schedule to perform at a civil rights rally on the campus of Tougaloo College in Jackson, Mississippi, alongside Sammy Davis Jr., Tony Bennett, Harry Belafonte, and Dr. Martin Luther King Jr.

July: Los Angeles civic leaders and social workers lead Brown on a tour of the Watts area, which had suffered a major civil disturbance during the previous summer.

August 16: Brown records "Don't Be a Drop-Out" and chairs a national media campaign encouraging youngsters to stay in school.

August 25: Brown befriends Vice President Hubert H. Humphrey at an Urban League rally and enlists his support for the "Don't Be a Drop-Out" campaign.

September: Brown signs new exclusive recording and production agreements with King Records under markedly improved terms. He is afforded complete creative control and the authority to sign and produce other artists. King agrees to provide James Brown Productions with office space in its Cincinnati complex.

October 30: Brown returns to the *Ed Sullivan Show* but is denied the opportunity to perform "Don't Be a Drop-Out" when the host deems the song too political for an entertainment program. Brown never again appears on the show.

November: New York governor Nelson Rockefeller and Senator Jacob Javits visit Brown for an impromptu photo op onstage at the Apollo Theater. Brown commends the pair for "recognizing the voters in Harlem" but stops short of any political endorsements.

1967

May: Brown records "Cold Sweat." The innovative disc introduces funk to the R & B canon and reinvents popular music along the way. It's also his fourth No. 1 single.

June 8: Brown hits the late-night talk show circuit with the first of many appearances on NBC TV's *The Tonight Show Starring Johnny Carson*.

June 24–25: Brown records his entire show for *Live at the Apollo, Volume II*. The two-record album includes a landmark, side-long version of "There Was a Time" that establishes his inventive band as the template for several generations of R & B musicians.

July 20–August 9: In his first major booking in the mainstream entertainment world, Brown plays the main show room at the Flamingo Hotel in Las Vegas.

September–October: The James Brown Show's first extensive tour of Europe includes appearances in Berlin, Copenhagen, Amsterdam, Stockholm, Paris, and London.

1968

January: Brown forms James Brown Broadcasting and purchases WJBE Radio in Knoxville, Tennessee, the first of three stations he would own.

Brown tapes TV appearances on *The Hollywood Palace, Happening '68, The Woody Woodbury Show*, and *American Bandstand*.

March 5: King Records owner and Brown mentor Sydney Nathan dies in Miami.

March 27: Brown tapes a syndicated TV special at the Apollo Theater. *James Brown: Man to Man* airs in various markets throughout the summer.

March 29: At the invitation of the president of the Ivory Coast, the James Brown Show flies to Abidjan via charter jet for its first performances in Africa.

April 4: Dr. Martin Luther King Jr. is assassinated in Memphis. Threatened by fears of civil disturbances, Brown arranges for a Boston concert to be telecast and encourages fans to stay off the streets and enjoy the show from home. His efforts are credited with minimizing unrest in the Boston area. On April 6, Brown walks the riot-torn streets of Washington DC, personally urging youngsters to return to their homes. Brown's influence doesn't go ignored by the media; newspaper editorials commend his activities during the days of national unrest.

May 8: Brown and his second-wife-to-be, Deidre Yvonne Jenkins, attend a State dinner at the White House. A handwritten inscription on Brown's place card reads, "Thank you for what you're doing for your country—Lyndon B. Johnson."

June: After two years of frustrating negotiations, Brown takes his show to Vietnam for a series of wartime performances for the troops. The trip also marks first-time visits to Japan and Korea.

June 22: Brown attracts an audience of 40,000 to Yankee Stadium in New York. The show is cut short when adoring fans lose control and rush the stage.

July 29: Brown endorses Vice President Hubert Humphrey's presidential campaign at a rally in the Watts section of Los Angeles.

Summer: Brown becomes an increasingly frequent guest on the busy talk-show circuit, often guesting on the shows of Merv Griffin, Pat Boone, Joey Bishop, Donald O'Connor, Mike Douglas, and Steve Allen.

August 7: Brown records "Say It Loud—I'm Black and I'm Proud." The disc is rushed into release and quickly becomes the anthem for young black America and James Brown's sixth No. 1 hit.

August 12: Brown's father figure and longtime manager Ben Bart dies suddenly of a heart attack on a golf course in New Rochelle, New York. While mourning the death of his beloved "Pops," Brown couldn't help but appreciate that he was now his own manager—with complete authority over every aspect of his career.

September 14–19: Brown spends several off days, taking business meetings and visiting old pals in Macon and Augusta. He begins to consider selling his home in New York and moving back to Georgia.

1969

January 18: Despite having supported Hubert Humphrey, Brown accepts an invitation to perform at President Richard Nixon's inaugural ball in Washington DC.

March: King Records releases "I Don't Want Nobody to Give Me Nothing (Open Up the Door, I'll Get It Myself)," a self-explanatory doctrine sung to a captivatingly creative musical arrangement by Brown bandleader Alfred "Pee Wee" Ellis.

April: Brown assumes ownership of WRDW, the Augusta radio station in front of which he hustled shoe shines as a youngster. He also announces his intention to buy a home and settle in Augusta.

May 25: Brown receives the 1969 Humanitarian of the Year Award from the Music and Performing Arts Lodge of the B'nai B'rith in New York.

June 23–26: Brown tapes a week of programs as cohost of the *Mike Douglas Show.*

July 11: Brown storms out of Los Angeles City Hall empty-handed when Mayor Sam Yorty delegates an underling to present a James Brown Day proclamation. The next day a humbled Mayor Yorty meets with Brown and apologizes.

August 21: The National Business League presents Brown with its Businessman of the Year Award in Memphis.

September 2: Brown presides over the grand opening of his first Gold Platter restaurant in Macon, Georgia, an ambitious but short-lived chain of soul food restaurants.

November 20: Brown and his band record "Funky Drummer." The single is just a minor hit when it's released but Clyde Stubblefield's drum break would live to become the most sampled beat in all of hip-hop.

1970

January 9–25: The James Brown Show follows Elvis Presley into the main show room of the sparkling new International Hotel in Las Vegas.

March 8: In Jacksonville, Florida, disgruntled members of the road-weary James Brown Show present an ultimatum. Unless their demands are met, they will consider refusing to perform the next night in Columbus, Georgia.

March 9: Not to be intimidated, Brown sends for a teenage band that he has been producing in Cincinnati. Beginning with their show in Columbus, Bootsy Collins and the J.B.'s replace suddenly unemployed veterans like Maceo Parker.

April 25: Brown and his new band, whipped into shape by his old sidekick Bobby Byrd, record "GET UP I Feel Like Being a SEX MACHINE." Brown's new sound transfers the emphasis from his horn section and to his dynamic young rhythm section. The record is a runaway hit.

May 12–13: Broadcasting over his WRDW, Brown plays the role of peacekeeper when a racial disturbance erupts in Augusta following a police shooting. Controversial Georgia governor Lester Maddox, elected as an avowed racist, met with Brown at the WRDW studios to offer his appreciation.

October 22: James Brown marries longtime sweetheart Deidre Yvonne Jenkins in Barnwell, South Carolina.

November 28–December 15: Brown tours Africa, including first-time visits to Nigeria and Zambia.

1971

March 18: Brown opens at the posh Copacabana in New York. The shows are sold out, but the two-week booking is cut in half when Brown and Copa management bump heads. Placed on half pay for their unexpected week off, several band members, including Bootsy Collins, give notice.

May: "Hot Pants" is the first release on Brown's own People Records. He also starts Brownstone Records, a partnership with Henry Stone of TK Records in Miami.

July: Brown signs exclusive long-term recording and production agreements with the German-owned Polydor Records. Polydor assumes distribution of the People and Brownstone labels and acquires the masters of all Brown's King recordings. Brown moves his recording operations to Polydor's New York offices and transfers his other businesses to a new headquarters in Augusta.

July 13: "Make It Funky" is Brown's debut single for Polydor and quickly reaches No. 1.

1972

February: Brown records "King Heroin," an antidrug song written by Stage Deli counterman Manny Rosen while imprisoned for defaulting on alimony payments. The unlikely pair plug the hit record on several television shows including Johnny Carson's *Tonight Show.*

March: Jazz legend Miles Davis intently watches a James Brown performance from backstage at the RKO Albee Theatre in Brooklyn, New York. Davis's fascination with the J.B.'s reportedly influenced his *On the Corner* recordings in June and inspired him to add rhythm guitarist Reggie Lucas to his own band.

May 11: Brown is recognized for his work against drug abuse by Georgia governor Jimmy Carter at the State Capitol in Atlanta.

August: "Get on the Good Foot" becomes Brown's third No. 1 single since moving to Polydor Records.

October: Brown visits President Richard Nixon at the White House and agrees to endorse his reelection campaign. Soon thereafter, Brown's appearances begin to attract picket lines of sign-carrying protesters.

December: Brown begins recording the soundtrack album for the Fred Williamson action film *Black Caesar.*

1973

January 29: Saxophone whiz Maceo Parker is welcomed back to the James Brown band with the recording of "Doing It to Death." The party anthem is released under the name Fred Wesley and the J.B.'s on People Records and becomes a No. 1 record.

February–March: The James Brown Show makes first-time visits to South America.

April–May: Brown and arranger Fred Wesley record the soundtrack to another blaxploitation film, *Slaughter's Big Rip-Off.*

June 10: Brown meets teenage preacher Reverend Al Sharpton after a concert in Newark.

June 14: Brown's eldest child, Teddy Brown, is killed in an auto accident in upstate New York. Overwhelmed with grief, Brown buries his son in Toccoa but wills himself to go immediately back on the road.

1974

February: Brown completes a third soundtrack album, for a film called *Hell Up in Harlem*. A film executive rejects the music as "not funky enough." Brown quickly releases it as *The Payback*. The single is his biggest seller in two years, and the album his most successful Polydor effort to date.

Summer: The James Brown Show maintains a barnstorming schedule of one-nighters although attendance fails to keep pace with previous years.

September 6: Brown performs at the Ann Arbor Blues and Jazz Festival along with John Lee Hooker, B. B. King, Sun Ra's Solar Arkestra, Cecil Taylor, and Gil Evans.

September 22–23: Brown headlines an all-star music festival in Kinshasa, Zaire, in conjunction with the Muhammad Ali vs. George Foreman heavyweight title bout. The concert is filmed and portions later appear in the film *When We Were Kings*.

October 25: Rolling Stone Mick Jagger and Atlantic Records mogul Ahmet Ertegun visit the James Brown Show at the Apollo Theater. Jagger joins Brown onstage for an impromptu performance of "Night Train."

1975

January: Brown returns to Africa for first-time performances in Gabon and Senegal. While in Dakar, Brown and his wife solemnly tour the slave-deportation point on Gorée Island.

March 24: Brown sings the national anthem and then contributes color commentary for the telecast of Muhammad Ali's title bout with challenger Chuck Wepner.

October: WTCG TV in Atlanta premieres *Future Shock*, a weekly television music series hosted by James Brown. The show is syndicated across America.

1976

January: Brown performs at the private birthday party of President Omar Bongo in the West African nation of Gabon.

June: Polydor issues "Get Up Offa That Thing." A comeback on the charts, the hit disc does little to improve Brown's fortunes on the road. Unable to sustain a prudent schedule of one-nighters, he accepts bookings in nightclubs like Atlantic City's Club Harlem and Fort Lauderdale's Bachelors III.

1977

January: Brown attends President Jimmy Carter's inaugural ball in Washington DC.

January–March: The James Brown Show musters more lucrative offers abroad than in the United States. Brown tours Europe and Africa with increased frequency.

November: Struggling for bookings, Brown takes his band off payroll.

1978

January: Mired in tax problems, James Brown Broadcasting sells off WJBE. The company is also behind on payments to the previous owner of WEBB in Baltimore. Brown ignores a subpoena to appear at a court hearing.

July 13: Brown is arrested while performing at the Apollo Theater and taken to Baltimore to answer charges regarding the financing of WEBB Radio. He is released following the hearing and completes the Apollo engagement.

1979

March: James and Deidre Brown separate.

March 10: Brown becomes the first R & B entertainer invited to perform at the Grand Ole Opry in Nashville. The controversial appearance is championed by country music legend Porter Wagoner but protested by many of the Opry faithful.

April: With his record sales at an all-time low, Brown appeases Polydor officials by recording with an outside producer. *The Original Disco Man* spawns a mild hit, "It's Too Funky in Here."

September: Brown loses his suburban Augusta home over a property-tax dispute. He soon buys a new property in nearby Beech Island, South Carolina.

October: Brown is baptized at St. Peter's Baptist Church near Williston, South Carolina.

November: Flanked by high-profile attorney William Kuntsler, Brown holds a press conference in New York leveling discrimination charges at the Internal Revenue Service, Polydor Records, and advertising agencies that didn't support his radio stations.

November–December: Brown ends the year with tours in Europe and Japan. He views a live album recorded in Tokyo as completing his obligations to Polydor Records.

1980

April: Brown films a cameo role as a preacher performing a gospel song for John Belushi and Dan Aykroyd's motion picture *The Blues Brothers*. Brown's zesty performance is noted as the film's highlight by countless critics.

September: Brown records a new album for TK Records. A single, "Rapp Payback" draws some attention. Thanks to the new record and *The Blues Brothers* Brown is suddenly embraced by the rock-club circuit patronized by young whites.

December 13: The James Brown "renaissance" continues with a dynamic guest appearance on NBC TV's widely viewed *Saturday Night Live*.

1981

Bookings increase and Brown visits Europe three times in 1981. Back home he sells out rock clubs and special events like the New Orleans Jazz and Heritage Festival.

November 12: Brown is scheduled to perform at Madison Square Garden in New York with the Rolling Stones but cancels when promoter Bill Graham refuses to send a charter jet to ferry Brown and his band to and from Augusta.

1982

March 20–23: Brown begins work on an album for Island Records with Jamaican producers Sly and Robbie at Compass Point Studios in Nassau. Creative differences abort the project.

July 12: Brown makes his first appearance on *Late Night with David Letterman.*

October–November: Brown and soul star Wilson Pickett team up for a successful tour of theaters and concert halls.

December: Brown films a cameo appearance for Dan Aykroyd's *Doctor Detroit.*

1983

March: Brown performs to more than 500,000 people at L'Humanité festival outside Paris.

August 20: Firmly reestablished on the U.S. concert trail, the James Brown Show sells out two shows at the Beverly Theatre in Beverly Hills, California. Contemporary superstars Michael Jackson and Prince make cameo appearances. The shows are taped for cable TV and eventually issued on home video.

1984

June: Brown records "Unity," a one-off project with hip-hop guru Afrika Bambaataa for rap label Tommy Boy Records.

September 9: Despite career revival, Brown's tax problems continue. The IRS seizes his Beech Island home. Augusta attorney Buddy Dallas later buys the property at auction and leases it back to Brown.

September 21: Brown weds Adrienne Modell Rodriguez, his third marriage.

September 23: The Black Music Association pays tribute to Brown at its annual convention in Washington DC. The festivities include performances by George Clinton's P-Funk All Stars with Bootsy Collins and film star Eddie Murphy.

1985

August: Brown records writer-producer Dan Hartman's "Living in America" for the motion picture *Rocky IV*. His elaborately staged performance of the song is a highlight of the hit film. The single becomes Brown's biggest hit in nearly twenty years and leads to a recording agreement with Scotti Brothers Records.

1986

January 23: Brown joins Elvis Presley, Fats Domino, Chuck Berry, Jerry Lee Lewis, Little Richard, Ray Charles, Buddy Holly, the Everly Brothers, Sam Cooke, Sam Phillips, Alan Freed, Jimmie Rodgers, Jimmy Yancey, and Robert Johnson as the inaugural inductees to the Rock and Roll Hall of Fame.

May: James and Adrienne Brown are received by Pope John Paul II at the Vatican during a stop on Brown's two-month European tour.

June 28: The City of Augusta proclaims James Brown Day.

October: Brown's autobiography, *The Godfather of Soul*, is published by Macmillan Books.

1987

January 10: Brown tapes a Cinemax television special in Detroit with guests Aretha Franklin, Robert Palmer, Wilson Pickett, Joe Cocker, and Percy Sledge.

July 5: Brown escapes injury when he wrecks a car he's driving in Augusta.

September 12: Brown is arrested for speeding and reckless driving in Augusta. Rumors of erratic behavior and substance abuse leak from the Brown inner circle.

November 8: Brown is arrested in Aiken, South Carolina, following another traffic mishap.

1988

January: Brown completes an album for Scotti Brothers produced by the hip-hop group Full Force. The LP spawns "Static," a mildly successful single.

April 3: A domestic dispute at the Brown home elevates to violence. Police are called and James Brown is charged with assault and battery. Following his release, Brown flies to South America for several tour dates.

May 18: Brown is charged with resisting arrest after a traffic incident in Aiken.

July: Brown inexplicably cancels some shows in Europe. His band is stranded in Italy.

August–September: Brown undergoes a series of dental procedures for which he is treated with prescription pain medications.

September 12: Brown is arrested in Augusta for speeding.

September 24: Brown invades an insurance seminar, brandishing a shotgun and threatening those who might use his office restroom next door. Police are called and Brown screeches off in his pickup truck, leading officers on a wild two-state chase. His tires are shot out, his truck stalls, and he is arrested. He is indicted on charges by both Georgia and South Carolina. Released on bond, Brown spends four days in an Atlanta drug treatment center.

December 15: A South Carolina court sentences Brown to six years in prison. Rev. Al Sharpton holds a Christmas-week Free James Brown vigil outside the prison.

1989

January 11: Brown is transferred to the State Park Correctional Center in Columbia, South Carolina.

February–March: Led by Rev. Al Sharpton and Rev. Jesse Jackson, many in media and the music industry express dismay at the perceived unfairness of Brown's sentence.

July: Otherwise described as a model prisoner by prison officials, Brown is disciplined when $40,000 in cash is discovered in his cell.

1990

October 28: Credited for good behavior, Brown is placed in a work-release program that affords him the opportunity to travel to and from prison for work-related purposes.

December: Brown receives an unusual four-day Christmas "furlough" in exchange for performing two shows for soldiers and their families at nearby Fort Jackson, South Carolina.

1991

February 27: Brown is paroled and officially released from prison.

March 6: Brown tapes an HBO TV special with hip-hop superstar MC Hammer.

April: Brown's freedom captures the attention of the media. In the first months after his release he tapes appearances on *Today*, the popular sitcom *Amen*, *The Tonight Show*, and *The Arsenio Hall Show*.

June 10: Brown's first comeback concert is a pay-per-view TV special telecast from the Wiltern Theatre in Hollywood.

July: Brown resumes full-time touring, attracting bigger audiences than ever.

1992

January 27: Brown makes an appearance at the American Music Awards in Los Angeles.

February 25: Brown receives a GRAMMY Lifetime Achievement Award in New York.

1994

May 3: Brown hosts his own sixty-first birthday gala at the Augusta Civic Center. Guests include actress Sharon Stone, Bootsy Collins, and rapper Hammer.

December 7: Brown is arrested in South Carolina for assault and battery resulting from a domestic dispute.

1995

May 14: Adrienne Brown is briefly hospitalized after overdosing on prescription drugs.

June–July: Brown spends half of the summer touring Europe, including performances at the Montreux, Pori, and North Sea jazz festivals.

September 2: Brown performs at Cleveland Municipal Stadium for the grand opening of the Rock and Roll Hall of Fame.

1996

January 6: Adrienne Brown dies from a drug reaction following surgery in Los Angeles.

1997

January: James Brown is honored with a star on the Hollywood Walk of Fame.

January 26: James is the featured performer in the Super Bowl half-time show.

August: Brown's tour itinerary includes first-time performances in Beirut and Moscow.

1998

January: Brown spends most of the month in his office, where his associates note his increasingly odd behavior. On January 14, he has an altercation with a longtime employee. Later that day, Brown's daughter finds him standing outside his home in a robe, holding a shotgun. She and Brown's attorney arrange to have him admitted to a care center for evaluation. A week later, he is arrested in Aiken for unlawful possession of marijuana and a weapon without a permit.

March 13: An Aiken court finds Brown guilty of the January charges and retroactively sentences him to the rehabilitation therapy he had voluntarily sought in February. A day later, the James Brown Show resumes a full touring schedule.

1999

November: Brown undergoes successful prostate surgery.

2000

June 15: Brown is inducted into the Songwriters Hall of Fame at a banquet in New York.

June 25: Brown performs with friends and former protégés Bootsy Collins, Bobby Byrd, Fred Wesley, Vicki Anderson, Marva Whitney, and Maceo Parker at the grand opening of Paul Allen's Experience Music Project in Seattle, Washington.

October 20: Brown performs with rock star Lenny Kravitz for the VH-1 /Vogue Fashion Awards at Madison Square Garden in New York.

December 31: Fans and media report strange behavior during Brown's concert at the Blue Note in Las Vegas.

2001

March: Brown is hospitalized in Augusta for "treatment of exhaustion."

June 29: Brown meets President George W. Bush at the White House to commemorate Black Music Month.

November: Brown films a cameo for the film *Undercover Brother.*

December 14: Brown marries Tomi Raye-Hynie in Beech Island, South Carolina.

2002

April 24: Brown receives the Jean Laney Harris Folk Heritage Award from the South Carolina Arts Commission.

May 28: Brown performs with opera legend Luciano Pavarotti at a televised charity concert in Modena, Italy.

August 6: Brown receives the BMI Icon Award at the annual BMI Urban Awards dinner in Miami.

2003

June 24: Brown is presented with the BET Lifetime Achievement Award by Michael Jackson at the annual BET Awards show in Hollywood.

December 7: Brown receives the esteemed Kennedy Center Honor for the performing arts in Washington DC. A national telecast of the ceremonies airs on December 26.

2004

October 3: Brown attends the fiftieth birthday celebration for Rev. Al Sharpton at the Apollo Theater in New York.

December 14: Brown undergoes successful surgery for a recurrence of prostate cancer.

2005

February 13: Brown performs with R & B star Usher at the annual GRAMMY Awards in Los Angeles.

May 6: A life-size statue of James Brown is ceremoniously unveiled in Augusta.

September: Brown makes his first appearances ever in Hong Kong and Kuala Lumpur.

November 21: Brown hosts a Thanksgiving turkey giveaway for the poor in Augusta.

2006

April 6: Brown receives the Martin Luther King Jr. Award from the Keepers of the Dream foundation in New York.

September 6: Brown performs songs from his 1969 *Soul on Top* jazz album at the Hollywood Bowl, with a big band led by bassist Christian McBride.

October 16: Appearing weakened from a year of steady touring, Brown attends the dedication ceremonies for the James Brown Arena in Augusta.

November: Brown's second European tour in six months closes with his induction into the UK Music Hall of Fame and a brief performance. The ceremonies in London are telecast around the globe.

December 23: Brown hosts his annual Christmas toy giveaway at the Imperial Theatre in downtown Augusta.

December 24: Brown drives to Atlanta for dental surgery and is instead hospitalized with pneumonia.

December 25: At 1:45 a.m., with longtime manager Charles Bobbit at his side, James Brown dies at Emory Crawford Long Hospital in Atlanta.

THE
JAMES BROWN
READER

A Few Words About James Brown

by Nelson George

One of the many remarkable things about James Brown was how his long, eventful life mirrored the journey of African Americans in the last century. His childhood and early career were defined by the restrictions of segregation. It was the Jim Crow time, the early decades of the twentieth century, when stifled dreams, cruel barriers, and institutional racism were the American way. Brown was just another dirt-poor Negro boy dancing for money in a redneck town, yet somehow cultivated strong self-esteem within a system devised to quell just such a quality. Not surprisingly, young Brown bumped up against the barricades of whiteness, entering the penal system, an enduring destination for self-satisfied black males who didn't know their place.

In the middle of the twentieth century, Brown was a member of a historic generation of entertainers who pushed the boundaries of American song, dabbling in gospel, blues, jazz, country, and the emerging sound of rock and roll. From barrelhouses and tent shows, from bars and churches, a new attitude toward performance was concocted, just as the civil rights movement was stepping onto the national stage. Brown would become one of the many to embrace "soul" as a style, making secular salvation his stock in trade. Along with impassioned vocalizing, he developed a flamboyant onstage persona—part street dancer, part boxer, part preacher— that would redefine showmanship for his generation, and which resonates to this day.

In the early sixties Brown (and all aspects of Negro life) existed in a parallel universe to the white entertainment world: a legend on one side, an obscurity to the other. The Negro press treated him with amazing reverence, but it wasn't until 1962, with the shocking sales of his *Live at the Apollo*, that he appeared on the radar screen of white media. Alongside the civil rights movement, Brown's career skyrocketed to prominence in the midsixties, becoming one of the ways white America came to understand the suddenly "black" experience. As *soul* became the all-purpose catchphrase for all things black, the entertainer (known as Mr. Brown to all in his orbit) was anointed Soul Brother No. 1.

The heightened sociopolitical atmosphere of the times emboldened Brown to release "Say It Loud—I'm Black and I'm Proud," an anthem for a generation, which placed Brown squarely in the vanguard of black leadership. With Dr. Martin Luther King Jr.'s assassination, blazing urban riots, and the conflicting philosophies that marked the black nationalists era, Brown's vision of economic self-reliance and his naive politics were respected and even envied. It didn't hurt that as a record maker / bandleader Brown had exploded the restrictions of soul, turning the singer-oriented music on its ear, creating a stripped down, intensely rhythmic music like nothing before it. Everything in the James Brown band became about rhythm, with melody an occasional, but far from defining, aspect of his work. "Funk," as it was labeled, changed popular music forever; its influence can be heard in every remix, every sampled snare drum, every time the beat drops.

Brown's rise from victim of Southern segregation to musical/cultural giant is stunning in its single-mindedness. His descent from that peak is equally memorable, as the ghosts of his innovations and power haunted him, maybe driving him a little mad. Just as quickly as Brown's innovations became absorbed (and expanded upon by a raft of freaky young inheritors), his Booker T. Washington–like, up-by-his-own-bootstraps narrative became viewed as exceedingly square and old-fashioned. The once undiluted praise Brown enjoyed gave way to critiques from inside his organization and ridicule from outsiders.

By the midseventies, Brown was struggling for relevance (*The Original Disco Man*) as black culture began its long descent into fragmentation along class, geographic, and aesthetic lines. In the articles and reviews of his work from this time forward there's a sense that Brown is a living symbol of a lost world, a landscape of noble striving obscured by the upward mobility of integration and the wreckage left for those who couldn't escape. Hip-hop, a musical aesthetic reliant on Brown's recordings for its essence, brought a slight return to respectability for him. His ego, by then not just outsized, but damaged, was somewhat soothed by the attention and, eventually, the revenue stream the sampling of his songs generated.

Still, Brown chafed at no longer being at the center of the culture and remained a man out of time. Tragically, drug addiction, an evil he railed against so passionately as a young star, ensnared him. In fact Brown became sadly contemporary again, since entrapment by crack made his just one of thousands of African American lives wrecked by "beaming up to Scotty" in the nineties.

After jail, rehab, and ugly romantic entanglements, Brown reclaimed his lost dignity by going home (aka back on the road). In the last section of his life, Brown found himself hailed as an aging icon, soldiering on night after night, grinding out bits of the old spark, his mere appearance conjuring ancient "chitlin' circuit" rituals for those who were there (or have seen the *T.A.M.I. Show* tape).

Brown played for so long that generations of grandmas, mothers and fathers, and grandchildren watched him shout, shake, and shimmy for their edification. Entire forests have fallen to build the newsprint mountain that recounts his exploits, declarations, and influence. Though his fortunes rose and fell, though he was ghettoized, deified, parodied, and reclaimed, Brown himself was a remarkably consistent man. His core values and views—sometimes inspiring, usually self-involved, and on occasion wacky—flowed from a dogged determination to be true to himself. Back when Jim Crow reigned and death by lynching was a daily threat, Brown saw that all a black man had to count on was who he thought he was, not what others did. Self-definition meant survival. It was no accident that so many of his songs were sung in the first person. James Brown was at the center of his universe, a universe he allowed us, happily, to dance in.

PART I

1960s

"Apollo, N.Y."

author unknown
December 16, 1959 • *Variety*

Little Willie John, Drifters (4), Flames (9), Laura Johnson, Stan Kirk, Reuben Phillips Band (12); "Return of the Fly" (20th Fox).

Little Willie John is not only the star-singer of this Apollo session but the m.c., and in both capacities attempts valiantly to make something cohesive out of what is otherwise a haphazard collection of acts. Young performer has an easy, winning way and provides show's best moments when he takes over the mike next-to-closing and belts out four numbers ranging from rock 'n' roll to pop to blues. He's an energetic but disciplined performer with a lot of the rhythmic drive that marks Johnnie Ray's delivery, especially in the sweet-tempoed "Talk to Me" and the bluesy "Anytime, Anyplace, Anywhere."

Laura Johnson opens the bill nicely singing three numbers each of which starts in soft, lazy style and quickly upbeats to a gutty conclusion that is a mixture of early, raffish blues and r & r. Thrush goes off to a good if not overly enthusiastic hand—the audience clearly impatient for the rockers to follow.

The four-man Drifters whet the r & r apetite a little more, providing four solid if almost identical numbers, with the Flames coming on for the show's climax.

Latter group, led by James Brown, almost blows out the walls to the obvious delight of audience. It isn't so much a group as collection of performers—singers and musicians—who seem just to have happened onstage at the same time. They use two mikes with three harmonizers deployed at one while leader Brown backed by two electric guitars, drums and two saxes occupies the other. The result is near-anarchy, with each man rocking in his little "big beat" world. Some stage direction to simplify all the movement, and mikes more carefully adjusted to the noise, might improve the act, but Apollo audiences probably couldn't love them more, no matter what.

Bill's comedy portion is handled in strictly so-so fashion by Stan Kirk, a young comic suffering acutely from lack of material. Imitations of Mortimer Snerd, the Kingfish, Liberace and Elvis drew only a few snickers. Reuben Phillips band gives good support to the entire bill. *Can.*

"James Brown Boasts New Tune And Dance"

author unknown
September 27, 1960 • *Chicago Daily Defender*

Curious individuals who so often seek "what goes" answers in their hope to discover how name of a dance like "The Madison" came into being occasionally come up with correct answer.

Frankly, there is no record at hand to explain why the latest dance craze is called "The Madison." However, in most cases the dance stems from tune of same name after it reaches the top in recordings. Such was the case with "Trucking" that produced both a dance step and a song. Later, the "Jersey Bounce," became a popular dance after someone had heard the song by the same name that made the late Tiny Bradshaw a top orkster.

Certainly old timers will remember that a song called "The Charleston" induced dance experts to come up with a dance routine by same name. "The Continental" was a top tune long before Hollywood chose to introduce Fred Astaire and Ginger Rogers in a dance by same name. And there have been countless others that can be catagoried likewise.

Now comes James Brown, a lad from Macon, Georgia introducing a song titled "Mashed Potatoes." Difference here is that Brown also introduced the dance by same name and at same time he came forward with the tune, a successful disc attempt for 1960.

Brown, at 27, is no stranger to disc circles even though a new comer to the dance introduction field. His previous discs on Federal label, including "Think," "Please, Please, Please" plus "Try Me" and "You've Got The Power" have already hit the top for the season.

While James Brown has gone places as a single he is perhaps best known to music lovers as founder of the "Famous Flames" back in his hometown several seasons ago. The "Famous Flames" have become national favorites and to James Brown goes much of the credit for the spot they occupy in the national spotlight.

"Dick Clark Spotlights James Brown's Flames"
author unknown
October 29, 1960 • *Chicago Daily Defender*

Dick Clark, the nationally known producer of ABC-TV's popular "American Bandstand" show, is making arrangements to spotlight James Brown and his Famous Flames on his nation-wide television program within the next month.

Clark, ABC-TV's standout talent show producer, became interested in Brown shortly after he first heard him sing his recordings of "Think," "Try Me" and "This Ole Heart."

Known for bringing the nation's top entertainers to his "American Bandstand" show regardless of race, color or creed, Dick Clark's presentation of an artist on his top-rated video program is widely considered as an indication that a performer has arrived at the "big time."

"James Brown: Vitality, Humility, Soul, Talent"

Eva Dolin
June 13, 1964 • *Chicago Daily Defender*

The name James Brown is easily the terse answer to the question, "What is talent?"

The amazing talent of Brown stands out from all the rest. He weeps the blues into a flaming torch and in a breathless change of pace swings his magic into a bouncing, rollicking song explosion of the power and blaze of an atomic blastoff.

An accomplished musician, he plays with startling brilliance the organ, drums, bass guitar and piano. A brilliant composer, his self-penned songs and arrangements rank with the world's great songwriters. There is no end to the James Brown talent. Year after year, Brown produced records score on the national pop and rhythm and blues hit charts, making him the record industry's ace producer. His instinct in seeing star potential in new performers has led to his discovery of such talents as Anna King and Bobby Byrd, and successful productions of their Smash Records chart-riding platters.

On stage, he is producer and star of the famous James Brown Show, the biggest and most successful road show in all America. He is Mr. Showbusiness—dancing out all the excitement that surrounds him. His incredulous versatility includes, too, leadership of one of the most powerful, most explosive bands in the nation.

Grossing well over a million dollars each year, the Brown show is big business and big talent. James has won national acclaim not only for his exciting performances, but for unbelievable endurance on stage—unmatched in the world of showbusiness.

He has been known to sing and dance a single routine or song for over forty minutes, electrifying not only the audience, but the musicians in his band. Millions of fans across the nation wonder how one person can have so much drive and energy and talent.

When asked why he stays on stage for repeated encores, why he will sing 12 or 14 songs in one set compared to six by other performers, James replies: "Because the people who come to see me are the ones who put me where I am today and satisfying them is the only way I can thank them."

James Brown has not forgotten that not too many years ago he hustled nickels and dimes on street corners as a shoe shine boy in Augusta, Ga., where he was born. Nor has he forgotten that his father, a talented blues singer and guitar player, had to move his family from town to town, looking for the "break" that was never to come.

Brown is grateful to millions of fans, for he learned early the lessons of hard work and showmanship, selling newspapers after school and far into the night, to help his father support the family.

Although James inherited his father's musical ability, plus his own special God-given singing talent, he was far more interested in pursuing a career in sports during his early youth. Perhaps his father's defeat in the entertainment world that refused to recognize him as a star, was responsible for James' own lack of enthusiasm for showbusiness.

Instead, the youth turned to the neighborhood gym and an intense interest in boxing. In Macon, Ga., where the family had moved, James met Beau Jack, former boxing great, while working out in the gym. Impressed with the youngster's boxing skill and amazingly fast footwork, Jack offered to help the boy and encouraged him to become a professional boxer.

However, destiny was reaching out for the hand of talent and without reason, James suddenly lost interest in boxing. He turned next to another sport in which he excelled—baseball. He was at his peak on the baseball field as a pitcher with a professional baseball team when he suffered a severe leg injury and was forced to give up his sports activities. It was then that destiny won her battle with talent and James turned seriously to his musical gifts and a career in showbusiness.

However, today, he gives credit to his early boxing training, footwork drills and swinging pitch on the baseball diamond as being responsible for his unique dancing style on stage, and unbelievable endurance.

Encouraged by his parents, James formed his own musical group and called them, "The Famous Flames." Singing jobs for groups were scarce in Macon, but the talented leader managed somehow to pick up enough odd jobs to keep The Flames working regularly.

Leaning toward gospel and spirituals, he built his early reputation in this field. But slowly, the musical excellence of the group caught the attention of local critics and rave reviews began appearing after each local appearance.

In January, 1956, James decided his group would get nowhere unless the world outside of Macon could listen and judge. So he arranged to cut an audition record in a local radio station without musical accompaniment. He found that after the quartet pooled their resources for the waxing their depleted funds amounted to a one-way bus fare home! Immediately after the recording session he hurriedly wrapped the freshly waxed dub and rushed to a disc jockey friend, pleading that he play it on the air. As a favor, the song went on the air. The tune was "Please, Please, Please." Minutes after it was aired the station's switchboard was ablaze with calls and requests for airplay of the sensational recording. The James Brown success story had begun.

"James Brown Just 'Sings His Heart Out'"

author unknown
September 4, 1965 • *Chicago Daily Defender*

James Brown, his orchestra and new stage revue appear in person at the Regal theatre starting September 24 for one week. What makes James Brown go? What is he like? "He's a business man. He sings his heart out." These two qualities have made Brown the most consistent rock and roll seller since the first record in 1956.

How did he break in: "Well I'd have to say it was a very hard thing; and it still got a long way to go", Brown said. "I started, actually, at a talent show in Augusta, Ga., this was sometime ago; I won't say when because I can keep my age that way, but it was kind of a luck thing, because at that time I was a prize fighter. I had won three professional fights and I had a chance to play pro baseball. At this talent show they were short of contestants and needed another. Just for kicks, I went up and started "screaming" also winning my first singing prize. From that day to this one I'm still "screaming.""

Bobby Byrd, who is the only original member of Brown's singing group, the "Flames" described how Brown made his first hit. "We recorded "PLEASE, PLEASE, PLEASE", which James wrote and arranged for an Augusta radio station. A talent scout for a record company was passing through and heard it. He had us cut our first album, "PLEASE" and "TRY ME". We didn't know it was a hit. About the time we cut our first album, "PLEASE" the Army had drafted the other Flames.

"The Flames have been reorganized twice since then but, I'm still around. James started me as a star four years ago and Anna King also. Lloyd Price and Bobby Bennett are the other Flames. Both will cut records for James Brown Productions soon."

Brown described his early years of singing: "We started out with a guitar and no drums. We use to stomp on the floor for time. Well, I've worked many nights earning one quarter, 25 cents a piece . . . after we paid our expenses, worked all night long, just like I'm working now . . . way before "PLEASE".

Brown has helped establish not only Bobby Byrd and Anna King. "We have another kid from Georgia—James Crawford. He's a good entertainer and he's going to be very big.

Remember the Five Royales, from Winston Salem, N.C.? I've just re-recorded them through Try Me Music, which he owns.

"Now I'm getting ready to do a movie the last of this month for Warner Brothers. I intended to be an actor, just anything that means entertainment; I want to be able to do it. Brown can play any instrument on the stage. "I've never taken music in my life. I learned on the road.

"I'm lucky to have following of teenagers, adults—everybody. I'm appreciative of the fact, and I don't mean to brag but, we're the only act that can and does work seven days a week, 365 a year . . ."

What makes him "the hardest working man in show business?" Two things. As a kid my family was very poor. Being poor will make you more determined." Second: "I try to please the people. What they want, I try to give. If I'm not able to do so I'll have to step back and give it to the younger ones".

Although Brown is in great demand as the acknowledged "King of Rhythm and Blues," he has not slowed the nightly, year-round pace he started 10 years ago. "I probably could select the shows and towns I want to play but, I don't want to feel that big. It's up to them to select the artist they want. If it's me, I'll be there. . . ."

Brown has written and arranged most of his material. It is this that has made him the most consistent record seller in eight years ". . . I want to tell you something I pity the cat that has to write it . . . you've got to feel everything you do.

"Go beyond me. Even when I arrange for the cats and girls in my stable, as we call it. I try to find their soul. Of course, you's got to give up some of yourself but, I still try to find what this cat or this girl feels."

Brown, today, has the biggest group act in the United States. Along with: Bobby Byrd, James Crawford, Elsie Mae (TV MAMA), and The Famous Flames.

The James Brown show includes an eighteen piece band. Five recently added members from North Carolina, and two: Melvin and Messeo, were with a local combo, the Bluenotes.

Commenting on the group's success, Brown said "I don't know how long this will last. I'll be doing my utmost to keep it in the same place but, you can't ever tell . . . I accepted stardom, I'll accept defeat."

"James Brown Meets the Nine Nobles"

Ron Courtney
May 9, 1986 • *Goldmine*

The period from 1960 to 1964 was a desperately poor time for rock 'n' roll music. By 1960 virtually all the '50s originators were either dead, in jail, or had become emasculated "pop" singers like Bobby Vee or Bobby Rydell, and it wasn't until the Beatles blew it all away in 1964 that real rockers began to appear again on Top 40 radio. The only way to hear any music with feeling was to turn your radio dial to the black R&B station and keep it there. That's where you could hear Bobby "Blue" Bland, Ike and Tina Turner, and the "hardest working man in show business," James Brown and the Famous Flames.

Three friends and I had a four-piece garage band in Richmond, Va., in 1960, known as the Confusion Combo, named after "Coffee and Confusion," a Washington, D.C. beatnik hangout. By the beginning of 1963, we had grown into a nine-piece R&B band with two tenor saxophones, a baritone sax, and a trumpet on top, and were known throughout the area as the Nine Nobles. We were nine middle-class white boys by day, but when those horns started gleaming in the spotlight, in our hearts we became blacker than a midnight alley in Harlem.

We bought our band uniforms from a little shop in the black section of downtown Richmond. They were a slightly iridescent beige with a black stripe down the outside of each pants leg, and short little waist-length coats with about 40 buttons down the tiny lapel. We looked like nine white porters in a run-down hotel.

At first we modeled our band on the local black bands in the Richmond area, doing a wide variety of R&B in a somewhat mild manner. But early in 1963, something happened that gave us a specific direction and made us one of the most popular white bands in the area: King Records released the *James Brown Live At The Apollo* LP and our lives suddenly acquired purpose and meaning!

Like Otis Redding and Little Richard, James Brown spent his early years kicking around on the streets of Macon, Ga. After spending a few years in boxing and semi-pro baseball, he began singing and playing drums with a group called the Famous Flames, and in 1956 they signed with King/Federal Records of Cincinnati and released "Please Please, Please," the first of a long string of R&B singles. In the late '50s, James became the star of the group and eventually eclipsed the other members completely and began to build a musical organization that became by far the most impressive one in black show business.

Fats Domino and Little Richard had superb touring bands but they basically just stood behind the star and played. James Brown's orchestra was part of a carefully choreographed show, fully integrated into the act and designed to have the maximum impact on an audience. Brown's every move was planned and rehearsed endlessly with the band so that it all worked so smoothly that it looked totally spontaneous. I once managed to get into an afternoon rehearsal at the Richmond Arena, where Brown was working out with his band. Dressed in a sportshirt and slacks, he mercilessly worked on a single routine for over an hour until he and the band were perfectly synchronized. An extraordinarily demanding taskmaster, he pushed his men to the limits of their ability, threatening to fire them on the spot if they didn't get it right. The result of this kind of precision drilling was the finest, tightest band and show in the business.

One day in early 1963, I walked into the Globe Record Shop, a small R&B oriented record store where I had worked the year before, and saw, prominently displayed on the wall, a copy of *James Brown Live At The Apollo*. There was a wonderfully moody watercolor of the Apollo Theatre marquee on the front cover, with some dark and mysterious figures moving through the mist. Just as I imagined life in the ghetto must be! The back of the LP had a small close-up photo of a very sweaty James Brown pleading into the microphone (*got* to be doing "Please, Please, Please!"), his shirt drenched with perspiration, his coat long since discarded with a great flourish, and his tie whipped off in furious abandon, but you can still see one of his cufflinks so you know the show is not quite over!

My parents nearly went into shock when I brought the album home and played it; they had never heard anything so black before. This wasn't just sepia or mahogany or burnt umber, this was darkest ebony, midnight on the Congo, kill-the-missionaries jet black! I thought it was wonderful.

The album was recorded with a piercing intimacy: you feel as if you're in the first row or even right up on the stage with James, prancing and grunting along with him, matching him step for step. The recording technique is a little uneven by today's standards perhaps, though this is probably due to poor mixing, but it is by far the best live rock or R&B LP done up to 1963, and it captures the electricity of a live performance as well as any live LP I've ever heard.

Side One starts off with Luke Gonder, Brown's rotund organist, introducing James Brown while the band plays half tones up the scale, punctuating each phrase that Gonder utters. Brown dances onto the stage as the band riffs on two frantic verses of "Hold It," the updated Bill Doggett song that James used as a theme at the time. Brown's opening words are "You know, I feel all right," the guitar hits the intro to "I'll Go Crazy," and they all take off in a mad frenzy from song to song without a letup. Brown croons a swaying "Try Me" and then jumps into a manic "Think" done so fast he can hardly get the words in. Following a haunting version of "I Don't Mind," Brown hits his stride in a 20-minute performance of "Lost Someone," his major hit at the time, a marvelously evocative rendering in which he wrings every ounce of anguish out of the pain of lost love. By this time, any doubters who may have been in the theatre are converted believers and James Brown has total control of his audience.

Everyone is completely mesmerized as Brown begs and pleads and cries and screams while the band repeats a single pattern until time almost seems to stop. Suddenly, the drummer gives out one staccato 'whack!' on his snare, perfectly timed as Brown drops to his knees and "Please, Please, Please" is born like some savage Phoenix from the ashes of "Lost Someone." By this time, you're well into Side Two of the record and Brown goes into a long medley of his hits, ending with a pulsing, driving version of "Night Train" that brings down the house. I'm sure everyone in the theatre must have been totally exhausted by this time.

This record, coupled with actually seeing James Brown perform several months later, had a powerful effect on the Nine Nobles: we were transformed from nine white high school boys who played a fairly tame brand of rhythm 'n' blues, into a tightly knit miniature Caucasian version of James Brown and his Famous Flames. Of course, we couldn't do it quite the way he could. At the finale of a James Brown concert, with Brown on his knees screaming "Please, Please, Please," one of the Flames would put a cape around his shoulders and attempt to lead him off stage. A totally despondent Brown is led docilely away until he reached the curtain, where he would throw aside the cape and dash back to the microphone for a few more verses, sending the audience into a frenzy.

We had no idea where to find a cape so we bought a fuzzy, bright blue bath rug. As we were about to go into "Please, Please, Please," Dave Dunville, the other lead singer in the band, would spread it out in front of the microphone with great dignity while I stood dramatically aside, waiting. Then the drummer would pop his snare and I would drop down with the microphone, knees on the blue rug, screaming "Please, Please, Please" at the top of my lungs. After several minutes of this madness, Dave would lead me off, the bath rug draped around my shoulders, tired but clean! Since the audience at a typical James Brown concert was 95 percent black and our audiences were always 100 percent white, virtually none of the kids who heard us had any inkling of where we got our frantic act, but they must have liked it because we were always booked solid.

Towards the end of a James Brown concert, he would yank off his tie at a suitable moment and throw it out into the audience, followed shortly by his cufflinks. Then, as the pressure intensified, he would take out his handkerchief, mop his sweat-drenched face and toss it out to his frenzied congregation. At such a show in Richmond in late 1963, the entire Nine Nobles band and our dates were seated in the first two rows in the center of the Orchestra section, the finest seats in the house, and when James hurled his handkerchief at us, it landed in the orchestra pit, not three feet in front of me! Seeing an unexpected opportunity, I vaulted over the railing and emerged triumphantly, handkerchief in hand.

I was a little disappointed to find that this was a plain white handkerchief;

I had expected it to have "JB" monogrammed on it in 24K gold thread. There was nothing to identify it as James Brown's handkerchief, but it was covered with brown pancake makeup and the entire Nine Nobles entourage had seen me snatch it, so I felt that my place in local rock 'n' roll history was secure. Flush with confidence, I placed my trophy in the top drawer of the bureau in my bedroom, where it could lord it over the other handkerchiefs. Except for when I took it out to show someone that I had James Brown's handkerchief, it lay undisturbed for four or five years.

However, never underestimate the power of a marauding mother. One day, after having moved to my own apartment, I had told the story of James Brown's handkerchief to some new friends and I went back to my parents' house to pick up the proof, the famous handkerchief.

To my utter horror, when I opened the drawer I saw half a dozen neatly folded, pristine white handkerchiefs—not a sign of the brown-stained treasure I had left there years before. A confrontation with my mother led to her confession (not at all contrite) that she had washed all my handkerchiefs, "particularly that nasty brown one!" and had put them all back in the drawer. Lost forever! One of those plain whities once had the honor of wiping the brow of the mighty James Brown, but which one?

Oh, well, I still have the album and the memories. Thank you, Mr. Dynamite.

"James Brown Is Out of Sight"

Doon Arbus
March 20, 1966 • *The New York Herald Tribune*

I've been waiting for ages. After all, he's very big now and getting bigger every minute, so it's not that he's oblivious or inconsiderate. It's a vital part of his social and professional dynamics to keep me waiting outside in the cold, sitting on the wrought iron bench in the front yard, gazing at the mysterious stone cupola with the two tiny, impenetrable cut-glass windows. It's his home, his strangely exotic home in the St. Albans section of Queens; part castle, part hacienda; and somewhere inside he is lying asleep. He works very hard so he likes to sleep as late as possible.

Well, he's a big man. Anyone familiar with the facts admits that. His two latest records, "Pappa's Got A Brand New Bag" and "I Got You," have sold over one million copies each. He tours the country with his own show 335 days a year, performing for an average of 5,000 people a day. Today, March 20, he will be at Madison Square Garden. He and his show will be the sole attraction.

He has never appeared in midtown Manhattan before—only at the Apollo in Harlem and at the Brevoort in Brooklyn, which is why few New Yorkers have seen him or heard him or even know who he is. It's strange, because he has gathered an enormous following throughout the greater part of the nation because of his records and personal appearances. But New York isn't with it when it comes to him.

I only saw him once, in the TAMI Show, JAMES BROWN AND THE FAMOUS FLAMES! It was filmed in Electronovision, which may account for his looking so peculiar; after all, so did everybody else: Lesley Gore and The Beach Boys and The Supremes. But he looked strangest of all—the giant head and broad shoulders, and the rest of him progressively smaller. Short legs. Tiny feet.

Someone finally does let me in the house, after he wakes up and says it's okay. Nobody does anything without orders from the boss, but when he wakes up and gives the word, someone lets me in through the back door into the den, which looks like a gymnasium all upholstered in black leatherette with a great post in the middle of the room. It's very bare. Photographs of him are crowded onto the wall above the imposing curved bar—photographs of him, beaming proudly as he accepts an award or demonstrating enthusiasm as he signs an autograph for a child or sweating luxuriously on his knees over the microphone. They hang in a cluster amidst the rows of bottles, and there are shelves with rows of plaques and trophies engraved with praise. "To The Hardest Working Performer." Three large white B's are emblazoned on the black upholstered wall at the staircase.

Every few moments someone wanders into the den and pauses in the middle of the room distractedly, standing there muttering about the cold or the time or a lost shoe or what car to take to the airport, then wandering out again. James Brown has to catch a four o'clock plane to Virginia Beach—there is a show that evening. A few people will fly down with him, the few that are still here, like Bobby Byrd and Bobby Bennett and Lloyd Stallworth, the three Famous Flames. All the other members of the show have already left: the musicians in the band and the band leader, Nat Jones; and James Brown's own girl group, The Three Jewels; and all the members of the unaccountably popular burlesque comedy acts. They have gone ahead in the private bus. The equipment and the instruments have left in the two-ton truck, and all the costumes have been packed away in the black plastic garment bags, each with a white B on the front, and driven down by car. That's the way it always is when the James Brown Show is on tour.

Nobody seems to know exactly how many people travel with the show, or if they do know, they're not sure if it mightn't be some kind of betrayal to reveal the exact number. So some say 40 and some say 50 and some just say "a whole lot." That's the way they are: cautious and guarded, afraid to say anything that might be used against James Brown. ("What are you trying to find out? You looking for the good things? Or you just wanna know bad things?") They believe in him. He *is* the whole show; he writes the music and the lyrics, he does the arrangements, and he does the choreography. He designs all the costumes and makes all the decisions. With some mystical, magnetic force, he keeps the whole thing together, all the parts working as a unit. He's got something, but they'll never tell what it is. Maybe they don't even know. All they know is that each has to be *best* in what he does. "The whole show has got to be the *greatest*."

Bobby Bennett, one of The Famous Flames, has come into the den from upstairs. He wears a shiny brick red suit, black nylon socks and a big jewelled ring that cost him $10,000, which he has to remember to give to someone to hold for him before he goes on stage. But it doesn't make him nervous, not a bit.

Bobby goes into a small room off the den. It has all sorts of black appliances in it: a black refrigerator, a black sink, a black washing machine. It also has an ironing board, which is what Bobby needs—he has come to iron his clothes. "Yes sir. You gotta learn to do everything yourself. No one's gonna do it for you. So you learn. 'Cause there's a $20 fine for having wrinkles in your clothes. Or making a bad goof on stage. Or gettin' in trouble. It's like the Army," he explains cheerfully. "You gotta have discipline. Otherwise, where are you at? Without discipline, nothin' gets done right." The fines go into the treasury to pay for parties and other good things.

Mr. Brown is upstairs in curlers under the dryer. Bobby has just finished putting Mr. Brown's hair up in curlers and Mr. Brown under the dryer. He does it every day, to get the kinks out, and to make Mr. Brown's hair big and round. Bobby says I can't go up yet. Nat Stillwell, the chauffeur, in an elegant blue-gray uniform, comes to collect the suitcases. There are three cars in the garage: the purple Cadillac limousine, the red Stingray with "Mr. Dynamite" painted on the side and the white '66 Cadillac. The Cad's the one Mr. Brown has decided to take to the airport, since it's very roomy. Bobby goes upstairs to check on Mr. Brown's hair. Nat Stillwell goes outside with the suitcases to check on the white Cadillac. I sink down onto one of the smooth, black couches to wait some more.

Bobby calls from upstairs, "You wanna come up now? It's okay." I go up the winding staircase into the main hall with the bright glass chandelier and the spongy green carpet protected with long strips of plastic. It is as if the whole house were being preserved against the hazards of being lived in, as if it were being prepared for a great future as a museum. It's embarrassingly exhilarating to look through the glass in the front door and see the outside and the wrought iron bench and the three teenagers standing by the white Cadillac, restless, intent on the house. From the outside all that can be seen in the glass is a reflection.

Bobby offers me some house slippers from the giant black suitcase or shoe box or whatever-it-is. It stands almost as tall as he does and has a very strange shape. In a way, it looks like a B, although it doesn't look like one at all. Bobby reaches way into the mouth of it and tosses the house slippers onto the floor, unmatching green and blue scuffs with Japanese-looking flowers or trees embroidered on the toes. I pick the two I like the best and hand him my own shoes, feeling as if I'm about to enter the doctor's office for an examination, or the holy sepulchre, or both. Bobby leads the way up a carpeted ramp through the living room with the Japanese prints and the couches all covered in plastic, into the kitchen.

Yes, he is there. He is enthroned after a fashion on a straight-backed kitchen chair against the wallpaper of orange and yellow flowers, his head of curlers resting lazily against the wall. He looks like the blackest man on earth. He seems to blot out the light where he sits, which may be what makes him appear so black.

"Just call me James," he says, smiling grandly, magnanimously. His teeth are set in a neat, gleaming row, a rectangular smile in a dark face. "How about a drink?" He uses my first name right from the start. It puts him in control, implying intimacy while remaining aloof. "Don't you want a drink? Something? Aw, come on. *Sure* now?" He has made himself the host, so *he* directs the conversation. *He* asks the questions.

The short kimono robe hangs open at his chest. A silver thing strung from a chain around his neck rests conspicuously against his chest, but he won't tell what it is. Like a spell, his not telling makes it impossible to guess.

A young woman sits massaging one of his feet which is stretched across her lap. It absorbs all her attention. He doesn't introduce her, but he treats her with a certain respect, as do Bobby and Nat Stillwell and the maid—as if, in the household, she were second only to James.

Bobby is ceremoniously taking out the curlers, one by one. He is a master. He teases each lock into place, leaning over from behind to get at the front, careful not to obstruct James' view of things. He has learned not to interfere with conversations when he's doing James' hair, creating the great round head. It looks terrific and I tell him so.

"Yeah?" James laughs modestly, as if I were putting him on. "I like *your* hair."

The radio is on and is playing his song: "I Got You" by James Brown. It is number 3 on WABC. "*I feel good. I knew that I would now. I fee-eel good. I knew that I wou-ould. So good. So good. 'Cause I got you.*" It makes him feel real good. He raises his hand and everyone freezes, silent and motionless, listening. But no one listens as well as he. He gazes deep into nowhere. He is part of it and it is part of him. He starts to sing with it. "I like that. '*Sugar and spi-ice.*'" The two voices of James Brown, the two incredible, hoarse voices of James Brown, are straining together. It is a Brown fugue.

We check in at the Admiralty Motel in Virginia Beach, the five of us: James and Bobby Byrd and Bobby Bennett and Lloyd and me. James has armed me with one of his suitcases and a pad and pencil, insisting that I carry the pad and pencil all the time, to prove that I'm a traveling reporter, and to guard against the assumptions of suspicious Southern minds: The pinched-featured white desk clerk with the plastered tan hair straightens up as we enter. He is marvelously meek. "Yes, Mr. Brown. Your room is all ready, Mr. Brown. Suite A 20, sir. It's all made up, and we have the three gentlemen in A 18, A 16 and A 14. But as for the young lady," he says, his eyes shifting uneasily from James to me and back again, "well, I'm terribly sorry, but the closest room we have is C 15. I do hope that's all right."

James winks. He knew it would be that way; he hadn't wanted me to come at all at first. Back in the house in St. Albans, when I'd asked him if I could, he tried to dissuade me, not just because his Negro fans in the South wouldn't understand if they got the idea he was going around with a white girl, but because he was worried for my *safety*. It's *dangerous* down there. "You remember what happened to President Kennedy." He even sent Nat Stillwell to explain: "Mr. Brown sent me. He wanted me to tell you—about Virginia Beach. He didn't want to tell you himself, didn't want to hurt your feelings. But the fact is you can't do down there like you do up here. Wander around any way you please. That ain't up North no more. That's the *South*, and they don't want you down there. *Anything* could happen. Oh, I ain't telling you what to do. You do like you want. But I'd think twice before going down there. I'd think twice if I were you. Mr. Brown just wanted me to tell you, just so you know what you're doing."

But James seemed to have changed his mind at some point, perhaps sometime while he was dressing, because when he came downstairs again in his shiny purple shirt and purple pants (two inches taller than before thanks to the heels of the pale suede boots) he winked confidentially. "Don't you worry about *nothing*. You'll go wherever I go. I'll look after you. And if you write this the way it really happens, it's gonna be like *I Passed for White*. Only the other way 'round."

So it was no surprise to him that they put me in C 15 a long way from his room; he had figured on it. After we'd all gone to our separate rooms, he sent Gert to fetch me. Dear, round, affectionate Gert is his wardrobe mistress and dresser and she has been with him 10 years. She has been through the whole thing with him, looking out for his clothes, looking out for his eating habits, looking out for his worries—everything, like a mother. There isn't anything she doesn't know. She has come to escort me to his room, back through the lobby past the comfortable businessmen, whose knowing eyes turn to watch us as we climb the stairs.

Suite A 20 isn't very grand for a suite, just a living room with a couch and two chairs, a dressing alcove, a bedroom and two bathrooms. Both television sets are on, one in the bedroom and one in the living room, and

James is sprawled opulently in one of the chairs, talking on the telephone. Bobby is doing his hair again, wielding the expert, inobtrusive comb. Gert is pouring champagne for all. James knows a groovy way to drink it—pour salt in it. It makes more bubbles and stings and also helps you burp. There is some fried chicken. "You dig *hot sauce?*" Eat. Drink. Have a ball. "So long, baby, I'll call ya." He hands Bobby the telephone to hang up. "She's in *love* with me," he laughs negligently. "Well, like I'm *all man*, you know." Lots of them are in love with him: it can sure make life *complicated*. He reaches for some more chicken, a real *hot piece*. It's *out o' sight*. "Hey, Bobby, come put my socks on for me, man, so I can spend these few precious moments talking. . . ." He fixes on me with those invincible black eyes, as if there's no one but him and me. He's giving me The James Brown Story.

You wouldn't *believe* how poor he was when he was a kid living in Augusta, Georgia. *Real* poor. He had to pick cotton and shine shoes and dance in the streets for people who would throw nickels and dimes and sometimes even quarters at his feet. "I had a *real* big family. I didn't have no brothers and sisters, but a lot of *close* relatives. Know what I mean? And I had to help support 'em." That can make a guy real determined.

He wants to *do something*. He wants to do something *real* bad, to find a challenge, something in which he doesn't feel completely sure. That's the whole trouble: he's always been confident, and that's no good. "Everything I've done I've always been the number one cat." He's done a lot. He started out as a prizefighter. Former boxing champ Beau Jack spotted his incredibly fast footwork and offered to coach him as a fighter. "Boxing, that's *all work* and none of the *fun.*" Later, he started playing baseball. "I was an extraordinary pitcher," he confesses, shaking his head. He had a chance to play professional baseball, but he injured his leg, putting an end to his career as a ball player. He organized The Famous Flames and started out in show business, singing gospel-derived songs for predominantly adult audiences in the South. But things really began in 1955, in Macon, Georgia. He and The Famous Flames made an unaccompanied recording of "Please, Please, Please" and a local disc jockey played it on his radio show as a personal favor to James Brown. Since then he hasn't needed many favors, because he is a talented singer and dancer and a "very sharp businessman." He works hard and knows how to make friends, and he is a "lucky guy." This is where he's at today: 34 years old and "the biggest Negro cat in show business right now." His record sales total well over five million and he has a huge following of adult and teenage fans all around the country and in Europe as well. "All that glamour from sun to sun. It's rough." Some guys might just sit back and take it easy at that point, but not James Brown. He's *ambitious*. He's gotta find the true challenge, expand to the limits of himself. Or further. He can't stop, not with singing; he's got to be moving on. "Maybe into the acting field. I think I'm gonna be an actor next."

"It can be pretty scary up where I am. I mean like everybody's watching. Know what I mean? The whole world. Black and white. I'm carrying the whole thing. Right now, in what I'm doin', I'm doin' more for the Negro cause than *any* of them *other* cats: I'm talkin' about *Soul*. Forgettin' that other stuff. That's silly. I'm talkin' about bein' *alive*, man. About *feeling*. That's what it's all about." But they're all watching him up there, and he knows if he messes up he's gonna make it rough for every other Negro performer and that's a frightening thing. Any sensitive cat, no matter how tough, would have to be a little scared sometimes, a little mixed up and very much alone.

"I am one of the most alonest guys. You hip to that? Like I'm a very serious person. Know what I mean? I've got *a lot* of problems. I'm real *confused*, you know. But I gotta keep it all to myself. All inside me. 'Cause there ain't no one I can really talk to. Not *really talk*. You dig?"

That's why he's got to do everything himself: he can't trust anyone to do it for him. He's got to know what's going on all the time, firsthand. That doesn't just mean with the songwriting, the arranging, the choreography and the designs for all the costumes in the show. Sure he does all that. But also, he's got a publishing company, Try Me Music, Inc., and he and his agent, Ben Bart, both own 50 per cent of a record production company, Fair Deal Records, Inc. On top of that, James Brown makes a special point of overseeing the whole business end of things: the publicity, the bookings, the contracts, everything. He has to be able to deal with all kinds of people in all kinds of fields. He has to keep his personality changing all the time. "A person who knows me from the way I am when I'm doin' the show would never recognize me as a businessman."

"I gotta be hip to what's goin' on all the time. Know what I mean? When you write songs it's the same with doin' anything creative. You gotta be able to *reach* people. So it ain't enough just to know all there is about any one special thing, like music. You gotta be diggin' *everything that's happening*. You gotta be *at least* 85 per cent up on everything. And you gotta try for 100 per cent."

He's trying to tell the real thing; it's not easy, but he's trying. "I don't know if you're gonna dig this. I talk *deep*. But when you reach a certain plateau, you can look back and see where you used to be. But when you're below, when you're down below, you can't see up. *Yeah*. I talk *real* deep. Hey, Bobby, I think she digs what I'm sayin', man! You know? She's a Soul Sister."

He knows that the best of James Brown is in his performance. It begins in that tremulous moment before he comes on stage, that moment when the whole audience knows he is about to appear. Those rows and rows of clean-cut white college kids packing the arena on a school night are all there to see James Brown. The girls in fuzzy pastel sweaters with their hair in pert flips, the languid-limbed boys in impeccably casual, open-necked shirts, all of them waiting. They are much more than just polite; they are revelling in the suspense, breathless with a tension they cannot explain. All 18 musicians are standing in a row, rocking back and forth as they play something soft and full of promise. The five dancing girls shimmer in the velvety blue and red lights, and small sad-eyed Danny, the quiet stage manager, the master of ceremonies, sits at a desk high up on some box, delivering his introduction. It doesn't much matter what he says; no one really cares. They're all too intent on waiting to be able to listen.

". ... And here he is, ladies and gentlemen. The star of many exciting television shows *and* movies. The *one* and *only* James Brown and The Famous Flames."

The audience screams. First come The Flames, in a row, trotting in time to the music over to the microphone where they dance the ritualistic dance. All three of them are doing the same step, simultaneously—leaning out toward the audience, leaning back, thrusting out their arms. The three of them look so hopelessly different, three different sizes, three different shapes, that even the identical gold jackets can't hide it. But they move as one, and the crowd never stops screaming.

When he appears at the opposite side of the stage in the glamour of a brown-checked, waist-length jacket, matching vest and sleek brown pants, it all gets wilder. Not just the screaming, but the music, too, and the gyrations of the dancing girls, and the enthusiasm of The Flames. He is coming out to give the audience all he's got, moving with a jaunty stride and a lot of purpose, as though he has come to do something he must do, something he knows how to do, something he loves to do. He is smiling at them, too, a huge, generous smile full of gleaming white teeth. He's magnificent, and he's no time-waster. He grabs at the microphone impatiently and starts to sing.

"Odansze ed*jerk*.
Pbapasinders*zing*.
Aindyuooo *hip*
Tdwotdat noobreeds*zayn*.
Ainno *draaaag*.
Pbap*pas* got*da* brannoooo*bag* . . ."

He has all the classic mannerisms: snapping his elbows to his sides to hike up his pants, flinging out his arms for a fresh start at the beginning of each new phrase, pantomiming the lyrics. His style is a phenomenal conglomeration of things: burlesque, gospel, sports, silent films. It is Super-Fine. James cups his ear: "Come on, John. Play your horn. Play your horn, your baritone." John rocks up to the microphone, feigning a limp, stepping with one foot and sliding the other to meet it, blowing his horn. John takes over at the microphone so James can do his stuff. He smiles at John. "Come on, John." Then his feet are shuffling quadruple time, never leaving the floor, carrying him miraculously all over the stage, so *easily*. His arms are outspread; he is erect. Now his knees are bending; he is sinking toward the floor; he is rising again. And all the while his feet are working with that phenomenal ease. He claps a hand behind his head, raises one leg, and watches as one foot moves him along with that slippery motion. Then he stops. He bends over his leg, smoothing an expert finger along the crease of his pants and the crowd howls its approval. He sidles back to the microphone to relieve John.

"Hehy*hey*
Come*ohn*
He*hey*
Yuhszetmeup*dtight*.
Yuhroutta*szight*."

There is no pause between the end of one song and the beginning of another, no pause at all. When James Brown starts giving, he really gives his *all*, gives 'em their money's worth. Once he gets started, nothing can induce him to stop for breath, not even the deafening applause which often drowns out huge portions of his song.

"Mebbede*lass* tdime.
Mebbede*lass*tdimeweshake*hand*.
Mebbede*lass*tdimewemake *roma-ance*.
Oh-o *whah*, Oh-o *whah*, Ah*dunnoh*."

The Flames are cooing, "Hup hup doo-wee-ooo. Hup hup doo-wee-ooo." The dancing girls are holding up their index fingers and saying, silently, "Oh why, Oh why, I don't know." The band takes over so James can dance with The Flames. They face the audience all in a line, each with his left hand on his left hip, watching each other. They hop right and bump; they hop left and bump. They each execute a smooth turn and face each other in two rows: James and Bobby Bennett facing Bobby Byrd and Lloyd. Each has his left foot forward, opposite toes almost touching: they are all bouncing their weight on and off the forward leg, smiling, really *looking* at each other and smiling. They love it, being *together*. It's intimate. All at once their heads bow and four arms shoot forward and then four more. "Oh why, Oh why, I don't know."

"Yiaaaaiih. Ahmalla*lohn*.
Ahaintgohtnoh*body* tocahlma*hohn*.
Causeahdoh*noh*ftmaybedelass*tdime*.
Lookahrounyahovahanhovahagai-*ain*.
Shakehanswid*yoh*bes*fren*.
Yahmighdt*nevahevah*seedemagai-*ain*.
Shakehanswid*yoh*bes*fren*.
Shake*hans*widyohbes *fren*."

He is back at the microphone, singing for his audience, his people, a modern Moses. He is telling them where it's *really at*. He is holding out his right hand to The Flames, and one by one they move toward it—first Bobby Bennett, then Bobby Byrd, then Lloyd. They each shake his hand and then, inspired, fortified, eager, they stroll cheerfully to the edge of the stage, stretching out their hands to the crowd. They want to shake hands, to shake *everybody's hand*. They move along the edge of the stage with their hands reaching out, inviting.

But it isn't only The Flames who want to shake hands. It can't be because two men in tuxedos are moving out from the wings, forbiddingly. Each grips one of James' arms as he goes to the edge of the stage where the crowd is waiting for him, swarming for his hands. A little shy at first, but frantic if they don't get their turn. They reach up for James' hands, which are scarred by the greedy fingernails of past crowds, as he moves all along the edge of the stage, gleaming and glowing, submitting himself happily to the contest as they try to drag him down to them and the men in the tuxedos tug his arms away. Lots of the time it almost looks as if the men in the tuxedos may lose him, but they never have. One girl faints, just collapses in a heap under all those frenzied feet, and the cops have to come and fight off her hysterical friends and pick her up and carry her out of the theater.

"Ahdlahktuhtellah*somemoh*.
So-*horry*. Ahgottago-*hoh*."

Then, suddenly, it all stops—everything. For a bare moment the musicians are quiet, the dancing girls frozen with their heads bowed. The Flames have turned their backs. The light is deep purple and James cries into the stillness, "Pleeeeeze. Pleeeeeze, pleeze. Pleeeeeeze." His shoulders heave and he flops to his knees, dragging the microphone with him, pleading over it.

The crowd is hysterical, shattering the stillness. The band music is sighing. The Flames are moaning. The five girls high up on their platforms are jerking in mourning. There are a lot of isolated screams from the audience, erupting out of its momentary silences. Sometimes a particularly long pleeeeeze is what does it, or a shake of his head, or a shiver of his back. When the pace is so insistently slow and the mood so sad, the balance is very delicate.

"Pleeeze. Pleeeze. Pleeeze.
Ohdahlin*plee-eeeze*dohngoh-who-aho-*owhoaaho-o*!
Ah*luhvyahsooo-o*."

He is in an ecstasy of agony, clinging to the neck of the microphone, dripping sweat, or tears, or both—screaming out his misery in that coarse voice which rakes relentlessly over the vowels. Bobby can't let him do it, can't let him do this to himself. Nor can Danny. They approach him, Danny with a great purple cape to drape over James' kneeling body. They raise him to his feet, swathing him in the robe. Bobby pats his back comfortingly, in time to the music. They guide him towards the wings, still singing, but he stops halfway there. He stops and they can't move him any further. He just won't go, he has to say more. He stamps his feet like a child having a tantrum. No no no no no, in quickening succession. He flings off the cape defiantly and stalks back to the microphone, grabs it and sinks to his knees with it again.

"Bay*bay*! Yahdone me*wrohng*.
We-e-e-eh. Yahdone me *wrohng*.
Yah*nohwyaduhn* duhnwe*wrohng*.
Yahtuhk*mahluhv* nowya*goh-hone*."

Danny comes out with a gold cape this time. He and Bobby pull James up from the floor, drag him to his feet, limp and still crying out his song, telling them about Soul. They understand. Danny and Bobby each put an arm around his shoulders, trying to tell him it's all right, it's all gonna be all right. He stamps his feet again. Again, he flings off the cape. He is back on his knees with the microphone, back where he belongs.

"Ahjuswannaheahyahsay Aaiii.
Aaaiii. Aaaiii. Aaaiii. Aaaiii.
Aaaiii. Aaaiii. Aaaiii. Aaaiii.
Dahlin*pleee-eeese*dohng*oh-whoah*-oho-ohyeah-*ohoo*.
ahluhvyahs*oh-hoh*."

The audience is still howling "Aaaiii," as they come for him once more. Danny and Bobby wrap him in a flowing black cape. They raise him very gently, very firmly. He is like a victorious fighter, exhausted by the contest, his shoulders are heaving spasmodically. He is weak with the strain of exorcising his misery. He stops again but it isn't possible for him to come back for more. It's just not humanly possible. He raises his arms proudly and the black cape slides off his back into Danny's waiting hands. Expertly, he unfastens his cuff links and before any one has a chance to guess what he is about to do, he flings them out to the audience in one last glorious gesture and all alone, without any help, he strides away into the wings.

The audience is overwhelmed by the relentless intricacy of it all. The music is still playing. The dancing girls are still swaying. The Flames are still warbling, and the audience is still wondering why they go on. What more could there possibly be? They are wondering until James appears again, triumphant in a clean tan suit, swinging a small suitcase at his side. "Out O' Sight" it says. He stalks across the stage with it, his parting benediction.

It is over, this elaborate personal dream out of the head and body and sweat of James Brown, who really believes in himself so fervently that the whole crowd is ready to follow him, even if he can only lead them to some private narcissistic vision of James Brown. They know it is not for them to ask what it all means. All that really matters is the sheer energy of his belief.

Backstage James sits at a long white dressing table cluttered with hair sprays and make-up kits and soda cans and packages of exotic cigarettes. He is transformed; the magnificence of his presence on stage has vanished, almost as if it had all been a dream. Grease-paint is congealed in the creases of his face, washed there by streams of sweat. It makes his face look cracked and stiff and undefinably cruel. The metamorphosis is shocking. Some open cuff link boxes are arrayed on the dressing table, displaying their goods. He uses 1,000 pairs a month to toss to his audiences. The boxes have been placed there by Gert or Danny for James to choose from—bold, jewelled links, shining in the mirror lights. A gold encrusted pair set with a small black stone in the center seems truly elegant. "Ya like 'em? Ah'll give 'em to ya," James says.

He strokes on fresh grease-paint, surveying the room in the lighted mirror like some feudal lord. It's very cozy. Not the room itself, which is stark and white, but the atmosphere they have brought to it. Bobby works patiently, repairing James' hair. Gert is hanging up the costumes, rearranging them on the rack, the 120 glistening shirts, the slacks, meticulously creased, the jackets, the capes. She attends each article with pride. Good old reliable Kenny is straightening the 80 pairs of shoes and boots, setting them out in neat rows against the far wall. He is harassed, he's always harassed, which is what makes him reliable and James knows that. "When a fellow stops worrying about his job, that's when *I* gotta start worrying. Right?" he says, turning to me, including me as a confederate. Danny is hiding something behind his back, a surprise for James. "Ya got a new ideah fer a costume ya wanna show me. Ain't dat it, Danny? Ah know. Cain't fool me, baby."

"Ah told ya," cries Gert triumphantly. "See. Cain't *nevah* fool James. Not dat *James*."

Danny unfurls the huge sheet and lays it before James on the dressing table. There are eight costume designs. One looks like a costume for Prince Charming, another as if it were made for Napoleon, another like a riding habit, and one like a Sherlock Holmes outfit. "Yeah," purrs James. He stabs a finger at the Sherlock Holmes. He really *digs* that one. Everybody agrees, it's out o' sight. He flips through the swatches of material Danny has given him. He wants it made up in brown, brown like this, with straight stove-pipe pants. "'Cause as long as it's tight from *here* to *here*, that's where the action is. That's where it's happening." Everybody laughs big, knowing and appreciative, doubling over and swatting their thighs. They take turns slapping his outstretched palm with approval.

It's the private world of the show, the James Brown World, warm, intimate and impenetrable. It even has its own language, spoken in a high grating voice, punctuated by squeals with an accent of elaborately broad vowels, stretching the best words out to the limits of a breath. And slang words and phrases and gestures: not just the classic ones, the ones everyone knows, but *special* ones, made up by James Brown, himself. It's very intoxicating.

He is very willing to teach it—more than willing, he's delighted. "Come on, lemme show ya. Watch this, Gert. Gert's gonna get a kick out o' this. Okay now. Lessee. Well, like when ya see a chick an' she's got a nice shape. Dig? So ya say, 'Man, dat yo woman? She's got a *muhthaah* on huh.' Ya hip to that? An' like when ya want somebody to give ya somethin', then ya say, 'Hey, man *maash* dat dollah bill on me.' An' maybe ya want someone to do somethin' *real fast*. You know, no messin' aroun'. So ya do like this." He reaches out for my hand and folds it into a fist, straightening out the index finger. "This fingah ya keep up like dis. An' then ya say to the guy, ya say, 'Git dat on ovah heah *riaaiight naaahw*.'" As he speaks, he keeps hold of my fist, slowly turning it over, directing it in a leisurely arc down toward the table. As he says "naaahw," he plunges the aggressive index finger against the table top. "Now *you* do it!" he crows. "Riaaiight naaahw." Everybody laughs again. "Ya dig dat? She's out o' sight man. Out o' sight."

But The James Brown Language can't be learned. It's solidly insulated, which is probably why he enjoys teaching it. It's his way of separating the insiders from the outsiders, his way of protecting his secret. The truth is that everyone who is on the outside and makes an effort to get inside appears hopelessly comical, like the white disc jockey who has booked the show. He keeps bobbing in through the stage door to check up on things, to record an interview for his show, to introduce his wife, to report the financial success, to extend his congratulations. He's tall and pale and emaciated with a sharp red nose. Next to James he looks almost translucent. He can't resist affecting his impression of The James Brown Language.

"Well, we really packed 'em in there, James, baby. Like, man, you were out of sight. They dug it like wild. Yeah, man. They really flipped. Sure was groovy, all right. Very out of sight, James. Cool, man. Boy, James, baby, we'd sure like to have you here during an Easter vacation. When all the schools are out. I mean like that would really swing. Of course, I know you're booked up solid. But at Easter, man, we'd really knock 'em dead."

The disc jockey rubs his palms together as he backs toward the door, almost bowing. No one laughs; that would be unprofessional, and the members of The James Brown Show are never unprofessional. Besides, laughter is superfluous: all they have to do is look at each other, just exchange a brief glance. That tells the whole story. He's an outsider. James flashes me a wink.

There's always something to rehearse after a performance, some little thing to go over. Maybe Bobby Byrd has to be straightened out about one of the dance routines. He will come to the dressing room and do it for James, go over it a few times until it's just right. Or maybe the leader of the dancing girls has to be warned to make sure the girls are covered up as much as possible—can't have it looking like a burlesque show, not when there's a fickle audience who could easily go either way, an audience that has to be wooed into the confidence that what they're seeing is something it's okay for them to like. Or maybe there's a phrase of music that's imperfect. Nothing gets left dangling; anything short of perfection has got to be repaired. Nat Jones, the band leader, is summoned to the dressing room for instructions on the introduction to "I Got You," because the way it is now, it's common, the way *any* old band would play it. It's not right for

The James Brown Show, where everything is *super-fine*. James shows Nat what he means. Hums it and beats it out on the surface of the dressing table. First the way it ought to be, then the way Nat's been letting them play it, then the way it ought to be again, just to show what a big difference it makes.

"You dig it, Nat? The way you're playin' it now, it's too easy. Hear it? It's right on the beat. Try it yourself. Try it both ways. See if I ain't right. It's gotta come *after* the beat. That way it's really got *Soul*."

Yes. Nat Jones sees it. He agrees, but something is bothering him. "What is *Soul*, James?" he asks earnestly.

"*You* know!" cries James, almost as if his feelings had been hurt. "It's *feeling*, man."

"Yeah. Yeah, I know. But remember that time we was talkin'? You and me? About Soul? About what it really is?" He glances furtively at me.

James tries to assure him. Tries to tell him it's okay to talk in front of me. But Nat Jones shakes his head.

"No. Some other time," he insists. "Sometime when we're alone, we gotta talk about that some more. Sometime when it's just the two of us."

"Yeah." James has to admit Nat Jones is right. He turns to me shaking his head regretfully. "I dig you. You know. You can see by how I treat you. But I can't let you hear about this. You hip to what I'm sayin'? This is *something else*. I mean like *this*, baby, this is *the whole secret*."

"James Brown in Paris: Sock It a Moi"

Jonathan Cott
November 23, 1967 • *Rolling Stone*

Your reporter disembarked from the Queen Mary—the penultimate voyage: the Beachcomber jukebox played "Land of 1000 Dances" to French-speaking Sweet Briar girls, while friends met friends in the Smoker's Room listening to Schubert's Ninth during High Tea. I got drenched coming off the boat, so I flew to Paris—the nicest time of the year, everyone coming back or going away, NLF newspaper girls on the

Rue de Seine where two British boys offered something special from Fez, but whom can you trust? (In Paris and London, the cops can frisk you on the street without a warrant.) The sun was shining, so I slipped into the shade to see two wonderful films: Godard's *La Chinoise* and Bunuel's *Belle de Jour*, the Living Theater's *Mysteries* production and the James Brown Show at the Olympia.

I wish I had saved *Le Monde's* review of *"Monsieur Dynamite"*— describing Brown with words such as *glittering, trembling, angular*, the point being that the James Brown Show—almost sold-out for its two-week run—is part laser beam, part hypertense machine. And so it is. The show is as stylized as it lacks what used to be called "shared spontaneity" between performer-and-audience. It's the same kind of show James Brown presents in Oakland, Winterland, Madison Square Garden. But the French audiences sit tight-lipped, tied and elegant, as French TV cameras quietly tape the concert.

The whole stage is wound up. The Famous Flames sing and dance robot-style, the musicians glide around, and the three J.B. girls, high on the altar, sock it to themselves. The lights, purple and white; the strobe effects, self-consciously and wonderfully timed. It's like an organism working at peak energy—at least for the second half of the two-and-a-half-hour concert—and at the body's center is that beautifully boyish compromise of heart and phallus.

James Brown sings "Prisoner of Love" for twenty minutes, falls to the ground as if in Satanic prayer, whispering "My hands are soaking wet . . . My face is bathed in sweat," rushes into "Break Out in a Cold Sweat" with that song's fantastic rhythmic suspensions, and keeps the *uhughs uhughs* going until he collapses again, the Flames bedizen him with lame, sable, organdy capes, James Brown flings them off, keeps it up some more, more capes, he throws his cuff links to the audience, shakes hands with the boys in the first row, dances off stage.

Everything is interiorized, narcissistic at the edge, if you want to labor the point. It's not that Black people aren't around to respond—as in fact they aren't at the Olympia—but that James Brown does all the work. He embodies followers, preacher, and church. And in the extraordinary "Prisoner of Love" section, he gives his body to Love. I suppose the audience protects itself with its detached magnetic field, but the point is that there is no need for protection. As James Brown says in his one French sentence: "Mon coeur est avec vous," but everyone knows he keeps it locked up as he offers himself to, and up to, an imaginary space of faces and cameras.

Instead of coming to London for a series of booked appearances, James Brown flew back to New York City, suffering from "nervous exhaustion."

"It's a New Day"

Harry Weinger with Alan Leeds
1996 • Liner notes from *Foundations of Funk,*
released by Polydor/Universal Music.

James Brown took many roads in the Sixties: recording the poppish "I Got You (I Feel Good)," embracing a slick studio band and strings with "It's A Man's Man's Man's World," digging into novelties like "Night Train." By the end of the decade, JB had driven himself to the cutting edge of a new Rhythm & Blues, a world of supernatural grooves called Funk, changing the sound of pop music forever.

But in early 1964, James Brown faced a crossroads. His enormous following in the black community was growing. The *Live At The Apollo* album had pushed him into the consciousness of white America. Yet JB was floundering for position.

He fought for economic parity with King Records and refused to record for them, signing instead an independent production deal with Smash/Mercury Records. But the first album was mostly big-band covers of R&B classics, a puzzling (and commercially unsuccessful) choice in an era of emerging black awareness.

Then in May, 1964, JB and a mostly new band wrapped a bass line around a street phrase and stepped into a whole new realm. The Smash single "Out Of Sight" sounds like improvised vocals; razor-sharp horns led by newcomer Nat Jones punch like crazy. Its final 30 second vamp pointed to freedom for James Brown.

Because soon, the vamp became all. Like the great African griots who told ancestral tales under the spell of drums and chants, James Brown could sit on that vamp as he spun ideas. Riffing with purpose, the band followed his every blistering move.

Their interplay on the vamp was the motherlode for Funk. But there was no immediate label for what Brown had begun to carve with his own hands. When "Papa's Got A Brand New Bag" hit in the spring of 1965, its emphasis on the rhythm in striking contrast to pop and R&B conventions, even the man himself could not explain.

"It's a little beyond me right now," JB told a radio audience upon the single's release. "I can't really understand it. It's the only thing on the market that sounds like it. It's different. It's a new bag, just like I sang."

"Papa's" pop success suddenly gave JB immense leverage with King Records. (The Smash deal evolved into an outlet for instrumentals and side productions only, but that's another story.) And his skyrocketing star afforded him a bigger and better band.

Nat Jones, music director from 1964 through January 1967, brought jazz sensibility and the facility to translate Brown's emerging sense of groove. Maceo and Melvin Parker were new additions in '64. Traditional blues guitarist Jimmy Nolen, nicknamed "Chank" for his strum, came aboard in '65, as did Bobby "Blue" Bland's drummer John "Jabo" Starks. Brown plucked unknown Clyde Stubblefield, and jazz head Alfred "Pee Wee" Ellis, who would eventually take the reins of the band from Jones.

As band leader, Ellis connected to the musicians immediately, instituting separate rehearsals for the rhythm and horn sections. "Cold Sweat" was their first serious test, affirming that JB was as much a musician as the rest of them.

"James called me in the his dressing room after a gig, said we were going to record soon and for me to have the band ready," Ellis says. "He grunted the rhythm, a bass line, to me. I wrote the rhythm down on a piece of paper. There were no notes. I had to translate it.

"James gave us a lot to go by. You got a musical palette from hearing him, from seeing his body movement and facial expressions, seeing him dance and from being up there with the band, seeing the audience. So you get a picture of that, and you write it."

"Cold Sweat" stretched into a jam session, propelled by a Clyde Stubblefield beat which upset the prevailing mentality. Because it was so fresh and captivating, radio had to play both sides of the single, introducing "give the drummer some" to the hip lexicon in the hot summer of 1967. It was as much of a wake-up call to R&B as Miles Davis' *Kind Of Blue* was to jazz in the Fifties.

(Preserved on tape is urgent instruction from JB how hard he wants Clyde Stubblefield's snare to POP. The alternate take illustrates how the song took one more stroke from the boss to gel. "I had written the guitar part for Jimmy Nolen one way," Ellis explains, "and James changed it to go against the grain. Which I think is better. It has more of an edge to it.")

From then on, nearly every James Brown recording was an extended *performance*. ("Let Yourself Go" begat "There Was A Time," for example.) His instinctive phrasing and clever lingo made spontaneous instructions to the band flow with the music. "That's right, you keep playing, Maceo, 'cause the *groove* is there," JB says in "Get It Together." "Tim! Help me out, Tim! Let me hear you walk a little bit," he yells to his bass player in "I Can't Stand Myself." "Start it over again," he implores the horns in "Give It Up Or Turnit A Loose."

Sometimes the instructions were less obvious. Listen how Brown coaxes, damn near *composes*, Maceo Parker's solo in "Ain't It Funky Now." Or how he elevates the entire band's performance by challenging Maceo to a duel in "Brother Rapp." And how his new formula could be adopted to a minor blues and create "Goodbye My Love," arguably the first funk ballad.

After rewriting the musical rules, the lyrical boundaries fell for James Brown during the social changes of the Sixties. The civil rights movement meant many things to many people. For James Brown, it meant manhood.

"A militant is just a cat who was never allowed to be a man," JB explained, while he asked his followers to sing "Say It Loud, I'm Black And I'm Proud." Gradually, Brown made the politics more personal: "I Don't Want Nobody To Give Me Nothing (Open Up The Door I'll Get It Myself)"—listen for his shouts of "let a man come in!" in the extended version here.

By the end of the Sixties, the message overtook the music. Brown was distracted; his band was disgruntled. The new day was done.

Funk was not. Building on these glorious performances, a brand new thang was tipping in, and the music would enter a Seventies heyday. Not surprisingly, a revitalized James Brown would lead the revolution.

"Does He Teach Us The Meaning of 'Black Is Beautiful'?"

Albert Goldman
June 9, 1968 • *The New York Times*

alk about your Black Power. Take a look at James Brown, Mister. That's right, James Brown, America's Number One Soul Brother. To whites, James is still an off-beat grunt, a scream at the end of the dial. To blacks, he's *boss*—the one man in America who can stop a race riot in its tracks and send the people home to watch television. Twice he worked that miracle in the terrible days following the murder of the Rev. Dr. Martin Luther King Jr.

It started at Boston, where Brown was set to play the Boston Gardens. When he heard the tragic news, he canceled the show. Then it was the Mayor on the phone—asking for help. The situation was desperate. Already people were in the streets, looting and burning. Some black politician, some guy who knows where it's at, told the Mayor, "Put James Brown on television." So the announcement was made: Tonight, TV, JB. Well, that got it. Everybody turned around and beat it for home. Who'd blow their chance to see the Man? That night Brown got out there—and he didn't stop. For six solid hours he held them. Out of that tube came the wildest shakin' and shoutin' ever seen. Brown sweated so hard you could almost smell him on the close-ups. When it was over, nobody had eyes for the street. The city was saved.

Next day it was the Mayor of Washington calling. The same number. "Save our city." Brown plunged right into the streets, grabbing gangs of marauding kids, talking to them like men but sending them back home like a tough uncle. When he hit the tube that night, he wasn't giving a performance in a cummerbund. He was just James Brown, standing there with a pained expression on his face yet bearing witness to America. "This is the greatest country in the world," he rasped. "If we destroy it, we're out of our heads. We've come too far to throw it away. You gotta fight with dignity." Next day, Washington was a quieter place. All of which explains why, when James Brown sat down to dinner with the President at the

White House recently, his place card bore this message: "Thanks much for what you are doing for your country—Lyndon B. Johnson."

That kind of power seems way out for a rhythm and blues man, a cat with a pushed-in face, a hoarse voice, a bag of tunes that sound alike and an act that is nothing new for the black vaudeville stage. But there you have the genius of James Brown. He is the greatest demagogue in the history of Negro entertainment. His whole vast success, which is measured in millions of records, thousands of performances and the kind of popularity that will have him touring the nation's ball parks with his "National Soul Festival" this summer—he will be at Yankee Stadium June 22—is based less on talents and skills than it is on a unique faculty for sizing up the black public and making himself the embodiment of its desires. James Brown understands, better perhaps than any entertainer or politician of the present day, that the price of authority is submission. He knows that you must sit down with the people to control them. Anybody who's going to stand even one step above them is not going to have them completely in his power. In fact, you must descend below the level of the audience if you desire ultimate mastery. That is why he identifies himself so emphatically as "a black man," setting himself apart from all the Negro entertainers (and all the Negro spectators) who dream of being Harry Belafonte.

That is why Brown has gotten so deep into the soul bag, dragging out the oldest Negro dances, the most basic gospel shouts, the funky, low-down rhythms of black history. He has made himself even more conservative than his audience. Nor does he ever miss a chance to talk about his humble origins in Georgia, where he was born 34, 36 or 38 years ago, and where he picked cotton, blacked boots and danced in the streets for nickels and dimes. Playing the shoeshine genius, the poor boy who rose from polish rags to riches, he makes himself one with the lowest and youngest members of his audience.

Success in the Negro world, however, is always equated with royalty; so Brown makes a great show of his clothes (500 suits, 300 pairs of shoes), his cars (blue-black Mark III Continental, purple and silver-gray Rolls-Royce, Cadillac convertible, Eldorado, Toronado, Rambler), his twin-engine Lear jet, his two radio stations and his moated, drawbridged castle in St. Albans, Queens. Until recently, he regularly had himself crowned onstage and sat cheerfully on a throne, wearing ermine-trimmed robes.

Now he has pruned his act of such gaudy features and begun to re-

shape his image in accordance with the current mood of public serious-
ness. Offering himself proudly as an example of what the Negro can
achieve in America, he has begun a tug of war with the radical black dem-
agogues, whom he feels are leading the people astray. Whether he has political ambitions himself, or whether he would be content to lend his
power to another man, is not clear; but the time comes in every great entertainer's life when he must decide whether he is going to grow old doing
his act or get into something else.

Certainly no words that Brown could speak from a political platform could
mean as much to his public as the thrilling image of himself in action onstage. A high-voltage halation crackles around "Mr. Dynamite" from the
moment he strides jauntily on until he is dragged off, one, two or three
hours later. Once a boxer, known for his lightning-fast footwork, Brown
carries himself with the taut muscular energy of a competing athlete. He
grabs the mike with a confident right cross, ducks and bobs with the beat,
lays a fist up beside his head, shuffles his feet in dazzling combinations
and winds up wringing wet, being swathed in a brightly colored, sequin-
spangled robe. A hitter hero, a scarred, bruised but triumphant Golden
Boy, he has enormous appeal for an audience that has been battered and
beaten and robbed of its confidence from childhood. Never angry or cruel,
he is a wholly admirable champion, a cocksure, carefree kid who is always
going out to conquer the world. The public gloats over him with parental
satisfaction.

Like all rhythm and blues men, Brown is a great stage lover, a man who
can take on thousands of women at a time and reduce them to screaming
jelly. In fact, he goes after the women in the audience a lot more directly
than do most entertainers. When he does one of his slow drags, like "It's a
Man's World," the rapport between him and the girls reaches scandalous
proportions. He shouts with killing sincerity, "Just be there when I get the
notion!" and the screams come back from the house like an enormous
trumpet section screeching in on the cue. Those screams, incidentally, are
not from teeny-boppers; they come from mature women who enter the
theater in twos and threes and at the great moments let themselves go.

Brown is always pouring on the love, but he often changes key or
tempo. He can command and he can beg. He can scream as loudly and
with as much anguish as any woman. And when the fit is upon him, he
drives his erotic frenzy right over the line that divides the secular from the

sacred. Like all the great soul men, his final station is in the church, right up there on the horns of the altar, testifying in an ecstasy. One moment he's the gladiator of the ring, taking a lot of punishment in the final rounds but hanging in there, battling his way to victory. Then, suddenly, he's an ancient darkie from the delta, shoulders up to his ears, arms stretched out like a ghost—and that face! Good God, the sweat is pouring down the man's face like a shower of diamonds, his eyes are rolled up wildly, his mouth is hanging dumbly open; but through all that agony there is a smile coming, a beautiful smile blooming like Easter morning.

James Brown ends in beatitude. He sacrifices himself and gives the pieces away. He wrenches himself out of his body and stands naked in the spirit. He concentrates his blackness and light comes pouring out of him. He teaches us the meaning of the phrase "black is beautiful."

Tonight at 9 on Channel 5, WNEW-TV, he will be presented in a one-hour telecast, "James Brown: Man to Man," taped at the Apollo Theater in Harlem. But the program will provide a view of the performer that could never be obtained in the theater, a view that alternates between the front of the house and the stage itself. Inevitably, some censorship had to be exercised on Brown's risqué lines, and an almost total blackout has been imposed on his famous go-go girls with their incredible rotary action. This constitutes only a slight dampening of a performance that is fascinating in detail and overwhelming in total impact.

By offering such a long and relatively unobstructed look at a great black entertainer on his home ground, Metromedia Television has initiated a policy that promises much for the future of the medium. Too long have ethnic entertainers suffered from the handicaps of studio productions controlled by ignorant or unsympathetic producers and witnessed by audiences who could not provide the understanding and enthusiasm that drive a great performer to the limits of his genius. Now that the path from the black stage to the national screen has been cleared in this brilliant inaugural production, we may expect it to stay open. Nothing could be more important at this time than the opportunity to penetrate the ghetto and its culture through the techniques of television. The integration of black and white America depends upon a new perception of beauty.

"1968, January . . ."

Chuck D

1996 • Liner notes for *Funk Power*, released by Universal/Polygram Records.

I was a second grader at P.S. 90 in Richmond Hill. We always hoped that the school ground would have its corner covered with ice, frozen flat from the melted snow that dripped from the drainpipes above. We would race to the corner at the recess bell to skate, slip and slide over the overnight rink. During the slippin' and slidin' a few of us had to turn it into the customary challenge, "try this move and swing like JAMES BROWN." To do the JAMES BROWN you had to start off with "I Feel Good, *Duh-DUH-dah dah dudda dat*"; I guess this style mighta started from his dances in "There Was A Time" and the unconscious, infectious style of "Cold Sweat." It's funny, because looking back on the school bus rides you sang Stax and Motown songs, like "Tramp," "Jimmy Mack" and "I Heard It Through The Grapevine," but you couldn't sing James Brown because it automatically meant you had to get UP, and to us kids the driver and the law said you had to sit your lil ass down.

By the end of the school year something was still making us do the JAMES BROWN. More than the funky drums, horn hits and the rhythm, James had put something in a young fertile mind to pick up and go to that other level . . .

April 4, 1968, Dr. Martin Luther King Jr. was assassinated in Memphis. School was out for a couple of days and the 6 o'clock news on the one black and white television in our house anticipated nationwide problems. Before then the turbulence of the decade had seen one assassinated president; political and civil rights leaders jailed, beaten or murdered for their beliefs. Vietnam was a blur on television, but the reality was my uncles receiving their draft letters. Another hero, Muhammad Ali, had proclaimed, "I ain't goin' to fight no Vietcong," and was willing to go to jail. Other black athletes were threatening to boycott the upcoming Olympics.

It was in this complex time that my young and simple mind remembers my family going from Negro to calling our race "colored"—that was my answer to the question of what I was in 1967 at age seven. After the King assassination James Brown's "Say It Loud—I'm Black And I'm Proud" came out (uhhh! wit yo badd self); he still had that thing we wish we had the ice for.

James Brown singlehandedly took a lost and confused nation of people and bonded them with a fix of words, music and attitude. After a hot summer of baseball camp, summer lunches and barbecues, "Say It Loud—I'm Black And I'm Proud" was the phrase that prepared me for the third grade, 1969, and the rest of my life. Black now signified where we was at, a new discovery of our bad self.

"James Brown Sells His Soul"

Mel Ziegler
August 18, 1968 • *The Miami Herald*

. . . not to the Devil, but to millions of Negroes, who hear in his plaintive singing an echo of their battle for emancipation. And, unlike Faustus, Brown's $20 million-a-year entertainment empire has shown that Harlem pays better than Hell

James Brown has done everything for soul but create it. There was a pilgrimage to Africa just to find it, and performances for the troops in Vietnam to share it. He has studied it, analyzed it, tested it, packaged it, and marketed it. He has given it style and personified its rhythm. He is an architect of its vocabulary, a supreme purveyor of its message. It has come with him from a shabby Georgia Baptist church and followed him onto stereo tape decks. He has brought it out of Harlem's Apollo Theater and put it into Yankee Stadium. He is its prize salesman, and the soul he sells reaps him nearly $3 million a year.

There are other soul heroes, the late Otis Redding, Aretha Franklin, Ray Charles and Wilson Pickett among them. But James Brown warms the throne. He is the King of Soul, Soul Brother Number One. Mr. Dynamite.

Soul Business Number One is James Brown Enterprises, which includes the Georgia radio station where as a youth he shined shoes, another radio station, a record production company, a publishing company, a road show, and acres of choice New York real estate. JBE grosses more than $20 million annually. It supports the entourage of 40 persons who travel with Brown for an average of 320 performances a year, appearances so rigorous that "The King" loses up to seven pounds each time he performs. His Soul Court includes a valet, a man who sleeps in an adjoining hotel room just to answer his telephone calls, a woman who plays mother, three more personal aides, a 21-piece orchestra including two drummers who just stand-by, stage hands, and a crew of five to handle the books.

James Brown's soul business is a trust in which millions of Black Americans have invested. They have bought most of the 50 million James Brown records, and last year alone they dominated crowds three million strong who turned out to see the King of Soul perform live. In return, Black America has made its own Horatio Alger.

The King zips from one frenzied stockholder's meeting to the next, night after night, in his $618,000 Lear jet, soon to be traded for a $2 million Jet Star. At each stop, advance men stake out the largest performing arena, plaster the town with posters and invade the pop music radio waves with heralding proclamations on the coming of Soul Brother Number One. Brown, who has described himself as "75 per cent businessman and 25 per cent talent," rarely fritters a day away from the crowds.

He has a mansion in St. Albans, Queens, with "J.B." monogrammed onto the front lawn, emblazoned on the chimney and etched into the furnishings, but he is rarely there for more than a month a year. In the garage are a Rolls-Royce, two Cadillacs, a Toronado, a Rambler and a Lincoln. Two large rooms are cluttered with nothing but hundreds of suits and shoes.

James Brown has built this empire on soul. Soul. To White America, soul is little more than the primitive screeching from the car radio when the teenage daughter is along. But to Black Americans, soul is the catchword of the new racial narcissism, something that elates them and ignites them, something they have for no other reason but for the color of their skin. Something all their own; something only a pariah Whitey can have—yet only if he waxes black, and only if he plays in reverse the same debasing color game Negroes have had to play for two hundred years.

"Soul is sass, man. Soul is arrogance. Soul is walkin' down the street in a way that says, 'This is me muh! Soul is the nigger whore comin' along . . . ja . . . ja . . . ja, and walkin' like she's sayin', 'Here it is, baby.

Come an' git it.' Soul is bein' true to yourself, to what is you. Now, hold on: soul is . . . that . . . uninhibited . . . no extremely uninhibited self . . . expression that goes into practically every Negro endeavor. That's soul. And there's a swagger in it, man. It's exhibitionism, and it's effortless. Effortless. You don't need to put it on; it just comes out," writes black author Claude Brown, himself a soul man.

The King of Soul grew up in Augusta, Ga. "I was nine before I got my first pair of underwear from a store. All my clothes were made from sacks and things like that," Brown recalls. He quit school after the seventh grade, and worked shining shoes and picking cotton to help his family meet its $7 monthly rent. He would sing gospel songs in those days—for a price—to local National Guard troops. But the pennies this brought him could not satiate an obsessive business ambition: Brown spent nearly four years in a reform school for stealing. Afterwards, he formed a trio and played at local engagements. By 1956, he had cut a record in a Macon radio station. Forty-three records (average sales each: one million) and a dozen years later, Brown is a millionaire. He is a soul millionaire who refuses to forget Georgia.

"Sheee . . . ," said Brown. "Soul is when a man do everything he can and come up second. Soul is when a man make a hundred dollars a week and it cost him a hundred and ten to live. Soul is when a man got to bear other people's burdens. Soul is when a man is nothin' because he's black."

There is even a gesture from the heavens on this hot heavy tropical summer night, as James Brown wails from the infield of Miami Stadium. Erratic flashes of distant, thunderless lightning pierce the black sky with quick psychedelic flickers. "It's the Lord approvin'; It's the Lord approvin' of J.B.," says a crippled woman in a wheel chair.

The eyes in the slight, five-foot-six, 135 pound, frame commanding the microphone emit intense alertness. His body vibrates, and the lyrics move between screeches and grunts, mumbling under the band's clamor.

The King's gyrations are clipped, sometimes brutal, always with a suggestion of the primitive.

James Brown's face mirrors the faces in the crowd—except that the eyes looking out at him are half shut in self-induced agony. Faces wrinkle in tormented joy. Soul brothers mouth lyrics the white ear cannot understand. Only a few, scattered white people are among the crowd, almost all of them in button-down collars and stylish miniskirts. They dominate the $5 box seats. In the bleachers above them, 12,000 blacks ($.99 children,

$3. adults) are brewing bugaloo from their seats. Some cannot restrain themselves, and bound from the stands into the aisles, dancing. Two girls in matching iridescent white and pink polka dot dresses stand on their seats and shimmy erotically to the rhythm. They have no words for soul. It is something between them and the King, something private. A white policeman looks on, puzzled.

The suggestion of rain looms. A drop. Two drops. The electronic equipment on the field is covered, but The King, in a frenetic dance, is still belting his soul into the microphone. The band continues to play behind him. The white people in the box seats cup their palms upward for early warning of the two more drops which will send them to cover. "Oh dear," says a blonde white girl, draping her long hair over the back of her chair, "I just set it, too". The sky bursts.

The Negroes in the bleachers dance down into the box seats the whites are abandoning. The King's hair flattens under the wetness; a dripping shirt grips his chest. The rain seems to inspire him. He is in a wild, drilling twirl, whipping the microphone from right hand to left, and back. With a swift, slippery ditch, The King collapses onto the grass. A bellowing "Oooooh" rings from the stands.

An aide rushes out with a sequined blue cape, which he drapes over The King's hunched back. He helps Brown up and guides him off the field. The crowd screams. Halfway off the field, Brown casts the cape off and rushes back to seize the microphone. The band starts up again and The King screeches his soul sound even louder, whips his body into another frenzy. Again, he collapses.

Again, a cape, this time red. Again, the feigned exit. Again, the triumphant return. Again, the shrieking of the crowd. Again, the collapse. The crowd begins to dribble on to the field.

The King does it again, from cape to collapse. The crowd is over the fence and storming toward him, through a barrier of policemen. The cape again, and he is off the field, into the dugout, and back in the dressing room.

Twenty-two thousand feet below, the lakes of Central Florida sew blue polka dots into the green quilt. A James Brown tape blares through the Lear jet's stereo. The King is shuffling his feet over the fire-red carpet to its rhythm, his eyes absorbed in his wife's heart-shaped diamond. With his fingers, Brown eats the hot sauce, soggy french fries, gripping a cold hamburger in his other hand. The comedian who performs with his show has a standard joke: "The soul brother got a jet because he couldn't get on the back of a bus."

"A lot of the things I got I got because it makes my people feel good to see me with them," he is saying. "Because it's an unusual thing to see a black man with a Rolls-Royce. Anything I want I get. This is what our people really dig. 'We may not be able to get it,' they say, 'but a soul brother got it, and it's not impossible.'"

This is the James Brown brand of soul. Beneath the frantic gyrations and the undistinguished lyrics, lies a message: I got soul and you got soul. I made it and so can you. Just work hard like I did.

It's the Protestant ethic, overhauled and with a color job.

"It's trust and confidence," said Brown. "James Brown is somebody. They believe in James Brown. James Brown ain't never gonna turn his back on his people."

Dr. Martin Luther King is dead in Memphis. First Malcolm X, then Kennedy, now King. Washington is under siege. In scenes reminiscent of a Latin-American military coup, armed troops stand guard at the political bastions of America. At his own expense, James Brown has cancelled performances and flown into the ravaged capital city. He is broadcasting a television message to his people, a message which will be rebroadcast time and again in the coming days, as the white man in desperation surrenders his expensive airwaves to a black man of whom he knows virtually nothing.

"I am not a speechmaker. I am not a writer. But I can tell you what's happening," Brown begins, and then launches into a capsule account of his own rags-to-riches story, embroidering it for the black ear. Dramatically, he concludes:

"I am not what we call around the country a man who would do anything anybody says . . . take sides. I am not what a black man describes as a Tom. I am a man. Nobody can buy me. I do what I want. I say what I want because this is America. A man can get ahead here. Through you, I got ahead. I've been able to say what I want to say. I say to you . . . get off the streets, go home. Take your families home. Turn on your television, listen to your radio or listen to some James Brown records. But get off the streets."

Ketchup oozes from the hamburger and onto James Brown's silver supershirt, a long-sleeved satin garment with a stand-up collar and ruffles in the front and at the cuffs. His wife dips a napkin into water and rubs the stain out. Suddenly, she is thrown back into her seat as the plane whips through air turbulence.

"Madison Square Garden called me today," said Brown, with a mouth full of hamburger, to Ben Bart at the conclusion of their airborne business conference.

"Yeah, how much?" asked Bart.

"Ninety-seven thousand. They said it would be good for $97,000," said Brown.

"They're crazy," said Bart, who obviously figured the show was worth more for a stand in New York during Christmas week.

Bart had sauntered aboard the plane in Miami, unshaven, in red felt bedroom slippers, and a flowered shirt (resembling pajama tops) open at the collar, like a man off to the drugstore for a cigar. He is a huge and flabby man, with white hair, and his belly uncomfortably jammed behind Brown's airplane dinner table. It was a dozen years ago when Bart, as he put it, "saw the act," in Macon, Ga., hitched on as Brown's manager and brought the Georgia bootblack to the gold-studded Kingdom of Soul.

Now Bart is only a "business associate." Brown, who is his own manager, still retains much affection for Bart, even though the two are so opposite in terms of physical habit and grace. (Brown didn't even offer Bart a hamburger, because he knew that his former manager is not a man to eat hamburgers.) The clinical efficiency with which James Brown Enterprises operates is The King's inheritance from Bart.

JBE is a business, and it is run like one. The King addresses his subordinates as "Mister" and, in turn, demands that they call him "Mr. Brown." Those who work beneath him are cautioned to keep up the corporate image. Brown imposes heavy fines on them for cursing, drinking, and unkempt physical appearance.

The jet whirred to the end of the runway and deposited Brown in a group of waiting fans, among them a trio of young Negroes who had come to seek the Soul Brother's aid in raising money for the construction of an Orlando youth center.

BROWN: Ain't no time to do nothin'. We're here for the show, and we're leavin' right after it. That's a drag. Wish you got to me earlier.

SPOKESMAN: We felt it was time for us to do something. Our parents didn't do nothin'.

BROWN: I got you. I'm a black man. Mine didn't do nothin' either. My father was afraid, you know. He say, 'sheeee, sheeee.' I say to him, 'sheeee, wha', Dad? I been hearin' that every day for twenty years. We gotta do somethin.'

The youths politely suggested that The King make an announcement at the show that evening, urging contributions. Brown replied, "I got you, man. I'm black. Be only too happy to do it."

James Brown never made that announcement.

No doubt, he forgot. But the Soul Brother has a highly developed business acumen which won't let him forget when it pays not to. He doesn't forget Georgia, because amid the thrust of the Negro revolution in this country, the prototype of a brother who made it and kept his soul sells records. He recorded a song entitled "Don't Be A Drop-out," hoping publicly that it would be an inspiration to Negro children, yet knowing well that more than a million of them would have a dollar out of their pockets for it. At his own expense, he has printed thousands of "Stay in School" buttons which are distributed as a bonus at performances, where the "Official James Brown Program" brings in $1.50.

With considerably less fanfare than Bob Hope, and with only the barest cooperation from USO, Brown was the first of his race to perform in Vietnam. He complained bitterly before departing, and when he came back, that black soldiers were not getting the black performers they would like to see. Yet, when some representatives from a group of Negro Vietnam veterans approached him for help after one of his performances, he turned them down.

"Soul is when a man is true to himself," Brown has said, and because he is a businessman true to his business, his people forgive him easily. The crowd that packed Miami Stadium to see him this summer is the same crowd that James Brown walked out on a year and half before. At that time, he had contracted to receive $20,000 for two shows, half in advance and half at intermission. When he didn't get his check at intermission, he cancelled the remainder of the show.

Another night, another show. This time the crowd, teased by the cape and the collapse, chases The King around the periphery of the Orlando Sports Stadium to a trailer, serving as his dressing room. Safely there, his aides undress him, comb out his hair and set it in rollers.

Outside, the guards at the door tell a disc jockey from Nashville that Mr. Brown will have no guests. James Brown himself had invited the disc jockey to the dressing room, because when James Brown was 20 years old and a nobody, this disc jockey promoted the show. That was when the soul man made $100 before he paid the band and the rent.

Now James Brown is 35 years old and somebody, and he is on the inside of an air-conditioned trailer with a half dozen helpers picking up after him, and the disc jockey who knew him when he was nobody is outside swatting the bugs off his complaining wife and their crying infant.

It is 3 a.m. He will wait. The show is over, and Ben Bart is in a small room with his glasses on counting out the gate receipts, and James Brown has forgotten about his friend, the disc jockey from Nashville.

"James Brown's 'Superbad'" (excerpt)

David Brackett
2000 • *Interpreting Popular Music*

Rhythm as a separate field of inquiry in Western music did not develop until the nineteenth century. Until then, treatises had regarded rhythm largely as a function of pitch. Partly as a result of this, rhythmic analysis has not developed to nearly the same extent as the analysis of pitch; when it does occur, it tends to contain many of the same epistemological biases as pitch analysis: the analyst searches for resemblances between small units; after locating these, the way in which they create a sense of "unity" or "coherence" is revealed; then attention shifts to the way the small units recombine "organically" to create larger structures with many "architectonic levels." Needless to say, these studies are based on spatialized observations derived from a score rather than a performance. Little work has been attempted on popular music; however, rhythmic studies are a bit more common in ethnomusicological literature, especially on West African music.

We may begin our consideration of rhythm by recalling Floyd's comment that "swing" is communicated by the way in which sound-events Signify on the time-line (i.e., a recurring pattern of beats based on the "metronome sense"). Olly Wilson, in his discussion of polymetric patterns in "Superbad," finds three different rhythmic patterns in the texture displayed in texture *v* in example 4.3:

(1) the accents of the horns and drums imply an alternating meter of 3 + 3 + 2;

(2) the bass, through heavy accents, implies a four-beat pattern beginning on beat two;

(3) the melodic goal of the bass, low D, creates a counter stress of a four-beat pattern beginning on beat one.

This last pattern is reinforced by the entrance of the guitar after eight measures (texture *w* in example 4.3), which begins its eight-beat pattern of 6 + 2 on beat one. The guitar part frequently features a slight anticipation of beat one, forming an upbeat-downbeat ellipsis similar to that noted previously in many of the vocal figures.

Although texture *y* (which dominates section B) shares many features with textures *v*, *w*, and *x*, it reorganizes them significantly. Following Wilson, we could analyze texture *y* in the following way:

(1) the horns and drums now play an eight-beat pattern which begins on beat two;

(2) the guitar plays a sixteen-beat pattern which features constant sixteenth notes broken off abruptly on the thirteenth beat; this accents the first beat of every fourth measure;

(3) the bass and bass drum produce a pattern that divides the first two beats into a pattern of 3 + 3 + 2 *sixteenth* notes, thereby producing a rhythmic diminution of the characteristic pattern of the horns and drums in texture *v*;

(4) the bass pattern for the whole measure divides the eighth notes into 3 + 3 + 4 (an eighth tied over to another eighth) + 6 (further subdivided into 3 + 3 when the bass plays sixteenth note fills);

(5) meanwhile the drums, in the second four beats of their pattern, engage in some extremely complex cross accents. Beginning on the second accented beat, the ride cymbal divides the twelve remaining sixteenth beats of the measure into a pattern of 3 + 3 + (2 + 2) + 2.

The third texture, texture z, provides a rhythmic antithesis to the preceding textures: it consists solely of eight evenly accented eighth notes, producing the only texture in the piece that consists essentially of rhythmic homophony. Texture z is also anomalous in other respects: it lasts for only one measure each time it occurs, compared to the extended durations of the other textures; and it is the only texture to occur with a "dominant" harmony.

We might say that Wilson answered the question implied earlier (how do the sound-events of "Superbad" Signify on the time-line?) by emphasizing the transmutation of West African polymetric practice in the music of James Brown. Another way of conceptualizing the effect produced by the song is to emphasize how the different accentual patterns create a complex, compelling "groove" by Signifyin(g) on the time-line of eighth-note pulses, "making the pulse itself lilt freely," which results in "swing," that elusive quality regarded by Floyd as the *sine qua non* of Signifyin(g) and the Call-Response trope. The web of accents is enhanced by the slight anticipations and delays within the patterns (e.g., where exactly does the second accent of the horn's "dunht, dunht" in texture v fall?). Snead's idea of the "cut" comes into play here in a nearly unmediated form: the matrix of one- and two-measure ostinati reminds us of Snead's claim that "the greater the insistence on the pure beauty and value of repetition, the greater the awareness must also be that repetition takes place not on a level of musical development or progression, but on the purest tonal and timbric level." Figure d4 from example 4.2, in the context of texture y in which it occurs, illustrates the way in which "sound-events" (generated by the voice in this case) can Signify against a time-line (already made complex by ostinati which are themselves Signifyin[g] on the time-line) creating an extreme, almost vertiginous sense of "swing." In example 4.4, which shows the rhythmic groupings in figure d4, Brown's voice briefly implies in the first measure yet another stratum in the polymetric matrix by accenting beats one and four, recalling the snare drum pattern in texture v. Brown contradicts this pattern in the next measure by accenting beats two and four (the only other time in which these beats are explicitly accented in "Superbad" occurs during the sax solo in section A5 when the guitar plays the figure shown in texture u in example 4.3). The rest of this example displays very complex rhythmic groupings, some of which fall into various combinations of three and two eighth notes beginning at different points on the time-line; these create a further sense of disorientation, obscuring the relationship between the voice and the underlying pulse.

Both the rhythmic analysis presented here and the analysis presented by Wilson in his "Significance" article imply that the presence of polymeter may be responsible for the kinetic quality of the music. Wilson's article implies as well that this is the source of the similarity between West African and African-American music. One of the major insights of Wilson's work is that he points out connections between West African polymetric practice and rhythms played by a single instrumentalist in African-American music which are not obvious. However, there is a risk that Wilson's idea might be misinterpreted, reducing it to a positivistic formula such as "multi-meter=groove." Discerning why some bands "groove" more than others is a complex affair. Besides studying further the already mentioned phenomenon of anticipations and delays within a groove, we need to understand better how performers communicate a sense of rhythmic freedom and play while at the same time communicating a strong sense of pulse; and how members of the ensemble primarily responsible for communicating the music's metronomic sense create a unified, yet relaxed, sense of pulse. An often unrecognized aspect of groove is the role played by the voice or lead instrument; the discussion of example 4.4 and the analysis of anticipations and delays in the vocal part hint at the importance of the lead vocal in the creation of vital drive. While there is much work to be done on how specific grooves are created, we must not forget the all-important factor of social "competence": a groove exists because musicians know how to create one and audiences know how to respond to one. Something can only be recognized as a groove by a listener who has internalized the rhythmic syntax of a given musical idiom. This assertion contains a degree of tautology, but scientific analysis of the rhythmic components of a given groove would be meaningless if the analyst (or the analyst's "informants") could not distinguish between a "good" groove and a "bad" one.

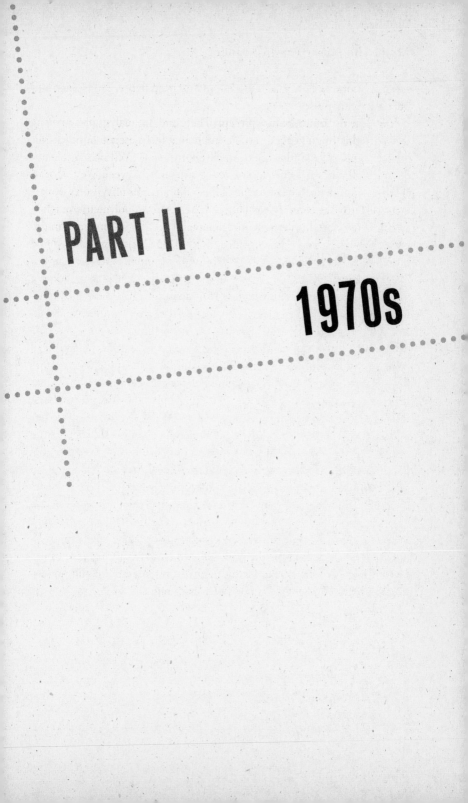

PART II

1970s

"From the Inside"

Alan Leeds
January 1991 • Liner notes for *Star Time*, released by Universal-Polygram Records

first met James Brown in July 1965. I had eagerly parlayed an obsession with his music and a fledgling radio career into an interview assignment. But my station's senior disc jockeys were quick to warn me of Brown's legendary tyranny—so by the time I knocked on the door of his hotel suite I was practically shaking.

A soft-spoken, exotic-looking woman escorted me into the bedroom, where Brown was sitting up in bed, a single sheet pulled halfway up his bare chest. His enormous process flowed over several pillows. He extended his hand and I barely managed to squeak some sort of greeting as I fumbled with my tape recorder. Brown immediately took control—using my first name, asking about my air shift and bragging about his latest hit record, the landmark "Papa's Got A Brand New Bag."

Within an hour I not only had the interview but a series of personalized jingles for my radio show. I was astonished. Unlike other artists I had interviewed, Brown had turned the tables and actually become a fan of *mine*. In fact, he had me firmly convinced that I was destined to become the biggest deejay in the industry.

Several years later I went to work for James Brown and I was able to reflect on my earlier relationship from another perspective. One of the first things he shared with me was his friend-making philosophy. Befriending deejays, he reasoned, was even more effective than payola. "Friends will play your records forever," he explained. Of course every time they played the records, they were not only selling those records but tickets to the ever-touring James Brown Show. Behind Brown's back, the gag went that if you had a ham radio in your bedroom, he'd do ten minutes with you!

At the time, James Brown Productions was housed in a modest suite of offices adjacent to the King Records plant in an industrial area of Cincinnati. Working there proved to be just short of joining a cult. Non-performers were expected to dress in conservative business suits and ties. Brown insisted that we all refer to each other by surname ("It's a respect thing," he would say), although we often lapsed into the ultra-slangy colloquialisms that peppered his song lyrics. And yes, we were liable to be fined for the smallest of "infractions." More than likely, though, if you were docked $100 on Monday, Brown slipped you $200 on Tuesday.

James Brown maintained complete control of his enterprises, despite (or because of) decisions seasoned with ego and emotions. His business approach seldom heeded departmental boundaries and he was surely aware that in deference to his mood swings, problems were sometimes concealed rather than brought to his attention. It didn't take me long to learn that Brown simply didn't want to hear certain things at certain times. Conversely, his rapt attention to detail and penchant for interminable grilling sessions prevented anything from falling between the cracks.

The business side of the James Brown "style" was made vividly clear during my first week working for him. We had learned that the boss would be spending several off days in the office, and suddenly everything in sight was dusted off, swept up or polished. Secretaries and agents quickly reshuffled their desks. Anything that might raise an eyebrow was put away.

An hour later the door ceremoniously exploded open. Brown strolled through the unusually sedate office without anything resembling a greeting and delved directly into tour business with agents Buddy Nolan and Bob Patton. In mid-sentence he bolted toward Patton's secretary and requested a copy of his latest record. Patton jumped up to switch on a stereo system, but Brown waved him off.

"I don't wanna hear it, I know what it sounds like," he said sarcastically. "I wanna look at that mutha!"

After a glance at the disc Brown turned back to the secretary. "Get Bud Hobgood down here," he growled. Then, switching to a sugary drawl, he added, "Pleeeze."

Production manager Hobgood whizzed into the office, looking apprehensive at best. Brown lashed right into him.

"Bud, all these damn records are pressed wrong," he said. "They're crooked, off center. Everywhere I go, the jocks complain. What the hell's the matter up there?"

The records *were* defective, but quality control wasn't Hobgood's jurisdiction. Brown didn't care. He knew Hobgood wouldn't rest until the problem was corrected.

Records were the core of our existence. Although a 1960s record deal wasn't generous enough to support a star and entourage the size of Brown's, the marquee value of the James Brown Show hinged on the success of his records. Not surprisingly, Brown insisted on daily sales figures of the records and carefully monitored ticket sales for upcoming tour dates. After digesting these reports, he'd call on his nearly photographic memory and compare the ticket counts to previous bookings in the same areas.

James Brown was a walking encyclopedia of cities and venues. When I became tour director, several times a year I'd sit with him and the agents to map out a tentative tour route three to four months in advance. Brown would first select larger, more lucrative cities and then build around them. We were all familiar with most cities and their regular venues, but it wasn't unusual for Brown to throw us a curve.

Stumped for a peripheral town to fill a vacant date, Brown would invariably come up with some obscure hamlet. Frustrated at being outdone, we'd have to listen to him victoriously proclaim, "There's an old theatre there, on the main street. It holds about three thousand people. Look it up."

He was always right.

Dependent on performance revenues for income, prior to the mid-1970s artists didn't "tour"—they worked. Big stars like James Brown had the "luxury" of working often. Arenas, theatres, stadiums, night clubs—the James Brown Show played them all, fifty-one weeks of the year.

The schedule sounds inhuman by today's standards, but unlike modern tours we didn't have scores of tractor-trailers full of gear. We carried a single truck for uniforms, musical instruments, a modest audio system, and a lone strobe light. Load-in never took more than a couple of hours. Local promoters supplied follow spots and the only microphones were for vocals and horns. None of the rhythm instruments were miked—and yet night after night, the band tore the roof off whatever venue we were in.

Brown traveled in his own Lear Jet. He sometimes offered rides to favored employees like merit badges. Business manager Charles Bobbit was normally on board and Bob Patton, Buddy Nolan and I frequently joined them to discuss business, but on one occasion Brown invited audio engineer Jerry Shearin to fly with us. Shearin jumped at the chance to swap an all-night bus ride for the opportunity to persuade his boss to upgrade the sound system.

We had cut things closer than usual that afternoon and didn't arrive at the gig until a half-hour before showtime. Shearin rushed to his post, only to be confronted by road manager Fred Holmes and informed that he had been fined for lateness.

Dumbfounded, Shearin asked Holmes if he was joking.

"No man, no joke," Holmes said, laughing anyway. "Mr. Brown says you know you're supposed to be on the job three hours before the show. He says you shoulda thought about that while you were layin' in that hotel last night, plottin' to spend his money on new equipment."

Worlds apart from the private jet was the band bus, an unassuming long-distance coach leased from Trailways. By 1970, with Maceo Parker and most of the "classic" '60s band suddenly gone, the entourage featured a diverse mix of rookies and old timers. Gertrude Saunders, Brown's long time wardrobe mistress, was in charge of the bus and ruled her domain with every ounce of her substantial frame. She refused to tolerate any behavior that compromised what little privacy existed aboard the "J.B. Express."

Everyone was assigned regular seats. Seniority dictated first choice. Most of the veterans, like drummer John Starks and roadie Kenny Hull, sat near the front, playing poker and sipping gin to lull themselves to sleep. Comedian Clay Tyson and emcee Danny Ray, graduates of the Harlem night club scene, appointed themselves the bus narrators. Mile after mile, they hilariously described every billboard, dilapidated building, winter-weary farm animal and downtrodden hitchhiker the bus would pass. Hardly anyone paid their incessant babble any attention. I don't even think they bothered listening to each other.

The younger musicians huddled in the back, sharing reefer and playing Jimi Hendrix tapes. A relatively inexperienced group of Cincinnati teenagers, they had been summoned hurriedly when their more famous predecessors had quit.

It didn't take long to discover what had attracted Brown to his new band. Among them were William "Bootsy" Collins, a gawky bassist with a strangely arresting rhythmic nuance and riveting stage presence, and his equally talented guitarist brother, Phelps. They quickly combined with drummers Starks and Clyde Stubblefield to form a rhythm section with a raw pulse that was fresh for even Soul Brother No. 1.

The transition from old show to new show had more than its share of fascinating offshoots. For example, less than a month after the band upheaval

I caught a show in Virginia and discovered a radically new arrangement of "Give It Up Or Turnit A Loose." I asked Brown about it afterward.

"Oh, that's my new tune," he said. I didn't understand how a two-year-old record could be his "new" tune, but all Brown would offer was, "Wait until we get to Nashville tomorrow. You'll see."

One day and another concert later, we were on our way to Starday-King's newly refurbished studio for the first recording session with Brown's new band. Too nervous to be tired, the fellas anxiously ran through the only tune they'd record that night. Sure enough, there were the licks I'd heard in "Give It Up." Only this time, the song was named "Get Up, I Feel Like Being A Sex Machine."

Brown called for a take, but stopped it when he stumbled over a phrase. On the second take a mysterious metamorphosis took place. We witnessed an instinctive musical genius that magically bypassed the normal thought process, evoking a vocalese from deep inside. When it was over, Brown broke into a wide grin.

He was ecstatic. He had transformed a simple groove into a piece of gold. Furthermore, facing criticism that his songs had become derivative, he had successfully altered his musical "formula." Maceo's soaring sax was replaced by a funky piano solo and Brown had written in a call-and-response with sidekick Bobby Byrd. But more significantly, the arrangement focused entirely on the polyrhythms of the Collins brothers and Starks.

Engineer Ron Lenhoff dutifully asked for another take. But take two was the bomb.

Everyone crammed around the monitors for the playback. Thirty seconds into the song the exhausted musicians started dancing in place, slapping fives and laughing. By the end the entire crew was cheering— actually yelling and screaming!

"Sex Machine" helped set the pace for African-American music in the 1970s. It wasn't the first or the last time James Brown would be at the evolutionary helm of his art form, but like the rest of his staff, I was too absorbed in day-to-day business to "think history." Of the five years I worked for Brown, however, those first two were probably the most exciting. He reclaimed his throne amidst an unusually threatening crop of competition that included Isaac Hayes and Sly Stone. The young, exuberant band, a timely new wardrobe and a handful of red-hot national television appearances combined to deflect any backlash from the Maceo mutiny. Meanwhile, smash hits like "Sex Machine," "Super Bad" and "Soul Power" ruled the charts.

The world was watching and listening again. Everyone who was anyone, from Miles Davis to Fela Ransome-Kuti, from a packed Olympia Theatre in Paris to New York's posh Copacabana, was checking out the "new" James Brown. All the critics who had prematurely buried the "hardest working man in show business" had to not only eat their words, but also come up with some pretty decent new ones.

It was a privilege to be there.

"James Brown: 'The Man' Vs. 'Negroes' "

Ray Brack
January 21, 1970 • *Rolling Stone*

Charleston, W. Va.—James Brown was dancing, screaming, sweating out his farewell to the shitkicker circuit. His appearance here was billed as the last of his almost-yearly caravans through hillbilly heartland.

He romped through his ritualized revue for an adoring crowd of 2,000 young blacks, then retreated to a dressing room to give several of the Famous Flames a dressing-down. (Brown may be cutting back on personal appearances, but he's proud of this band and won't brook any sloppiness. Like Louis Armstrong or Little Richard, he doesn't dig on-stage improvisations.)

He dismissed the chastened Flames. Then, showing none of the exhaustion and dehydration said to afflict him on the road, Brown waved his visitors into his room. The ensuing rap went on for two hours.

Upshot: Soul Brother Number One, "The Living Legend" (as he's billed for concerts these days) is into Hollywood—and militancy.

Not that Brown, who boasts 29 million-selling records, is going to quit recording (his next album, due out next month, is called *Broadway Funk*)—and he isn't retiring from personal gigs, either, as he had announced in Memphis in September. "I'll be doing about 30 dates a year. That's cutting off about 85 percent of public appearances. You don't see

Sinatra out on the road 300 nights a year. Still, I don't want to be a myth. I'll do New York, Los Angeles, Detroit, other big towns . . . and Las Vegas.

"I'm just taking my music into movies and television," he continued. "I start filming my life story in March, working with Dick Clark. I have control and ownership of everything, including the soundtrack." The story of James "The Man" Brown.

As for TV: "I was closed out of television for a long time because I went for manhood. They were afraid of losing sponsors. Now, I could have my own show five days a week anytime I want it. I don't; I'd over-expose myself. But I'll do some specials, and I'll probably be forced to have my own weekly show some time. I could do a lot for the country. I could bring people together."

Someone suggested James would be bringing manhood to Hollywood. He liked that.

"Manhood." To Brown, this denotes blackness with balls. He'd already denounced Leslie Uggums and Robert Hooks on the Mike Douglas show, calling them "Negroes" who really "want to be white." In the resulting flap, the FCC backed Brown up.

"They didn't have to back me up. I was right."

Brown's contempt for most of the big-name black entertainers that have preceded him to Hollywood is undisguised. While they have demonstrated that black-skinned talent can cut hit albums and handle movie-starring roles, TV specials and variety shows as well as whites, Brown feels that none of them have stimulated improved racial understanding by bringing brazenly, unretouched blackness to the business.

In his dressing room rap, Brown enlarged his indictment of black Hollywood.

"Robert Hooks, Sidney Poitier, Sammy Davis Jr., Bill Cosby, Leslie Uggams, Diahann Carroll—they're all Negroes. They're ashamed to be black. Trying to be white. They have a chance to do something for the country, but they won't do it. So why should I attack whites before I attack these Negroes? They're my enemies."

Brown believes his Hollywood entry will open the way for a new breed of screen star, ethnically authentic.

"I'll play myself in my life story. All the real people will play themselves. Burl Ives doesn't know my life. Black youth don't dig Dustin Hoffman any more than John Wayne. I am an actor that is now."

Brown's disdain of pseudo-black Hollywood is part of his growing militance.

During the ubiquitous urban riots of recent years, Brown was on the side of the angels, cutting more cool-it radio spots than any black entertainer. But in his concert here he got the biggest rise out of the audience with, "I'll fight for the country, but if it doesn't give me my rights, I'll fight the country." For James Brown, that's radical.

Privately, he confided, "Me and Nixon don't get along. He asked me to go along to Memphis in the campaign. I didn't want to be his bullet-proof vest. I didn't want to protect him from my people, deceive them. Make them think he's with me and I'm with him." That's just not the same Brown who was winning human rights awards from liberal groups.

"Here's the problem."

He walked over and put an arm around a chubby white chick deejay. She, being emotional, started to blubber.

"We got to free up people until she and I have a chance. The man has the white woman and the black man uptight. She's trapped in the house and I'm trapped in the field. We're going to break loose.

"Until a black man and a white girl can walk in here and nobody thinks about it, we're in trouble.

"Take me. I should be the biggest in the business right now. I would be if I hadn't had to fight the establishment. I will be the biggest. When I retire, I'll go out on top."

"Take It to the Bridge"

Alan Leeds

1996 • Liner notes for *Funk Power*, released by Universal/Polygram Records.

It was March 9, 1970. The funk vine quickly spread the news: James Brown lost his entire band.

Disgruntled and burned out, the musicians had confronted Brown with a list of ultimatums just before a show in Columbus, Georgia. Instead of mulling over their demands, Brown called his Cincinnati office and set his staff in motion: "Mr. Patton," he told his agent, "you gotta find Bootsy and those kids now!"

Bob Patton tracked down bassist Bootsy Collins, his guitar playing brother Phelps, horn players Clayton Gunnels, Daryl Jamison and Robert McCollough, and drummer Frank Waddy, at a dive called the Wine Bar. Veteran JB sidekick Bobby Byrd made the call. In a matter of hours, a teenage band that had only briefly toured behind Hank Ballard and Marva Whitney was on its way to Columbus in Brown's Lear jet.

The Pacemakers (or Blackenizers or New Dapps, depending on what month it was) didn't find a pretty picture in Columbus. The show was late, the crowd was restless. The old band was in uniform, defiantly refusing to play. Byrd led the scraggly teens to the boss' dressing room. After a brief huddle, the houselights went down, and James Brown hit the stage with a brand new band.

We'll probably never know if Brown was bluffing—using the youngsters to put the old band in its place. But Maceo Parker, Jimmy Nolen and the rest of the Sixties veterans packed up and sullenly disappeared into the Georgia night. The sound behind them was thousands of fans screaming their approval for Soul Brother No. 1.

But the transition wasn't neat and tidy. Those of us who recognized that James Brown's funk magic owed much to his state-of-the-art band were devastated at the loss. And I was even more devastated the first time I heard the new band.

Two weeks into their new jobs, the "New Breed Band" (soon to be dubbed The J.B.'s) struck me as everything the classic Brown bands were not—loose, unpolished, occasionally out of tune and small. No regal line of hornmen spread across the stage, just two tinny trumpets and a lone, hoarse-toned saxophonist. The rhythm section consisted of a single guitarist, a gawky bassist, loyalist John "Jabo" Starks and a second drummer who seldom played.

While Brown's other-worldly vocals and unbeatable energy level were still at their peak, musically the show was disheartening. "It was quite scary at first," recalls Byrd, who coached the new lineup from behind the organ. "They basically knew James' licks but it wasn't the way it's supposed to be done. I wondered whether they'd ever be able to do it."

Yet a few weeks later in Virginia, something had happened. Sure, the horns were still a bit sour and they seemed swallowed by a huge arena, but this time my eyes and ears were on the rhythm section. With a big confidence boost from Captain Byrd, and an exuberance that all but obscured the rest of the band, the Collins brothers had forged James Brown's funk into the sound of the Seventies. "All I had to do was lend an ear to what they were doing and start there," says Byrd. "They had a kind of radar together that was electrifying."

Using Larry Graham of Sly & The Family Stone as a prototype, 18-year-old Bootsy commandeered the rhythmic edge of the band. "Bootsy had a different concept of playing his instrument," says Starks. "When he would sit in a groove, everything on you moved."

That wasn't all. Bootsy's enthusiasm turned "gawky" into a statuesque stage presence, giving his boss a natural foil. He soon became one of the only bassists to earn a solo spot in a James Brown Show. "I was just happy to be around," Bootsy told me recently, the enthusiasm still in his voice. "James was our hero. To be up on stage with him was mind-blowing."

The new groove did wonders for the standard Brown repertoire. Fresh arrangements of "There Was A Time," "Bewildered" and a fierce "Give It Up Or Turnit A Loose" became highlights of the show. Then, in the wee hours of a Nashville night, I heard "Give It Up" gain a new set of lyrics and magically become "Get Up I Feel Like Being A Sex Machine"—the J.B.'s first session as the official Brown band, and a smash hit.

It was, as Brown is apt to say, "a new day." "Sex Machine" brought him out of a slump, both on the charts and at the box office. And the funk vine lit up with chants of *Bootsy!*

Bootsy wasn't the only foil to Brown. Since dissolving The Famous Flames, JB depended on various alter egos to spice up his music: In the late Sixties, Maceo Parker's landmark sax solos were the centerpiece; sometimes the Basie-inspired horn section answered the leader like a choir. Other times, James called on band members to spontaneously devise beats or riffs. In 1970, the inexperienced J.B.'s offered little opportunity to explore funk's uncharted territory. So Brown turned to Bobby Byrd, his musical partner since 1952, who became a more visible co-vocalist and co-writer than ever before.

James Brown reinvented himself again. He spent the next year accumulating an enviable string of hits, each of them a reservoir of incredible drive: following "Sex Machine" was "Super Bad" ("*I wanna kiss myself!*"), "Get Up, Get Into It, Get involved" and "Soul Power." (JB's personally political "Talkin' Loud And Sayin' Nothing," a prime example of the locked rhythmic communication between Bootsy and Jabo, sat on the shelf for 18 months.) But typical of Brown's business sense—moving so fast he'd leave things behind, or jumping on trends and mixing agendas—this period was never properly compiled on LP, until now.

Sex Machine, for example, was a hugely successful double album, yet did not include the original hit single. Brown had assembled a disc of 1969 concert recordings, then called an impromptu session at King Studios to create a second disc from his new show. Without a qualified engineer available on short notice, King label president Hal Neely and a petrified trainee manned the board. It was a tense evening, peppered with technical glitches and false starts, but a determined Brown led The J.B.'s through killer re-makes of "Sex Machine" and "Give It Up Or Turnit A Loose," which were later overdubbed with canned audience reaction to simulate the live atmosphere on disc one.

James Brown also had several recording careers going on at once. Besides his J.B.'s, he recorded ballads and pop songs with jazz combos or studio orchestras. In 1970, Brown even tried his hand at what he called "underground" rock, with an album, *Sho Is Funky Down Here*, that's better left ignored.

James Brown's mixing of genres was never more apparent than on the *Super Bad* album—a potpourri of filler and excess flawed by another attempt to fake a concert recording with cheesy overdubs. There wasn't anything on *Super Bad* that remotely resembled the hit title song, and it failed to duplicate the success of *Sex Machine*. It turned out to be Brown's final album for King Records.

King was in disarray—barely keeping the doors open—and Brown was about to jump ship to Polydor. A proposed live-in-Paris album with The J.B.'s was cancelled, and the "Get Up, Get Into It, Get Involved" and "Soul Power" singles fell between the cracks, never making it to an album at the time.

There were other changes afoot. Veteran saxophonist St. Clair Pinckney returned to the fold, joined by guitarist "Cheese" Martin. "Soul Power," the original J.B.'s final studio date with Brown, marked trombonist Fred Wesley's return and his rise to band leadership.

If that wasn't enough, marathon touring was taking its toll. The J.B.'s had followed their mentor everywhere—to arenas in tank towns and theaters in big cities; to ghetto taverns like the Sugar Shack and posh nightclubs like the Latin Casino; to Africa where they found their roots and finally to Europe where they found the latest fashions.

But when they returned to New York in March 1971, for an important two-week engagement at the Copcabana, morale was shot. "It really began in Africa and continued through Europe," Bootsy Collins remembers. "The band was rappin' about money all the time."

Jet lagged and irritable himself, Brown argued with Copa impresario Jules Podell over the opening act, then had a more serious dispute over a cash advance to cover his payroll. When Podell held his ground, Brown played hardball and cancelled the second week. When the band was told they'd have to go on half-pay, they too played hardball. "When James did that," Bootsy explains, "I knew I had to leave."

Many of the fellas walked with him. After a year and 16 days, James Brown again found himself without a band.

A few weeks later, Bootsy, Catfish and Chicken were in the audience watching James at Cincinnati's Taft Theatre. Outlandishly garbed like the Funkadelic with whom they'd later tour, they smirked and giggled as the nervous new J.B.'s struggled to find grooves on "Sex Machine" and "Super Bad." If they had waited a few more weeks, Bootsy and his gang might have been surprised, as Pinckney turned Robert McCollough's John Coltrane imitations into something musical, and Wesley transformed their enthusiasm into the more versatile band that would escort Brown through the next four years.

"After all," Wesley insists, "Whoever you put James Brown in front of becomes a great band."

Maybe so. But never again would James Brown be at the helm of such an unwieldy, raw, yet exciting group as the original J.B.'s.

" 'I have two selves and one is black' "

Juan Rodriguez
July 18, 1970 • *The Montreal Star*

James Brown was a relaxed man as he walked into a dress-room before his show at the Forum last weekend. He looked around, saw many young, nervous white faces, and swaggered to a chair at the front of the room. He's a small man, compact, well-conditioned. He dominates. He's tough and he lets you know it. He was in a talking mood and he wasn't about to get uptight about it, but there's this toughness about him, this battling spirit, that gives every word he speaks its punch.

He starts off with, "I don't know what I'll be doing next year, I don't know what I'll be doing tomorrow, man, cause I'm gonna live from day to day, you know. I can plan for tomorrow but I still gotta live today." That's just an opening preamble. From then on, he shifts back and forth about being black and James Brown in a white country.

"I've been a victim of the establishment, that's all. I'm not a victim of nothing else because I can communicate with people . . .

"I've just released three records at once, man. But the establishment ain't gonna recognize that. But there are stations that I can talk to, that understand, because if the records are selling that's all that matters. If I have a record that sells 800,000 copies it wouldn't even make the Top 50, but one of the establishment-owned groups can sell 100,000 and be in the Top 10.

"It really *amuses* me, it don't humiliate me, just *amuses* me to see a cat be so stupid because like the truth is gonna come out anyway, man. I feel a little bit hipper than the cat, I don't have to do it physically cause I can outthink the cat and make him blow his own thing, cause he's gonna like, spend most of his time trying to keep me in a bag, but he'll be in the bag, man, trying to hold me there. Like, you look in the bag and I won't be there!

"I feel pretty good to be in a country where every day is history with me cause everything I do, man, it's like the first time that a brother ever did it independently. It's a groove, man. I just enjoy living. It's history every day. They can write it up if they want to or not, but it's a groove. But it's nice when you got something to do and the other cat got nothing to do but see what you're gonna do. It knocks me out . . .

"To me, black is an attitude, it's an attitude from black people, to be completely independent in their thought . . . I'm just doing what the Italian people, what the Jewish people have been doing, I'm just fighting for my identity, that's all, and it just happens to be a black man doing it . . . I don't want black supremacy or white supremacy, I want *people* supremacy. Let a man go for himself. That's the way I'm going.

"Cats get angry, man, and they do a lot of things and there are reasons for cats getting down. When you look at one race that's been oppressed for 300 years, man, it's too bad. I mean, a lot of cats' actions are justified. He don't know nothing better. But for some strange force of reasoning, I just know there's something else. I just believe that *people* will win out over *bums*, regardless of who they are. I figure a cat's a bum if he don't want another cat to make it. I don't have time to stop nobody, I don't wanna stop 'em cause *I'm* gonna get away, you dig?"

James Brown has made it on his own in more ways than one. His father only finished the second grade, Brown made it through the seventh, he was a juvenile delinquent at 16, did four years of an eight-year sentence, and spent 10 years on parole. For the last 17 years, he's been THE soul leader. There's Ray Charles and B.B. King and Sam Cooke and Otis Redding, and then there's James Brown. White radio stations won't play his music and white charts won't recognize it, but it's there just the same. He's been a major cultural force for years.

"We got an album called Raw Soul. R-A-W, that means everything is like it is, man. It's not the same as "tell it like it is." It *is*."

He's always been in the forefront of his kind of music. He says that what people are doing now, he was doing 10 years ago: dances, fashions, music. He doesn't listen to other people's records because "they're not gonna give me what I want. It's *old*, man."

James Brown Enterprises controls a radio station ("The black man has been completely denied the mass communications . . ."), as well as working with the poor. "We'll do *anything*, man, but there's not many things open, man, because if you're black you've either got to be an entertainer or a ballplayer . . . I've had 31 million-sellers and I've never had a TV show offered to me, up 'til last year. I've set new precedents in music over and over, I've showed myself as a countryman, as a humanitarian, but I've never been approached with nothing. It's a bad scene . . ."

He's been speaking rapidly, not letting any of the questions get in his way, sometimes chuckling at the naiveté of his interrogators. Suddenly, there is SILENCE. Brown loks around, says "You guys wanna ask me questions . . .", chuckles at the situation again, and continues.

"I'm moving back South. I'm giving up my apartments, I'm giving up my stuff to the underprivileged people and going South. I'm going there to face it, I'm not gonna run away from it. I feel that if you don't face it, you're running away . . ."

Perhaps James Brown had gone *too* far, because the questions started flying.

"How much time do you spend with underprivileged people?"

"Well, I spend 365 days a year with 'em." SILENCE. "Too heavy, wasn't it?"

"How do you figure that?"

"Because I *am* the underprivileged." SILENCE. Brown chuckles. "How do you feel brother? After everything I got I'm still the underprivileged."

"Why?"

"Don't ask me why. You shouldn't even be in the room if you're asking why."

"You can have anything you want—"

Brown cut him short. "What do you mean? I can have anything I want except freedom. I still don't have that."

Someone decided to get philosophical. "I think we are all stuck with ourselves."

"Naw, I'm not talking about that, I'm talking about equal opportunity. I'm stuck with my color. What are you stuck with?"

"I bet you're stuck with yourself first."

"Naw. You see, you can't tell where I'm coming from, you can only imagine. You can walk in there and be any race you want. But I'm a black man and they know who I am . . . You know, the only area in the world where I've got to *kill* you in every time is the black area. David Susskind found that out, he's supposed to be an authority on a lot of things, he tried to rap to me about black and he was *lost,* man. How can he talk to me about being black? How can I talk to you about something I don't know about, man?"

Mr. Philosophy was persistent, though. "You don't have to have a knife in your back to know how much it hurts . . ."

"No, you're wrong there, brother . . . You said a man has to face himself. Well, unfortunately for me I have *two* selves and one of them is black. That's taboo in this country."

"Supposing," said the same fellow, "you were in America before white people."

"I was in America before a lot of white people; I'm 37 years old and anybody under 37, I was here first. But that don't make no difference. Leave me alone brother, you're gonna get hurt. You'll look very *weak.* If you've got any standards in this city, you'd better *ask* me instead of trying to *tell* me . . ."

"What do you think of Stokely Carmichael?"

"I think Stokely's a man who made a move."

"Good or bad?" A last gasp.

"It was good. It made people aware . . . Everything boils down to prejudice. And it's bad. It's a man's world, not taking the ladies out of it, but
that's the way it goes. And it shouldn't be color. If I become a bum, let me
become a bum by my own choice; then if I become a bum, don't label me
a nigger-bum."

There was a fanfare from the stage. James Brown got up quickly, smiled
and sighed at the same time, and said "I gotta go. Anyway, I enjoyed sitting, talking, rapping. . . ."

And off he went, another battle won, but the war far from over.

"James Brown Speaks to 'Observer'"

Mike Ogbeide
December 13, 1970 • *Sunday Observer*

The American Negro musical culture exists in several active simultaneous layers of which now one and now another is lifted into importance
by a complexity of circumstances.

The co-existence of these various layers makes possible the surprising
situation that continuity and discontinuity are simultaneosly present; that
the ends and the beginnings of epochs overlap; that revolution and evolution co-exist.

As long as Negroes are denied the opportunity to become fully integrated into America life, and are subjected to isolation in the physical and
psychological ghettos where communications and participation are more
and more concentratedly Negro, they will have race consciousness and distinctive characteristics.

Negro music has had almost as profound an influence in the life of
white people as it has had in that of the Negro.

As a "collective representation" it has provided the American people
with a documentary of social comment, criticism and protest from the
Negro people, for it is an important body of literature.

Its success is evidence of the potential of the Negro, if given an opportunity to develop.

It has provided composers everywhere with raw materials of styles, forms, content, spirit.

Negro music has been a social process, conscious at times and unconscious at others, which has nevertheless been effective in altering the functional relations between Negro and white individuals and groups, establishing communication, reducing conflict and promoting reciprocal adjustments, altering attitudes and behaviour patterns to the end of a better accomodation of the races.

Today, Negro music is providing an effective social device for channeling into nonviolent, creative action, the energy which legitimate discontent, impatience, and often anger, have created.

Perhaps no man is more qualified to talk about what it is to be a black musician in a white world than James Brown Soul Brother No. 1.

Famous James Brown is black.

He is a highly successful musician, having made 34 records that hit top chart and sold over a million each.

I talked to James Brown in an exclusive interview at Hotel Bendel, Benin, on Friday December 4, the day he set foot on the city.

This musical genius and black millionaire answered my blunt, deep searching and thought-provoking questions with amazing calm and dignity.

"There is no truer truth obtainable by man, than comes of music.

"The beauty of life lies in struggle and change and taking tough decisions.

"There is no easy way to success, you've got to work hard and struggle."

James Brown told me that there are three kinds of Negroes:

"Coloured people afraid to face responsibility.

"Negroes who become white oriented, get rehabilitated and care no more.

"Blackmen who want to make life to the top, but still want to remain black."

JB belongs to this class.

"I think my greatest record has been 'I am black, I am proud.'

James Brown said that unlike Nigerians and other Africans the blacks in America have lost their pride and dignity.

"You have your pride.

"You possess your culture.

"The white man couldn't rob you of it."

What is it like being a black musician in a white world? I asked.

"I lead the only successful black musical group, not controlled by whites.

"Mine is the only group of its kind.

"You know, I have made 34 top chart records.

"Each of these records sold a million plus thus selling about 34 million records and more.

"This is rather unprecedented.

"The interesting thing is that if I were a white, each of my 34 top chart records could have sold over 5 million copies.

"I never had television recording: You know whites run the country, and so I never had the chance."

James Brown contributed a lot of wealth and power to the ghettos.

But what does this mean in terms of dollars?

"In five years I made ten million dollars.

"You know a great part of this amount was spent for charity.

"Many of my business are ghetto based and many black people are on my pay-roll.

. James Brown is reputed for giving more of his money and time to the ghettos than any other black performer in the United States.

He is against violence.

He is equally against oppression of any kind.

When I asked him about racial crisis in the United States, James Brown replied:

"I will not pray to be violent, but when a man slaps me on one of my cheeks, I will never turn the other side either".

"You can say I am a man that stands up to fight and die for others, if need be."

Asked about the bitter youth revolt and the question of generation gap in the United States, he replied:

"Of course the entire world is in a mess.

"The youth want a change for the better.

"There's got to be changes made.

"But they don't know how they can make the required changes.

"The older generation knows how, but they don't have the guts, the pride and dedication."

Yes there is soul in James Brown, but there is more than that.

Asked about his attitude towards women and sex, he said:

"I am a man

"You can't fight nature"

James Brown told me that Women Liberation Movement in the United States does not bother him.

"Every day that I live, I live for the black man."

Asked what was his feelings when he set foot on African soil, James Brown said:

"I can hardly explain my feelings.

"You meet brothers that you know live somewhere but you have never met.

"The feeling is sacred.

"It is just like a religion."

"Is it not a shameful thing that you have accepted from a white-owned company to visit the biggest black nation?"

I challenged him.

"Africans have tried to sponsor my trip to Africa, but they could not pay the bill.

"It is true that I came on the invitation of Phillip Morris—a white-owned company.

"Sad enough.

"May be next time I will love to come here for Nigeria and her people."

James Brown believes that the relationship between Afro-Americans and black people in Africa could be improved.

To him, it is a two-way traffic.

"Both sides have something to gain.

"I would suggest both should meet and talk as frequently as possible.

"Regular conventions here and there will promote goodwill and understanding which has existed from time immemorial."

James Brown who once said proudly: "I'm 25 per cent talent and seventy-five per cent business" observed that Nigeria has tremendous economic potential, but woefully lacks the knack for business.

"Nigerians need to be taught how to succeed in business.

"They need the skilled manpower.

"I think proper education is very necessary in this respect.

"The Government should educate her people so that Nigerians can control their destiny.

"You only could build your country, no one else can do it for you."

Asked what he intends to do with his future he told me he cannot tell.

James Brown revealed:

"I have invested millions of dollars in viable businesses.

"I own three radio stations in United States.

"Looking into the future, I think I would have loved to go into the film world—Hollywood in Carlifornia.

"But I have my pride and dignity.

"I detest playing an inferior role in a motion picture which is always the lot of the black actors and actresses in the so-called white world".

James Brown is mighty.

He is magnificent.

He deserves a top role.

He deserves respect.

"Mister Messiah"

Philip Norman
March 7, 1971 • *The Sunday Times Magazine*

James Brown will die on the stage one night, on the moving staircase of his own feet in front of a thirty-piece band; and then who knows what may be unloosed between black Americans and white? In Baltimore or Washington or Detroit, cities where the very peace between them has a quality of angry breathing, merely the presence of Brown has been reckoned to equal 100 policemen. Harlem, on the sweltering night after an atrocity, he can cool by one word. At the end of each performance he sings the chorus "Soul Power" over and over again with bass guitar equalling a tribal tom-tom in rhythm that locks up the mind; but he doesn't cause a riot, he empties the theatre. The audience dances out into the street.

Oppressed people are the ones who need heroes in the deepest sense of idols that come from among them and can show them a way upwards to release and happiness. James Brown is the greatest American black hero; more than any of their dissenters, more even than Dr King. He is so much to them because of his distance above them as the most famous of all Soul and Rock singers; because he started life far below them, shining shoes on the doorstep of a Georgia radio station; and because this ascent has given him a bulging conceit which, like an itchy ectoplasm, reaches black audiences, somehow transformed to pride that they deserve to feel in themselves but have been denied. He is great, above all, for his music, for never having withdrawn, as the Beatles did, to be cut and issued from record studios by scientific means. After 15 years, every night he is miraculously re-created on the stage of one desperate city or another.

When Dr King was murdered in 1968, the Brown revue was appearing at the Boston Garden. It was the televising of this three times during the following 24 hours that kept streets throughout the Republic relatively clear of the destruction that police and National Guard had anticipated. Brown himself made a public entreaty to black people to contain their grief— "you ain't going to tear up the streets and throw your shoes in the trash can"—that was afterwards entered on the Congressional Record. Therefore, black politicians sustained by hate say he is an Uncle Tom, just a catspaw of the white law agencies. They monstrously resent Brown for what he does for morale. He has given black people not theories or systems of aggression but a phrase from the soul that they can speak and be uplifted by and yet smile at—"Say it loud, I'm black and I'm proud." What can white culture offer to give a glow like that to the spirit?

I first saw Brown sing at the Apollo Theatre in Harlem three years ago; in a winter when the sauerkraut relish from the hot dogs steamed on the breath of queues stretching two blocks either way down 125th Street. And the Apollo audience is exquisitely critical and it has tranquilly watched the decline of many who fancied themselves Brown's equal in soul-size. There was Little Richard, whose stage company finally exceeded any fee he could possibly be paid, who sang flanked by mock Grenadiers and demanded that a carpet be unrolled before him as he walked. There was screaming Jay Hawkins, carried onstage in a coffin (which shut him in one night), and Solomon Burke, who always had the catering franchise. His followers used to sell pork sandwiches and popcorn in wrappers that bore Burke's image wearing a crown.

And then a new generation of perfectly good people, like Sam and Dave, Joe Tex, Arthur Conley, has from time to time produced a challenger to Brown, emboldened by the thought that he was making records in 1965, when *Please Please Please* sold a million. There have even been tournaments, with Brown and his younger opponent as mailed knights and some gigantic Southern stadium the tilt-yard. Always the challenger has been danced off the platform, roared out of sight, unable to comprehend that Brown has lungs and legs like a normal man.

He could tear down a theatre on his own; yet the turning of a short man of 38 with a perceptible heart condition into this colossus is the product of an organisation as quaint as it is profitable. Brown is a business tycoon and multi-millionaire; a condition that his soul-brothers readily pardon because of the thousands of dollars he gives back to Negro charities and schools. He owns buildings and three radio stations including the one where he was shoeshine boy, and a chain of restaurants called The James Brown Gold Platter, which do quick-service soul food. His few leisure hours have a baroque quality—in the ornate mansion in Queens, New York, that is soon to become a museum of black history, at his estate in the lushest portion of white Georgia next to the links where they play the U.S. Masters, and in a black private aircraft named The Sex Machine after its owner's most characteristic song.

When I reached Washington last month for his appearance at Loew's Palace, the Brown organisation had struck the District of Columbia already. Detailed sheets had been drawn up of exactly how much the four-night engagement should earn, allowing for the usual percentage of children let in at a special rate of 99 cents. The theatre management had received exact, if slightly misspelt, instructions as to the advertisements required, the size of Brown's name in relation to his supporting acts, and how many promotional spots should be engaged on soul radio stations around the city.

It was only in the wings of the theatre, watching the show for the sixth or seventh time, that I began to appreciate Brown's full size as a star: that is, how many arms and legs existed round him to do their utmost to stop us meeting. There was a U.S. Marshal with white hair, a camel coat and eyes and eyebrows cast into the same dangerous dark nuggets; there were dozens of other acolytes wearing suits and sometimes hats, addressing each other as Mr Bobbit, Mr Hall, Mr Holmes as their employer insists they do—he once corrected Hubert Humphrey for omitting that courtesy. I was also counselled not to drink to excess, since Mr Brown disliked the smell of alcohol, and told to have faith. In the succeeding 48 hours I must have shaken as many black hands as the Chief Scout at an international jamboree.

The show is Brown—virtually nothing else. Even the three go-go dancers who pump their knees in ghostly red light on a dais behind him seem to have been chosen for perfect inconspicuousness. There is a comic and a supporting group, in this case The Chi Lights, who astonished me by saying they had worked 10 years together. But the band is splendid. Splendour is forced on them. There is an Afro-Rock section, a formal octet of brass and strings, two drum kits, talking drums. Good billing is also deservedly given to an old friend of Brown's, Bobby Byrd, who was in his classic group of the early Sixties, The Famous Flames. Byrd plunged offstage in a glaze of exertion and was at once introduced to me. "*The London Times!*" he exclaimed. His hand shot out. "Talk it up!"

Because of his heart condition, each of Brown's appearances has an element of brilliant suicide: each is like his first big chance or his last, and yet he has probably done two shows tonight already. It is as if he is gripped by demons and poltergeists, themselves in the grip of drums. Hot whips seem to turn him: the eye can only follow him when he stops but he can't bear to stop. *Get Up, Get Out, Get Involved* with its chorus "Soul Power" stretches into parts of an hour, not with the effeminate self-indulgence of a group like the Rolling Stones but because there truly is no end to such a rhythm. Brown is wrapped in a cloak which he casts from him again and again, precisely on the drum-roll. Is the only thing he really loves the velvet space he sees beyond the mirage of the stage lights?

Finally at four in the morning I was beckoned through the crowd of supplicants into Brown's dressing-room. It remained, however, difficult to enter, because of the number of black men in suits respectfully crowding the walls. Reverence hung like the smell of an altar. The next thing I saw was some two dozen pairs of boots and shoes, from the 80 pairs Brown wears out onstage each year, in patent leather and piebald and snakeskin, giving the impression of a harbour crowded with picturesque craft. Next to the shoes sat Brown himself, drinking beer from a can. After the way he looks in performance, coiffed and tailored in beige or soft blue, he is a man of surprising shortness and plainness.

He was engaged with a disc-jockey in tape-recording programme flashes for his most recently acquired radio station, in Baltimore. That and WJBE in Knoxville and WDRW in Augusta, Georgia, are among the very few soul stations in America which are actually black-owned. "Hi," Brown said into the microphone, "this is James Brown. *Hello Brother!* Now," he ordered the disc-jockey, "you reply 'Hello Sister'."

"Hello Sister," repeated the disc-jockey.

"Hey no—they'll think I'm some kinda' faggot here. Say after me. *Hello Brother!*"

"Hello Brother!"

"*Hello Sister!*"

"Hello Sister!" said the disc-jockey.

"I think the people are beginning to understand," Brown recited. "Get outa' that *bed* and into that *bread!*

"Now li'l brother and li'l sister, if you' on your way to school and you' feeling bad—a education can bring you the things that you never had—so don't feel bad, but say it out loud . . ." Brown produced a variation on the axiom that has passed into the literature; "I'm going to *school* and I'm black and I'm proud."

He started to talk, but this was as much to his attendants as to me and his voice, to begin with, was silted up with distrust. "I'm preaching revolution. Some preach revolution for land and some for politics—I'm preaching it for *awareness*. If I'd of had an education I wouldn't be where I am today, wouldn't know nothing about land, business, but not everyone can have my advantages. Most important teacher I ever had? He was my manager, Mr Bart of Universal Attractions. He was manager to a lot of famous people, Jackie Wilson, Little Anthony and the Imperials, but he told me I had something no-one else had—intelligence. I was a *whole* man. Now you rarely get a whole man. A doctor or an attorney, he's a doctor or an attorney 150 per cent. of the time. How can he satisfy a woman?"

Brown turned to one of his men and said, "Now Mr Patton, you shoulda' told this young man 'fore he came in here that I was super-hip, you shoulda' primed this man up. I can tell what he's going to ask me 'fore he asks it."

I replied that this was untrue. For the first time I felt Brown's complete attention settle on me, with a body-weight. There was a little shudder from the door. The interview ended and for the next 24 hours it was intimated at second and third hand that I had blown the whole of it by contradicting the star: he was as a result 'leery' of me and, anyway, I had already enjoyed as much of his time as had ever been granted to *Look* magazine or *Cosmopolitan*. Therefore it was surprising to me—not to mention those of his followers trying to see me off—when Brown told me to go up to his suite at the Hotel Sonesta when he rose in the early afternoon.

Brown was eating a tangerine in a white-carpeted parlour, somewhat complicated by cream-coloured wrought-iron tables and chairs. All the ashtrays had peel in them and the room smelled sharp with it. At first Brown appeared to be by himself: then the soft movements were added of a woman in slacks whom I took to be a chambermaid. It was only when she gave Brown his heart-pill that I realised this was his wife Deirdre. She came back into the room with two of the long wastepaper baskets peculiar to American hotels, and Brown put one leg into each. They were filled with warm water and salts. Then she rubbed his feet with ointment. Sitting beside him on the couch she took one of his hands under her arm and began to trim all the cuticles of his nails. In this apparently servile posture, all at once she looked strong and influential, and Brown not lordly but quite small and vulnerable.

"When I'm on my own on the road I behave just like a teenager, 19, 20 years old—bang, bang, bang," Brown said. "I'll eat a hamburger before the show that I won't even finish, but this afternoon I ate almost a full meal with salad and Black Forest dessert. We could get a maid to do all this but she won't have it. People sure like me if Didi's visiting. She salts my feet and rubs 'em and takes the ingrowing hairs out of my nose that I'd cut myself if I tried.

"She gives me a lot of room in the bed. I don't do karate tricks but I have to spread out. If my wife and I are together in bed I'll dream—95 per cent. pleasant dreams. If I eat late I may dream about an accident and that's not pleasant. And I wake up and see the outline of her there, and I feel like I did sleeping at the back of the aunt I boarded with when I was 12 years old. She gets up to bring me a soda. I drink a little of it. I can relax and feel like my spirit goes and lies on the studio-couch in the next room 'till morning."

Brown grew up in Augusta; in red clay country where the white word 'Boy' can have the most evil sound in the world. "It was a country home—water outside. I was nine years old before I had my first store-bought underwear, my clothes having been made out of sacks and things like that. My first memory is unpleasant. If it were pleasant I wouldn't remember it." His mother left home when he was scarcely walking; his father greased and washed cars and was a sporadic parent. James helped him and picked cotton and gathered coke from railway lines, danced for the soldiers at Fort Gordon or cleaned shoes. "I'd come home at one or two a.m. and there was nobody there."

His cousin Fred Holmes, now with the Brown road show, says, "We'd steal anything—groceries, hub-caps. All I could think of then was that James was going to be a hoodlum." At 16 Brown was sent to reform school; at 19 he was paroled and became a lightweight boxer. The cleft over his right eye that the stage make-up conceals is a souvenir of that. "I trained with Beau Jack and all the fighters I was with went on to spar with Ray Robinson. I only ever lost one fight and that was because I was a chicken." Today, in extreme displeasure, he will still aim a punch at somebody.

When he sang spirituals in a church in Toccoa it was not from any promptings of the soul but because "I was trying to get a foothold in *anything*." His early professional years were spent touring Southern dives, he and eight musicians and their equipment all junked into one station wagon. It was that life which gave Brown his extraordinary notions of how orderly and punctual a touring Rock show must be. His employees, as well as addressing one another formally, have to wear suits. Even the road-managers with their filthy nails have to operate in jackets, sometimes with *three* rear vents. The available females that pursue Brown after each show are used with the same relentless courtesy. Brown himself makes little secret of benefiting from their company. "That racehorse—he don't run if he ain't got no lust." According to someone else, "there can be three different women in three motel rooms but he's polite to 'em; he calls 'em 'Miss' and puts 'em on a pedestal if they put him on one."

The band is ruled by iron. Rock musicians must forsake their dilatory ways if Brown employs them. He devises each phrase they play and remembers everything. He designs their suits. He is capable of rehearsing them 12 hours at once. With him, recording is not simply a lazy, artful process on individual tracks: he wants everything played straight off as if it were live onstage. He governs by a system of fines: 25 dollars for dirty shoes, 100 dollars for lateness; it can be as much as 1000 dollars for what Brown considers some gross breach of order or courtesy. The astonishing thing is, the bandsmen pay. They believe Brown leads them to play beyond their capabilities.

Possibly his equation of business acumen with pride of manhood is whimsical: even so, it beats political harangues or the vagaries of someone like Chester Himes, the novelist, whose vision is that blacks will engage whites in total war. "We ain't won," Brown says, "until any black man can walk down the street and nobody turns their head to look at him." But how about looking at his clothes, his shoes or his car? At this question Brown's features parted into a brilliant grin. "Yeah," he said, "*right*. I put all o' my people into Cadillacs. Miss Sanders my wardrobe mistress I gave a Cadillac Bro'ham. I got a Buick Riviera '71 that there's only seven of made at a time 'cause of the recession, and when I'm sitting in that sometimes I wish *I* was the car so people would look at me that way."

By the third night of his engagement at Loew's Palace, a vast number of people had assembled outside his dressing-room. There were several U.S. Marshals now, police and local disc-jockeys, most of whom professed intimate friendship with Brown, and one insufferably earnest white youth from the Boston Philharmonic Orchestra, and the pilot of The Sex Machine. At one point, Deirdre Brown was also there, holding their two-year-old daughter: the child's hair rose up from her face in a cataract and she stared at all the people while her shoulders moved in intimations of rhythm as thrilling to watch as a first step forward.

And there was a preacher named 'King' Coleman with a bald head like a Payne's Poppet and a character named Rufus—"folks call me Catfish"—Mayfield who was intent on outpreaching him in the small hours, while Brown was still lecturing the band musicians on their night's performance.

"I," Catfish shouted, "am the sergeant-at-arms, I am the chairman of the board and the master of my own soul and there ain't no white man on his Ajax horse gonna' come along and say to me 'down Boy'."

"Rufus," King Coleman said. "You been brained."

"No I ain't, no I ain't," Catfish shouted.

"You a militant . . ."

"No I ain't," Catfish shouted. "I'm only doin' what J.B. says to do. Get out, get involved and take care o' business."

At last Brown released his guitarist and bass guitarist and came out of the theatre himself. He is very short but somehow conveys a sense of someone on a litter in an old illustration. He was intercepted by two boys, their hair shaved into black stooks, who clamoured that they'd been made to leave their shoeshine boxes outside during the show, and somebody stole them.

Brown gave them a 20-dollar bill.

"Oh—hey, thanks," said the larger boy. "I was meanin' to come talk to you James Brown while you was appearing."

"*Mister* Brown," Brown said. "When I come back tomorrow I want to see you here and your shoeshine boxes full of shine. Then I'm going to call you 'Mister'."

"James Brown is Super Bad"

Vernon Gibbs
June 7, 1971 • *Rock*

We're sitting there rapping, a little before camera time. This evening James Brown is making one of his increasingly frequent television appearances, and he's gettin ready to reincarnate himself as Mr. Soul, The Super Bad Sex Machine, or any of the other lucrative images he has required over the last three years. Before that it was something else, the strange enigma who could dance better and longer than anyone else, the man whose "do" was tougher than anyone else's, the man who could claim without too much difficulty that he was undeniably the King of Soul. No one disputed it then, and no one disputes it now.

But the extra flashy days are in the past, the seamy images buried with all the other paraphernalia of a hard working entertainer who could slide all the way across the stage of the Apollo on one foot. Times have changed, and J.B. has had to change with it; now he gets asked by Lester Maddox to help him cool down the streets of Atlanta. There is a great picture showing James with a satisfied look on his face, seated behind his desk, while Lester Maddox stands in front of him with a shit eating grin, his arms outstretched in a pleading gesture. President Johnson invited him to the White House to eat fried chicken and talk about the "racial situation," and the Sunday Times of London has called him the "soul singer who could stop an American revolution."

James Brown has become more than a good dancer.

So it is to a fairly content person I am speaking, one who has overcome many of the problems an entertainer with his roots normally faces. He is presently at the top of the world of soul music, the one individual whom *no one* has ever succeeded in imitating, the one who creates a kind of excitement that no one else can. He is doing limited touring now, and his concerts always sell out. He has just finished a successful run at New York's Cheetah, drawing some of the largest crowds in its history. In other cities where he is now something of a rare sight, he has been known to draw incredible crowds. At one concert in Milwaukee, in a facility designed to hold 8,000, they somehow had to squeeze in 57,000. At large stadiums it is not unusual for Brown to draw 50,000 and even in Africa, where he is even more loved and respected, hundreds of bands naming themselves is his honor, he packs huge stadiums whenever he appears. James Brown is then an international hero, an international symbol for Third World consciousness.

So we are sitting there in the dressing room doing a little medium-weight rapping, talking about music, politics, The Situation, James admitting that in spite of all his travels, he still loves to work at the Apollo first and the Cheetah second, because the Apollo has his roots and the Cheetah the groove.

In the middle of our conversation a dude walks in. He has been asked to wait outside the door until we finished talking, but he doesn't look like the kind of man who likes to wait for anything. He is dressed in yellow, wears shades, and has dull blonde hair starting to wear out at the top. The evil slash that he calls a mouth is now working double time. He has entered unasked but we ignore him, pretending he didn't exist. James Brown just says to me "Keep on rapping."

The intruder doesn't like this. He doesn't like being asked to wait outside the door, he doesn't like having had to follow Brown around until such time as James comes to a decision.

"When we gonna get together, James?" he says. I pause in mid-question.

"We already got together," James replies, ending the conversation.

"Well it's on your end that we're having difficulty, not ours."

"Oh yeah?" James is profoundly bored.

"The director we have in mind just did a picture that was nominated for an Academy Award."

"It doesn't mean nothing; George C. Scott showed you all that."

"Well, I just wanted to show you the kind of person we have in mind."

"It doesn't matter. He couldn't produce me, all he could do is just follow. You can't find a cat who knows my thing. How can a man direct something when he doesn't know what he's talking about?"

"Well, who are we gonna get? Some guy from 116th St. sitting on some curbstone to do it?"

Our enterprising movie maker has lost his cool. A purple tinge starts to creep across his face, and James doesn't even do him the honor of becoming upset, he continues to get his afro together.

The thin slash continues fumingly, "We got the right man, what do you want us to do?"

"You got to let me get the man. You see there is one thing you fellows forget, you can't do anything you want with anybody no more."

"James, I'm not trying to do ANYTHING with you."

"You see I'm busy, you can't come in here trying to run my life."

"I'm not trying to run your life, all I'm saying is that I have a legitimate motion picture deal for you."

"Well I don't want your deal. Talk to me like a man. Just because you come in here and raise your voice, that don't mean a damn thing."

Time is running out, so thinking the matter is settled I say, "I'd like to ask a few more questions."

But James isn't quite through yet.

"Hold on a minute brother. These things have got to be talked about; this is something you got to hear. He can't come in here talking like that. Just because they come in here running their mouths, they think that they are gonna scare cats into a Uncle Tom bag, but they don't mean a damn thing to me. You live as long as I have, I been dead all my life anyway, so they don't mean a damn thing."

He has been addressing me and referring to the man in shades as a third person. The shades speak up.

"What does that have to do with me?"

"Well, I'm just letting you know, man." James is still ignoring him.

"Well, I'm the one fucking white man that probably did anything for the black people."

"Well I'm black and I don't know anything about that."

"I have programs going where I help people. I don't bullshit people, I help them."

"You can't prove nothing to me."

"Well I'm not here to prove anything to you."

"And I'm not here to listen."

"Well then, no motion picture deal."

"Fine," says James still combing his hair, "there's the door."

He slams the door as he leaves. We have a good laugh, slap fives and continue to rap. "They still think they can walk in with their little pieces of paper and we gonna jump sky high to sign. But I don't want their deals. They seem to think that I'm here to make money for them."

* * *

Appearances by James Brown are starting to become rare occurences. There was a time when they took up 365 days of the year, but King James isn't touring anymore. He is busy trying to give some economic validity to his concepts of Black Power. Not that James believes in Black Power the way it is manifested by the Panthers; he is more into "People Power." A lot of his time is spent with his businesses and deservedly enjoying the rewards of many years of brutally sweaty one night stands in thousands of smoky dives all across the country. He is enjoying the fruit from the years when, in spite of the justifiable boast that he was the "King of Soul," the biggest stop on the itinerary would be the Apollo; that aging dried-paint-crackling-on-the-sagging-walls symbol of the continued enhancing of the pockets of outsiders, with the talent of black music.

The Empire Room and all those lavish palaces, choking on their own lushness, are open to him now, and fat businessmen from Dallas can sip their extra dry martinis and enviously watch him dancing above the jingle of Las Vegas, but all this really means nothing. James Brown sums it up by saying, "Yeah, it took me too long to 'make it,' but by the time I made it to those places, it really didn't mean anything . . . I still like the Apollo most of all because it has my roots."

But there is a sense of bitterness connected with having taken so long to rise to the top of America's mythical road to stardom. He has always been a star up in Harlem, and in all the Harlems that create themselves whenever poverty and oppression come together. But it has taken a long time for James Brown to be "recognized." As he told one reporter, "I've been a victim of the establishment, that's all. I'm not a victim of nothing else because I can communicate with people . . . If I have a record that sells 800,000 copies it wouldn't even make the Top 50, but one of the establishment-owned groups can sell 100,000 and be in the Top 10 . . . I've had 31 million sellers and I've never had a TV show offered to me, up till last year."

Maybe now that the extensive touring is over, it has given people an opportunity to observe all the things James Brown is into, as well as given him a chance to involve himself more in other aspects of what he is into. He suggested that when he said, "There are a lot of things that I have to do that take up so much time. Touring wouldn't give me as much time to handle my business well. My business is what's really important right now. I didn't always want to be an entertainer, but it was almost the only thing I could do when I got out of reform school. I was basically into sports when I got out, but it was a matter of survival, I had to get into something, so I chose entertainment. I guess I learned a lot of things in reform school, it really got me together and a lot of things that have come out wouldn't have come out if I hadn't gone."

Reform school. That's only one of the many interesting things that go into the James Brown legend. Everyone knows about his owning the building in front of which he used to shine shoes, and becoming the premier citizen from Augusta, where he first learned all about poverty and the rough knocks that come from being defenseless. When he left reform school at nineteen, he immediately got into entertaining, evolving through stages into the symbol he is now.

But aside from being a symbol, he is also the world's most dynamic entertainer, and on this particular night the Cheetah is packed. The Cheetah was a strange place for James Brown to make his first New York appearance in a long time. It is a gaudily wrapped rhythm palace, unimpressive and ungainly, lurking off to the side of New York's theatre district. It's a prowling area where Pink Cadillacs and outrageously attired females on the lookout mix with party-minded jivers, in for a night of fun from the provinces. With James Brown there, the entire scene is even more unreal. Upstairs the Otis Redding Room has been transformed into a madhouse. The Pink Caddies have disgorged their loads, and they're all trying to get into James Brown's dressing room to say hello. Everyone has a different story. Some are fellow entertainers, others claim to be life long buddies. There are quite a few pimps who seem to be trying to rub shoulders with money that isn't tainted. Many of them never make it in.

Downstairs on the scared dance floor, the little people whom James Brown calls his "friends" eagerly await him, having yawned through the ritual of a few non-entity bands, who only serve to show how good James Brown is.

If you were there Saturday night, you may have wondered as to how the $9 tab may fit in with James' philosophy. But he had nothing to do with it. The Cheetah is always expensive, but this time around it has been rented by rip off promoter, Joe Cavallero, the unctuously mustachioed little man who squinted from behind his pseudo-hippie long hair as you walked in. He paid James Brown a flat rate and then proceeded to charge whatever he thought he could get away with.

The James Brown Band always warms up the audience. They are meticulously trained, every note they play being authorized by J.B. When prepar-

ing the audience they usually play hits made popular by other artists, waiting until James appears before getting into what they are best known for.
The J.B.'s are a big, flashing display of glittering brass and funky elegance.
Most of the band travels with Brown, but sometimes a few local musicians
are hired. They form a separate contingent and are directed by a trained
conductor, playing from sheet music while the rest of the band has it all
memorized. The size of this band within a band always varies, depending
on the size of the stage and the auditorium. The J.B.'s fit very snugly around
their leader. Once he is on stage they never take their eyes off him, playing
with a tightness befitting their reputation, hopping and jumping with
Brown's every breath, just as if they were an extension of his voice.

When James Brown comes on stage, he is all rhythm, he hardly ever
stops moving. Admittedly he isn't as flashy as he once was—after all, he is
thirty eight and has been on the road for seventeen years. But he still is the
"greatest showman on earth" and "the hardest working man in show business." His energy output might not be as constant as it once was, but he
still puts more into every wiggle than all his imitators put together can
come up with in one hour. When he starts to work his show, all you can do
is stand back and watch in wonder; it's hard to imagine where it all comes
from. He doesn't spend the entire show dancing anymore, but he still has
those moves, and that careless hipness that he wears like a king everytime
he makes a move is still his and his exclusively. He puts all the others in
their places just by sliding across the stage and listening to the girls responding on cue. Even when he is only standing behind the mike, shaking
with that powerful band gestures, he is still a very dynamic figure.

One would think that with all those years of wear, the voice famous for
those piercing screams would have started to show signs of wasting away,
but it is still in top condition and when he says, "I feel like I could scream,
do you want to hear me scream?" he can answer his own question without
too much difficulty.

It is true that he doesn't ask the question too often; he isn't screaming
that much anymore, and the entire tone of the act is more relaxed, a mixture of this week's hits, with standards like "Please, Please" and "Papa's
Got a Brand New Bag." James explains a few things about his new policy,
"I think the trend for dancing has pretty much caught up with itself. What
can I do in showmanship that I haven't done already? So I've got to go the
other way, I've got to do more singing. I've got to move into different
things. For instance, my latest album is called, "Sure Is Funky Down

Here" and it's what you might call rock or underground music. It is really underground jazz. I've been into this a long time, but this album is really a new thing. I think soul music can do a lot more for jazz by mixing it in so that people can start to become aware of jazz once again. Straight jazz is hard for many people to take unless they have been brought up with it. But when you mix it in with soul you have a new thing that people can relate to. This is what's happening today and I'm getting into it."

As everyone knows, James Brown is very much into mixing music and politics, a mixture which he considers very necessary in these times.

"I don't want you out there just dancing and not thinking about nothing . . . I think communication is one of the strongest areas for revolution in the world . . . I want a cat to be able to make a move and know that he has been across that ground before. The revolution in the mind is what's happening. If a cat's mind is a little softened up to what's going on, he can set to fight what's happening. If I can get everybody thinking right, if I can get 'em to the bridge, I got 'em . . . I'm not hung up just on black, I'm hung up on right. There's a lot of white kids out there that are really together. It's tradition that we are fighting. We're not fighting white, we are fighting tradition."

James Brown has been called many things. Now that at the height of his career he is being hailed as a "messiah," an inspiration, the leading black man in America, there must be a feeling of responsibility attached to the acquisition of all these titles, especially the one calling him a living legend.

"Whether I'm a legend or not is up to you to decide; you know what I stand for. I do feel a certain responsibility, first to myself as a man, and I think if I just exercise that, it will serve as a tremendous force to revolution, to identity, respect, dignity and pride to the black man. Because that's what I want to be, not something else. Black people have got to be able to go anywhere and do anything. We always just wanted to be Americans, but they forced us to be black Americans. By the time my kids come up I want them to become president if they want to. It's a terrible thing not to be able to do what you want. I wouldn't run for office because I might win and then I would have somebody telling me what to do. But black Americans should be able to do anything they want. One of the things that really bugs me is when I get on the plane to Europe and I get there, I'm a man. When I come the other way, I'm a black man."

"The Man Behind the James Brown Myth"

Sharryn Watts
January 17, 1972 • *Soul*

There was, (once upon a time) a mighty little giant, who was not only a king . . . he was a soulful Black King. Hailing from Macon, Georgia (as did some other soulful kings) he brought to his people a declaration, a message, a tiding of utmost importance. His message? "Soul Power" . . . "Black Power" . . . "Power to and for the People" . . . "Be Black and Be Proud." The message to his people was to encourage the development of more Black soulful kings. This mighty little giant was a Black man; and rather than be called, "Your Majesty, Black King," he preferred the title James Brown, Soul Brother No. 1.

For one weekend and four concerts, SOUL was granted permission to be in the presence of the No. 1 Soul Brother in order that the people might know the king off, as well as onstage.

330 DAYS OF CONCERTS A YEAR

For more than 330 days of the year, James Brown and his troupe (this year consisting of the J-B's, Dramatics, Lynn Collins and the Soul Twins, Bobbie Byrd, and Clay Tyson) are delivering a message to the Black people in the form of a dynamic James Brown Stage Show. Unlike most leaders who send ambassadors to the people, James Brown goes himself, leaving the business management, promotion, production, and follow-up work to trusted individuals working out of the New York and Georgia offices. And unlike most leaders, he doesn't limit himself to the people of one state, one coast, one country or one nation. James Brown takes his message to people—Black people—all over the world. He doesn't preach militance or hate, just Black Soul Power through pride in Black consciousness. And, though the message averages about three hours in deliverance, it is easy to grasp and exciting to behold.

The promotion for a James Brown concert is more than any politician can boast of receiving. For more than three weeks prior to his shows, people of all ages are informed by radio, billboards, flyers, and word of mouth, that the Soul Brother will be in town.

It has been more than two years since the fans in Los Angeles had seen the James Brown show. And on hand in Inglewood's Forum the evening of October 19, was a crowd of eager adults, teenagers, mini-fans and the well-known Jackson Five (Michael, especially anxious to see his idol).

LOS ANGELES' CONCERT

The announcer for the shows who travels with the troupe, Danny Raye, began the evening with a brisk welcome and words of good feeling. Promising a great show, he introduced James Brown's band, The J-B's, who played a few numbers to open the show. The band, under the apt direction of Mr. Fred Wesley, is an outstanding group. Working tightly together, they warmed up the audience with their opening number "Theme From Shaft." Special mention goes to the trumpet section which is quite animated as they produce their sharp uptight sounds.

The other performers and performances were also outstanding, each doing more than justice to the dynamic James Brown show.

The major criticism of the Los Angeles show was the sound system. For some reason proper equipment hadn't been set up and all the performers came through the system sounding tinny and badly distorted. Probably for this reason the audience was restless. Throughout the entire show there was unnecessary milling about. It was rude and very immature, but people so often are thoughtless when all isn't right. It seems that it would have been better to have corrected the sound before continuing with the show and I am sure had it been possible, that would have been done.

The first half of the show completed and intermission behind, James Brown was introduced to the eager and anxious crowd. Running out on stage, while an ocean of people surged to get close, the opening bars of "Can I Get A Witness?," were drowned out. He became what they had anticipated as he sang such favorites as "Bewildered," "Make It Funky," "Try Me," "Super-Bad," "Sex Machine," and "Breaking Up Is Hard To Do."

He wore a pale blue jumpsuit with matching jacket accentuating a low "V" neckline in front and revealing a large circle cut out in the back as he ripped the jacket off. But unlike most crowds, instead of screaming and dancing as he performed, this audience stood as though mesmerized by this special man on stage as he stepped and stomped in a flickering strobe light to the music. With Bobby Byrd accompanying him, he sang hits past and present and left the standing crowd filled. Though some felt disappointed because the sound was so bad, they all left still fans of James Brown.

CONSTRUCTIVE NOT DESTRUCTIVE

Some of the young people who come to see the James Brown shows seem to come because it is a big event for them so they can dress and style. They don't seem to come to hear the message or grasp it's pertinence. At concerts they feel it's necessary to either show off or tear down and break up the Man's property. And it was no different the evening at the Forum, where people were hurt and property completely destroyed. Some of the kids even think it's hip to figure ways to get by the guards and police to break into the show and see it for free. But these destructive games are some of the things Mr. Brown speaks against.

Before really getting to know what Mr. Brown advocates and why, this reporter was one of the people who would yell "pig" and harass the guards just on GP. And though there is still no love for them, at least it was explained that we should respect them as men with their job to do, and not make it necessary for them to have to bother with us. "Suppose you need one to help you one day in an emergency?" the question was posed. So the issue of Black pride was raised—pride in who we are as young Blacks and pride in being Black enough to be constructive, with no time to be destructive.

The concert in San Diego's Community Concourse Auditorium on October 22, was a totally different experience. Getting to an auditorium while it's still empty, watching technicians set up the sound system, workers arrange platforms, performers practice dance steps, and musicians go over chords, is a part of the show fans do not get to appreciate. There is the setting up of concession tables, rapping to guards and officers about the "if" things, and counting estimated ticket sales. People forget that the work isn't done only on the stage when the floor lights go out and the stage lights come on; for the people behind the scenes, the show really starts about three hours before the lights go out off-stage, and all isn't over till about two hours after the last song is sung.

THE SPECIAL WOMAN BEHIND THE SCENES

Mrs. Sanders supervises the backstage dressing rooms of not only Brown, but all the performers on the tour. Like a great special Mammy, she is that type of strong-leader, loving-protector Black woman who is not only behind the Black man who makes it, but she is the one who kept the plantation running well, who led the Blacks from slavery, who is today the symbol of Black female leadership. Mrs. Sanders is all of this and indescribably more, as she organizes the unpacking and repacking before and after a show; as she keeps intruders out of the Star's dressing room; as she sees all runs smoothly backstage to be carried off properly onstage; as she checks to be sure that everyone gets on the bus on time and much, much more. All homage goes to this great special lady with her insisting bark and her infectious laugh. And under her strict direction, the hustling in preparation continues right up until the curtains open to an eager crowd waiting for that first dynamic chord.

THE SHOW IN SAN DIEGO

The next night in San Diego, the auditorium was filled predominently with high-styling young Blacks who received the J-B's first number ("Shaft") with roars of excitement. But it was when the Dramatics ran onstage in their colorful outfits, doing syncapated stepping and singing the melodious tunes to bouncing sounds, that the crowd resisted control and flooded to the front dancing the "Break-Down" and the "Rubber-Band." As the Dramatics closed their performance with their hit, "What You See Is What You Get," they left the audience screaming above the band's final chords.

Security guards in San Diego are just that . . . Security guards. No hassles, no bad vibes, just men with uniforms on to be identified by, there to protect the right-on people from the right-off people who shove and push, and act niggerish instead of Black. The feelings there were greater than the Forum concert, the vibes better (because of the security), and when Mr. Brown appeared there was no holding anyone back. The entire audience filled the front section and the floor lights immediately came back on.

James Brown stopped singing and asked everyone to please go back to their seats. Hesitantly, his fans proceeded to obey. He began again, and again he was forced to stop. Explaining that it was for their safety that they needed to be seated, once again he began his first number, "Bewildered." And this time a Black dude decided he should take the front row center seats occupied by a white couple, and the fighting ensued.

It was as though guards fell from the sky to stop the skirmish. Yet with the fight terminated, the officers merely released the two and asked if they would please return to their respective seats. During the disturbance, Mr. Brown became calmly incensed. Shaking his head slowly, his hands on his hips, he stepped to the microphone and asked, "Why? Why do we act like this in front of the Man? This is the very type of thing they love to see from us. We don't need this kind of thing at a show. You all sit in your seats at a movie or in church. So do the same now! We just don't need this. What we as Black people need is Soul Power. Power to the People. Come on repeat with me. We need Soul Power, Power to the People."

Repeating the chant again and again, he asked everyone to return to their seats to show that "We are all too Black and too Proud to act disorderly." The majority of the crowd quietly retreated, but quite a few just backed to the walls of the auditorium and stood. Mr. Brown remained still a moment, then with voice a bit strained, he pointed out to three rather large Brothers to act as "our police force" and they were to put anyone who wasn't sitting in a seat, out of the place. Needless to say, there were only security guards and ushers still standing within the minute. It was truly beautiful to see such a Black action and reaction rather than the usual gestapo tactics. But it took someone like James Brown to think of it in an emergency.

The concert resumed and each person though they remained seated, bobbed and bounced in enjoyment as James Brown performed. And though sitting, the excitement exuded by the crowd was more than could have been contained if they had been up and dancing. When concluded, about 4000 completely satisfied fans filed out in orderly fashion.

Tired, yet eager for the San Francisco show on the next day, the 135-lb. 5 ft.-6 in. James Brown prepared to leave, only to be halted by about 30 to 50 fans, who waited almost three hours, enthusiastic about getting a glimpse, a touch, or maybe an autograph. Still able to smile in appreciating, he paused to give out autographs, touches, and Black Power waves.

The troupe boarded the bus after the San Diego concert, on their way to San Francisco. It would be an exhausting 10 hour drive before they would arrive at the Holiday Inn on Market Street by early morning. (Mr. Brown flew up in his new, all-black, private Lear jet.) Completely beat, no one got up till time to set up at the Civic Auditorium.

SAN FRANCISCO OVERLY ORDERLY

The people that filled the auditorium October 23 were of all ages, sitting orderly as they waited for the curtains to part and the long-awaited show to begin. The completely Black security force seemed almost as excited. At 8:30 the band began, as did a medium amount of applause for them. During the first few acts the crowd acted more like a congregation of Catholics in church than like an auditorium full of James Brown fans. One of the exciting moments came when some people couldn't see past some of the guards who were also straining to see. The people started shouting, throwing paper balls in order to get the guards to move, as they of course did.

Third on the show after the J-B's were Lynn Collins and the Soul Twins. The trio, though, practically unknown, is exceptionally good. In mellow tones they sing hits like "Mr. Big Stuff" and "Goin' Outta My Head." Every song is superb, however it's on their last number—"I Don't Wanna Do Wrong"—that they really open up and leave the crowd screaming for more. This is one of the groups Mr. Brown is personally pushing and we should be hearing from them on their first album in the near future.

As Mr. Brown entered, there was a thunderous applause and an instantaneous surge toward the stage. The security guards merely blocked the aisles and the show continued undisturbed. This show was just as good musically as the great San Diego show, however the audience was practically the opposite through the entire first half. It is very interesting to observe the differences in crowd reception according to areas.

DRESSING ROOM RAP

All over and all filled with good feelings from good music, James Brown invited this reporter from SOUL and one from Muhammed Speaks into his dressing room to interview him. Entering the oblong, grey-walled dressing room, filled with his family, his business and promotion managers, the two reporters were escorted to seats near where he leaned on the mirrored dressing counter.

With Mr. Brown the use of profanity is forbidden—especially in the presence of ladies. Everyone is addressed by surnames. And all are treated with respect as it is due. Mr. Brown feels that there flows an atmosphere of greater respect when adults address one another more formally. Though there is always a mood of business when in his presence, there exists a feeling of honesty and warmth. He looks each person directly in the eye when speaking, in a sincere desire to be clearly understood. And he leans forward listening with his entire body when he is being spoken to. When he smiles, his head tilts back a bit as he exposes opaline white teeth, releases a hum of a chuckle, and radiates the ability of a Black business man to get down.

"I'm 75 per cent business and 25 per cent entertainer. I believe Black-owned business is the only way we as a People can make it. It's time we stop crying about the white man oppressing us and buy him out; stop trying to kill him and getting killed and use him for our purposes; stop preaching hate and revenge or peace through submission and build our own businesses. Then we can hire whites to work for us. We must come together in business, because Black business Power will help us establish power for our people."

BLACK RADIO

When asked how we could get started in the right direction, Mr. Brown felt that, "The best way is through our own Black-owned radio stations across the country. This way the young people can be encouraged to think and grow through Black orientation. Now I don't mean any form of militance. Just the importance of school, no drugs, and Black businesses. Pride, real pride in Blackness is something most Blacks don't realize. They can give the Power sign, preach white overthrow, and push drugs for quick money, but most can't spell, read, or write well. Most can't hold down jobs working to try and save for the future. And most don't think they can be creative without drugs. Most of them drop out of school before they are sixteen and school is where the foundation is formed. This is why I wrote 'Don't Be A Drop-out.' There were other songs to encourage them to think, like 'Get Involved,' 'Blackenized,' 'I Don't Want Nobody To Give Me Nothing,' and 'I'm Black & I'm Proud.' Black young people should be made to understand that the most effective Black power is brain power. The Black college students want to do something. Something special for the future of their children. They've looked to violence only to see their leaders killed or silenced. They tried demonstrations, only to be beaten and jailed. Some of us even hoped integration would be the answer, but integration was one of the biggest mistakes we've made. It allowed the white man to think he could be equal to us. I don't hate the whites. But we must get ahead in business and then use the white man to work for us. Everyone must have his place and it's time we took our place as the boss.

"I own my own company (James Brown Enterprises), live on my own estate in Georgia, own my own private bus for our tours, have my own private jet, and have three radio stations (WEBB in Baltimore, WRDW in Augusta, and WFBE in Knoxville). This is not boast, but business. Black owned business is the only way we can ever be on top."

Time was lost with all the talking. When informed that we all would have to vacate so the custodians could lock up the building, Mr. Brown asked that I be escorted to his car so we could continue talking. I was still tingling from the conversation with Mr. Brown as I waited comfortably in the backseat with his 18-month-old daughter, Deanna, and her two puppies, his sister-in-law, and his attractive Creole-looking wife (in the front). On the way to the hotel, as he was driving, Mr. Brown explained that, "The Black woman has been together from the beginning. It's time the Black man got himself together. The Black woman wants and needs a man, and she is usually more than willing to help her man be a man. It's taking us, as men, too long to get it on and if I were a Black woman (as much as I hate to admit it) I would probably have to have a white man, too. Black men, trying so hard not to be like whites, don't show respect to their women by opening doors for them, or getting up when they enter a room, or other such courtesies. We must respect our women and treat them well in order to have them stand beside us as we climb to the top. There is nothing worse than to have your woman against you. We should also start wearing suits and ties and dressing neater as we prepare ourselves for business. We have got to not only act the part, we've got to look the part."

Driving up in front of the Holiday Inn, Mr. Brown slowed and stopped, put the flashers on, got out of the blue cadillac, and helped me out of the back seat of the car. We stood in the crisp (really cold) San Francisco morning at almost 3:00 a.m. and continued discussing Black awareness. After one half hour of rapping, Mr. Brown asked this shivering reporter to stay over another night to attend the San Jose concert to be able to finish talking.

ON TO SAN JOSE

Boarding the JB Enterprises bus on time is very important, because the policy is "business must be carried out on schedule" and the bus has been known to leave without anybody on board. All aboard by 3:00 we arrived in San Jose a little early. Around 5:30, while technicians were setting up equipment in the Civic Auditorium, Mr. Brown was on stage rehearsing with the J-B's and Fred Wesley. One quietly watches the Taurus persistently go over various notes and chords with perfection in mind. Though he is definitely the leader of the entire show, the one who chooses the tunes and supervises the dance steps, and clarifies the sounds, he doesn't lord this authority over the people working with him. Standing around backstage before the show, the subject of how he felt about the woman's role today was discussed. Especially in regards to business. Or if he felt she should give up being the strongest and stay home or just what.

"That depends on the man and woman. If a Sister is well taken care of and can trust and respect her man and if he wants her home, she should stay there. If not, she'll go out and work anyway. But young Black Sisters should still stay in school and learn all there is to learn cause she never knows what she'll be required to know. The few Brothers who will make it will want more than a pretty Black face to make it with them, you know.

"Women today have heavy heads: They are ready to do the man's business if he can't carry it out, but there's so much she can do—and then what does she do when she needs someone? It, of course, requires heavy Sisters to produce and rear heavy sons. But you see, school is so important for all of this."

He explained that the reason he has quite a few songs like "Sex Machine," "Ain't It Funky Now," and "Hot Pants" is because it draws the attention from the masses and is needed to get them in to hear "Don't Be A Drop-Out."

The small conversation circle began slowly to grow as showtime drew near. Showtime was scheduled for 8:30, yet a crowd was forming at the door by 6:30. An hour before the show began, the front doors were opened and like some great tidal wave, Black and Brown young people crashed into the auditorium, running, rushing, grabbing seats, yelling across to one another, laughing in excitement and scheming for front row seats.

8:45, the lights went out and the wave surged to the stage. The lights came up and after only one request that they do so, the crowd returned to their seats.

FOR THE YOUNG

Mr. Brown was behind the curtain watching his overeager fans with a pensive expression. These were the young people that love him. He could start a riot just screaming "Please, Please, Please!" These are the young people to whom he must be careful to give just what they want in a performance, so that when he says "Stay in School"—they'll listen.

These are the same young people that he dances for and appears sexy to, so when he sings "Get Involved" they don't drop pills or drink just because everyone else does.

These are the young people to whom he says, "Hot pants are to say,

'What You See Is What You Get,'" and they know he means, "You've got to use what you got (your mind) to get what you want . . ."

It must be more than desire for riches that makes a Black man spend more than 330 days traveling around the world performing and still find time to attend political functions and appear on talk shows. It's quite a bit more than just lust for excitement. It's pride in being a Black Man capable of generating influence. Of course, some people still insist that it's his desire to be a millionaire that makes him push on. But, according to Mr. Brown, "The only way the Black man can get ahead is with enough money to buy, own, and/or sell his own businesses. That way we can produce the commodities we need."

James Brown is proud that he is Black. Because of this he's had to work very hard—but the pride that comes with hard work is what pushes and drives him on day by day as he attempts to reach every Black listener.

During the show the audience was more than responsive. They were contributory. All of the performers were caught up in the electric excitement of the night and gave incredible performances. From the first chord by the J-B's to the dynamic Dramatics to the breathtaking Bobby Byrd, to the luscious Lynn Collins and Twins, through the sidesplitting Clay Tyson, the crowd was never still.

Clay Tyson is a comedian whose style is geared to youthful audiences with mature heads, more so than in the past. Though the subjects all deal with man/woman relationships (sex) there is never any smut or "dirty" joking. He merely takes everyday situations and reconstructs them humorously. The crowd gave him a standing ovation when he left the stage. An ovation mixed with laughter.

Intermission wasn't long enough to make anyone impatient and as soon as Mr. Brown was introduced the stage was ringed by squirming, excited young fans. Turning on the entire audience, Mr. Brown danced as he sang their favorite songs. He fell to the floor emphasizing a line and the girls would scream in loud soulful tones. Even males reached out in hope that Soul Brother Number One would give them the soul shake. Even though the performance was great the audience was one of the best that an entertainer could have.

COMING DOWN

Once the concert was over, while autograph seekers milled about outside and photographers, reporters, promoters and civic people stood around waiting for James Brown to change clothes, he came down off the high that he gets from performing. The feeling of exhaustion is good to him for he knows then that he's given his all. The sound of fans outside does not frighten or bother him for there is always the possibility that his giving the one autograph may spur a youth to stick with school and become successful as an end result.

It's no hassle for him to push on because Mr. Brown has a message to deliver to all of his Brothers and Sisters.

The climb to the top for James Brown has been long and rough. There were dark crevasses and sky-high mountains, and as he continues to cross rivers to reach his people he must experience moments of woe as well as joy. Destructive criticism is something he doesn't need, though he receives a lot. Constructive suggestions are all welcome, and as we look to suggest, let us first look to ourselves, for James Brown is out there acting as a soulful ambassador of Black Consciousness.

"Out of the Brown Bag"

Bob Palmer
September 12, 1974 • *Rolling Stone*

In 1965 James Brown altered the role of the rhythm section in black popular music radically and irrevocably. White listeners, understandably enthralled by the innovations of groups like the Beatles and the Rolling Stones, paid scant attention at first. But black fans understood immediately, perhaps because the components of Brown's new bag had long been a part of their aural environment. The chunky, broken-up bass patterns, sprung against the downbeats, had been common currency in Latin music since the Forties and had turned up in jazz classics such as Dizzy Gillespie's "Night In Tunisia." The trebly, insistent chicken-scratch guitars were a legacy of Fifties R&B as played by Mickey "Guitar" Baker and by Brown's own Jimmy Nolan, who had served his apprenticeship with Johnny Otis. The tight staccato horn bursts were prominent on soul records coming out of Stax studios in Memphis, where Al Jackson was already a past master of hustling, dynamically understated, excruciatingly even drumming.

But James Brown put those elements together in a way that sounded perfectly natural, for all its newness, and further emphasized them by stripping away any elements in his music that might interfere with their impact. Before "Out Of Sight" and "Papa's Got a Brand New Bag," the rhythmic elements Brown synthesized had been used to drive home songs, harmonic structures with choruses and bridges and dramatic modulations and all the other devices which black pop had borrowed from white pop and from its blues and gospel roots. With "Sight" and especially "Bag," the rhythmic elements *became* the song. There were few chord changes, or none at all, but there were plenty of tricky rhythmic interludes and suspensions, and Brown used his voice more and more as a rhythm instrument, putting affirmative slogans in stream-of-consciousness fashion over an increasingly elaborate counterpoint of pulses. The approach probably wasn't inspired by African drumming (in which rhythms are orchestrated as if they were melodies in a fugue) but it was certainly analogous and soon Brown was the most popular recording artist in Africa. In the U.S. he was Soul Brother Number One.

Sly Stone arrived in 1967 and soon dispelled any lingering traces of the walking bass line and the shuffle beat. He is often credited with having singlehandedly booted pop rhythms into the Seventies, but his new kind of momentum would have been impossible without the scores of James Brown singles which preceded and shaped it. As Sly temporarily took over the partying crowd's fancies, Brown began singing more and more about the need for black ownership, self-determination and pride. He was singing directly from his own experience.

As long ago as 1958 Brown knew what he wanted to do on record. He wanted to use his crack road band, but Syd Nathan of King records said no. Brown's reaction was to record the band himself under the nominal leadership of drummer Nat Kendrick and in 1960 Kendrick and the Swans—the J.B.'s in fact—had a national hit, "Mashed Potatoes." Nathan relented and Brown's records, with his band, sold better than ever. In 1964, concerned that King's distribution was inefficient, Brown and his manager gave "Out Of Sight" to Smash, a Mercury subsidiary. A year of legal wrangling followed, Nathan gave Brown the guarantees he wanted and artistic autonomy as well and Brown bounced back, on King, with "Papa's Got a Brand New Bag." By 1970 he was managing himself, had purchased several radio stations and was in the process of forming his own production company. At present he records for Polydor and runs his own People label under the Polydor banner.

The indomitable ego which helped Brown get to where he is today is abundantly evident on many of the records he produces. *"Damn Right I Am Somebody"* by the J.B.'s includes a long consciousness-raising session, Brown asking each band member, "Are you somebody?" with predictable results. On *Us*, by saxophonist Maceo Parker, Brown takes up most of the ten-and-a-half-minute "Soul of a Black Man" with a meandering rap and an exhortation: "Maceo, I want you to blow." Maceo does, for around three minutes. To many album listeners these lapses will be unforgivable, but they are as much a part of James Brown's contribution to the concept of soul as his rhythms, his song lyrics and his empire.

Hell, a double album by the man himself, is remarkably free of self-indulgence. The title tune, "Coldblooded," and "Papa Don't Take No Mess" are sure-fire disco smashes, the kind of no-nonsense party music one expects from Soul Brother Number One. But there are some interesting variations in the Brown formula as well. "Please, Please, Please" is reworked as a very catchy calypso, which combines an irresistible momentum with harmonic and melodic charm. "These Foolish Things" sheds its warhorse image and becomes one of Brown's most lyrical and affecting ballad performances. Resurrections of "Stormy Monday" and "When the Saints Go Marching In" feature chord progressions and rhythm lines which have been considerably altered and are much the better for it. There is a studied avoidance of monotony throughout. The instrumental work is superb.

In fact, the current J.B.'s are Brown's best-ever band as well as his most successful. Their *Damn Right'* LP contains two hit singles, "Same Beat" and "If You Don't Get It," both of which are worthy followups to the million-seller "Doin' It to Death." For the first time in his career, Brown has allowed one of his coworkers, trombonist/arranger and J.B.'s leader Fred Wesley, to front the band in name as well as in fact, and the results are salutary. Wesley is a brilliant trombonist. His solo lines never stray far from the blues but they are delivered with such authority, rhythmic accuracy and exemplary control of the instrument that they never become tedious and usually generate as much fire and drive as the rhythm section. Maceo Parker performs ably on tenor, as he did on "Papa's Got a Brand New Bag" and so many other James Brown hits from the Sixties, and veteran guitarist Jimmy Nolan continues to grow with the times. His tasty

Wes Montgomery/Roland Chambers octave work is particularly impressive. That anonymous "freak" tenor saxophonist who added so much raw energy to several Brown singles from the "Hot Pants" era is back on "Same Beat," and drummers John "Jabo" Starks (traps) and Johnny Griggs (conga) are as usual crisp and penetrating. There are a few weak spots but most of *Damn Right* is as much fun to listen to as it is to dance to.

Maceo's own album is a burner in the tradition of the J.B.'s. Brown dictated that the saxophonist switch from tenor to alto for these sessions and thus his work has a singing quality which contrasts refreshingly with the heavy funk backup. Parker's sound, which often takes on a crying edge reminiscent of Jackie McLean's, is as powerful in its own way as the sound of Brown's voice, and occasionally it grabs the viscera the way King Curtis used to. With the exception of "Soul of a Black Man" the production is understated and supportive. Much of the band's work is slicker and more flowing than on the J.B.'s album, lending credence to the studio gossip that guitarists John Tropea and Cornell Dupree, bassist Gordon Edwards and other stalwarts played on most of the tracks.

For Sweet People from Sweet Charles is Brown's lushest production yet. Charles Sherell sounds like a Smokey Robinson / Al Green hybrid and very unlike an original, and the disparate material—everything from "Strangers in the Night" to "Soul Man"—doesn't add up to a direction, but there are enough references to Gamble/Huff and Barry White in the arrangements and overall sound to suggest that Brown is now listening closely to his competitors. He hasn't absorbed these influences yet. The derivative nature of Sherell's style is accentuated rather than glossed over by the production; there is even a direct cop from the O'Jays' "When the World's at Peace" on "I'm Payin' Taxes" by the J.B.'s. But as Brown's first venture into the lucrative sweet soul field, *Sweet Charles* is doubtless a harbinger of things to come. Having created a rhythmic idiom that lends itself to endless permutations, Soul Brother Number One is now diversifying the surface of his music. He will doubtless continue to grow without sacrificing the energy and urgency on which his reputation rests.

"Papa Takes Some Mess"

Pat Kelly
December 1, 1975 • Crawdaddy

James Brown struts in high style while bandmembers complain of bitter treatment and threaten mutiny. Has the New Ministry gone all Bad?

In every society, if we examine the lives of famous people, we will discover flaws, exaggerations and myths passed down for generations to follow. The American dilemma reflects an interesting paradox; while there exists a desperate need for true leadership, America supports false images, assassinates her prophets, worships idols, semi-gods and superstars whose power includes the will to influence our very lives. Instead of searching within, we look towards men and women whom we are programmed to emulate. This produces two profound problems, one relating to the nature of racism, the other to the disease called egomania. From the exposure that Abe Lincoln really didn't give a damn about slaves, to the acceptance of the "Godfatherness" of James Brown, racism is a bitch that must die; ego, a sin, her sidekick.

The reinforcement of the slave–master relationship continues to exist as America promotes blacks as sexual objects to be toyed with but not taken seriously, or, even worse, as tar babies with a funky beat. James Brown is a metaphor for this society, and basic to its slick sickness. He is a paradox, a poem of excess imagery, an entertainer who has passed his peak, who's been crowned with wealth, international fame and the power to influence. If happiness is equated with money, if happiness is equated with riches, if happiness is a tight girdle on a fat lady dying to be somebody else, then happiness *is* James Brown.

But offstage as well as on, James Brown is not only the center of attraction, he is its victim. After traveling and talking with him; after witnessing his drastic decline as a concert attraction, record seller and musical innovator—after being told by sources close to Brown that I might "disappear from earth" if I told the truth about him—I can say that James Brown is no more willing to relinquish his "throne" than that other Godfather, Don Corleone. A neo–King Lear is King James, as much a part of the American institution as violence is to television, McDonald's to hamburgers. James Brown is a lost spirit, but indeed, Brown's stubbornness, his unwillingness to pass on his crown to a new "King of Soul," has made him an even more fascinating phenomenon. His innovations in music have been co-opted; he's imitating himself now and there's nothing left to do except "Give it up or turn it loose."

May, 1975. JFK Airport, New York. The scene is chaotic. I'm preparing to depart for Cameroon, my fourth visit to the continent in five years. (I'd seen both "Soul-to-Soul" and "Festival '74," two previous concerts in Africa.) While waiting for James Brown, I recall what former Watts poet Quincy Troupe had told me about a near-tragic encounter he'd had with Brown some six months previous during a flight to Zaire.

Before take-off, Brown apparently had begun by belittling Bill Withers. "You ain't shit, you can't sing, you ain't nothing, motherfucker," Troupe had quoted Brown.

Then Brown's sound equipment arrived, with record producer and director Stewart Levine and later a friend of James, singer Lloyd Price, both making vain attempts to inform Brown that his equipment wasn't necessary. (They had already built a $600,000 stage.) Brown said, "Fuck you. If the equipment don't go, *James Brown* don't go."

"Everybody wants to kick his ass, not just me," Troupe continued. "But then the wine starts flowing and everybody's having a good time. They don't want to lose James because he's the star attraction, so other luggage is removed—the Crusaders and Johnny Pacheco lived in the same clothes for four days. The plane *barely* takes off, it's so overweight.

"When we stop to re-fuel in Madrid, Brown and his entourage rush out to the airport lobby. He takes out a portable record player and a stack of his own records and turns the volume all the way up. I'm in the lobby with the Crusaders and all of a sudden we hear this *da, da, da, da, da* . . . and all these people are standing around James saying, 'Yeah, you sure was getting down on that one. . . .' He must have had at least a thousand people around him. At this point, back on the plane, Stewart Levine tells us what's happened. We find out the plane is 5,000 pounds *overweight*, the pilot almost crashed in the water and now James is holding up the fucking plane. But while he's gone, to balance the weight, the stewardess has tied down the first twelve rows of seats. Everybody's laughing because these are *Brown's* seats. B.B. King, the Spinners, everybody's being themselves and James is fucking up the whole scene.

"When he comes back the stewardess explains. Brown says, 'Fuck this,' and he sits down. Then he says, 'Oh Lynn [Lynn Collins], you sit down.' Then, 'Sweet Charles, you sit down,' so Charles's right-hand-man got to sit down too. Then *everybody sits down*. 'Let's get this motherfucker off the ground,' Brown says.

"And that's when I came to *really* dislike James Brown *personally*. Then, a well-known singer, whose name I won't mention, pulls out a knife he'd bought in Madrid and says, 'I wish I was the sheriff of this mother-fucker. I'd put the desperados off.' The stewardess gives up. The plane *barely* takes off again.

"His actions were suicidal," Troupe had asserted. "But James Brown's attitude, from the beginning, was insane. Some of it being show biz, part of the mask that's expected of you, but James Brown went *beyond that*. It was incredible. I had to admire the flight velocity of his ego."

Born in the red-clay Georgia hills near the South Carolina border, James Brown has said of his background: "I had no real mother, no brother or sister, a father only on occasion." As a youth, he collected pieces of coal from the railroad tracks to warm the family home, and also helped his father wash and grease cars and pick cotton. He claimed to have received his first store-bought underwear at the age of nine. At ten, he danced for nickels and dimes for soldiers at Fort Gordon, Georgia. In the seventh grade he quit school and at sixteen he was sent to a reformatory for stealing. Paroled three years later, Brown toured with a Baptist gospel group to support an early marriage. He said: "I was trying to get a foothold on *anything*. I just wanted to be able to sit down and eat a good meal."

From the gospel group, James Brown formed his own trio and the turning point in his career came with the release of "Please, Please, Please," in 1956 on the King Records label in Macon, Georgia. His hits continued with "Cry Me," "Bewildered," "Lost Someone." In 1966, Brown was titled "Soul Brother Number One."

As a musician and performer, there is no doubt that Brown is, as he is introduced in his act, "one of the hardest working men in show business." He writes most of his tunes, designs the costumes not only for himself but for the group. In those early days, Brown would appear after three or four other acts. Part acrobat, part exorcist, Brown would challenge the audience: "Ain't I clean?" After 45 minutes, his would exit and return with another costume change, sweating profusely, screaming and (this used to always crack us up) covered with his cape, which he would immediately throw away. The music blared with trombones, horns, drums and guitar. Bathed in blue spotlight, James was King, throwing his microphone, spinning it around, catching it before it fell. As he was draped with the cape for the final show and led away, women would grip the arms of their seats, threatening: "I'm going to tear all of his clothes off!"

1968 was a controversial year for James Brown. He produced "Say It Loud, I'm Black and I'm Proud" and saw it banned for a long time on white stations. In April, Martin Luther King died, a book appeared entitled *Black Rage*, and in June, *The New York Times* published an article, "Does [James Brown] Teach Us The Meaning of Black Is Beautiful?":

To whites, James is still an off-beat grunt, a scream at the end of the end of the dial. To blacks, he's boss—the one man in America who can stop a race riot in its tracks and send the people home to watch television. Twice he worked this miracle in the terrible days following Martin Luther King's funeral. It started in Boston.

"This is the greatest country in the world," he rasped. "If we destroy it, we're out of our heads. We've come too far to throw it away. You gotta fight with dignity."

Next day, Washington, D.C. was a quieter place. . . .

If one were to drive through the area where the '68 riots occurred, one would know the shallowness, the weakness of such "dignity." But for his efforts, James Brown was rewarded with a card from LBJ—"Thanks much for what you are doing for your country." And Brown really believed the President from Texas loved him.

In 1968, James Brown became the "White House nigger." When Soul Brother #1 decided to take these crumbs from his masters' tables seriously to promote his own brand of black capitalism, he threw in with the State Department. The Voice of America began pushing James Brown and spread the concept abroad that Brown's was the only Afro-American music. In a report on Brown's tour for the USO, the State Department verified his new status as politician/spokesman:

*James Brown, dancing and singing soul music . . . with a throbbing
beat that is somewhat primitive and savage. He was so anxious to make
the USO tour he cancelled more than $100,000 worth of bookings. . . . He
is well-known . . . for the power to cool it for peace, as he proved in
Washington. . . . He is living proof of what opportunity can do; he is a credit to his profession and his country. . . .*

Brown's act now grosses over $3 million a year. He has lived up to his
black capitalist pretensions, employing 85 workers in his New York production office, James Brown Enterprises. In addition to co-ownership of a
music publishing company, Brown's holdings include three radio stations,
a share of Polydor Records, two jet airplanes and many land interests.

The audience to which Brown appeals most is the so-called "grass-
roots" segment of the black community. Contrary to popular myth, this
never included nearly all black people. Many of those I grew up with in
New York considered him the "ugliest colored person in the world." Some
hated him because of his "negroid" features, because he made them conscious of their "inferior" African roots. Bleaching creams and other reflec-
tions of self-hatred were the order of the day as the children of concubine
slaves and their masters were favored over the darker brethren.

But then there were others who, regardless of his looks, knew Brown as
a human captive who did not have to go to the extreme of his conk and
flashy clothes. He sang about nothing but sex; his message songs were superficial. If you had asked a cross-section of the many young people who
were not his fans what they thought of James Brown, you would have gotten comments like: "I think he's a slob" . . . "I know some bloods who'd
like to kick his ass" . . . "He's so dumb he really thinks white people love
him" . . . "They really want us to look up to that toe-dancing nigger?"

In my neighborhood, James Brown was (and still is) referred to as the
"famous fag." The brothers made jokes about his "contorted face" and
since they believed the rumors that he was gay (just look at the covers of
his early records, they'd say) he was given no slack whatsoever. They
wouldn't support his obvious hang-up on "straight" hair. He was/is "em-
barrassing."

There were, of course, others who loved him simply because he was a
life-giving force in their lives. During adolescence, James Brown's music
never failed to start a party off. No one could deny the African roots in his
music, nonsense lyrics or not. So we mostly ignored the rumors that he

was undergoing a sex change so he could marry a popular male singer. His house in St. Albans, Queens, drew curiosity only in winter, when Brown would display a black Santa Claus and everybody'd try to get a glimpse of his wife to see if the gossip were true.

Charles Bobbit became James Brown's manager in 1966. "It was love at first sight," he laughs. "I saw him at the Apollo and admired what he said about drugs and school; his hit song then was 'Don't Be A Dropout.' I asked to be a part of his organization; started out as a valet and presently I'm the president."

Bobbit and I met briefly in Kinshasa, Zaire, during the Ali-Foreman bout, and again in Cleveland, Ohio. In Cleveland, the critics were down on James for messing up the "Star-Spangled Banner" and adding his jazz version of "Lift Every Voice and Sing" at the Ali-Wepner fight.

"Personally," I told Bobbit, "I don't see the reason for all this fuss. So what?" Bobbit, listening intently, told me that Brown was a frequent traveler to Africa and asked if I'd be interested in making a tour. He asked me:

"Are you ready for the James Brown experience?"

I had returned from Zaire only six months earlier, but as the plane rolls off the runway heading for Duala, I know things are going to be . . . different. This is my first experience traveling to the continent with any kind of group, and this group belongs to *James Brown*.

Onboard, the band members have no intention of going to sleep. They play cards, drink, tease the stewardesses, talk about the food and wonder *who is the blue dungarees?*

A writer? "You think James Brown is so important?" Fred Wesley asks me. "Check out the library and see when they list his name in *The New York Times Index* or any of those bibliographies.

"Watch and see if James doesn't come back here to see if you're talking to us. Here he comes now . . . the nigger's scared you'll write more on us than him . . . look how he's grinning at you."

The JBs, his band, his back-up men, are the cornerstone of James Brown. Unfortunately, they don't receive much credit after individuals such as Maceo Parker and Fred Wesley; they are just a part of the chopped meat behind the steak.

Prior to take-off I can feel the pulse, and once in flight, the scene has the aura of play. Even though we are actually *in the air*, we could very well be on a Greyhound bus going to Alabama. Everybody is letting his or her shit *hang*. The Jokers, two of Brown's aides, are challenged to strip and run the length of the plane into the first class section to "surprise the Lord."

"I'll give you a hundred dollars, nigger, if you take off and streak in front of the 'Boss.'"

Feliard, the 200-pound sound man, almost does it, but the band is really after a big, red-haired woman who is the wardrobe mistress. They say she's also Brown's private eye and ears. They make her the same offer. She laughs and ignores them. "She's the Big Momma," someone says.

Fred Wesley, the bandleader, is also the ringleader. He introduces the rest of the group: Maceo Parker (saxophone) and his brother Melvin (drums), Charles Sherill (vocals and keyboard, also known as "Sweets"), Jimmy Nolan (guitar), Fred Thomas (guitar), Jimmy Parker (no relation to the other two; sax, horn), Russell Sinclair (the veteran, "Cheese") and Johnny Griggs (congas).

For 17 hours *nobody sleeps*. They say they are a "family" and talk about James like I've never heard before. I learn his other names: the "little nigger," the "greasy nigger," "King James."

All big groups make sarcastic remarks about the hand that feeds them, but only Fred Wesley can talk about the tragic change in James Brown; only "Sweets" can imitate and impersonate James's "sugar" ("sugar" is when he's getting into the gay bag). They complain about Brown's rules and regulations, mock his monumental ego, his delay in paying, his fines and lack of respect for them as human beings (he reportedly smacked one musician in the face for not laughing at his jokes), and his attempts to create factions within the band.

Finally, at 35,000 feet, I see the drenching beauty of the landscape, the miracle that sends chills through my body and soul each time. Africa. I know I'm still sentimental as I witness night become day as we approach Dakar, Senegal. I'm thinking, too, about James; I wonder what he feels as the jet nods down to greet this earth.

Dakar-Yoff International Airport is filled with young, mostly tall and enthusiastic Senegalese who engulf Brown almost immediately as he deplanes. It is a quick layover and an hour later we are back in the air.

The plane stops every 35–40 minutes, like a Greyhound bus: Accra, Monrovia, Lagos, and finally, Duala, Cameroon. Fans have flooded the tiny airport, hundreds and hundreds of people are everywhere. In the background, "Payback" blasts in the lobby. With all due respect, it's about the last thing you want to hear.

The bags are collected, taxes on Brown's stack of records are taken despite the protest of two aides, and we are directed to separate vehicles and driven to a modest hotel. The show's dancer, Gidget, and I are roommates. Brown and Bobbit live on our floor.

There has been some misunderstanding about our rooms, as the first news leaks of trouble on the Cameroon promoter's end: he hadn't left a deposit to reserve the rooms. Through the window lies an almost unbelievable view of paradise, giant palm trees surrounding a tranquil river. I laugh to myself; the world is nowhere near as serene as this perfect picture.

I am shaken from my reverie: the hotel scene becomes extremely wild, local people roaming around, knocking on doors, looking for "discs" and hair oil, James Brown shirts, asking if my roommate and I are singers . . . "*Non, je suis une . . .*" They run—someone has caught a glimpse of James. But James is having dinner; he has brought along his own food. The rest of us dine in the top floor restaurant, then return to roam from room to room with tales of youngsters who want to trade bracelets and local Muslim jewelry for our shoes and clothing. Armed soldiers are everywhere.

Several people assemble in Maceo and Charles's room, rapping about everything from new musical groups to the likes of the "man," James Brown. He dominates 90% of the sarcastic conversation.

Around 3 o'clock Maceo says: "Wait a minute. What's this I hear? Somebody's singing." He opens the door so we all hear:

> *Please . . . Please, please, please.*
> *Please don't go.*
> *Please, please, please, please.*
> *Honey, please don't go.*
> *Oh, yes, 'cause I love you so . . .*

"It's that nigger James! What's he doing singing at 3 o'clock in the morning? Don't nobody want to hear that! He didn't even offer nobody no food!"

The Republic of Cameroon is a *former* French colony, yet one wonders about its "independence." The daily wages are twenty cents an hour; most business is still in the control of Frenchmen (one owns this hotel), who date the "best-looking" women. We are told the "President" is a puppet controlled by France and that the people are tense. There is no television; progressive newspapers are banned and political activists, once uncovered, face deportation, imprisonment or execution, depending on nationality. That is why a visit from James Brown is regarded as an event so important people travel from all over the country to witness it.

Yet it becomes obvious that the promoter here hasn't been taking care of business. The publicity is rather low-keyed, due to James Brown's two or three previous cancellations, caused, as Bobbit puts it, because "they didn't have it together enough for James to risk it." Tickets for the first night's show are $25.

The evening of the concert is a comic strip. Twice loading and unloading the van, going back and forth with instruments and horns and drums for at least three hours, we finally arrive at the auditorium. The group is speechless. The hall has a seating capacity of 2,000 but there is a crowd of only about 200. The building is ultra-modern, very impressive, and so are the people who've come to hear James at $25 a head. They are waiting patiently. Ladies in elegant, sequined gowns, braids and wigs, make-up and natural looks. Couples of all varieties and racial composition—seems like the elite, the sects of a divided race.

The word gets out that James, *James*, is not coming. No. He is *not* going to appear for just 200 people. "Feliard!" shouts the wardrobe lady. "The Boss said to tell Sweets, Maceo and Fred and that writer to go and tell the people Mr. Brown won't be able to play 'cause de 'quipment broke."

I decline the offer to translate the message into French. Someone else agrees and immediately there is a strong murmur in the crowd. Because they are well-to-do, most try to be cool, but they are obviously disappointed and hurt as the young woman explains that they can either come to the big concert tomorrow outdoors, or they can wait five days for when Brown is scheduled to come through Duala again. As they exit some demand instant refund, but the promoter can't produce—he's already banked most of the money. The police arrive and carry him off to jail for his own safety—some in the crowd threaten to kill him.

There is an overcast the following evening as the concert begins on schedule and thousands of people pour into the outdoor stadium. Almost as soon as Brown appears there is rain, but the show continues. In spite of the weather and potential danger, James, for once truly "Mr. Dynamite," comes down off the stage platform onto the wet grass and performs his best trick, a split and turn catching the microphone as he revolves. The mike sparks out electricity. . . . *Whew!* My admiration is on the brink—courage or cuteness? An exhibition of loyalty to fans or self? Whatever, he puts on a *show*. As Brown continues to sing, and the people cheer fanatically, a man is being beaten—most likely, someone says, because he is struggling to be nearer the stage. He is a hundred yards away.

Yaounde. Capital city. A sweet coolness in the air. The landscape is hilly and wet; there has just been an early morning rain. The people at the airport this time include Peace Corps volunteers, hundreds of locals, and Europeans. The drive is nearly 25 minutes through town, which resembles the *favellas* of Rio de Janeiro. The road is a misty red clay, like the earth of Ghana and also, ironically, of Georgia.

Two days pass. James decides to call a press conference. Rhetorical questions on African politics, on which Brown is encouraged to be a spokesman and of which he knows little. When I ask about the situation here in Cameroon, Brown says: "I don't think the people in the States should know."

Why?

"Because, this will make the Black man look bad; we don't need to look bad. I still say people will accuse the Black man, saying he isn't ready."

The night of the final show, I am told I will ride *with James*. Accompanied by two valets, Brown enters the van, very clean in his black short-sleeved suit. He turns around and says, "Hi." It seems as if he's lost weight; he's grown a moustache and his hair is back to process. I really don't think he's ugly, but I don't *say* that. He smiles like he can almost read my mind and begins talking to me like a father.

"You know," he explains in his deep husky voice, "it's too dangerous for you to be in here. The people be jumping in front of the car, you know, trying to get to me. But don't worry . . . I'll make sure you're escorted after we get there. . . . This is too dangerous . . ."

"Thank you, Mr. Brown."

"You in school?"

"No. I've finished."

"That's wonderful . . . now see, you traveling with James Brown . . ."

"How about that . . ."

He turns around again and laughs. I laugh with him. He's quiet for the rest of the way . . . looking out the window, waving to his fans, chewing gum and smiling.

When we arrive, the voltage is being changed from 120 to 220. There is no platform stage so they will perform at ground level. 40,000 people, the largest crowd so far, paid $6 for these tickets. At this point, however, the government has taken over the handling of the affair and the people wait patiently for more than two hours as repairs are made.

The band enters in black suits with gold frills. Gidget wears a denim and studded hot pants and halter outfit. She struts onstage, giving the Cameroon soldiers a fit. (Offstage, she has come to learn one does not dress as freely in this Muslim nation-state, and Brown has criticized her for going to the beach alone with two white Peace Corps volunteers.)

The JBs start the jam off with "Pass the Peas"—"You can have Watergate, just give me some bucks and I'll be straight." Cameramen get closer; soldiers and policemen in green berets and uniforms line the entire ring of the stadium and have the best seats.

The musicians continue to pour out the sound born of southern men—the two drummers and congas beat the rhythm, the famous "funky soul" just as familiar to the local people as Kentucky Fried is to America. "Give Me Some More" sounds like the plea of men who thread a thin love-hate line for their leader. Wesley's trumpet solo turns the crowd out!

Finally, James makes his grand entrance. Dressed in a skintight body suit with "G.F.O.S." inscribed on his stocky chest, Brown begins with "Soul Power" as people are being clubbed by police. The crowd chants in communion, oblivious to everything but the "Godfather from America." "Cold Sweat" drums in the ears, the song of former bandleader Alfred Ellis. "I can't stand it!" Morgan, Melvin and Johnny on drums and congas are really making their pulse felt. Brown raps, slides, glides on the wooden floor. The horns go up and down . . . *Bammmmm* . . . "Papa's got a brand new bag!" Good God!

Another incident. A soldier is beating a young woman, pulling her arms and twisting them. She is screaming and succeeds in kicking him. No one stops them. James keeps singing:

This is a man's world.
But it wouldn't be nothing
Nothin' without a woman or a girl.

The seductive sound of the saxophone. Brown cries, pleads . . . "Maceo, blow your horn. Maceo, brother . . ." Brown's passion is sincere . . . the audience responds with pleasure. Gidget teases with her hips, shakes her pigtails, widens her red-coated lips with a smile.

The mood changes to "Get on the Goodfoot," as Gidget and James do the Robot together. He cuts into "There Was A Time":

Now there was a dance
That I used to do
The name of the dance
They call the boog-a-loo

"1962!" Mr. Dynamite shouts. He hits "Make It Funky," "Try Me," "Money," and then closes with "Say It Loud, I'm Black and I'm Proud."

"James Brown, ladies and gentlemen, James Brown!" "Sweet Charles" exclaims. Brown makes his exit, runs around the stadium track surrounded by aides and policemen, pursued by fans screaming and yelling his name.

Yaounde airport the following evening. The flight to Duala is three hours in the waiting. I seek "the man." I ask the wardrobe mistress: "Where's your boss?"

"Oh, he's in the V.I.P. section."

Brown appears only slightly surprised when I enter, as if he knew I was looking for him and also that I would find him.

"You know," he begins, "Mr. Bobbit told me about you, said you are a good writer. Here, meet this young Cameroon teacher. I'm going to build a school, you know."

"That's nice," I comment. "I taught for three years."

He looks shocked: "You're quite a young lady. Do you smoke?"

"No, I don't."

"No?" His guttural voice gets personal. "What *do* you do?"

"Right now I'd like to ask some questions."

He puts his hand on my knee. ["It's his way," one of the band members had warned, "don't be upset."] I move my knees away and think, *he's trying to mess with my mind.*

"If you tell the truth about me," he said, half grinning, "nobody would believe it."

"Some will and others won't. It doesn't matter."

"Yeah, you a good writer. Would you like to go to Europe with us in September? We'll be touring 65 countries."

I try again, searching for substance. He interrupts. I want to know why he refused to appear for 200 people at $25 a head. What's the story with the group? Does he treat them like captives? What are his reasons for not exposing the talent within his band? Technical questions—why can't they play without him? But "Mr. Dynamite" insists on interviewing the interviewer.

"Are you in love? Do you have a boyfriend? Well, let me give you some advice: If it's not a cat like me or any in my band, and he's a musician, I'm telling you, you'll have a hard time 'cause he's probably not worth it."

"Is that right?" I see he likes to play games persistingly.

"I'm the only black man in America who's done what I've done. Whose name is known *everywhere in the world.* My music is known in Russia, Poland, in Germany, in England, all over Africa. . . . Everybody knows James Brown. They all know the music of James Brown. . . . When they had the riots, the State Department called *me personally* and said, 'Mr. Brown, what should we do to stop these riots?' "

"The U.S. State Department *called* you?"

"Yeah. It was in all the newspapers, they asked me to talk to the people and I did. . . .

"Look," he said abruptly, "we'll rap some more on the plane. You tell 'em to let you up front, first class with *Brown* after take-off."

I nod, we shake hands and I walk away. We didn't say much on the flight.

In Geneva, Switzerland, we stay at one hotel, James at another—same one as Frank Sinatra, $400 dollars a day. Ten days seem like ten years.

Here comes Melvin: "Fred Wesley? Where's Fred Wesley?"

"He's in the john," someone answers.

"Fred Wesley?" teases Melvin, "what are you doing in the john?"

"Oh," Wesley says casually, "I'm taking a James Brown. . . ."

Later in the evening, Fred, Maceo, Melvin and Sweets are invited to have dinner with James. Sweets doesn't accept; James hasn't paid them their money, but he says, "He gave me $200 to go buy shit for his little girl. Told me to go and get for her what I would for mine."

"If you don't come," says Melvin, "I'm going to tell James when we left you were in here sucking pussy."

"Tell him whatever you want, I'm not going."

Charles and the rest get paid and fly home. But only for five days; then it's on to Shady Grove, Maryland.

The first show in the States and the crowd totals only about 450, the final show, 600. The press says James is tired. The "Godfather" monologue is too long, over 20 minutes: "I'll never forget who I am, where I'm from and who put me there. Poor boy from Georgia, got two jet airplanes . . ." Some people yawn. There aren't enough there for a mass exodus.

July. Madison Square Garden is next. Bobbit is driving to New York. "There was a time," Bobbit begins, "when he wasn't like this, when he didn't have such an unbearable ego. It was an achievement to do what he did. When it was hard [before the era of black consciousness], people like James had it hard, and he *made money*. Normally, we keep writers from getting too close to him, because some of them don't understand. He's a 'tainted genius.' He's in trouble now and we just can't seem to get it through to him that he doesn't need all of this now. He's made his mark. He's accomplished a hell of a lot for a man who had nothing. He just refuses to let go. . . ."

New York City. It's 9:30 at night and the band hasn't arrived from the 800-mile trip from North Carolina. An aide says the men haven't slept in three days.

Around 10, weary, with disgusted looks on their faces, the JBs arrive. They change and perform. The same songs, the new song . . . "Do the Hustle." The "Godfather" informs his fans he wants to run for President. "I'll change the White House to the 'Funky House,'" he says. People are laughing, but they don't know how serious he is.

After the concert, gripes come to a head. Fred Wesley, the man behind the music, announces that he isn't going to Tunisia. "As a matter of fact," he tells the group, "*I quit*. As soon as I get paid, I'm going back to L.A. where I belong."

Someone else adds: "James needs his ass whipped. He didn't even come in to say, 'Dogs, you did well, thanks.'"

When I see Bobbit, he's not in a good mood. Everyone says the change comes when he's near James. "You can't go to Tunisia. No more writers. You can't write a book, he'll take all the money. Brown is in no mood to talk."

I sit there and just look at him. I haven't asked to go to Tunisia, and could care less about Brown's mood because I haven't even asked to speak to him. I shake my head. "I've seen enough." He nods, but adds: "and you haven't even *written* anything."

James and the JBs go to Tunisia and tour California before we get together again in New York. Sweets says Brown is hampering his singing career; he's recorded an album but it's not being promoted like it should.

The JBs cannot perform without his consent. They are unknown without James. When they joined, they knew of his rules and regulations but the opportunity seemed like a "once in a lifetime thing," a chance to "make it big, because he was big."

Jimmy Parker is long-legged, dark brown, with a process, and very attractive. Fred Thomas and "Cheese" are also brown-complexioned. All the band members are near to the color of James, with the exception of "Sweet Charles," who's light-skinned, tall, with a "superfly" hairdo.

Cheese: "Well, the biggest change has been since Fred Wesley left. You see, James used to give Fred things to do and Fred would alter them into something more musical. Now, there's nobody to do that. We definitely miss him. And when he stepped out of this thing he just knocked a big hole in this circle. When Wesley split, cats said there must be something wrong when the *band leader* cuts loose.

"When we went to California, we didn't even have time to stop at the hotel, we didn't even have time to *check in* . . . we got to go to rehearsal, we leave rehearsal, we got to go straight to the studio and, just like an orange, he squeezes the juice. . . . We see Fred's not starving and he's *out there* . . . and musically, things are falling apart."

"Have you decided to leave?"

"I haven't decided yet. I'll do a few more gigs and then I'll quit. You stay because you think you got a thing going. We're caught in a vacuum."

Jimmy Parker: "I've been with James four years. When I first met him, he had a few bucks and I wanted to make some. . . . It was a *job* from jump street."

Fred Thomas: "But you can never make *much*. Just enough to keep you hanging or thinking you gone make some shit."

Parker: "My influence? Forget it. I must have been fired at least ten times."

"How do you stand it?"

Fred: "Try and stay there and make some money and don't let it hassle you, just block the shit out. Hey, the most positive thing is to make the money. I've always thought of it as a job, a gig, because you had to work according to how *he* wants you to play and not according to your inner feelings. I like to venture out. Now [he had just quit] I have a chance to play. . . . Cameroon was just like all the rest—we try to enjoy it, but it's hard to work for somebody like James 'cause you know something is going to set you off, something is going to make you *mad as a mother fucker.* . . ."

Cheese: "It's a mind-bender. He will *bend your mind.* It really gets so far out . . . when 5 o'clock comes and it's time for us to play, we dread it."

Parker: "With James, it really doesn't mean nothing. In and out, the same ol' shit. I like him because he's *silly.* I like to see him when he's into his thing. [He laughs again.] He's got a complex, *boy,* an envious kind of thing. Envious of who? *Anybody and anything that's done right.* It's the most unusual thing. Curious because he can out-talk . . . he loves to talk, you don't know. He don't be saying nothing at all . . ."

"Who told him he's so great?"

Parker: "He did, he did, [laughter] who else? Yeah . . . the cat was lucky," he says more seriously. "He had a little thing, came up with a nice dance. The cats he got involved with were popping his music above all else. On top of everything he did, he made *a lot of money.* No education, no brain whatsoever. Now he wants bigger and better things . . ."

Thomas: "He wants to be on top."

Parker: "He confuses his profession with politics. Instead of being an entertainer, he thinks he's a politician." He laughs loudly, and continues, "Sometime, you go out there in them front rows and see what's happening. You see it's them fat women making him do that."

"What fat women?"

"His clientele. His drawing crowd."

Cheese: "About his being homosexual . . . as far as I know, he's all man. But this is how he draws people. He wrote an article saying he was a faggot. This was to draw people to come and see if he really is. Because I know it's a gimmick . . . just like his retirement thing. 'This is my last show before I retire.' Somebody will come *just* to see him do his last show.

"Let the people see who is the 'Godfather.' None of his band has profited from association. St. Clair Pinckney—he's been with Brown for fifteen years. You think he should have a big house somewhere. Maceo . . . check it out. Maceo did a lot, a whole lot.

"And like the fines—a person can always get back at you by taking your money. That's the *only* thing he can think of . . . a fine. Like if you're late, take his money. He likes to break you, as if he *knows* you're starving already, take some more. He continues to take the money, it's *always* money . . . keep you from getting over."

Parker: "I remember one time he told us how he spent—how many years in jail? He said he wants to run his whole group like a prison camp. . . . *Crazy.* And he wants to be the warden, and the motherfucker wants to tell you to do this and that and report and live your personal life *and* the life you're living when you're working with him. Like, if he could get into and live your personal life, he'll get in and control that too. If you're smart enough to stay away, fine. If you're not, let him in and see if he don't destroy it."

Thomas: "The 'Lord' knows everything, he knows *everything.* He wants to know about *everything,* he can tell you how to go about doing *anything.*"

Cheese: "The wardrobe mistress, Gerdy, she's been with him a long time. She catches as much hell as anybody else, now. She use to *spy,* but she don't be carrying too much word these days. She use to tell on us a lot of times. You wouldn't even know until James called you. Once, James told us to ride the bus to a gig, we passed her in a car, didn't know it and she runs and tells James."

Parker: "I'll never forget when he told Thomas [Jimmy imitates the husky voice], 'So you didn't ride the bus? You know I'm gone have to get you, don't you? I got to charge you a yard [$100].' The stars like Wesley, Maceo, got charged $300. The reason nobody ever goes on strike is because the group has never really been together. You got a group of three over here, one by himself . . . well, that comes from working for a very rich man and everybody thinking he's going to get a piece of the pie. He preaches an individual thing with the group members."

Cheese: "He tried to make me the band leader after Fred quit. He knew me, Jimmy and Fred are close and that if he gets one he can hold the other two. 'You can go and make some money, all you have to do is keep your mouth shut and keep the cats together.' Then if he hears trouble he'll call you and say: 'I know *you're* not involved in this.' Like the time he told one cat he heard he was smoking reefer . . . 'can't have that.'"

Parker crosses his legs and says: "Sometimes I look at him and say . . . 'Peace.'"

Cheese: "In North Carolina, somebody threw cups of ice at him. At another place, somebody threw apples. Believe me, I'm whipped."

"You still haven't told me about California," I tell them.

"I freaked off very heavy," says Parker.

"I can hardly remember from one gig to another," replies Cheese.

"Yeah," laughs Fred Thomas. "You're going to need reels and reels of tape. I can give you an encyclopedia on that nigger."

"James Brown: Back to Africa — Seventies Style" (excerpt)

Vernon Gibbs
1975 • *Penthouse*

Since the heyday of black nationalism in the mid- and late-sixties, the "Back to Africa" movement—long a central issue in black ideology—has remained unresolved. The advocates of migration have become less vocal; the many black Americans who did go back in the sixties found their cultural values so changed in three hundred years that "assimilation" was next to impossible.

Today, however, many black entertainers see Africa as a lucrative market for their product. CBS Records is already making plans for an "African Market" campaign. Parts of Africa have already developed a pop sound—termed "highlife"—with historic roots in military and European dance bands, which gave colonial Africa a sound to imitate and the Western training to facilitate it. With the coming of African independence, more and more black American music began influencing "highlife"; the demand for real live Americans to fit the bill has grown steadily even though the performers have not always been willing to make the trip. When the trip is made, it usually takes the form of some special event. In 1971 Roberta Flack, Eddie Harris and Les McCann, Wilson Pickett, the

Staple Singers, Ike and Tina Turner, the Voices of East Harlem, and Santana were flown to Ghana to perform for the country's fourteenth Independence Day celebration. More recently, the Jackson Five did some shows in Senegal. The Spinners, Sister Sledge, and the Fania All-Stars were among the performers at the music festival held prior to the postponed Ali-Foreman fight in Zaïre. James Brown went on tour in Senegal and was invited to perform for the president's birthday celebration in Gabon.

In the United States, James Brown is regarded as the King of Soul. In Africa, he is king of all he surveys. An African visit from James Brown takes on all the ceremony usually accorded to a visiting head of state. Indeed, Brown does regard himself as an ambassador from black Americans to black Africans. For his most recent (January 1975) visit to Gabon, an oil-rich West African nation, he was met at the airport by screaming thousands and an honor guard. Motorcycle-escorted limousines whisked him to an audience with the president at which they exchanged gifts and patted each other on the back. This was followed by an audience with the king's pet lion and an appearance before the screaming thousands of the capital city—James Brown blowing kisses from the back of a Mercedes-Benz convertible. After his exhausting afternoon, Brown was ensconced in the presidential villa. For the next five days he was involved in a constant round of press conferences, special receptions, and command performances. At the conclusion of his Gabon visit, Brown was invited by the president to accompany him on a goodwill tour scheduled for later this year.

On his way back to the States, Brown reflected on his newfound audience and power:

"This is the first time I've ever received *this* kind of treatment. I've been to Africa many times but this is the first time I've ever received this kind of treatment in my life *anywhere*. It's a new experience, it's a new awareness, it's a new awakening, and it's a new beginning. I have a new concept as a man."

However, Brown sees his involvement in Africa as something more than a new outlet for his career: "This is not just an ordinary engagement. Every century has a messiah; people look on me as a messiah in Africa because they see I can bring all black people together. The Africans may have the money to save black people."

Brown insists that his current interest in Africa is not directed towards enhancing his personal wealth: "Everything I do is for black people. I don't need the money. I've grown into a *world* figure, international sounds too small. From now on I'm gonna be involved with the world. When I stopped the riots in Washington, one of the national magazines called me the most powerful black man in America. They've also said I'm the most powerful black man in the world."

"After 21 Years, Still Refusing To Lose . . ."

Cliff White
April 1, 1977 • *Black Music*

A monthly magazine cannot attempt to match the ephemeral topicality of a weekly news-sheet, particularly a monthly magazine that works within the rigid structure of one of the world's largest publishing corporations. It has to have a different function. Ideas for issues are mooted months in advance of publication, assignments are allocated when it's still not certain whether they'll be relevant on the day of judgement, editorial deadlines are many weeks before the final copy hits your local newsagent.

Despite these cumbersome logistics we at BM believe that the diversity of taste, knowledge and experience of our contributors and editorial staff has provided a more perceptive publication than others in the field, not only in anticipating the direction of black music but, just as important, illuminating where it has come from and where it has been between "then" and "now".

That's where we come to the true function of a monthly mag. We try to give everyone a forum; superstars and budding newcomers, sadly neglected names from the past and even some who've never really made it at all. And when we hit on a name we try to do it right, the full works, as definitive a piece as we can muster at the time of writing. Therefore once we've told you all you need to know about a subject you can fairly well assume that we won't be repeating ourselves because for every one there's another hundred or so who deserve the spotlight.

Sometimes, however, a personality is so consistently powerful that we find ourselves inexorably drawn back to take another look, and of all the black music giants that we've covered in the 41 months since our debut, James Brown must surely be the most powerful of them all.

Whether we're examining the roots of black music, the underground growth and influence of black music, the emergence of black music into the reluctant embrace of mainstream show-biz, the flowering of black music as a dominant part of the business or the possible future developments of black music, James Brown is the name that seems to crop up more often than any other. From his lowly origin in the poverty and degradation of pre-war, segregated Georgia to his unprecedented success as an independent superstar Brown has paralleled, exemplified and occasionally stimulated the social and musical changes of modern black America.

Acknowledging his importance we have previously summarized his entire career (BM. 7), catalogued his prodigious output of albums (BM. 7) and singles (BMs. 15 & 16) and reported two instances of his changeable but resilient grip on success, from New York (BM. 16) to LA (BM. 35).

So why another piece on James Brown? Well primarily because February 1977 was the 21st anniversary of his recording debut, a landmark in everybody's career, emphasising just how remarkable is his story even when compared with artists of similar longevity.

Only a small percentage of artists' recording lives last that long anyway. Of those, most groups survive in name alone, changing personnel behind the corporate image. Of the few groups who've remained more or less intact and the solo artists, almost all have suffered periods of severe slump (in popularity and/or quality) and a great many have compromised themselves and their music. NONE have stayed so aggressively individualistic while maintaining such a consistent and prolonged liaison with the nerve centre of popular music, the scrum of energy and ideas that is essentially the province of the young, virile, or imaginative.

James Brown has been around so long now that it's easy to take him for granted. But just stop and consider for a moment. He was arguably the first rhythm & blues singer to break through to fame and fortune and hold on to them without diluting the spirit of his music or alienating his original audience.

The success of rock 'n' roll stars like Little Richard, Chuck Berry and Bo Diddley was short-lived at its peak, erratic in the long run, has been largely dependent on white interest and nostalgia for survival and has rarely been as great as legend suggests. Perhaps only Fats Domino's lengthy run of good fortune could be said to predate Brown's achievements but Fats refined a traditional musical style rather than creating any new ones, his success came more by an accident of timing than by design, and it only really lasted about a decade.

Ray Charles, on the other hand, did begin to have a fundamental effect on black music, as Brown was to have, but like countless others before and since he was sidetracked just when he could afford to be most creative, a blind alley from which he's never fully emerged. Other immediate predecessors and contemporaries like Jackie Wilson, Bobby Bland and B. B. King have variously been influential and/or successful but not at the level or with the consistency of Brown.

And do you notice how all of the artists mentioned above reflect a bygone age? Blasts from the past, oldies but goodies, all that kind of jive . . . whereas James Brown rolls off the tongue with Sly Stone or Stevie Wonder or Parliament or . . . well, you know, the seventies heroes. He may not be making music that's directly comparable with the newer names but he's just as cogent and still in there with them.

That might just be his most amazing achievement. Setting aside the record breaking details of his career, his spectacular run of hits and his legendary stage show, the influence of both on others, and the fact that he did it all through an independent record company and his own little independent organisation, it's the fact that he's still charged with the same complex emotions as when he started that boggles the mind.

It's as if, instead of now appealing to a certain percentage of his old fans on account of nostalgia and a vast MOR audience on account of their naffness, Elvis was still a rebel, shaking society with raw aggressive modern rock that not only excited a lot of his old following but grabbed the young punks too.

In other words I don't think it's misusing a devalued epithet to claim that the James Brown story is unique. And from that you can rightly deduce, so is the man himself. He—as an individual, divorced from his musical reputation—is literally a legend in his own time, and an extreme one at that. Subject to about equal amounts of praise and abuse he is the victim of a lot of scurrilous myths or a lot of home truths, depending on your viewpoint.

It seems like very few people who know of James Brown are indifferent to him. Whether they be record-buying members of the public, entertainers, DJ's or other people in the business, or those who have had more intimate contact with him, opinions are nearly always dogmatic. Folk either

Billed merely as the Flames, James Brown and his group open for Hank Ballard and the Midnighters in Atlanta the week after their first record, "Please, Please, Please," is released.

James Brown's first publicity photo.

After several failed attempts at a second hit record, Brown saved his career with a self-financed low-budget demo of two songs, "Bewildered" and "Try Me." The scratchy, one-of-a-kind disc was discovered at a storage liquidation auction in Florida.

Brown and the Famous Flames reach Kansas on their first West Coast tour. Top-to-bottom, Sylvester Keels, Nash Know, Johnny Terry, and Bobby Byrd. Brown is to the left of the group. Macon organist Luke "Fats" Gonder led their early backup band.

With a photographer convenient on hand, Brown bought Girl Scout cookies from a young fan outside the King Studios in Cincinnati.

An Apollo Theater handbill advertising the shows that were recorded for the classic album *James Brown Live at The Apollo*.

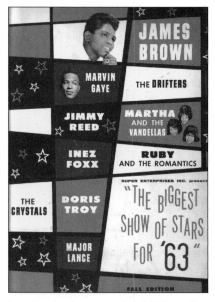

James Brown headlined promoter Irvin *Feld's Biggest Show of Stars* for '63.

The most recognizable group of Famous Flames. L-R: Bobby Byrd, Bobby Bennett, and Baby Lloyd Stallworth.

James and the Flames film a performance of "I Got You (I Feel Good)" for the Frankie Avalon teen movie *Ski Party*. Despite the unlikely garb, the appearance marked Brown's growing appeal to mainstream audiences.

Rehearsing for the *T.A.M.I. Show*. The guitarist is Les Buie and Fats Gonder is at the organ.

Brown being led back to the stage by valet James Pearson during a show staged in an old tobacco warehouse in rural Virginia. Brown had split his pants during a wild version of "Signed, Sealed and Delivered" and had to dash off to change outfits while the Flames and the band vamped on.

Brown's performance in the all-star *T.A.M.I. Show* is widely viewed as landmark by any measure. L-R: Bobby Bennett, Baby Lloyd Stallworth, Les Buie (guitar), Bobby Byrd, Melvin Parker (drums), and their mighty leader.

Brown and manager Ben Bart show off his sleek new Lear Jet.

Brown visits Vice President Hubert H. Humphrey and presents him with a copy of "Don't Be a Drop-Out."

The James Brown Show debuts on the Las Vegas strip with a three-week engagement at the Flamingo Hotel.

The incomparable saxophone section from the band that helped invent funk. L-R: Maceo Parker Jr., St. Clair Pinckney, and Alfred "Pee Wee" Ellis.

The original Vox Studios tracking sheet from the "Say It Loud—I'm Black and I'm Proud" recording session in Van Nuys, California.

Mixing another hit record at the King Studios in Cincinnati.

The first (and only) James Brown Gold Platter Restaurant open in Macon, Georgia.

Green power = black power. Say it loud.

Autographs for fans in Lagos, Nigeria.

Brown moves his business home to Augusta, Georgia, and opens his newly named Mans World Enterprises at 1122 Green Street.

Olympia Theatre, Paris, France.

Pittsburgh, Pennsylvania. Holding court with a branch of the Black Panthers following a show. Behind Brown are tour manager Alan Leeds; personal manager Charles Bobbit; and popular Pittsburgh radio personality Brother Matt (both partially obscured).

Brown cohosts *The Mike Douglas Show* for a week.

Cooking up something other than funk on *Dinah's Place* with Dinah Shore.

Georgia Governor Jimmy Carter officially commends Brown's work against drug abuse. The singer's father, Joe Brown, is the gentleman on the left.

Brown's Summer Fall tour is called the Soul Bowl featuring the newly anointed Godfather of Soul.

Early in his first "post incarceration" tour, Brown visits with three ex-employees. L-R: Alan Leeds, unknown, Vonnie Sweeney, and Bob Patton.

Brown portrays a singing preacher in *The Blues Brothers*, the vehicle credited with a renaissance in the singer's popularity.

Twenty-six years after his first appearance, Brown returns to Harlem's legendary Apollo Theater. The theater appropriately hosted a public viewing after Brown's sudden passing in December 2006.

LOVE him or LOATHE him or as often as not fluctuate wildly between the paradoxical poles of emotion. And so on this 21st celebration of his first recording let's dwell awhile on the man instead of his music or career.

For this I have to break the rules and get personal. With the possible exception of obituaries, first person involvement is generally frowned upon in journalism, but although this is far from a final tribute—for I believe that unless he misjudges his physical power and disintegrates on stage Brown is gonna be around for a long while yet, even if in a different medium to the present one—I have to admit that, overall, James Brown and his music and achievements have impressed me more deeply than any other artist. But I don't think I've witnessed the phenomenon through rose-tinted glasses. To paraphrase my comments in BM. 7:

In battling his way to the top Brown forged about himself a shield of ruthless steel to brush aside scorn, prejudice and any would-be competitors. As a result, bitter remarks and unsavoury rumours have churned in his wake for years. On examination most of these allegations can be seen as pure jealousy but there are undoubtedly deep-rooted reactions in the man that set him apart from contemporaries.

Anyone else would have long passed the point where they needed to prove themselves to the world, yet he has never allowed himself the good humoured civility of others who took their chances at a more leisurely pace.

Public slanging matches with challengers like Joe Tex and Wilson Pickett have dogged his career, the claustrophobic atmosphere of his autocratic empire has led to a constant flow of personnel, particularly band members seeking greater artistic liberty (and recognition), and a blind insistence in his own judgement has produced some horrendous lapses of taste on record.

And yet without the years of blinkered perseverance the James Brown legend would not exist, with each change the band grows tighter, moving along with the tide of time, and it is precisely the unwavering egocentricity of the man that gives his music its unique flavour. If there are flaws, who's the loser? Perhaps only Brown himself, bound to the isolation of self-styled omnipotence.

"You know" he reflected hesitantly, "I wish I wasn't er, dynamic or legendary . . . star . . . with so much. I think I'd like to be just a little less fortunate." Then smiling almost embarrassedly at his lapse he quickly added, "Sounds bad, don't it?"

James was talking to me on the way to Heathrow airport at the end of his recent trip to Britain. During his four-day stopover I'd made the opportunity to witness him in several moods, both off and onstage, and now that he was within an hour or two of departure he was probably more relaxed and open than at any time since his ride in from the airport on the day of arrival. There was only the boarding procedure left to supervise and that should be a formality. For the time being, in the back of a limousine in limbo between hotel and takeoff there was nothing to worry about. (Unlike a lot of entertainers James is not bothered by air travel, in fact he owns his own aircraft.)

I was interviewing him for Charlie Gillett's *Honky Tonk* broadcast on Radio London, an assignment that called for concentration on the early part of his career, a period he is reputedly reluctant to discuss. So much for that particular myth. He was pleased to talk about his formative years and I'd like to include you in the conversation later on. But first, back to square one.

It was friday afternoon, the day of his two London performances, and things weren't shaping up as intended. James was scheduled to arrive at the West End hotel at 2pm in time to freshen up for a music press conference at 3pm, a national press conference at 4pm, and then the possibility of either a meal or a quick visit to the theatre for a sound-check with the band before the first show at 6.30pm. But it was already just after 3pm and he was still stuck out at the airport, stymied for what turned out to be a two hour delay because of some finicky regulation or other, nobody seemed sure exactly what, that had to be cleared with America.

The natives were getting restless. James's awesome reputation spreads before him like a bad case of halitosis, so while Polydor's press officer tries to keep abreast of events and silently prays for an even break the small assembly of journalists and photographers debate amongst themselves whether or not to stick around and what to expect if they do. On his previous trip to Britain, four years earlier, James had stipulated "No interviews" (although one enterprising journalist got one) but this time around he'd readily agreed to be cross-examined; a good omen. On the other hand his unpredictable fire-cracker temper is a legend in its own right and a two hour hassle at Heathrow would aggravate a lamb let alone a lion; a bad omen.

Finally the message comes through. James has cleared customs in high spirits and good humour, all is cool. The press conference (by now a single one) was on, everybody on their marks. Cameras and cassette recorders are made ready and before long we're tipped the wink that he's arrived at the hotel. The promoter and a gent from Polydor who've motored in from the airport with James join us in the suite that's been reserved for interviewing, apologising for the delay but confirming that everything was now all systems go.

Then a cloud of doubt swirls in. Rumours of a megaton explosion echo down from on high followed by another delay and then the succinct instruction "No photographs". Cameras are packed away again but everyone stays (the one national journalist having come and gone a long time ago) until eventually there is a bustling of bodies in the doorway, admitting the short but sharp figure of Mr. James Brown.

Dressed in an elegant three-piece suit and with his hair more conservatively styled than before he is looking nattier than dread. After brief introductions and further apologies for the hang-ups he assumes command of the room by sitting majestically facing the gathering and we're in business.

As it turned out it was a routine affair. James was affable but nobody seemed to want to ask anything worth relating (least of all me because I was hoping to get the private interview) and so after about 45 minutes of irrelevant chit-chat enlived by brief flashes of the notorious ego we all shook hands and dispersed.

Myself, I trucked on down to the theatre in order to catch both shows and was not disappointed. Trying hard to be objective, and without detailing the whole thing, I'd say there were minor flaws in the evening's entertainment (like the hammy "Woman" introduction to "It's A Man's World", the superficial version of "The Payback", and the GLC regulation that oppresses dancing in the aisles) but basically the Brown revue lived up to expectations and was gratefully and rapturously received by 99% of the audiences.

Telling it from the heart I'd go further and confess that I enjoyed the concerts more than any other since the last time I saw him. Even though he's slowing down the maestro still makes most other performers seem static and his voice has as much character and power as it ever had. Although I'd like to have heard a bit more slow soul and a little less funk I wasn't expecting it, current trends being what they are, so I just got off on the music that makes the lame to walk, the blind to see and 7-stone weaklings leap over tall buildings in a single bound.

His band, the latest in an ever-changing combination of JB's, was particularly impressive. Perhaps not so diverse as many modern outfits but then Brown's music thankfully doesn't require the synthesizer pyrotechnics and prolonged shapeless layers of instrumental virtuosity that mar a lot of other bands' performances. There is a place for such music but it's one thing to drift away in the privacy of your own home to skilfully mixed recordings and quite another to be confronted by directionless interludes in concert, where they invariably bore the pants off everyone and deflate the pacing of the show.

Brown's bands have always been good solid R&B combos, with sometimes a little unambitious jazz thrown in for their own pleasure during the opening segment of the show. The current line-up is as tight as any he's ever had, driving the funk with immaculate precision so that Brown and his musicians become as one as they shift up from underlying rhythm to intersperse his repeated and gradually fragmenting phrases with sharp horn riffs. As Brown reaches the point where he becomes like another instrument he'll then swing back into a dance with a warning scream or command that brings forth a blistering sax solo or an unexpected key change introducing a contrasting riff and perhaps a unison chant from the band.

This keen relationship between Brown and his musicians has played a major part in the evolution and influence of his music, linking the era when solo stars fronted anonymous bands to the present trend for self-supporting, interacting singer/musicians.

Sly Stone took the process one step further by making his a more dramatic group (everybody is a star?), writing and arranging tunes that featured them all, and generally presenting the image of all-for-one, one-for-all togetherness. But long before Sly hit the charts with Family Stone, Brown was referring to his troupe of musicians, singers, dancers and other assistants as his "family", the one big difference being that there was only room for one star in his—JAMES BROWN. It was, is and probably always will be a rigid autocracy, with the predictable result that over the years it's been ravaged by in-fighting, back-biting and outright rebellion.

Brown has had a band of his own since the end of 1958, varying in size from his first regular half-dozen musicians to the larger assembly in the mid-sixties, when he was carrying three drummers, and back down to his more manageable current eleven pieces. (It probably should be a dozen but he was missing a rhythm guitarist.) At the last count nearly seventy musicians have flowed through the corporate identity, making the personnel turnover of vocal groups like The Platters and The Drifters seem slow by comparison.

Twice Brown has lost about 80% of a band in one fell swoop and both times it was the music director that instigated the mutiny and led the walkout.

This hive of talented discontentment has fostered quite an impressive alumni of ex-JB musicians, like the MD/arranger/writers: J. C. Davis (saxes), the leader of Brown's first band, who went on to work with Etta James; Al "Brisco" Clark (saxes), who went on to work with Otis Redding; Nat Jones (saxes, keyboards), who went into a mental home; Alfred "Pee Wee" Ellis (saxes, keyboards, guitar, bass), who went on to become a respected session musician/arranger; Richard "Kush" Griffith (trumpet), who went on to obscurity; and of course Maceo Parker (saxes, keyboards, flute) and Fred Wesley (trombone, keyboards), who are both currently flirting with George Clinton's Parliafunkadelicment Thang.

Other Clinton sidekicks who came from Brown include guitarist, bassist and burgeoning superstar, William "Bootsy" Collins; his guitarist brother, Phelps "Catfish" Collins; drummer Frankie "Cash" Waddy; plus, I believe, saxist Robert McCollough and trumpeter Clayton "Chicken" Gunnells played a stint with Funkadelic too. Hey, I've also just noticed that Richard Griffith has returned from obscurity to play on Bootsy's latest album. If he carries on the way he's going Bootsy will soon have a complete set of ex-JB's around him.

As well as the acknowledged MD's many other musicians have played crucial roles in Brown's band(s), particularly: Bobby Byrd (vocal, keyboards), Brown's main ally from pre-recording days until 1972; keyboard player/MC Lucas "Fats" Gonder (his is the famous intro on the first 'Live At The Apollo' album); drummers Nat Kendrick (who was credited as leader of the band's instrumental hit "Mashed Potatoes"), Clayton Yillyau (a contemporary of Kendrick who contributed as much to the distinctive sound of that era), Clyde Stubblefield (the original "funky drummer", the kick in "Cold Sweat" and other hits of the period), John "Jabo" Starks and Melvin Parker (both intermittently long-serving stalwarts); guitarist Jimmy Nolen (ditto); and saxman, flautist St. Clair Pinckney (who deserves some kind of medal for surviving in the Brown band with only one ten month break since March 1961).

"The thing is", he offered philosophically, "to be with Mr. Brown you've got to take the rough with the smooth and not let any of it bother you. It's kind of hard to accept sometimes, but then it's not always as bad as you might have heard. There have been a lot of good times too, you know."

I'd caught up with St. Clair and the rest of the band backstage at the

California Ballroom, Dunstable. On the Friday of his London concerts James suddenly decided to compensate for some cancelled German gigs by playing over the weekend in the first three British ballrooms that agreed to accommodate the revue at such incredibly short notice.

The following day's gig in Birmingham apparently went off alright but Sunday's proposed appearance in Wigan was blown out by what seemed to be a combination of late arrival and early closing. Monday's gig in Dunstable was late starting, too, but there was no curfew at the club and the manager had miraculously rustled up a sizeable audience. Into the wee wee hours of Tuesday morning we bumped and sweated and cheered and although the overall show was uncomfortably presented on such a small stage, on balance the gig was as much fun as the theatre date and a grand time was had by all. Except perhaps by the performers.

None of the musicians and dancers could have been particularly happy with the cramped conditions and James looked decidely edgy towards the end of the show. Not that his performance was affected much, if anything he dealt a more intense hand than on the previous Friday, but I'm sure I occasionally detected that glazed *What am I doing here? Why do I keep subjecting myself to this? What is it all about?* look that all artists tend to get when they're pushing themselves to the limits of their endurance in the back of beyond while normal mortals lie cozily abed.

Backstage after the show it quickly became apparent that all was not well. In fact there was a minor riot going on, all of it emanating from the star dressing room. This week's court of enquiry is what it was, James Brown style. It's these notorious after-show trials and the equivalent confrontations concerning other aspects of his organisation that have been the main bone of contention in the Brown camp all along, and source of most of the public bad-mouthin' about him since it was first revealed that he fined any of his personnel—or indeed, often *fired* any of his personnel, if only temporarily—for seemingly trivial reasons that generally only amounted to anything that rubbed him up the wrong way.

This particular night it was drummer/bandleader Melvin Parker who was catching the brunt of the flak (possibly because he'd missed a beat that was supposed to coincide with one of James's knee-drops) and sure enough before long the door burst open and out stormed Melvin. "That's it, I quit, I'm not taking that shit anymore. It's all over", and bang goes another member of the JB's. No doubt Melvin will soon be cropping up on Bootsy's albums.

"It's insane", if I may quote Jerry Butler, "for a man of his talent to lower himself to that line of bullshit." Indeed it is pretty ridiculous.

I have met James five times now (if you count three times in two days as separate occasions) and each time has been a pleasure. He has been friendly, courteous, to the extent of seeing me safely back to my hotel in New York, and quite willing to talk about himself or his career. But then (a) I respect him and his work and have said so (b) our meetings were not on a business level, and (c) for better or worse I am a member of that loud-mouthed institution, the press. I'm also well aware that if you don't comply with any or all of these qualities you're liable to catch a tiger by the tail when you run up against this volatile schizophrenic.

But there are two sides to every story and every complaint. For instance a band member caustically observed, "It's well known that guys leave the group because they're not getting their just reward. I mean, apart from the fact that other artists pay their bands better, James'll use *your* ideas on record and put his name on 'em!"

The following day James mentioned in passing, "I put a lot of people's names on arrangements because I figured it would motivate them by giving them some of the sub-titles, you know, help 'em out. But I found out that it didn't help because all you do if you're too fair with 'em and include 'em in some things, you're really hurting them all down the line. It winds up being detrimental to the person, fooling them totally, because for some reason they take the credibility that I had given them and use it as though they could fluently think on their own in that same capacity. And it would always wind up disastrously.

"I was giving of myself and they were taking that and using it fraudulently like they done it themselves. I hate to see that happen but it happens over and over again. That's my reason for explaining to you that 99% of my recordings that have somebody else's name on them, I did all the recording, wrote all the lyrics."

Well, whatdya think? Who's fooling who? Personally I'd say it's about 50/50. Various band members have very clearly had an effect on Brown and his music, so much so that there are definite stages in his recording career that coincide with arrivals/departures of key personnel. On the other hand, with the exception of Bootsy (via George Clinton), no-one who has quit the Brown troupe has ever achieved great things on his or her own, unless you count Tammi Terrell and Yvonne Fair's brief spasms of success at Motown. Even with my earlier short-list of Brown's talented ex-sidemen I'd cite their periods in his band as the most fruitful of their respective careers, suggesting that he has had as much influence on them as vice versa.

Only Maceo Parker got close to the James Brown sound when he first walked out with most of the band in March 1970 to form Maceo And All The King's Men. Their first album (on House Of Fox) was pretty good but the follow-up (on Excello) was mediocre and the band soon fell apart, several of them, including Maceo, eventually rejoining The JB's.

"Yeah" said a band member, "but Maceo didn't make it 'cause James had his record suppressed." Really? It's just about possible I suppose, but hardly likely considering that James has enough trouble getting his own records played. I don't think he would claim to have any special influence with the programme directors of North America. Far more likely is that, without James Brown upfront, Maceo and his men turned out to be just another anonymous group in the grand scramble for success.

It's a fact that a large number of the musicians and singers who have left Brown over the years have returned . . . if only to leave again, return again and so on and so on. He'll always take them back, providing they recognise the basic facts—and this is what all the friction boils down to really— that if you're on the bus you keep your place, do as you're told, and try to understand that the whole organisation, musicians, singers, dancers and assistant personnel, is intended to be a projection, an extension, the alter ego of its creator—JAMES BROWN.

And while it's obvious that that's a frustrating position for an ambitious musician to put himself in, to an outside observer it's also clearly why Brown's music has stayed so personal and his career been so unique.

What it is is what it is. There's a Catch 22 law in operation. If James Brown was an even-tempered, easy-going, unassuming, all-round good guy, ex-members of his staff and others who've tangled with him would have less cause for complaint and he might have received the same sort of critical acclaim that's been awarded R&B/Soul stars with wider appeal. On the other hand, if he was that other personality there would be no James Brown story, with its legacy of exciting, distinctive music and unprecedented achievement.

James Brown is a complex mass of paradoxical emotions, attitudes and qualities. He thrives on commercial success and public adoration but has never really compromised for either, always pulling back from total commitment to the establishment, achieving his aims by exaggerating himself rather than disguising his true nature.

In the late '60's for instance, when his political involvement and musical direction were getting ambiguous (he recorded an album with a cocktail-lounge style trio, 'Gettin' Down To It'; a big band jazz album, 'Soul On Top'; and a 'rock' album, 'Sho' Is Funky Down Here') he suddenly stopped campaigning, shukked off his tailor-made suits for wilder stage gear, grew his conservative afro longer than was thought fit in polite society at the time and recorded a series of hard-driving funk classics, the first of them ("Sex Machine") immediately shattering his respectability and the consecutive follow-ups ("Super Bad", "Get Up, Get Into It And Get Involved" and "Soul Power") laying his conscience on the line.

At close range he's so unpredictable that all in his vicinity step lightly, never knowing whether they're in favour or not. In the long run he's dependable to the extent that he's become an institution. He is certainly egocentric and at times vainglorious but he also concerns himself more deeply with life outside of his own stylised world than most other performers. He is poorly educated and given to making socio-political statements, on record and in person, that have been attacked as being superficial and naive by deeper thinkers. And yet a lot of what he has said and done makes more sense to the man in the street, be it you or I, than the pretentious and obscure bullshit spouted by a thousand others. He is seemingly the most self-confident entertainer in the business but he clearly draws on a well of insecurity to fuel his persistent and aggressive determination to stay the course, the reason for his unremitting conflicts with other artists. And also the source of his soul power. When Brown is troubled, as he usually is by one thing or another, his records are fired with a restless spirit. On the rare occasions he's become complacent they've been less inspired.

Not a comfortable man then but a distinctive man, his own man. Even though the public naturally see more of his positive qualities than his bad points he is essentially the man you'd expect from hearing the records. There are no secret skeletons in his closet (whatever bones there are having been loudly rattled in public on numerous occasions), he is—taking into account the changing personnel that's assisted him over the years—the self-made, revolutionary and innovatory success that legend describes. Take him or leave him.

If, to his chagrin, many do choose to leave him, well brother, it's hard but it's fair.

At the airport on the day after the Dunstable gig he was cheerful but subdued and more than a little thoughtful. We'd rejoined the band in the departure area and I sensed that James was regretting the previous evening's dust-up.

"You can't really blame musicians for wanting to make a name for themselves", I ventured, "after all, they're only doing what you did. Taking charge of their own careers and looking out for number one".

A pause. "Well, in some ways," he countered. "But you know, I never wanted so much for myself, I never even really wanted to leave The Famous Flames behind." Perhaps realising that I didn't believe a word of it he opened his heart a little more. "I wish you'd try to tell the guys why I am like I am sometimes. You know what it was like when I was coming up, the sweat man, the Hell it was to get over, how hard it is to stay on top in this business."

True. There are plenty (although a rapidly diminishing number) of black entertainers from Brown's era who are still around but none of them achieved what he did and it must be increasingly difficult to maintain his position amid fresh talent. In fact, let's face it, although nothing can take away his past he is no longer the supreme attraction he was. He's now one of the top acts in black music as opposed to THE ultimate main man.

However, if he's having to gradually hand over his crown jewels to younger men and new generations of audiences he's still in there fighting at present, performing less frequently than at his peak but still putting on a full-length revue that rivals any act in the business. With him on this trip were, St. Clair Pinckney (saxes, flute, arranger/writer), Phineas Johnson (1st tenor sax), Joe Poff (saxes, flute), Russell Crimes (trumpet), Hollie Farris (trombone, trumpet), "Sweet" Charles Sherrell (keyboards, vocals, m.d.), Jimmy Nolen (guitar), David Weston (bass), Johnny Griggs (congas and other percussion), Tony Cook (2nd drummer), and Melvin Parker (main drummer, bandleader).

Five members were recruited over the last year, all from the South, Farris and Poff being the first two white musicians in his band since bassist Tim Drummond in 1968. The rest are intermittent old hands: Crimes on and off since May '71, Sherrell since August '68, Griggs since September '70, Nolen and Parker (Maceo's brother, incidentally) since 1964, and

Pinckney since 1961. St. Clair has recently registered Touaar Music publishing company to augment his livelihood with his own songs and ideas, an interesting new venture for this talented and versatile stalwart of the band.

As familiar to regular Brown fans as the older musicians is MC/master of the cloaks, dapper Danny Ray, who's been introducing "Jaayyymm-mmes BROWN" since the early '60s; and backstage there's the imperturbable bosom of Ms Gertrude Sanders, James's wardrobe mistress and general mother figure to everyone on the show.

The generous hulk of a man who appeared on stage during the finales of the London shows but whose main job was to shepherd the members of the revue turned out to be none other than ex-drummer Clayton Fillyau and James's other personal assistant/valet, William Starlling, has been around a few years now, too.

Back in the spotlight there's also his three dancers, Yvell "Gidget" Richardson, Lola Holman and David Cairo; and singer Martha High (Hyer, Harvin) who first joined the revue as one of The Jewels in late '65, left when the group broke up a couple of years later, then returned on her own in 1972 as backup vocalist for Lyn Collins.

Lyn is no longer with the show so for this tour we were treated to a reappearance by Vicki Anderson, possibly James's most popular female vocalist who joined him in 1964 and stayed for the best part of nine years, during which she recorded 22 singles including 3 duets with James, until she left with husband Bobby Byrd in 1972. Unfortunately London audiences missed her because she slipped, stumbled and fell just as she was about to go on the stage of The Odeon, Hammersmith. The Dunstable crowd were luckier, she appeared that night and sang her heart out. Before the show she told me that she and Bobby are doing fine in a modest kind of way and as soon as she finished her temporary return gig with the revue she'll be pursuing her solo career. Bobby is of course already recording again, most recently with "Here For The Party" (released in Britain on Contempo).

So that was the state of the James Brown revue in January 1977. But what about the interview? Well I'm not going to take you through all of it but I thought it'd be appropriate in this 21st anniversary feature to highlight how vital a link is this man between the past and the present by quoting some of his comments about the early, and generally undocumented, part of his career. For instance James recorded a couple of the songs made famous by his namesake Roy Brown so I assumed Roy must have been an early favourite of his.

"Very early favourite, and I just wish that I would be able to have the type of drive he had. He was a very strong man in singing, *very* strong . . . along with Wynonie Harris as well."

At the same time as these R&B/Rock 'n' Roll shouters were popular The Five Royales were one of several outstanding and influential black groups, James recording a fair number of their own songs, either himself or on someone in his revue and eventually producing them himself in 1965.

"And I wish I could find them today to produce 'em because they were probably one of the most singing groups I've ever heard. Them along with The Dells and The Manhattans. You know these people could sing, but I know The Manhattans have changed their style a little bit because they became afraid and they had to go where they thought it would be safer."

Along with The Five Royales James has recorded his debt to Little Richard, The Dominoes, The Midnighters and Little Willie John, for whom he released a tribute album in 1968.

"The public didn't get the whole concept of what I was trying to do because it was on a small label (King) and they was limited to promotion. But I would like to do that again and I'd also like to pay tribute to Hank Ballard and The Midnighters as well, and I'd like to pay tribute to The Five Royales. It's astounding for me to say that but I can sing their songs from memory, from love, and from total involvement to where you would almost believe it's them."

I can believe it alright, and it's also very apparent—from bits of his stage performance if not from most of his current hits—that he could still work wonders with many of his own past triumphs if the climate was right to slip them back into the repertoire.

"I would love to do 'Oh Baby Don't You Weep', I'd love to do 'You Got The Power', 'Prisoner Of Love', 'These Foolish Things', 'Lost Someone' . . ."

"The only problem is", I muttered disappointedly, hoping that James will consider resurrecting some of these classics but realising that it's highly unlikely, "do you think the modern audiences would accept them now?"

"No they wouldn't", he agreed, "because they don't understand 'em and that's where they're missing real show-business. You know it's funny but you can get on the stage today and do less and impress 'em more. If they could see me do a real James Brown show (as it was at his peak) it'd open their heads. They would see how much they're being robbed by the other entertainers. I say it that way openly and it's not that the other entertainers realise that they're robbing them, it's just they don't know no better.

"Their managers are taking advantage of the people, don't hold the entertainers responsible. 'Cause the entertainers today wanna break so bad they don't realise that they're not really doing a good show and they're never learning show business."

At my instigation James went on to talk a little bit about his relationship with Syd Nathan, president of King records, before recalling the struggling days between his first recording, "Please, Please, Please" (Spring 1956) and his big hit "Try Me" at the end of 1958. In particular he confirmed his affection for the southern United States, where he is still primarily based in his home town of Augusta, Georgia.

"I used to perform 8 months out of a year in one state—Florida. Back in The States the people in Florida, South Carolina, Georgia, Alabama . . . the southern places are real soulful, so you could sing one song there for 10 years, you know, 'cause they get locked in and they appreciate it. They remind me of European audiences, they remember you for your good things. But the northern part of The United States, they forget over night, you're only as good as your last record.

"Talking about the struggling years, after 'Please, Please' the record company wanted me to keep in that style so I cut a couple of tunes (actually 9 more singles) that didn't make it because they sounded like 'Please, Please', such as 'I Won't Plead No More' and a few other things. Then I cut a few things that really didn't relate. I cut one comedy song (the very fine "That Dood It") and I even copied another man's style to get a hit record . . ."

"Chonnie-On-Chon?"

"That was one, that was right on Little Richard, I copied off Little Richard one time, and I also copied one time off of Hank Ballard and that started me, 'Begging Begging'."

The follow-up to "Begging Begging" was his classic original "Try Me" that hit both the R&B and pop charts and introduced him to a broader audience across America. It also foreshadowed the run of progressively unusual hits that led up to him being crowned 'Soul Brother No. 1' in 1962/3.

"I began to hit somewhat of a different feel. But the thing that made that was my eyes start opening. As long as I stayed down south I would have cut the other kind of songs but the minute I start seeing different things and my brain started to intercept the new ideas and new thoughts I became a big-city thinker. And I started tying that in to bring the people together, thinking of what they need most and what would really be some contentment for them. What could I offer?"

The answer was a string of great records, but even more spectacular in those days, the most dynamic road show ever to hit the boards of popular entertainment. In 1962 at his own insistence his segment of the show was recorded 'Live At The Apollo'.

"I even had to pay the money for it, they didn't believe that it would go down. I paid my personal money to record that album."

It was well spent. The album was an artistic and commercial triumph, not only selling in truckloads to black audiences but breaking through to a considerable white market as well, an avenue James cemented shortly after with his fervent interpretation of "Prisoner Of Love".

"Which just made it better for me. There I was with the biggest R&B album ever to be recorded, strictly R&B, then I came right back and cut a pop tune so I had a dual market going."

Within another year James grabbed both audiences simultaneously with the double-sided smash "Out Of Sight"/"Maybe The Last Time" that sparked off the heady run of hits that is still being maintained by scorching sides like "Get Up Offa That Thing", "I Refuse To lose" and "Body Heat". But looking back to the early days James was ready to acknowledge that, despite a few turmoils, his unusual relationship with King records enabled him in the long run to develop the individual stance that is part and parcel of his legend.

"One thing about Mr Nathan when he was alive, he had a very unique respect, an outstanding respect . . . I had a free hand to do what I wanted, when I wanted, how I wanted, when I wanted my releases to come out and everything. That had never happened before in the world of music. That's the reason he was so successful, because I had my hand on the pulse and he knew that James Brown was not gonna let himself get cold. So he made money on me constantly.

"Hal Neely, who later became president of King, he was like my father. Hal Neely is one of the finest persons I've ever met. During that time it was like I became part of the family, it was a whole different set-up then. If you had a problem you could call the company president at 5 o'clock in the morning, tell him what it is, he would be concerned. He'd be on the next plane down there. That's what it's about. Personal feeling, personal touch, personal involvement. There isn't much of that now."

As if to emphasise the point James rounded off this anniversary examination with a personal message for readers who are fan enough to have persevered this far:

"I'd like to say to the European audience that you have definitely proven to me that there are people out there that respect a man for his belief, appreciate him for his work and certainly showed me that you been satisfied . . . and that you're concerned about me continuing. I want you to know that I may not always be able to give you a dance but I can give you a song and I'll give you a lot of good times. I wanna say thank you for without you my life wouldn't have been near as fulfilling as it's been with you. I hope that through the press and through the word of mouth of people you'll know that James Brown didn't love black or white, he loved people, wrong or right."

If that's a bit too much hearts and flowers for you I'd like to leave you with one last quote, "People ask me why I've made so many records. All I can say is, why did Henry Ford make so many cars?"

PART III

1980s

"James Brown" (excerpts)

Robert Palmer

1980 • *The Rolling Stone Illustrated History of Rock & Roll*

Through 1001 nights, 1001 shows, Superbad James Brown keeps on keepin' on. His band locks into a chopping rhythm riff and Brown strides purposefully from the wings, wearing a red jumpsuit with the word SEX stitched across the front. His head jerks to the beat, his hips shimmy, and suddenly he's snaking across the stage on one foot, his other leg windmilling along with his long, limber arms. He does a split, erupts into a pirouette, whirls like a dervish, and ends up at the microphone just in time to shriek "bayba-a-ay" as the band modulates into the introduction to his latest hit. As Brown moves into his late 40s, the dates become more selective, the act slightly less acrobatic. But the energy, the pandemonium, and the great, rending buzz saw voice remain.

Brown recorded his first single, "Please, Please, Please," in 1956 for the Federal label, a subsidiary of King Records, and during the next few years his grainy gospel voice became a fixture on Southern radio, inexorably affecting the development of rhythm and blues, pulling it away from show business sophistication and back into the orbit of the black churches from which it ultimately derived. The grittiness of Brown's late-Fifties/early-Sixties output—"Think," "Night Train," and "Shout and Shimmy" were a few of the hits—paved the way for the emergence of Otis Redding, Wilson Pickett, and the other soul shouters who followed. For while Ray Charles was already tempering the rawness of his early recordings with uptown sweetening, Brown was injecting some of the hysteria of sanctified church services into each of his releases.

Pervasive as Brown's influence was during the Sixties, he has shaped the music of the Seventies even more profoundly. The chattering choke-rhythm guitars, broken bass patterns, explosive horn bursts, one-chord drones, and evangelical vocal discourses he introduced during the mid-Sixties have become the *lingua franca* of contemporary black pop, the heartbeat of the discotheques, and a primary ingredient in such far-flung musical syntheses as Jamaican reggae and Nigerian Afro-beat. Various producers and arrangers have added lush string arrangements, flugelhorns, bass trombones, and sighing female choruses; Sly Stone, the Isley Brothers, and others have overlaid whining, distorted guitars, wah-wah clavinets, more complex cross-rhythms, or chunkier drumming, according to their tastes. But the basic band tracks—"the wheels of the car," to borrow a metaphor from R&B producer Willie Mitchell—continue to follow Papa James's directions. . . .

The change was probably determined, at least in part, by the structure of Brown's new songs. He continued to work in gospel and blues forms, but he also added another kind of composition: Brown would sing a semi-improvised, loosely organized melody that wandered while the band riffed rhythmically on a single chord, the horns tersely punctuating Brown's declamatory phrases. With no chord changes and precious little melodic variety to sustain listener interest, rhythm became everything. Brown and his musicians and arrangers began to treat every instrument and voice in the group as if each were a drum. The horns played single-note bursts that were often sprung against the downbeats. The bass lines were broken up into choppy two- or three-note patterns, a procedure common in Latin music since the Forties but unusual in R&B. Brown's rhythm guitarist choked his guitar strings against the instrument's neck so hard that his playing began to sound like a jagged tin can being scraped with a pocketknife. Only occasionally were the horns, organ or backing vocalists allowed to provide a harmonic continuum by holding a chord.

The chugging push-pull of the Brown band's Brand New Bag was the wave of the future. Its impact was obscured initially by the English invasion, which consisted of white bands covering R&B hits from the previous decade; and by the Memphis sound, which resembled Brown's music in its gospel orientation and harmonic simplicity but had a much more conservative rhythmic bias. By 1968, however, psychedelic rock was replacing the older English R&B styles, and the Memphis sound was becoming diluted. Sly and the Family Stone were purveying a psychedelicized, more rhythmically complex variant of the Brown sound, and Brown himself was at the height of his powers, preaching stream-of-consciousness sermons like "Cold Sweat," "I Can't Stand Myself," and "Say It Loud—I'm Black and I'm Proud," all of them pulsating with polyrhythmic power.

During the late Sixties Brown became a politician of sorts, encouraging black capitalism, hobnobbing with would-be president Hubert Humphrey, touring Africa, entertaining the troops in Vietnam and Korea, urging rioting ghetto youths to cool their passions and build instead of burn. He acquired a large house, a fleet of cars, a jet, several radio stations and other businesses. Militants, suspicious of his vested interest in the system, accused him of Tomming. The ghetto ignored them and bought more and more of his records, even after they had begun to sound alike, as if each were merely another installment in one very long discourse on the state of the nation and the state of mind of its Number One soul brother.

Brown has never been a critics' favorite, principally because of the apparent monotony of so many of his post-1965 recordings. But attacking him for being repetitive is like attacking Africans for being overly fond of drumming. Where the European listener may hear monotonous beating, the African distinguishes subtle polyrhythmic interplay, tonal distinctions among the various drums, the virtuosity of the master drummer, and so on. Similarly, Brown sounds to some European ears like so much harsh shrieking. White Americans have rarely bought his records in large numbers. In fact, he has never had a Number One pop hit. Only six of his singles have made *Billboard*'s Top Ten, and all of them were released during the years of his most intensive media exposure: 1965–1968. But subsequent Brown singles continued to place high on the R&B charts well into the mid-Seventies.

Characteristically, Brown responded to the rising tide of sweet soul from Philadelphia by sweetening his own recordings with strings, horns and vocal groups. The emergence of the disco fad found him making harder, more aggressive records again, but the public seemed tired of the James Brown formula. For the first time in over ten years, Brown's singles did not get automatic airplay on black radio. But he was still a successful producer of, among other acts, his own backup band, Fred Wesley and the J.B.s, who had several hit singles in a disco dance vein.

During the late Seventies, Brown fell from prominence. He titled a 1979 album *The Original Disco Man*, an ironic comment, perhaps, on his inability to profit from the success of an idiom he helped create. But, true to form,

Brown kept working. Apparently, he was still the same suspicious, hard-pushing, self-absorbed man who built the Famous Flames into a moneymaking proposition and eventually built an R&B empire for himself.

But criticizing Brown for his drive or his ego is like criticizing his music for being repetitive. His fierce determination to get to the top and the hypnotic insistence of his sound made him what he is. What he is, whether you love him or hate him, is Soul Brother Number One.

"J-a-a-a-ames Brown!"
Thulani Davis
June 9, 1980 • *The Village Voice*

"James." By 1971 my friend Nim had us all calling him James, just James, like we knew him, cause we did. James was big and we thought he was forever, but also unaccountable like Nixon but still familiar—somebody you could "call outta they name." James. (Not like Muhammad Ali, for instance, who was *never* called just Muhammad. Which Muhammad would that be?) There was only one James.

James Brown has been in my life so long that I associate him with "party" like I link Smokey with I-would-die-for-you love. This is a subjective thing. James Brown gave me my first rush off a horn section. James Brown made me want to be old enough to go to the Apollo. JB was why clothes were in the cleaners so often. Proof that you could leave the church and still be saved every once in a while. He was the reason my friend Red wore hot pants through nine months of pregnancy, which I thought was real strange, and hard to do. He made the word "bewildered" sound sexy and saying "please" sound hip. JB! JB was proof that black people were different. Rhythmically and tonally blacks had to be from somewhere else. Proof that Africa was really over there for those of us who had never seen it—it was in that voice. When I was in college I liked to speak of his Africanness by claiming Brown was the embodiment of the phenomenon of the Diaspora. Baraka couched his interpretation of it in terms of "Form" and "Content"—but it was just a sound that black folks knew.

We could get the screams lots of places, a bop beat to dance to was easy, even horn players who stepped and crooned in the back, but it was the polyrhythms that snared us. The horns on a half time from the drums, rhythm guitar alternating riffs that slapped the bass line once or twice, horns popping little accents and James in the middle. His left leg would be on the fastest time going while his voice got the long notes, holding a scream and everything in-between—it was too much. That's why when people ask, as they often do, why they don't see throngs of black Americans at reggae concerts, I say, "My theory on that is James Brown." If they look confused I add, "He leads 15 pieces with his knees." Add to that an old work tradition, "call and response," the audience scream that is part of the song, and James's hairdo. These contrasting rhythms, the honking and shouting, all dressed up in frilly shirts, cuffs, and heavily treated kinks are part of Afro-American language and iconography—they reaffirm. Yes, George Clinton wears a giant blond wig—he's from Here.

So far, 25 years' worth of dances have boogied through the career of James Brown. While we were doing that old basic bop, James was putting two, three, more beats on it. His early "Night Train" started out so fast it became cool to do it in half-time, break it down somewhat. (It's still a *tough* bop!) James made you do something to loosen your body, so your head did one thing while your feet obeyed other laws. The Twist was never the answer—James knew that was still one-two.

At 52, he has songs on the radio again and is trying to recapture an audience estranged perhaps by disco. Go to one of his concerts (the last few in New York have been great); try to control your body when you get there. It's still "too funky." And JB is not exactly on the replay circuit. Now that everybody's spent 10 years learning how to dance, they're ready to get out there and sweat—intricately. James Brown says he's back and he's packing them in. Certainly some of "them" are those of us who were there before. Others are young people who never ventured, for whatever reason, into the Apollo's territory. James Brown comes to them as the myth spoken of in certain sincere tones by rock stars and the loyal underground. In 1980 one is not seduced by James's power, but chooses to give in. This audience seems to come out to give some credit where credit is due. The King of R&B, the Godfather of Soul, Soul Brother No. 1, Mr. Dynamite, Mr. Please, Please, Please, the Hardest-Working Man in Show Business. Where did this dude come from? He comes from Here.

* * *

Biographical material and legend have it that James Brown was born either in Macon, Georgia, or Pulaski, Tennessee. Brown has always said he's from Macon but grew up in Augusta. Books and interviews say he once picked cotton, shined shoes, and danced in the streets for change, had no brothers and sisters but belonged to a large "extended family." His father wanted him to be a filling-station attendant, but he wanted to be a prize-fighter, and later, a baseball player. In the '40s he worked with gospel groups, where he learned to play drums and organ.

Then came the Famous Flames. James Brown and his Famous Flames toured the R&B circuit in the South, performing gospel-influenced rhythm & blues. He played those run-down theatres with nine lives that were named after black folks all around the segregated South. The champ of that circuit was, of course, New York's Apollo. (In my hometown it was the Basie, an enlightened choice. Couldn't we name the Apollo the Ellington? Or even the Brown? "Yeah, we're going up to the Brown to catch Marley.") Little Richard is quoted as saying *he* put Brown in the business, but I can't track down anybody else who says that. In any case, Ralph Bass of King records heard a dub of the group, went to Augusta, and signed Brown to the Federal label on King Records. The Flames recorded "Please, Please, Please" in 1956. It hit.

This was still an era of "race records" and "race radio," the chittlin' circuit, the local band with a 45, the Platters, Little Richard, Chuck Berry, Bill Haley, Etta James, Ivory Joe Hunter, Hank Ballard. 1956 was a big year for Screamin' Jay Hawkins, who came onstage in a coffin, with a cape and wand, to do "I Put a Spell on You." Brown remembers Buddy Johnson, Roy Brown, and Louis Jordan and the Tympany Five. Jordan had a big band and a string of hits like "I'm Gonna Move to the Outskirts of Town" and "Is You Is, or Is You Ain't (Ma Baby)?" And there were others, like King's Five Royales, who first created two big ones, "Think" and "Dedicated to the One I Love."

James Brown did not come out of nowhere, but he did do it like there was no one else. He wrote songs, arranged, choreographed his whole show, taught more than a few how to dance. He decided on the "look" for the band, inspected for wrinkles, and kept his eye on everything else— even when he worked 300 nights a year.

On stage he has always made the competition look stiff and stingy. He shimmied and boogied, bopped, slid, spun and did splits. His show was the best. He had those champeen hornplayers—the Flames, the JBs, the New

Breed. Black kids all over the country could catch their individual sounds on the first note, like naming any model car by spotting the grill: Bobby Byrd, Bobby Bennett, Lloyd Stallworth, Fred Wesley, Maceo Parker. Brown's band kept the powerful front line that is one of the great traditions of black music and we participated by always checking it out. In the '50s and '60s the solo work of the Flames and Junior Walker allowed a whole generation to get ready for Ornette Coleman without having to dismantle our view of history. We had danced to it before, we are dancing to it now. The continuity affords us the opportunity in the '80s to be eclectic in the best sense—to create a whole music from disparate sources.

> *The hard, driving shouting of James Brown identifies a place and im-age in America. . . . If you play James Brown (say, "Money Won't Change You . . . but time will take you out") in a bank, the total environment is changed.*
>
> —*Baraka*, Black Music

This always struck me as, uh, restrained, very cool. What is this sound that would rock a bank? James used to call for the "groovemaker" when he wanted the rhythm guitar to get something that would be irresistible. From the vamp came the groove, where all the elements of the band fell together in a steady rock.

On early records there are different elements than those you hear today: organ, lots of singing of the kind a cappella gospel groups might do, modula-tions like preachers make as they improvise words and sing the sermon. Brown's voice could even lilt in the early '60s. Some of those things could not survive the wear and tear of 25 years on the road. He has more gravel and scream left than sure tone. The Chuck Berry–style guitar became quickly overused and Brown gave it up. The bands now are smaller and the show is pared down. As Brown himself admits, some of the rawness is missing.

The new music, on *The Original Disco Man* and *People*, is hemmed-in, slowed down. It aims to pick up production styles currently in favor without pushing Brown into a limbo where his outsized rep could not sur-vive. Brown suggests he had to "clean it up so everybody can take it." This is one way to put it. But what's happening with his career now appears to be a case of taking the LPs up the low road and the shows up the high one. These two recent Polydor records represent Brown's concession to being produced by someone else. The producer chosen, Brad Shapiro (who also produces Millie Jackson), may be aiming the discs at the large not-so-urban black audience with whom he has been successful.

The concert tours of the past year, however, have taken Brown into halls not well attended by blacks, where he draws a crowd that might just want to see the "legend" one time. In the concerts I've seen he got down on those oldies, but couldn't quite make the covers and the new tunes get off. While I can understand his not wanting to do Oldies but Goodies shows, the rough stuff sounds awfully good these days. At the Lone Star his inclusion of Chuck Mangione songs in the JB's opening set made me fear that what I came to see was gone, but his entrance turned it all around with the old ingredients.

Sliding on to the stage, his feet just a blur of things we have all tried to do, he completely controls the sound if he raises his right hand. One could speak of modulations—or simply remember "git it in D," "take me to the bridge (& drop me off)," "give the drummer some!" and, most famous, "can we git some head right *here!*" The time is in his legs, the changes in his arms, and the constant surprise comes out of his mouth. Suddenly in the middle of "Super Bad" he whoops, "I wanna jump back and *kiss* ma self!" Improvising in the traditional style of blues and gospel singers, JB has come up with some real twisters. A classic King recording of "Cold Sweat" has my favorite: "I don't care about your thoughts / I just wanna satisfy your faults." I had to live with that one a long time before it seemed that he had just interchanged two words.

James really can't croon the way he used to, except for an occasional roof-shaking version of "Man's World." "Regrets," on the *People* LP, is sentimental, nice enough but not at all compelling. (It was written for Marie Osmond originally but given to JB—hmm.) The young James Brown had a tender side that was not calculated like this one is. "I Found Someone" became a killer as he pleaded, "Don't go to strangers / Come to me . . . Help me, I'm so weeeeaak." All the papers used to judge that he was raw, rough, basic (or the more snooty "visceral"), but Sam Cooke wasn't the only one giving vulnerability. And Brown didn't miss Jackie Wilson's number either. He listens to everybody, it shows. In recent shows at the passe-chic Studio 54 and the Lone Star, he did "remembrances" of Cooke, Wilson, Redding—which never failed to be a reminder that he has outlived them in several ways. He has transmuted the sound to fit what was in the street and expanded the rap way beyond blues and romance. He has also had a thing about bringing back his old songs in new times and arrangements. "Think," "Money Won't Change

You," "Please, Please, Please." And Aretha was listening and so was George Clinton. James knew.

Never ask an artist what they think they've done for you. When they get through telling you, you may be wondering how they knew your mama so well. James Brown isn't shy about taking credit for his influence over countless musicians. George Clinton; Fred Wesley; Maceo Parker; Bootsy Collins, the whole P-Funk contingent; Sly Stone; BT Express; Earth, Wind & Fire; Average White Band; War; Mick Jagger; Tower of Power; James Chance; Ohio Players; the Isleys. As I was listening to *Live at the Apollo*, hearing so many vocalists, my friend Jessica said, "Janis Joplin. Forget the Bessie Smith bit, it's James Brown." Yes, the list is very long.

While he says he's proud, he has also been forced by the market to contend with his godchildren. His own records have to get over in three minutes with the kid with the giant radio on his shoulder, just like everybody else's. And his proteges are doing mighty well. The musicians who got something from James Brown did not just rip him off. Unlike him, they have kept up with what's happening on the street. James Brown's heirs have created a sound that's more complex both substantively and musically. They have added everything from strings, spaceships, and social commentary to humor and hybrid cosmology. They have had to, but James doesn't see it that way. James Brown, I think, takes himself more seriously than any of these people and because of that has been more difficult to deal with.

James Brown went to the riots in Boston and D.C., had something to say about a boycott in Augusta, bought black radio stations, and is now struggling to keep them, speaks in terms of his "first" Lear jet, supported Nixon, and is still integrating nightclubs. He became much more than a singer, more than some of us wanted or needed him to be. In many respects he has been out of step with the generation raised on his steps. You might say he's always been a little late.

His recent acknowledgement of disco came at least two years later. Even songs made almost two decades ago were more like recognitions of popular feelings than catalysts for them. And these songs, especially those of the late '60s, made him a great deal of money because they worked as anthems for attitudes that were already widespread. "Don't Be a Drop-Out" and "Say it Loud—I'm Black & I'm Proud" were acknowledgements, stamps of approval for a nationalism among blacks that ran much deeper than Brown's commitment to race pride. In the same year that he cut "Black & Proud" (1968), he made "Lickin' Stick" and "America Is My Home." Maybe this chronology has to do with the fact that black people were bopping and fighting at the same time, or maybe Brown was aiming to be all things to all people. His attitudes would not have been so unsettling or even noticeable had he not been asked to speak for black people and taken it upon himself to do so. The world that I hear James Brown speak of is still very much like Georgia in the '50s and fearful of self-acceptance.

While I have always loved James Brown by ignoring his unsophisticated notions about what is good for the race, I have had to keep dancing with the idea that he is not alone and that my generation did not manage to change the world (yet!). I wonder why he's told some interviewers that white people are the best friends blacks have ever had, that Jewish people "taught" blacks about their rights, that blacks are "crippled," that "you got to open up the farms again and put black people back to work with what they can work with—their hands." These ideas are very hard to ignore.

I got in a cab the other day, and the driver, a black man who had been a lifer in the Army, started rapping about his past. He first served under Truman—"but Nixon was my BOY!" "Really?" I said. "Why?" "He was a nice guy, he just got caught." He told me that James Brown is his boy, too. They are both from Mere, same place I come from. In West Africa there are children whose last names belonged to ancestors and whose first names are James Brown. Something has to be said for just being able to take those polyrhythms back where they came from.

Brown gave us a sound that led us to many other musical places but that we cherished for not being diluted, not influenced by things outside the tradition, language, and unspoken understandings of our black American world. We called him James cause with his 44 gold records, with all his "Form" and "Content," his embodiment of Us and Here, he made a stomp and holler analysis of ourselves. It was narcissistic and wonderful, selfish and fun. What's great about James Brown is still in that left knee, where the time is.

"A Consumer Guide to James Brown"

Robert Christgau

June 9, 1980 • *The Village Voice*

At around the time of "Mother Popcorn" in 1969, James Brown began to concern himself more and more exclusively with rhythmic distinctions, thus leaving himself ever more open to the all-sounds-the-same complaints he'd always been subject to. Having enjoyed his interracial vogue, he quickly faded from the consciousness of most white people. But between 1969 and 1971, while whites danced (if at all) to Creedence and the Stones and maybe Memphis soul (Motown was out too), Brown scored 17—17 in three years!—top-10 r&b hits that changed black dancing and paved the way to disco. That most of these were on Brown's own King label, which had no press list, did nothing to increase his access to journalists. But when he signed with Polydor in late 1971 it got no better. Vince Aletti wrote a prescient review of *Hot Pants* for *Rolling Stone*, Richard Robinson did something in *Creem*, I gave *Get On the Good Foot* a B plus, and that was about it for the rock press.

What follows, then, is my attempt to make up. I overrated *Good Foot* because I'd missed many much better LPs, and here's a rundown on everything he did after dissolving King. The King stuff has disappeared almost completely (though I still see *Super Bad*, a pretty good one, here and there), but most of the Polydors, while officially out of print, are available in discount bins and used record stores. I would like to thank Pablo "Yoruba" Guzman for raising my consciousness, Carol McNichol of Polydor for compiling a discography, Vince Aletti for lending me records, and James Chance for ripping off "I Can't Stand Myself."

'Hot Pants' (8/71) Is it rolling, James? The hit vamp (can't call it a tune, now can you?) "Escape-ism" was supposedly cut to kill time until Bobby Byrd arrived. The title track follows and it's a killer too, one of Brown's richest Afro-dances. "Blues and Pants" suggests that the title track is a mellowed-down takeoff on "Sex Machine," which is good to know. And "Can't Stand It" is not to be confused with "I Can't Stand Myself." If you say so, James. Only he doesn't. I don't think he cares. And neither do I. **A MINUS.**

'**Revolution of the Mind**' (11/71) Ever the innovator, Brown here presents a live double-LP, "Recorded Live at the Apollo Vol. III." Good stuff, too—a consistent overview of his polyrhythm phase. But "Sex Machine" is sharper and "Bewildered" deeper on 1970's live double. And with the medley on side three the tempo gets so hot that anybody but JB will have trouble dancing to it. **B PLUS.**

'**Soul Classics**' (5/72) Brown recorded nine of these ten cuts for King; every track is good and many—"Sex Machine," "Papa's Got a Brand New Bag," "I Got You"—are great. But they're so jumbled chronologically—side two jumps from '71 to '65 back to '71 to '69 to '66—that it's a tribute to Brown's single-minded rhythmic genius that they hold together at all. Hearing his classic '70s dance tracks in their original three-minute formats, you begin to pine for the extended album versions; devoid of verbal logic and often even chord changes, these patterns, for that's what they really are, are meant to build, resolve. And the great formal advantage of top-forty strictures is that they force speedy resolutions. Time: 28:25. **A MINUS.**

'**There It Is**' (6/72) A generous four r&b hits here, three of them—"There It Is," "I'm a Greedy Man," and "Talkin' Loud and Sayin' Nothing"—ace JB grooves. (Who's on congas, James?) The fourth is the "King Heroin" sermon, which together with its ten-minute offshoot "Public Enemy # 1" is stuck cunningly—Brown has been reading his Alexander Pope—in the middle of the dance stuff on both sides. Plus an actual song, the first new one he's recorded in years, and a JB composition called "Never Can Say Goodbye" that asks the musical question, "What's going on?" For junkies, this is an A plus; for the rest of us it's somewhat more marginal. **A MINUS.**

'**Get on the Good Foot**' (10/72) Only two hits on this studio double, though it takes Hank Ballard five minutes to describe its riches on side two—"he comes from all sides on this one." Lines repeat from song to song—"The long-haired hippies and the Afro blacks / All get together off behind the tracks / And they party"—and so do riffs. The hook on the

12-minute "Please, Please" (not to be confused, of course, with "Please, Please, Please") repeats one hundred forty-eight (and a half) times. I love the hook, I even like the line, and if this were the world's only James Brown album it would be priceless. But there's a lot of waste here, and the ballads can't carry their own weight. **B MINUS.**

'Black Caesar' (1/72) You listen to Brown for music, not songs, but that's no reason to expect good soundtrack albums from him. He should never be allowed near a vibraphone again. **D PLUS.**

'Slaughter's Big Rip-Off' (6/73) As movie scores go, this rip-off is only medium-sized. At least it apes Oliver Nelson rather than Henry Mancini, and sometimes it even breaks away from the atmosphere into something earthier. Worth hearing: "Sexy, Sexy, Sexy." **C.**

'Soul Classics Volume II' (8/73) In absolute terms, Brown has declined on Polydor. Even if you don't insist on great songs (never his strength) or great singing (where he's waned physically), he just hasn't matched rhythmic inventions like "Mother Popcorn" and "Sex Machine" for the big label. And this compilation inexplicably omits "Hot Pants," which comes close, in favor of his ill-advised revivals of "Think" and "Honky Tonk." Still, eight of these 10 tracks have made the soul top 10 over the past two years, and except for "King Heroin" you'll shake ass to every one. **A MINUS.**

'The Payback' (12/73) Because more is often more with JB, a studio double comprising eight long songs isn't necessarily a gyp. Especially when all the songs have new titles. Not only does most of this work as dance music, but two slow ones are actually sung. "Time Is Running Out Fast," however, is a spectacularly inaccurate title for a horn-and-voice excursion that shambles on for 12:37. **B PLUS.**

'It's Hell' (6/74) Great stuff on the two good sides—tricky horn charts, "Please, Please, Please" with a Spanish accent, law enforcement advice. Then there's the side of ballads w/strings, which might be all right if they were also w/voice, and the side that begins "I Can't Stand It '76." **B.**

'Reality' (12/74) Talkin' loud and sayin' nothing, Brown's streetwise factotum intones: "He's still the baddest—always will be the baddest—that's why we give him credit for being the superstar he is." A bad sign (really bad, I mean). As are "Who Can I Turn To" and "Don't Fence Me In." **B MINUS.**

'Sex Machine Today' (4/75) If someone were to airlift this one tape to you in the tundra, the remakes would be godsends. But if you own another version of "Sex Machine" you own a better one. Ditto "I Feel Good," ditto every aimless solo, and ditto the reading from Rand-McNally. Which leaves us with the symphosynth, the complaints that other musicians are ripping him off, and the putdowns of hairy legs. **C PLUS.**

'Everybody's Doin' the Hustle and Dead on the Double Bump' (8/75) In which JB eases the tempo and stops using his voice as a conga drum, thus fashioning a languorous funk that I guess is designed to compete with Barry White. It's not horrible, but I'd just as soon hear the competition—after all, what's JB without intensity? And then suddenly he says fuck it and closes the record with a seven-minute jam on "Kansas City" so sharp it could bring back the lindy hop, at least in dreams. **B MINUS.**

'Hot' (12/75) This record has a bad rep. Most of it was reportedly cut with arranger Dave Matthews by New York studio musicians and then dubbed over by JB, and the title hit didn't do as well among blacks as David Bowie's "Fame," where its guitar lick first went public. But side one really works. If Brown did cop that lick, he certainly had it coming, and except for the sodden "So Long" everything else is touched with the extraordinary, from the cracked falsetto that climaxes "For Sentimental Reasons" to the stirring male backup on "Try Me" to "The Future Shock of the World," a high-echo rhythm track on which JB does nothing but whisper the word "disco." Unfortunately, the dance vamp and ballads overdisc are nothing new, though "Please, Please, Please" (with more male backup) sounds fine in its umpteenth version. **B.**

'Get Up Offa That Thing' (7/76). "I'm Back, I'm back?" is how JB begins the commercial message on the jacket, and the title track is his biggest single in a year and a half. "*I can see the disco now,*" he emphasizes, and even the blues and ballad cultivate a groove designed to reintroduce him to that strangely hostile world he discovered. But he sounds defensive because he has a reason to be — he can't hit the soft grooves the way he can the hard ones. When he starts equating himself with Elvis Presley (just before the fade on "I Refuse To Lose"), you know the identity problems are getting critical. **B MINUS.**

'Bodyheat' (12/76) Two or three functional dance tracks and Brown's will always be tougher than MFSB's. But not than Brown's. "Woman" is unlistenably sanctimonious, "What the World Needs Now Is Love" is the raggedest singing I've ever heard from him, and "Kiss in 77" is "head to head and toe to toe," — in other words, as "brand new" as the *New Sound!* he promises. **C.**

'Mutha's Nature' (7/77) When they start writing songs called "People Who Criticize," you know they're *really* worried. And the anxiety always comes out in the music. **C.**

'Sex Machine' (9/77) This is the same *Sex Machine* Brown released on King in 1970. Some doubt the claim that it was recorded in concert in Augusta, Georgia, but everyone believes in the music. On "Get Up I Feel Like Being a Sex Machine" he creates a dance track even more compelling than the 45 out of the same five elements: light funk-four on the traps, syncopated bass figure, guitar scratched six beats to the bar, and two voices for call and response. When he modulates to the bridge it's like the Spirit of God moving upon the face of the waters. After that he could describe his cars for three sides and get away with it (hope this doesn't give him any bright ideas), but in fact all of it is prime JB except for the organ version of "Spinning Wheel" (horn bands will out) and the cover of "If I Ruled the World" (thought he already did). Side four, with its powerful "Man's World," is especially fine, closing with a soul-wrenching scream that says it all. **A.**

'Jam/1980's' (3/78) Free of the pretentious bluster that has marred so much of his work in the disco era, this is the groove album Brown has been announcing for years. He's finally learned how to relax his rhythms without diluting his essence, and the A side is simply and superbly what the title promises, though he may have the decade wrong. The B side is less of the same, and I bet no one ever chooses to play it. I also bet they'd get dancing if they did. **B PLUS.**

'Take a Look at Those Cakes' (11/78) The title cut is a great throwaway—an 11-minute rumination on ass-watching, including genuinely tasteless suggestions that Ray Charles and Stevie Wonder join the fun. The rest is just throwaway—with a beat, of course. **B MINUS.**

'The Original Disco Man' (6/79) In which Brown relinquishes the profit-taking ego gratification of writing and producing everything himself. Those credits go to Brad Shapiro, Millie Jackson's helpmate, who thank god is no disco man himself. Sure he likes disco tricks—synthesized sound effects, hooky female chorus, bass drum pulse—but he loves what made JB the original disco man: hard-driving, slightly Latinized funk patterns against the rough rap power of that amazing voice, which may have lost expressiveness but definitely retains its sense of rhythm. Plus: disco of the year, "It's Too Funky in Here." And a renunciation of "It's a Man's, Man's, World." **A MINUS.**

'People' (2/80) Once around with Brad Shapiro was a treat; twice is an American cheese sandwich. Although "Regrets" is the strongest new ballad Brown's had to work with since coming to Polydor, Shapiro apparently went with his best uptempo tricks last time. Not that the new ones aren't fun. But even "Let the Funk Flow," a valiant attempt to create a classic can't-stand-it-rhythm, tries too hard. **B.**

"Anything Left in Papa's Bag?"

Steve Bloom
September 1, 1980 • *Down Beat*

I'm riding in an elevator at New York's elegant Sherry Netherland Hotel with James Brown, the world-renowned Godfather of Soul. As we descend some 20 floors to the lobby, Brown kibitzes with the operator.

"May I ask you a question, sir?" he begins. "Am I the greatest soul singer to ever stay in this hotel?"

The operator, sensing a perfect opportunity, smiles and drapes his arms around the Godfather's muscular shoulders.

"Pendergrass stayed here, sir," he says, staring directly into Brown's unblinking eyes. "But he couldn't even shine your shoes."

Everyone in the elevator bursts with laughter. Brown, totally ingratiated, shakes the operator's hand and thanks him "very much." As if on cue, the car suddenly lands. Two well built members of Brown's predominately male entourage fan out to the left and right, each holding a door. Brown takes the lead and bounces on through. The contingent follows the Godfather of Soul into the lobby.

There is little doubt that James Brown, whose career now spans four decades, is *the* legend of modern black popular music.

There is little doubt, too, that James Brown especially enjoys letting people know all about it. In conversation, he repeatedly compares himself to Elvis Presley, but that's not all. One of his favorite braggadocios goes something like this: "My contention is that there were three B's, and now there's four: Beethoven, Bach, Brahms and now, Brown."

That Brown insists on informing others of his talents and of the inestimable gifts which he has bestowed upon mankind is often laughable; his words, however, are also pointed and usually contain bits of the truth. Certainly if egos were balloons his would be a blimp. Still, James Brown hasn't shined anybody else's shoes since he was a young turk growing up in Georgia. That is, not until the last few years.

There was a time when James Brown records were fixtures on every turntable in every black home across America. A tune called *Please, Please, Please*, recorded by the Cincinnati-based King Records, started the ball rolling in 1956. Soul classics like *I Got You (I Feel Good)* (1965), *Papa's Got A Brand New Bag* (1965) and *Cold Sweat* (1966) followed, bringing James Brown to the attention of millions of listeners. He shouted and hollered; he wore sequins and wigs and makeup. Like his peers Little Richard and Chuck Berry, his appearance was that of a rock and roll star.

But there was one difference. Brown's music—an amalgam of gospel testifying, backwoods funk, and even jazzy innovation that had never been heard before—was a modern twist on rhythm and blues. Though it really was just a stone's throw from early rock and roll, Brown was relegated to second class status, confined to the chitlin scene. James Brown didn't go for that at all—instead of touring low pay, funky nightclubs, he wanted a piece of the concert action that rock and rollers took for granted. Since no one was about to steer him in that direction, he grabbed the controls himself.

According to his manager Al Garner, Brown decided to foresake a club engagement he had scheduled for Houston back around 1965. Brown asked Garner, director of a local black radio station, for help in promoting his own Civic Center show. An artist promoting himself was—and still is—relatively unheard of, but Brown felt it was time to test whether or not a black performer could fill a concert arena. "We went to work one month ahead of time," Garner recalls in his native North Carolina accent, "and sure let everyone know about it. Why, we not only sold out the concert (14,500), but even broadcasted it live over my station." This story is only one of many that detail Brown's strong mindedness when it comes to taking care of business.

Says Polydor Vice President Dick Kline, whose career includes a sales stint at King in the late '50s, "Working with James has always been a trip in itself. He's always had his own methods, his own thoughts and his own direction. He's always done everything on his own because he's rarely trusted anyone in the business. I will say one thing about him, though—James Brown is the greatest promoter of James Brown that there ever was."

As of 1980, all Brown's commotion and promotion has done little to revive his sagging sales. James Brown, much to his own disbelief, could no longer sell out Yankee Stadium on any given summer night as he did in the late '60s much less Carnegie Hall, or even the Bottom Line. Disco was something he was not prepared for.

While the Bee Gees and the Doobie Brothers jogged to the bank, the Godfather (who claims Sex Machine was the original disco song) continued laying down those infectiously funky tracks on albums titled Jam/1980's and Take A Look At Those Cakes (both released in 1978).

That these releases were very much in the original funk tradition of James Brown, but still did not produce healthy sales, proved that the market was even further bottoming out for the waning Godfather of Soul.

By '79, changes had to be made. In some very confidential meetings with Polydor (he signed with them in 1971), Brown was urged—for the first time in his career—to accept the common practice of employing an outside producer. Polydor felt that his technique had been slipping. (Conversely, Brown would say the same about Polydor's promotional work or lack thereof.) A studio ace might be able to transform Brown's sound without radically altering it. In what amounted to a major compromise, the Godfather agreed to stand a disco trial with Miami-based producer Brad Shapiro (Wilson Pickett, Millie Jackson) presiding. It was TK Records President Henry Stone, one of Brown's confidantes in the business early on, who negotiated this agreement.

The result was *The Original Disco Man*, both an album and a promotional gimmick. On the surface, Brown was pleased with it, especially when the single, *It's Too Funky In Here*, momentarily bulleted on the black sales charts. At the time, Brown said of Shapiro, "Brad has the sound we need today—technique. I can do ten times more arrangements than Brad can, and he knows that. But I don't have the sound. So Brad's my right arm. Brad can produce James Brown better than James Brown can produce himself. You cannot take that away from Brad."

But it didn't take long for their romance to ebb. When it came down to recording a second disco-styled project with Shapiro, Brown began to holler. "The problem with Polydor is that they're followers, not leaders," he told me, blasting the label for which he has recorded 19 albums in less than a decade. "They wait for somebody else to do something and by the time they jump in it's all over with. That's what they did with disco. Right now they're not doing anything.

"What the Germans should do," he continued, referring to Polydor's German-owned parent firm, Polygram, "is give me a label on the side like Gamble and Huff [Philadelphia International, a division of Columbia Records], and then let me go and do what I have to do.

"They delayed me because they wanted to sell disco. Now it's over with. They've sold as many of my old licks as they could and now they want new ones," the Godfather grumbled. "I'm not going to give them no complete albums of funk, they ain't gonna get that no mo'."

"Never again?" I cried.

"No, never."

"Do you mean that we'll never hear the real James Brown again on record?"

"I didn't say that," Brown snapped back. "I said I'll never give you a full album of that 'cause they copy too much. I can only bring out one single at a time. I know what I want to cut, but I'm not going to cut it right now. I made that mistake with *Groove Machine* [A song Brown produced and recorded, but which was never released. Another song by the same name then came out, sung by Bohannon. They were both recorded in the same studio, so Brown believes he was robbed.] I should've held it back.

"If I don't record it," he said, chuckling to himself, "then you won't hear it. They may come up with a synthetic, but it won't be James Brown original funk."

Earlier this year, Brown begrudgingly recorded again with Shapiro. What could he really say to Polydor after *The Original Disco Man* posted his most impressive sales stats (175,000) in nearly a decade? But with the followup album, *People*, mastered and ready for pressing, Brown took still more potshots.

"It's not funk, but it's good. It's different. It's a new direction, but it's still not James Brown original funk," he pointed out. "It's a very establishment all-funk sound."

Had he not just returned from a tour of Japan where he recorded his first live concert since *Sex Machine*, the Godfather might have had a few more kind words about *People*. But James Brown has never been noted for his patience. In a telegram to Dick Kline, Brown asked that the live package (two records, though Polydor pleaded for only one) be released in tandem with *People*.

"The live album is unbelievable," he repeated several times. "If Dick Kline and them were smart, they'd release it right now. They'd put *Regrets* [the single on *People*] and *Let The Funk Flow* [also on *People*] on it and release it. They wouldn't take time messin' with that other stuff. They're wastin' time with that.

"See, they were committed to the *People* album first, but they're stupid for doing that. They are very stupid for doing that. The people in Europe are smarter than the people in America when it comes to records, 'cause people in Europe release what they hear. Americans release what they are told." Our conversation closed with Brown once again laughing to himself.

Despite Brown's urgings Kline decided to stick with his plan, one which he hopes will raise Brown from the murky mess he is in.

"Since James appeals to a core audience," Kline explained, "the trick is to expand that core. Having a Top 15 hit on the r&b charts with *Too Funky* has already begun to revitalize his career. I am hoping that *People* will further expand that core. Then, with that interest built up, we will go with the live record [planned for release this summer]. James has to trust me now. I'm doing what I think is best for James and at the same time trying to sell records."

Did *The Original Disco Man* and *People* arrive too late, as Brown said, on the disco scene?

"Maybe it was too late, maybe it was too early—who's to know?" Kline replied. "The music business is extremely volatile today. Everything is timing. And, of course, it has to be in the grooves."

James Brown's life has not always, so to speak, been "in the grooves." Born more than 50 years ago in Augusta, Georgia (where he still resides), the son of a gas station attendant, young James grew up fast. Before the age of ten, he washed cars, picked cotton and shined shoes. Whatever change he could scrape up was added to the family stash that covered the $7 rent for their broken down shack of a home.

"My family was so poor you wouldn't believe it," he remembers. "In the afternoons during the winter I'd walk home by the railroad tracks and pick up pieces of coal left behind by the trains. I'd take that home and we'd use it to keep warm."

Entertainment was a natural path for the enterprising young James to follow. Brown recalls:

"I always loved to dance, especially as a little boy. When I was eight years old I used to go dance for the National Guard soldiers who camped outside of town. They threw nickels and dimes and sometimes even quarters at me."

In 1956, James Brown was "discovered" by Syd Nathan, the owner and founder of King Records. With each hit a new nickname seemed to arrive: first "Soul Brother Number One," then "The Godfather of Soul" and finally, "The Minister of the New New Super Heavy Funk." "Mr. *Please, Please, Please* himself" (as he is most affectionately called by his personal emcee, Mr. Danny Ray) has been plain funkin' down ever since.

Where does that unmistakable James Brown sound come from? Asking Brown himself is like imploring a magician to explain his tricks. He does acknowledge childhood favorites like Roy Brown, Buddy Johnson and Louis Jordan, but that's usually as far as he's willing to consult his memory. Otherwise, the Godfather likes to give much of the credit to God.

"*He* gave me a knowledge and built the antennas in so I can recognize what I should be saying. From a conversation, I can record. Just write something down and I can sing it in tempo. Other people can't do that. I can sit down at a piano and show you so many things it's frightening.

"All that stuff I'm playing, I taught it to them—I did it years ago. That's why when the young acts go into the studio today they say, 'Gimme that James Brown sound.'

"The James Brown sound I didn't learn from nobody. It's from me."

Brown rates his work with the greatest American musical innovations of the 20th century. He maintains that his music has been so far ahead of its time that he had no choice but to restrict the complexity of the compositions and arrangements. Otherwise, James says, we never could have understood it.

"A lot of times I used to do arrangements and they'd be too good," he thinks back, "so I would take the one that was less precise 'cause I knew the one I was shooting for would've been too sharp. Like when I did *I Got The Feelin'*, I took the very first cut, which was the weakest. And I remember the first time I cut *I Feel Good*—it was like jazz.

"I went back and made it slower and the sound muddier. I did that on purpose. People were not ready for that sharp sound.

"But everytime I came out the box it was gold or platinum 'cause I always cut James Brown," the Godfather continues, relishing each and every thought. "I can cut at four o'clock in the morning. When I get an idea I call everybody to wake up and the engineer rushes right over. I wrote *Sex Machine* on the back of a placard when we were playing a gig in Nashville. Afterwards, we went right on over to the studio and cut *Sex Machine* and *Super Bad*.

"King needed me and depended on me, so they let me do it. It just made them more money after money."

According to Brown's management, he has sold over 50 million records, 44 of which they claim are gold singles. But the Recording Industry Association of America, which certifies gold records, says that Brown has had only *two* gold singles (*Get On The Good Foot, Part 1*, 1972, and *The Payback*, 1974) and one gold album, *The Payback*. As with many aspects of James Brown's career, the truth is elusive. But the sales discrepancy may be explained by the practice, particularly common among r&b record labels, of under-reporting sales. Whatever the facts, Brown's greatest hits never achieved their expected RIAA certification levels.

Brown is dissatisfied with his current, larger label for other reasons.

"See, conglomerates can't afford to take many chances," James explains. "They got to move according to the GNP. Gross National Product, that's what they go by. It's very bad. Try to move in the safety zone, but when you move in the safety zone your profits are very small. That's why it's so hard being an innovator. Big companies don't feel that they can take that big of a risk. But small companies just don't have all that much to lose."

Sweet Georgian Brown paints an almost idyllic picture of his days at King, but he admits it wasn't *all* peaches and cream.

"No matter what," he strains to recall, "every song I ever cut with that strange sound—like *It's A Man's World*—they said was no good. *Live At The Apollo*—I had to spend my own money to do it. *Prisoner Of Love*—they said I couldn't sing ballads. They always said, 'Why sing a song that you've sang all your life?' I said, ''Cause when you do it live it's never the same.'"

For "James Brown The Entertainer" (as he calls himself when dialing strangers on the phone), live performance has always been bread, butter, and lifeline in a very fickle business. When Americans decided to stop listening to him, Brown began accepting countless invitations to travel abroad. The Japanese, Italians, Germans, Mexicans and British and others can be credited with supporting the Godfather during his worst moments of professional distress.

During the '70s, Brown's empire suddenly caved in; not only was his ego blown, but his pockets were empty. Gone were the personal Lear jets, the extravagant expenses, the mansion with a moat in Queens, New York. Also lost were two of his three radio stations, victims to bankruptcy. James Brown, forever the Godfather of Soul, had painfully fallen to earth.

His most recent problem is with the Internal Revenue Service, which is assessing Brown $2,100,000 for unpaid taxes covering the years 1975–77. It has erroneously been reported that Brown has already been indicted for this sum; however, the parties are negotiating and Brown claims to have lost money during this period.

Meanwhile, on the concert trail, things have begun to pick up for the irrepressible Brown. As of May, he began touring the rock club circuit for the first time in his 24 year career. After years of playing to mostly black audiences, it has finally come to his attention that hordes of teenage rock and rollers have been digging James Brown for quite some time. This realization crystalized during spring of 1980 when Brown flew to Chicago to play Reverend Cleophus James in the recently released *The Blues Brothers* movie. There he was greeted with the kind of respect he had not received in the States for years. Says James, "It was deeper than respect: it was love."

I next saw him and his eight man band at one of New York's new wave rock palaces called Irving Plaza, a former Polish meeting hall now disguised as a high school auditorium. Brown, as always, was most candid.

"I know what this place is and I'm proud of it," he told me. "I'm proud that even though I was acting under instruction with my last two albums, the younger people have demanded that James Brown do what he's noted for. They want to hear that again 'cause," he said with emphasis, "it's authentic. They want the real thing—they want it *raw*.

"See, blacks know what I was doing, but they don't know as much as they think they do. They never knew that I was making history then. But you whites know I'm making history because your schools are better. See what I'm saying?

"When someone makes history, it's current until you're reminded that this is history. But like I've said before: everyday I live is another day added to history."

Black, white, purple or green, the fact remains that Brown's two day engagement at Irving Plaza was his most successful appearance in the New York area since he arrived back in town about a year ago. The packed houses danced with the kind of fervor that used to mark every James Brown and the Famous Flames show. He could've literally pleased them playing all night.

The same, however, could not be said for one particularly disconcerting series of dates last winter. On a Saturday night he was only able to fill one-third of the seats at Newark's Symphony Hall. The next evening he barely sold half the tickets for a gig at the Westchester Premier Theatre. Prior to both concerts, Brown was visibly upset. Poor sales at halls where he had once sold out—like Symphony—does not exactly raise the spirits of the very sensitive Godfather. He responded with performances that were simply not up to par.

Brown's new-found new wave audience is all well and good, but blacks are still not buying James Brown. *People* has failed miserably, unable to even locate a spot on the top 75 black album charts in the trades. At a time when black acts like Kool & the Gang, the Spinners, Ben E. King, Gladys

Knight & the Pips, the Whispers and many more are recouping with hits after years of silence, James Brown—in terms of airplay—is in the dog-house. Some say James Brown—who's not the easiest person to get along with—has made too many enemies in radio over the years; others simply believe *People* is not "in the grooves."

Says Dick Kline: "He's definitely disappointed with the results so far. The street response has not been that good. But there are many things that enter into the picture with James as to *why* his records don't sell. It becomes difficult putting the normal situations together that you would with any particular artist that you release. He constantly wants to do things his own way. Evidently, in the past few years, that's proven limitedly successful for him."

According to a spokesman at WBLS-FM, New York's top-rated station (which is also black owned and operated), *People* is "not what people are listening to now. James seems to still be into that old sound. But that doesn't mean we wouldn't play a tune like *Escape-ism* on which James does a lot of improvising. He should go back to rapping because people are into rap records now.

"I know for a fact that Frankie [Crocker, the station's manager and one of the major tastemakers in black pop] is into James Brown. It's just that he probably hasn't heard what he wants yet."

What blacks don't want is a reminder of the days when black entertainers wore wigs and matching suits with sequins. Times have changed. Chic and GQ, upturned collars and upward mobility—as long as it has the beat—are now in. James Brown's raw, original funk is definitely out.

Maybe Brown's next studio release will do the trick. He's already announced that it will be "James Brown from the '60s in 1980. It'll be the way I feel in 1980. Polydor wants me to be myself again. Even all the executives are saying that they want me to do my thang. It's gonna be fantastic."

So much for Brad Shapiro, who Brown says "had good intentions."

And so much for Dick Kline, who claims he has "no idea what James is talking about."

I'm sitting in New York's City Hall. Mayor Ed Koch is two seats to my right. James Brown, the Godfather of Soul, reclines in a couch directly across from me. Dick Kline, Al Garner, Brown's personal Reverend Al Sharpton and several other members of the retinue are either seated or standing around the room.

The main purpose of the meeting is to introduce Koch and Brown, who've never met. Another function is to discuss the late Dr. Martin Luther King Jr. in respect to the government's unwillingness to declare his birthday, January 15, a legal holiday. Koch agrees that something should be done, then shifts the conversation into Brown's lap. The Mayor asks how he's doing, how his career is going. Brown is uneasy with the prospect of discussing his problems, but decides to anyway.

"What does it take for a man to get true recognition in this country?" Brown asks, apparently referring to both himself and Dr. King. "What does it take for a black man to totally succeed?"

"Wouldn't you say that you've totally succeeded?" Koch returns.

"No, sir."

"Why do you say that you haven't?"

"Because I'm still economically doing the same thing."

"But aren't you one of the most noted, accomplished people in your field and universally . . . ?"

"So was Jesse James, sir."

"I don't understand," Koch says. "You are someone who has risen to the very top of your field, not as a black but as a performer. Isn't that so?"

"I feel that."

"So then what is it that you're saying is missing?"

"James Brown is a legend, sir. Kids see me in the dark and they say, 'That's James Brown.' Again, I ask what does it take for a man like me— who is rated only second to Elvis Presley in the statistics—to put a record out and have it played? There should be no question."

"Do you think that the stations are not playing you?"

"I don't want to single out no stations, sir," Brown says. "I didn't come here for that."

What James Brown, Soul Brother Number One, the Godfather of Soul, the New New Minister of the Super Heavy Funk, Mr. *Please, Please, Please* himself asks is one very simple question: What does it take?

"The Renegade & the Godfather" (excerpts)

Gavin Martin
September 1, 1984 • *New Musical Express*

What do you think of when you think of James Brown?

A stretcher case raddled with emotional pain dragging himself back from endless encores of 'Please Please Please'?

The self-proclaimed, undisputed Godfather of Soul roving across his kingdom in his robes and finery giving strength and supplication to the weak and weary masses? The man who stopped a race riot? A pompadour quiff dripping a sheen of sweat over his face? Rubber limbed knee jerks, full length splits and heel swivels? One of the finest musical brains of the past 25 years? A larger than life presence. The speed. The grace. The glory?

Laydeez and gennelmen—the star of the show, hardworking, Mr. Dynamite . . . Jaaaaaymes Brown.

Or, are you ready for this James Brown wrapped in a bathrobe, cooly appraising himself in front of his bedroom mirror with his hair wrapped in pink rollers. Would you believe it? The Man's Man Sex Machine Brother Rapp Minister of The New Super Heavy Funk with huge plastic combs to give his nylon textured locks that permed flounce and parting!

If you were around his hotel room the morning before the start of his three day assault on The New Music Seminar in New York's Hilton Hotel, you'd see how the rollers are just part of his elaborate and well established process of readying himself to meet the press and public.

Inside their bedroom, his wife Alfie busies herself with the various make-ups, toners and highlighters that will improve his features without making him look like one of those over-painted honky faggots who seemed to have colonised the charts while James has been elsewhere.

Then there is the extensive wardrobe of clothes designed to make this small, corpulent 56-year-old look solid and imposing rather than the glutinous overweight mass that one suspects lies under the carefully tailored cloth. He is also on a diet specially planned by Gertrude Stein, his wardrobe mistress and weight watcher for the past 20 years.

Obviously no spring chicken herself Ms Stein, a tall quiet lady in a white crimpolene frock with a mild case of varicose veins, had quite a hard task. Because while Mister Brown, as everyone in his select entourage refers to him, nibbles on cornflakes and sliced bananas at breakfast and delicate little canapes for a lunchtime snack as he plays Funky President in waiting, when at home in his Augusta Georgia mansion, he is no stranger to the joys of Southern style home cooking.

The extra flesh is there to prove it but the careful preparation pays off and Mr Brown looks smart, cool and, yes, imposing.

It's still a bit disconcerting when you see him swagger across the floor of his hotel suite or strutting downtown New York with the butt wriggling and that rolling cowboy gait in full swing. Still, pink rollers! That wasn't going to be too easy to forget. That was a real shocker.

On the Hilton's 44th floor is the Presidential Suite. Richard Nixon stayed here with his wife Pat in the middle of some of his corrupt dealings. The main room has oak panelled book shelves with a veritable library of American literature, various items of engraved antique furniture and a swish polished ballroom floor. Windows the size of a small football pitch look over the broad sweep of the Manhattan skyline, and beside the windows sits a large Steinway.

Various people from Tommy Boy Records and The James Brown entourage mill around the main room and kitchen (where there's a bar with an extensive supply of Perrier water). At the top of the spiral staircase James finishes off his preparations.

As I wait for his arrival the girl from Tommy Boy introduces me to Alfie, the fourth or fifth Mrs Brown who's now busying herself with some knitting. A good few years JB's junior she's fairly plump and squat with a bouffant of back-combed black hair and a well powdered white face. Later in the day somebody tells her she looks like Joan Collins and she's not amused, at all.

Also there throughout the three days is Mr Henry Stallings, hardest working manager of the hardest working man in show business, and Willie Glenn, a friend of James since schooldays, now employed as a general assistant. His chief function seems to be to give wholehearted support and agreement to the craziest statements and conjectures made by his friend and keeper. Some of Brown's male offspring by previous marriages and his newset collaborator—Overlord of The Zulu Nation, self-proclaimed, undisputed King Of Hip Hop Afrika Bambaataa—are also present.

It's only after flying 3,000 miles from London and about three minutes before the interview that I'm taken aside by the girl from Tommy Boy and told there are three areas to avoid—politics, religion and colour. A James Brown interview without politics or religion wasn't exactly the sort of interview I'd been preparing for. The thought that I'd had when the trip was first proposed began to niggle. It was that Brown had only decided to do interviews as part of the deal struck with Tommy Boy for his collaboration with Bambaataa on the megamix 'Unity' (it was rumoured he was given an unconditional payment of 30,000 for his part in the recording) and not to delve into the brilliance and complexity of one of the most amazing success stories and catalogues of recorded work in the whole of history.

Suddenly there he is descending the stairs in a wide flapping casino hustler suit, aviator shades, and a ruffled red shirt. Patent leather shoes click on the floor as he strides over to the piano to run through an old song that he never got round to recording. Tune called 'Honeydripping' and it's a fine version.

"*Boogie Woogie,*" yells James as he goes for an extended run between verses.

"I wish I could see his eyes; his eyes say it all," sighs Alfie.

He looks in my direction. "You wouldn't know 'bout hings like that, recorded before you was even born," he says removing his shades and coming down to sit beside me. Afrika Bambaataa takes a stool on my other side, but remains mute while Brown is speaking. Although it was his idea to approach Brown to make 'Unity' and he's followed him for years, it soon becomes clear that there are several issues on which Bam is prepared to be more forthright than The Godfather. His silence seems only to avoid contradiction and ensures the courtly respect flows smoothly.

In the past you've been critical of new funk groups, why have you decided to work with Bambaataa?

"No, I'm not critical. It's an extension of what we've done and it's another way to get to it. I'm never critical of no one. One thing we are critical of, Bambaataa and myself, is people killing each other. Now you live as long as you can and die when you can't help it but we don't want you to plan nobody's death."

But you must have had offers from people before?

"Yeah, I have; I won't call their names, they're good people, good faith. I think one of The Rolling Stones wants to do an album with me now, Nona Hendryx also. They want me to work with Aretha, but I choose Bambaataa. When I first talked to him I knew it was what I wanted to be involved in. He's about people looking out for the underdog and looking out for the small man. That's what I get from him, that's what he told me, anything else he's thinking I don't know about but that's what he told me. He's got a reputation for helping the young and that's what I'm about also."

The sound of inner city hip hop is an extension of the sound of American geography. When you began making music the various regions had clearly defined 'sounds'. Were you conscious of wanting to integrate all these elements?

"It's like travelling, some takes the autobahn, some takes the service road, some take a train, some take a plane. Everybody's going the same place—survival."

Baffled, I repeat the question.

"No, I wasn't. I was conscious about eating and sleeping. I wanted to live. All that came after. But once you get what you want you shouldn't be so hung up on yourself that you won't help other people. That's why I love him because he's concerned about people other than himself."

Weren't you influenced by people. I hear you like the blues singer Little Willie John?

"No, he didn't influence me. I like some of the things he was doing but he didn't influence me. Louis Jordan influenced me, *Lew-iss* Jordan. It was the show as well as the music, very vibrant, very entertaining."

Your show was very stylised, how did you go about putting it together?

"I think organisation is the key to everything. Organise—that's what Bambaataa's talking about. Organise people's minds toward peace. Organisation. What's wrong with the entertainers today is that they walk onstage and they're not organised, then they ask the audience which one shall we play. We know which one we're going to play when we get up there. Entertainment, that's what its about—E-N-T-E-R-T-A-I-N-M-E-N-T, entertainment."

Was it important that your show was very rootsy; it came from local communities and ordinary folks could relate to it.

"I don't understand your terms of words so I'm not going to agree with you."

* * *

After a while it becomes clear that James Brown isn't so much interested in answering questions as using the spaces in the conversation as an opportunity to propagate his flaccid, ecumenical clichés. He tells me later that I'm too young, got no wisdom, that I'm dragging down the horizons of the interview. Well, excuse me.

I'm not quite used to adjusting to the neo mystical rarefied verse required by Ye Gods of entertainment. Oh sure we could get into one of those dopey religous flip top dialogues but it would get us nowhere fast. This is JAMES BROWN forgodsakes, a real bleeding hero. I want to grapple with the reality of the man who had me motivated and fortified with his music for as long as I remember. A man whose music has travelled further and stayed sharper than anyone involved in the (r)evolution of modern music, whose gut bottom pained shriek on 'Cold Sweat', 'Please Please Please', 'Bring It On' (fill in your favourite) is the epitome of soul music's sonic powerdrive. A man whose esteem seems to diminish every time he opens his mouth to do anything other than use The Steinway. I decide I might have more success with a reverential pitch.

You went through a lot of hard times touring the South, recording great music that never charted, getting ripped off. Did you always feel that you'd be popular?

"I thought I would get to the top. I knew I had something to offer and that I was as good as any man that wanted to do something and a whole lot better than those that didn't want to do nothing. Heh heh heh. You understand?"

You became a real hero to many, like young Bam here. Was that the intention?

"I must have done something he liked. I hope I became a hero to him. I hope I became a hero to his family and that he's a hero to me. The intention was to be a hero, to make everyone like me. In the beginning it was for me then I got mine and I started to think of other people. Any man who doesn't think of himself first is not very intelligent. When you eat food do you eat for yourself or someone else? I rest my case."

You developed at the same time as Elvis Presley . . .

"I didn't develop anything Elvis did. I was singing before I met Elvis. We wasn't allowed to play together during that time, there was a separation thing called prejudice. Elvis and I got together when we weren't working, we were good friends, we was religous brothers. Both sung gospel."

Were you to black folks what Elvis was to white folks?

"We was equivalent to people but the system wouldn't allow us to be together—not as white and black people. But we had to say what we said during those times, even though people don't really have a colour. But since they separated us we dealt with what we had. But, by the same token, when he'd get off work Elvis would be peeping in the window watching BB King and T Bone Walker like I used to watch Tommy Dorsey, Bing Crosby and Frank Sinatra."

You met them as well?

"Yeah I met Sinatra. Sinatra's a very good friend of mine. I like a lot of things he did. I like the way he stood up for himself and defended himself when he was publicly attacked."

Would you like to have recorded with Elvis?

"I think it would have made a good record—me doing what I felt and Elvis doing what he felt. I think it would have been good for humanity— like Bambaataa and me together is good for humanity. I'd love to record with Streisand, that would definitely be good for humanity and for artistic merit. I would still like to record with Sinatra and hopefully, I wish, he would like to record with me because I think we could bring a lot of things together."

You created a great showman that you seem to have to be 24 hours a day; is that easy to live with?

"James Brown is forever because he do as God tells him to. Yes it's great to live with, all you got to do is think of the time before. To be so important is easy to live with."

Does the world need heroes today?

"Sure, everybody needs heroes. Heroes are role models."

Are the heroes of today the sort the world needs?

"The world needs what it has, the world don't produce nothing it don't need."

It produces famines, nuclear waste, wars.

"Wars? I guess it needs wars. Wars is a way of debating. Killing—they don't need that. But they have wars, the whole of the Olympics is war. A war of art. Heh heh heh."

Have you seen The Jacksons show?

"I didn't get a chance though I was invited there. But Michael is doing very good and well enough without me not to bother seeing him.

"I don't want to distract attention away from him. Kids need to look at

Michael, not me. We got Michael going, now we got to work on Prince and Bambaataa."

Jackson regularly checks you as major influence but the elements of sexual ambiguity and childlike wonderment in his act seem at odds with the masculine tradition that you celebrated. Would you agree with Black Muslims who've said his image is "Sissified"?

"I haven't anything to do with that. I'm not here to talk about that. I think you've run out of questions, haven't you? Don't get fresh when you come back to me. I don't want to talk about other people. Don't ask me those sort of questions. I'm here to talk about this thing (points at a copy of 'Unity'). You talk to Bambaataa now."

Woops, think I just blew the James Brown story. The great man ups and walks off to complain to Mister Stallings. As I shot the breeze with Bambaataa—a sweet guy with his own story to tell—I can hear Billy Giddens shouting "Yeah, you right, you right, you damn right."

Bambaataa had met James Brown several times in the '60s and '70s when he came up to the Bronx, sometimes making an appearance at one of the special annual Brown tribute nights that Bam DJ'd. Just as James Brown stopped a race riot by going on 24 hour TV in the late '60s, so when the calm of his club was one night disturbed by an outside shooting incident Bambaataa quelled the crowd by playing nonstop JB.

The Godfather recorded what is probably the first rap record—'America Is My Home'—and later, when the '70s scene took off, made one of his greatest records in years with 'Rapp Payback'—semi-taunt, semi-tribute to the youngbloods. While he'd obviously been keeping tabs on the New York scene—he'd been snapped hanging out with Kurtis Blow during the early days of The Roxy—it wasn't until the young man who he remembered from way back (Brown's photographic memory is legendary) made him an offer that he decided to join forces.

But it's not all that Bambaataa's been involved with or plans to be involved with. A list of his ventures crisscross the cornucopia of modern music. Firstly he has his own groups on a variety of labels—Shango, Soul Sonic Force, Time Zone and then the people who are interested in using his beat advisory service—John Lydon, Thomas Dolby, George Clinton, German rapper Falco, Yellowman, Nona Hendryx.

He hasn't actually met Lydon but in preparation he was watching all available videos of The PiL lynchman and reading as much as he could about him. Whatever love he once had for Lydon's former manager was washed away by McLaren's comments on a recent Hip Hop documentary.

"Anybody asks me about Malcolm and I always start talking about Malcolm X, McLaren is a liar. He met me in a housing project in South East Bronx—it wasn't burnt out or looking raggedy or nothing. They show the same piece of The Bronx all the time in the movies and on the box but it's only a small part of it that is like that."

For a guy so young and so much in demand Bambaataa seems in control and not afraid to let his tongue loose on issues like South Africa when these days The Godfather would rather keep schtum.

I ask why he recorded so many of his old songs again in the late '70s, and he says "I just do as God tells me."

And what of his collaboration with Sly and Robbie?

"I wanted to go in one direction and they wanted go in another. But he and I did something together because we went in the same direction. Heh heh heh heh. Aint't that funny Bam? Hehh heh heh heh heh, that really funny . . .

"I ain't metcher mam yet Bam, got to meet your mam."

"That'll be a trip for her," says Bam.

"It'll be a trip for me, too, to see where a fine young man like you come from. You come from a special breed of people to go through all the things you went through and still draw a happy medium. But you're still into that black thing real strong, aren't you Bam?"

"I check for all world things. I'm looking out for everybody. But especially for them that are where I come from."

"But you got to take everything in your stride. You'll see a lot of things but you don't want to limit your conversation when you say you're black, white German or Jewish you're going to turn off other nationalities and limit it. Your rap will begin to change and modify itself but you'll still be talking about the same things. I'm not telling you what to say but I will give you both points of view and let you make your own decision because you're going to make both decisions later anyway. You make one decision now, what's known as a right decision, later on you'll make a left decision. Later on you'll make one that's right down the middle. That will come from experience, nobody can teach you that."

As Joe decides to take some snaps Brown pushed away the packet of Kool cigarettes resting on the table beside him.

"One thing, we don't want pictures with cigarettes in them."

Still throughout the course of the day he regularly filches a few fags from Alfie's packet. Even soul giants have their vices, I guess. He also tells Bambaataa to hide his wallet; "You don't want to associate yourself with money."

Later the next day I see him talking to Tommy Boy label boss and 'Unity' executive producer Tom Silverman. They are comparing hands and Silverman comments on Brown's lack of jewellery. "That's good, that's right," says JB, "we don't want to alienate the poor, don't want to show our wealth. . . ."

In the green room at MTV Alfie preens Brown for his appearance—fixing his shirt collar, removing dust flecks from the back of his jacket and flicking his hair curls into perfect shape. James and Willie decide to try their hands at the pool table in the middle of the room. "Well I dunno I use' to be pretty good but I ain't shot for some time," says Willie.

"Weren' I bad, Willie, weren' I bad," says Brown.

"You sure was bad, James. You sure was," says Willie.

"When James and me get together we're the baddest team there is. Ain't that right baby?" says Alfie on the sidelines.

"That's right baby, that's right," says James.

James gets beaten on the game of nine ball and as Willie walks away he playfully mutters under his breath "Ya jive ass mutha fuggin' nigger." Bambaataa had disappeared into the kitchen on arrival but as they'd rode the short distance from the hotel to the TV station Brown had continued to give him advice on presentation.

"You speak kind of low Bam, I don't want to undercut you. When you say the words 'LOVE' 'PEACE' and 'UNITY' say them loud like a DJ."

But just before they are due to make their appearance, there's a hitch which is finally resolved when MTV (the cable channel notorious for extremely dodgy, implicitly racist programming) agrees to draw up a specially worded contract. James objects to the wording that says MTV *permits him* to appear on *their* channel. "I'm not signing that, I didn't ask to be on this show. There might be some kids begging to go on the show but it's not me, not James Brown. Rick James may have begged to go on it but where is he now? If I go on, their ratings go up and they get millions of viewers. I'm doing them a favour. . . ."

"James Brown & Afrika Bambaataa"

Glenn O'Brien
October 1, 1984 • *Interview*

*S*ay it loud. I'm black and I'm proud. It's a man's world. But it wouldn't mean nothing, nothing, without a woman or a girl. Stay on the scene like a loving machine. For goodness sakes, take a look at those cakes. Get up offa that thing, and try and release the pressure. Peace, unity, love and having fun.

James Brown needs no introduction. Mr. Dynamite. The hardest working man in show business. The Godfather of Soul.

I met James Brown at the New York Hilton, where Brown occupied the Presidential Suite while attending the New Music Seminar. Mr. Brown was joined by Afrika Bambaataa, D.J. and recording artist, who collaborated with him on his new record, "Unity" (Tommy Boy Records).

Meeting James Brown was a great honor and a thrill. He radiates wisdom, kindness and positivism. I was a little nervous meeting him, but Mr. Brown put me at ease by shaking my hand every time I said something he liked. He is the most naturally regal person I've ever met. He is majestically funky, full of awareness, knowing, cool, proud, but with a reverent humility, the total picture of a cosmic executive.

GLENN O'BRIEN: *How did you and Bambaataa get together?*

JAMES BROWN: A lot of people want to make records with James Brown—they want the name. But Bam and Tommy [*Silverman, president of Tommy Boy Records*] came and said they wanted to do something really positive. Bambaataa had the fruit from some of my labor. He wanted young people to say, "I want to do better things, I want to go a step further than James Brown had a chance to go. I want to tell people what we're about." Now that they've heard James Brown we've got something to build on.

I want to help to extend life. I see a great danger to people in small countries who might be oppressed. I want to get into the mainstream. The people who have enough money to buy nuclear weapons, we want to try to talk them out of using them. We want to talk with the world leaders and sit down with the small countries and not force them into using something that could be detrimental to all of us. We want to stop the terrorists and guerrilla warfare, and use that same energy diversified into planting, farming, feeding people, hospitals and things of a more positive concept.

GO'B: *Had you heard Bambaataa's music before he approached you?*

JB: Not a lot of it. But Bambaataa always came and talked to me at all the different shows. He always said to me, "We play your music. We believe in you." I don't know all of his songs like he doesn't know all of mine. I'm sure some of my songs were hard for people to digest. I know when I said, "Say it loud, I'm black and I'm proud," it kind of separated some of my fans. A lot of white people or people of different races may have thought that I had left them. What I was trying to do was clean up some of the mess that they couldn't clean up. I think that mess is pretty well got together. You see a crowd of people now and you don't see color or race or religion, but you see *people*. If we can get those overtones across to everybody then we're in business. I haven't always said what I'm saying now, and if Bambaataa hasn't always said what we're saying now he was on his way to saying it.

GO'B: *Do you listen to the radio?*

JB: A lot, yeah. I think some of the songs out there are a little rough. They need to be changed. I think we're going too far out in protesting; I think we're going too far out in profanity. The profanity on the records should just be cut off totally. Any time a person cusses on a record it should be taken off the air—*period*.

GO'B: *They used to be really strict about that.*

JB: They'll get back to it. I'm going to work on that. People shouldn't have to use four-letter words to sell themselves.

GO'B: *It's interesting what's happened with hip hop music. It has really become a great vehicle for people with something to say. There used to be a lot of bragging and now the messages are a lot more interesting.*

JB: I made rap tunes in the '60s. Now, young people like Bam, Grandmaster Flash and Kurtis Blow realize that we *can* get a message across. Curtis Mayfield came behind me and he did a real good job and then the Staple Singers and gospel singers, especially gospel singers today. They've been doing it. Even in the country tunes, people have been doing it. I don't hear the classical people doing it so much, or the middle of the road people, but the Latin people are doing it and a lot of other countries are doing it. I'm very proud of that.

GO'B: *You made so many great message songs. I really like the one you wrote and produced for Bobby Byrd, "If You Don't Work You Can't Eat."*

JB: That's probably one of the most direct messages in the world. You know, a man looking for a job today looks for a special kind of job; he should first go get *a* job. I started as a janitor, a shoeshine boy. I shined shoes in front of a radio station—27 years later I came back and bought the station.

GO'B: *I saw you at the Howard Theater in Washington in the late '60s, and when you slid across the stage sparks flew.*

JB: That's right. They wanted to wire me up one time so I could fly. I wouldn't do it. All that has to happen is some cat blows a fuse and there you are, *bam*, on the ground. That stuff is dangerous. And another thing, they wire you up and you are subject to shortwave, breakers, a whole lot of things. I just left Italy and every time I came offstage my hair would be hard as a brick, all the oil would be gone. Do you know why? Because they've got you wired up. All that electricity going, and you've got different systems in different countries and you know what takes the beating? The human body. Skin be dry, hair be dry, lips get parched. Just like being electrocuted. That happens all the time. You've got to be prepared. I put on certain braces and things, to stop that thing from taking completely over. The human body cannot stand that kind of stuff; you've got to be geared up for that.

GO'B: *Do you work out or do you get enough exercise performing?*

JB: I exercise and I think. To exercise you have to have the discipline to think that way, you've got to think that way. And if you don't eat a heavy meal past six or seven in the evening you're alright. You look good. You look *good*.

GO'B: *I do?*

JB: You do. You look good.

GO'B: *Are you doing a record with George Clinton?*

JB: I have a record that should have been released already called *Go For Your Funk*. I think I'll go back and get it now 'cause it's unbelievable. George Clinton and Bootsy (Collins): it's unbelievable.

GO'B: *Bootsy, Fred Wesley and Maceo were in your band. Was George Clinton ever in your band?*

JB: No, George was a hairstylist in Washington where I used to get my hair fixed. He's a barber. He was on T Street.

GO'B: *That's how you met?*

JB: Yeah, I didn't remember, but he reminded me of it. George and I never did a lot of things together. The only thing he did was pull a few of my musicians away. It was good for me. If they'd have stayed with me too long they'd have become stale. He just did me a favor.

GO'B: *You cut quite a few records with spinoff groups—the JBs, Fred Wesley, Maceo, Bobby Byrd. I guess you were one of the first artists to produce his band members.*

JB: One of the first.

GO'B: *What happened to Bobby Byrd?*

JB: You see what happens is that you can make a man big, but not *experienced*. Young people just chop themselves off. They get too smart for themselves and then they blow it. We were hearing some of the young entertainers last night: they want control of themselves, they want this, they want that. That's good for creativity, but it'll kill you in business. You can't control yourself. You've got to have somebody with the knowledge. You go out on the road and you'll be a babe in the woods out there. I could go up against a newcomer and beat them every time.

GO'B: *Yesterday you said you had done something like 832 songs—I don't remember the exact number.*

JB: A little bit more than that.

GO'B: *Were you aware of that all along or did you find that out later?*

JB: No, I only found out when the tax man got behind me. I didn't know I'd got myself into so much trouble. Success is trouble.

GO'B: *Anyway, I think it's great that you have written all those songs. Do you write on a piano?*

JB: I play piano.

GO'B: *Yeah. I used to love your organ playing. I have this jazz album called* Grits and Soul.

JB: A very good album. I write 'em from different things, but a lot of my songs I got from my children. When they start coming out with sayings and things I take the lyrics and make a song out of 'em. If I say I'm singing a song of mine I'm kidding myself. The idea is where the song is from. I just put on the music. But the song is first an idea. I wrote "It's A Man's World." I wrote everything about it. But a girl gave me the idea and you know I gave her 50 percent of that song. She didn't write nothing, but the idea is really the song. It doesn't do you any good to know all the chords if you haven't got any ideas. The idea is the song.

GO'B: *How do you feel when you hear someone on the radio who copies you?*

JB: I feel extra good. Bambaataa; George Clinton; Sly; Earth, Wind and Fire; Chicago—all of them people are following James Brown's act. I could have been forgotten, but they went and started cutting my songs. They brought me back.

GO'B: *I think the first time I ever saw you was on the television show* Shindig.

JB: I did "World." That was a song that should have made it and they killed it. I was talking to all of the races and all the nations of people.

GO'B: *I was really impressed. You were up there singing and your band was sitting down. I'd never seen a hot band sit down. They looked serious.*

JB: It was real serious. "World" was real serious.

GO'B: *A lot of the new records use new technology—computers and things. Were you exposed to those things before working with Bambaataa?*

JB: I knew about all that. I know about studios. You need a studio that's on the first floor, that's in contact with the surface. A studio on the fifth or sixth floor is a joke.

GO'B: *For the vibration?*

JB: That's right. No bass. I'm the man for bass. Nobody gets bass but me. Rock people get more bass than soul acts because soul acts don't understand equipment that well. My guitar players never did learn how to play the wah-wah. We had the first effect sound guitar, the Vox, but none of them ever did know how to play the wah-wah.

GO'B: *Did other people produce you before you produced yourself?*

JB: I always produced myself. I've been forced to have other people produce me.

GO'B: *Why would they force you to have an outside producer?*

JB: To control you and take a piece of the song. They want their in-house man to produce it so they get a piece of the copyright.

GO'B: *Do you ever think about producing other artists now?*

JB: I'd love to. I'd love for a record company to get me in there and let me show these young kids how to perform.

GO'B: *Who would you like to produce?*

JB: At this point I'd like to produce Diana Ross, because I think she's a great talent who's lost her direction. I'd like to produce Aretha Franklin. I'd like to help Dionne Warwick; she's a fine lady. I'd like to produce Lloyd Price, Hank Ballard and B.B. King. I'd really like to produce the Dells, too. They need help because nobody can produce the old sound. It takes somebody out of that other era. And I'd like to produce my wife. She's one of the greatest singers in the country. She's not really interested in it, but she's got a fantastic voice. When I'm singing on stage she sings high parts offstage. She sings so high it's scary.

GO'B: *Bam, as a D.J. do you see yourself as an educator?*

AFRIKA BAMBAATAA: I love to see the reaction of a dance floor, people getting vibes off other people's music. I like to catch people, like people who say, "I don't like no rock music." So I'll play something funky by the Rolling Stones like "Hot Stuff." People say they don't like Latin music, but I'll play something by Eddie Palmieri and they're dancing like crazy to it.

JB: I said I didn't like squash and one time a lady prepared some squash for me. It looked like sweet potatoes and I ate a whole plate of it. She said, "You don't eat squash?" I said, "No." She said, "You just ate just about all you can handle."

GO'B: *Bam, in all these D.J.-oriented publications they list the number of beats per minute a song has. Do you pay any attention to that kind of thing?*

AB: Not really. I don't like to programmize. I'm educating the people to different cultural styles. What we had in the Roxy brought all walks of life, all cultures together. You saw the new wave people learning now to do the smurf dance that was popular in the black and Hispanic community, and you'd see the blacks and Hispanics learning to do the stomp that the new wavers were doing. It was an exciting thing. Nobody was worrying about no colors or nationality. Everybody was in there to dance and have a good time.

GO'B: *I'm sure you've been told this a million times, but your records have been played in clubs constantly for years.*

JB: I don't blame 'em. They ain't playing nothing new on the air. They put a damper on
the airwaves. You write something and it'll never get on the air, never see it on television. You're in the zero time, the reorganization time. It's like a lawyer once had a son and this man was working on a case and he worked on that case for 25 years, put his son through college, bought a home, bought a car and insurance and annuities. The boy finished college and law school and his father said, "Well, I've been working on this case for 25 years and I'm gonna give it to you, son." So the fellow went off and came back the next day and said, "I closed the case. I cleared the matter up. I did something you couldn't do, Dad, I solved the case." His father said, "You know what you just did? You broke yourself. That case put you through school, bought this home, the car, the insurance policy. Now you've got to find another case." It's unfair, but that's business. Business prolongs things. Everything that you can think of is put together. Everything is organized. The only thing that's not organized is spirit. That you can't put together. God controls spirit. Everything else is organized. *Everything.* I can go in your church right now and give a thousand dollars and you

give twenty dollars and everybody's gonna talk to *me*. It's organized. That's bad. But that's the root of all evil, money.

GO'B: *You were probably the first person to make long singles. Now
everybody does twelve-inch singles, but you used to do a song in
part one and part two. Were you forced to cut them in two
because they wouldn't play anything longer on the air?*

JB: I made part one and part two because when I make a record I
want to make the B side as good as the A side. I get tripped up
by my own perfection. I started making the same thing so you
got no choice. I'm the one that started coming out with double A records. The A & R man told me, "James, don't ever
make a bad record." I would never make a bad record. When
you put a good record on the flip side you blow it. The flip side
of "It's A Man's World" is "Is It Yes or Is It No." It's as good as
"A Man's World." The flip side of "Please, Please" is "Why You
Do Me Like You Do." The flip of "Try Me," "Tell Me What I
Done Wrong," hit first. The flip side of "I Can't Stand Myself"
was "There Was a Time." The only way you're going to get
results is put the same thing on both sides.

GO'B: *We've just been attending the New Music Seminar, and I think
there's something strange going on with the whole idea of "new."
It seems to me that there are so many great artists out there who
can't get a deal and it's just because there's this demand for new
faces. I don't know if it's the record companies or if the public is
that way, too. This is the fifth year of the New Music Seminar
and hardly any of the artists who started new wave or new music
or whatever they call it are still around and doing well.*

AB: It's not just the record companies. A whole lot of it has to do with
radio, the programmers. It's a shame that a programmer can
control what a whole city will hear and some of them be playing
games. Some of them say, "I don't like that, I'm not going to play
it for the city." Or, "I don't want to hear no more funk, so I'm not
going to play it for the city." Or, "I don't want to hear rock."

JB: Frankie Crocker [*former program director of WBLS in New
York*] hurt an awful lot. I love Frankie and you can quote me.
Frankie's done a lot of things, but Frankie hurt this city im-
mensely. He made people like Bam find a new way out. They

had to go to the clubs to get their stuff played. I think he won't
play things sometimes only because he don't like the man who
owns the record company.

GO'B: *Are you making a video for "Unity"?*

JB: I don't care about making a real video, because it takes a lot of
money to do what really needs to be done, to do it the way it
should be done. You'd have to go take pictures of Africa, the
major conflicts in the world, the destruction, the blast of the
atomic bomb in 1945.

GO'B: *Have you toured in Africa?*

JB: More than any other artist in the business. To go to Africa now
would be a little dangerous for almost any act because you've
got two or three forces. You've got to remember that Russia
takes care of a lot of Africa, like the American people and the
French people. If you go in there and try to Americanize, the
Russians might not like it.

GO'B: *It's hard to imagine Russia having a long-term or deep connection with Africa, or even with Cuba, because there's much more
affinity between American and African cultures. If you pick up
an African record you can hear James Brown on it and if you
pick up a James Brown record you can hear Africa on it.*

JB: But in Africa, you've also got presidents, and you've got guns
in those countries, and they run those countries. We were born
in this country and we still ain't got no control over it. The
Afro-American has no control. We've got to face it. You can't
keep hiding behind it, that's what's going to bring things down.
Let a man become a bum of his own choice. And then if he
becomes a bum don't label him as a special kind of bum. Give
a man a right to fail. We have to give people a right to control
their own destinies. Not a right, because everybody has the
right, but we have to let them control their own destinies. I got
a letter where the Russians asked me to perform, but the
American people wouldn't let me. For some reason they won't
let me over there. I wouldn't go over there and get into their
politics. I would go there to sing. But you have to be careful. If
I went there and then I came back and the press said, "How do
you like Russia?" That's a loaded question. You tell 'em you

went to play music and they enjoyed it. If I say I liked Russia then you're messing with American politics. I don't hate nobody. I'm like Will Rogers: "I never met a man I didn't like." But I still wouldn't mess in their politics. I wouldn't go there and try to Americanize and I wouldn't come back here and try to Russianize. I'm not in politics. But your appearance isn't politics.

GO'B: *Have you ever heard African music and noticed connections — like something tribal might sound like B.B. King or Robert Johnson?*

JB: It's in the air and it's in the genes. You can go to a country where you've never been. I went to Liberia, and I saw people who looked just like my mother and my dad and my uncle. I saw people who looked just like me. I was in Senegal and I saw a kid walking down the street that looked like my dead son Teddy, identical. You must remember when God made bodies and souls he made man in his own image. So in every country there's somebody who looks like you. All you've got to do is change the pigmentation of their skin and they look just like you, talk like you, walk like you, think like you and act like you. In every country in the world you have a double. Or a triple. I've seen people who look just like you. Identical.

GO'B: *Yeah, I saw a picture of a guy getting arrested in a riot in Ireland and he looked exactly like me. . . . Do you know where your ancestors are from?*

JB: My ancestors, I think, are Asiatic.

GO'B: *How do you mean that?*

JB: Asian. There's a lot of different people in my line.

GO'B: *Spiritually?*

JB: Gene-wise. On my father's side and my grandmother's, I have a lot of Asian in me.

GO'B: *In African music there are beats that are for specific purposes or associated with particular gods. Do you think the change in beats in popular music reflects some popular mood?*

JB: I'm the champion of that. Most any rhythm they've played since '65 is based on my rhythm.

GO'B: *People always trace funk back to you, but where would you say funk was before you?*

JB: Funk is blues, as interpreted by Webster. Funky is James Brown.

"James Brown: The Godfather's Back, with a Bullet" (excerpt)

Ben Fong-Torres
1999 • *Not Fade Away*

Could it be true? I was going to have a chance to meet the Godfather of Soul? In 1986, after almost two decades of writing about pop, rock, and R&B artists, I heard that James Brown was coming to town, to play, of all places, the Venetian Room in the Fairmont Hotel.

I'd been a fan since who knows when. Brown was ageless, and, from the first time I heard him, singing "Night Train" and "Try Me"—please stop me before I start writing like one of his MCs—he was timeless. I played his record on my college radio station, and on KSAN, and at home.

Now, I was going to interview him. It didn't matter, either to him or to me, that it would be at the Fairmont, which had begun to book pop acts that had—shall we say—begun to appeal to people who'd come of age in the sixties.

Brown was riding high on a new hit record, and I was riding high on the idea of meeting this icon of American music. This was Ray Charles, all over again.

As things turned out, the visit, stretched over several events—rehearsal, press conference, personal interview, and showtime—took a couple of contentious turns. And, when all was said, I felt that the Chronicle article, with its space limitations, didn't reflect the many shades of Brown. I welcomed the opportunity to rewrite the piece for BAM (Bay Area Musician), a local magazine with which I'd become friends. In fact, when the publication decided to launch an annual awards show to celebrate our music scene, I was one of the first hosts. And when, one particularly sad month, it found,

*itself without any possible subject for a cover story, BAM plastered my photo
on the cover, and tried to turn my career into a story, down to details like the
green BMW I was driving.*

It was an Audi. Damned irresponsible journalists.

"Call him Mr. Brown," a colleague advised me on the eve of my first meeting with James Brown. "Or he might not talk to you."

I put "Mr. Brown" right on top of my list of the things James Brown has
been called, or has called himself: the Godfather of Soul, the King of
Soul, the Living Legend of Soul, Soul Brother Number One, Mr. Dynamite, the Sex Machine, and the Hardest Working Man in Show Business.

But it'll be Mr. Brown to me. After all, I've heard a few stories about the
man. Legend has it that he's a General Patton of music. He runs a tight
band, levying fines for showing up late, dressing wrong, or fluffing a note.
In fact, during a two-week engagement at the Fairmont Hotel in San Francisco, he fired and rehired a horn player within an eight-hour span. James
Brown is the boss of bosses.

But if the man demands respect, he also deserves it. Brown is a true pioneer of rock and roll and R&B. He mixed gospel and jazz in the mid-
fifties and came up with a sound that's been echoed by several generations
of musicians. He blazed more trails with his fiery stage show, a mix of the
intensity of Baptist evangelism and the raw animalism of sexual abandon.
His spins and knee-drops; his ritual exits with the routine of the corona-
tion by capes; his absolute control of the big band and singers, added up to
theater of blood, sweat, and tears.

In recognition of his influence, so obvious in such peers as Prince and
Michael Jackson, Mick Jagger and Tina Turner, Sly Stone, Parliament
Funkadelic, and a host of urban, funk, punk, rap, hip-hop, Afro-pop, reggae, Salsa, and fusion musicians, Brown was one of the first ten musical
acts inducted into the Rock and Roll Hall of Fame last month.

This month, thirty years after his first record, he is on top again, with
his prefight appearance in *Rocky IV*, and, especially, with his song from
that film, "Living in America." . . .

FIRST VISIT: 10:30 A.M., NOB HILL SUITE, FAIRMONT HOTEL

JAMES BROWN OPENS TONIGHT in the hotel's posh supper club, the Venetian Room. In his two-floor suite, complete with baby grand, Brown is

guarded. In public, he's always surrounded by attendants. Here, he maintains a polite distance—even after I've called him "Mr. Brown" several times.

But when I appear to have some knowledge of his past accomplishments, he warms up. And when I tick off a tally of the musicians he's inspired, Brown's suddenly on fire. "You're well-versed!" he declares in a low growl. He helpfully adds Lionel Richie to my list, and he claims to have influenced fully 80 percent of the popular music of today.

He wears shades, a light blue scarf, a silk robe over an aqua shirt opened to the waist, and sports slacks. The pompadour that used to pile high over his head is now generously settled over its sides.

I mention his induction into the Rock and Roll Hall of Fame. "I didn't deserve to be in," he says. "I came with soul music. I did record 'Please Please' right in the rock and roll era, [but] I felt my career has spanned much broader than any entertainer that ever lived."

"Living in America" happened, he says, because "Stallone wanted James Brown. They'd mentioned a couple of other artists—Lionel . . . Ray Charles . . . but he said, 'No way; it can only be James Brown.' He felt that *Blues Brothers* and *Doctor Detroit* (in which Brown did musical cameos) were the beginning of what should have happened to me."

For James Brown, these are the best of times. Besides the place in the Hall, the hit record and the life story, he's being sought for commercials. "Coke and Pepsi are fighting over James Brown," he says. "All the car companies want me."

"You gotta admit one thing," he says. "God has been very good; something's been working in my favor, because 'Living in America' is the biggest record I've had in four or five years."

It's actually been thirteen years since Brown penetrated the Top 20 (with "Get On The Good Foot, Part 1"), but he doesn't admit to any dips in his career.

Consider Brown's stand at the Fairmont (he was, in fact, the first act to bring contemporary music into the Venetian Room, in 1983). When Tina Turner played the room, just before her *Private Dancer* album became a hit, she said she couldn't wait to escape the supper club circuit, to get back to the rock concert halls. The insinuation was that the Fairmonts were only a handy, rent-paying gig.

Brown says he's not here to make money. "We do so much business here," he says. "My problem is we lose $100,000 a week when we play here, with my expenses." (A spokesman at the Fairmont disputed Brown's claim, but agreed that he might be earning more with separate shows in bigger facilities elsewhere.)

At the Fairmont, Brown says, "You test your skills. The audience here is 75 percent the same as Vegas and Atlantic City. You play here and you're ready for those halls."

So Brown isn't here for the money. Still, it seems, a year ago, he could have used some. Last January, he testified in a Baltimore court that he couldn't afford to pay $170,000 to creditors; that he ate at McDonald's restaurants. (In 1984, the IRS sold Brown's furniture and three cars to obtain $100,000 in back taxes.)

Brown sits down to a breakfast of pastry, bacon and eggs, juice and coffee. He shakes his head at the unpleasant story I've just brought up. "Somebody came up with some bad information," he says. "I haven't been poverty-stricken since 1952. I haven't been off; I just went out of the country. Three years ago, we played twenty-six miles outside Paris to a million and three thousand people, three times Woodstock." Brown is loved all over the world and has always made money, he says—at least "enough to stay out of unemployment lines. Somebody's trying to write me down."

Somebody—Brown accuses an unspecified "they"—took his radio stations away "because I was a revolutionist . . . they're afraid I'd come back and do what I did in the sixties. The system thought I got a little too strong, helping communities survive, teaching kids, guiding them from what I did."

Being friends with well-placed politicians was no help, he says. "The system works for or against you. It's something Hubert Humphrey told me. He said, 'James, there's no room for an independent. If there had been, I'd have been president.'

"I'm very close to the Reagans," he says. "I converse with them a lot."

Brown says he was one of the first people to call for a national holiday in commemoration of Dr. Martin Luther King, Jr. Reagan, I remind him, was originally opposed to any such legislation. Reagan also made speeches on Dr. King's birthday this year representing himself as a longtime civil rights supporter; the record differs. "Somebody told you that I was poverty-stricken," Brown counters, "and we're playing to more people than ever in my life. Your information down the pipeline has been false.

"I'm not political," says Brown, "but I give a man his due. Naturally [the press] attacks the President. But Mr. Reagan signed it into law. Did anybody else sign it?"

James Brown is the Godfather to the hilt. When a room service waiter requests payment for breakfast, he pays, then gets on the phone, identifies himself as "Mr. Brown," and gently explains that he'd set aside $500 with the hotel for such expenses; that he was asked for cash. "I have a fellow interviewing me and it didn't come off right, you know."

Returning to his table, he says, "It's not important, but sometimes it rubs me wrong."

But appearances are important. When two of his longtime assistants enter the room, they are formally introduced, and Brown addresses them as Mr. Ray and Mr. Stallings. They, of course, call him Mr. Brown.

He and his band are highly disciplined, says Brown, because "I watched the other way fail. Nothing that way ever made it. You don't see people marching, one with dungarees and one with shorts." He indicates Danny Ray (his MC, cape-draper, and road manager) and Henry Stallings (hair stylist and general manager). He says he trained Ray's voice (a booming echo of Cab Calloway at the Cotton Club) and spends hundreds of thousands on suits for his entourage. "Look how they dress," he says, while the two men sit silently. "I can send my men anywhere, and they can handle it."

Brown may be self-absorbed, but he's also willing to give credit where it's due. His influences, he says, include Louis Jordan, the stylish blues and jazz artist of the forties. His cape routine, done to "Please Please Please," has its roots in church—and Gorgeous George, the colorful wrestler of the fifties. "I used to come back on stage carrying a suitcase, and they threw a towel around me; I threw it off. And I thought of Gorgeous George. He had capes, and that was flamboyant, so I put that in the act." It's still there. And at the age of 56 (Brown says he'll be 53 in May, but that's disputed by various biographical sources, and during our talk, he said he was 9 in 1939), he has no thoughts of retirement.

"Retirement from what?" he demands. "When I see the president of the United States, or George Burns or Bette Davis . . . Thank god, I have the greatest track record in the world, and now I got the biggest record of my career. I just got started."

SECOND VISIT: 2:30 P.M., THE VENETIAN ROOM

JAMES BROWN WANTS TO TAKE CARE of the rest of the press in one loud, fell swoop. He opens his rehearsal to a group of reporters and sits for a quick interview. At the rehearsal, he noodles on the piano for the TV cameras while Maceo Parker, Jr., the saxophonist—who's back with Brown after a stop with Parliament Funkadelic—teaches a riff to the Fairmont Orchestra's horn section.

For "Living in America," Brown wants a flag on stage to unfurl behind him as the song begins. But, given only a few hours' notice, the best the hotel can do is call up a modest-sized Old Glory from room service and hang it up at the back of the stage.

Brown repairs to a side room to talk with reporters.

He is revealing. "My own [musical] arrangements hit a lot harder than 'Living In America,'" he admits. "That was a lot softer, but it was good for airing.

"It sounds so funny when I listen to my old stuff," he says. "Today's stuff don't drive as hard. I'd like to see music get back to that."

He is generous. Asked how he feels about Prince's success with a latter-day version of James Brown, he says, "I feel good about that; I hope he and Michael Jackson and David Bowie and Mick Jagger and Tina keep doing a female James Brown act—keep on." It is clear that he's just listed some people he believes he influenced. For good measure, he adds, "Certainly the rap music didn't hurt me because I started rap a long time ago [with the record, 'Brother Rapp,' in 1970]."

Asked how his music has changed since "Papa's Got a Brand New Bag," he says, "I don't see anything different; people are just late catching up. I was twenty years ahead of my time."

THIRD VISIT: 9:45 P.M., THE VENETIAN ROOM

THE FIRST SHOW OF OPENING NIGHT is stunning. Brown and his band— eleven pieces, a female singer, and the musical director—seem to be celebrating their success. They do "Living in America" not once, not twice, but three times. In the process, they run half an hour overtime, and get the audience rocking the Venetian Room as it's rarely been rocked.

Onstage, Brown is in charge. His strong voice is gritty on the funk, high, clear and sustaining on the ballads; when he does "Try Me" from out of '59, I expect to hear scratches. His trademark moves have been cut back; short shuffles and shimmies have replaced the multiple spins, splits and one-legged, across-the-stage skittering of the old days, but even if he's just toying with a mike stand, he's worth watching.

Most impressive of all is his absolute command of the band, whose members pick up cues from his slightest twitch. The endlessly repetitive, one-note riffs of some past shows are gone; now the band teases with bits of familiar tunes, then delivers long, inspirational dance grooves. The Godfather seems to have a formula: the tighter the band, the looser the crowd.

And the formula works. Score one for discipline.

A few minutes after the show, Brown is in his hair stylist's room, sitting under a dryer between shows, his hair in bright blue rollers. His glittering cape sits draped over a chair. It's nearly midnight, but he's still got his shades on. He laps up an appraisal of the show, especially the part about his mastery of the band. But some of the follow-up questions I have don't go over as well.

I show him a newspaper clipping about his testimony a year ago about being broke, about having to eat at McDonald's, and he nods recognition. "The judge said he was broke, too," he says. "Can you name me somebody who doesn't have to pay bills? God bless this country. They can say you owe $50 million, but you got a chance to make $300 million."

I ask again about his friendship with the Reagans. I'm curious: What do they talk about? "I don't want to get into that," says Brown. He recalls my negative remarks on Reagan, and knows I'm not just curious. His guard is up. "I say one thing. There's so many things he wants to do; everybody needs to get to know the President. . . . He's not there to stop you; he's there to enhance what you're about.

"He may not be your style," says Brown, who suddenly shifts gears. "I know whatever you think about James Brown is right, so I'm not gonna fight you; I'm just gonna lay back and let you write.

"I'm gonna leave you alone," he says, by way of ending the interview. "You want to know too much." Brown flashes a wide, disarming smile. "You're a very observant person, and I'm very fond of you. You came to see me the other day [actually, it was only this morning] and said, 'Wait a minute—I know about James Brown, but I see some more things here.' And after the show, you said, 'I see something else.'

"And I don't want to talk about it."

He smiles again and extends a hand. He can't help asking one more time about the show. Praised again, he shouts over the hair dryer: "I love you, I love you! You're so hip!"

And I'm glad to leave Brown—Mr. Brown, if you please—on the upbeat. After the performance he's just given, it seems only fair.

—April 1986
BAM

"James Brown, up and down"

Michael Vitez
February 9, 1989 • *The Philadelphia Inquirer*

Augusta, Ga.—As humble as he once was bold, James Brown stood in the courtroom, his back to a corps of hungry press, and mumbled an apology. "My life has always been a model," he said. "I just don't feel good about it now."

The voice that had made him legend—that first howled "I Feel Good!" almost 25 years ago—was barely audible. He rambled. Small and pot-bellied and dressed in a three-piece black polyester suit, sandwiched between drunken drivers and petty thieves on a crowded court docket two weeks ago, Brown was just another man seeking mercy. Gone was the aura of the self-anointed Godfather of Soul, Mr. Dynamite, His Bad Self, who broke down the barrier to wealth and fame for black entertainers, who considered himself one of the "Four Bs" (Beethoven, Bach, Brahms and Brown) and danced so hard he would sweat through the soles of his shoes.

Three rows back sat his mother, who had abandoned him as a baby but who had come back when he was a star. Tears welled in her eyes. With her index fingers, she formed the sign of the cross.

Brown was here to plead guilty to charges stemming from a two-state police chase that began after he barged into an insurance seminar with a shotgun last September. In late December, a South Carolina judge sentenced him to six years in prison for failure to stop for police. Now, on Jan. 23, it was Georgia's turn to punish him, on charges ranging from carrying a deadly weapon to reckless driving.

But Brown was confused. He had trouble comprehending that a Georgia prison term could be piggybacked onto South Carolina's.

"Mr. Brown, do you understand that?" asked Richmond County State Court Judge Gayle B. Hamrick.

"No, sir, I don't. . . ." he murmured.

Hamrick ended up giving him six more years, to be served concurrently with his South Carolina sentence. Brown was led out by deputies, and has since been unavailable for comment.

So James Brown, at 55, was back where he started, the same way he started—in debt, behind bars, in the South. Augusta is the city where he was raised; the city that sent him, at age 15, to prison for three years for stealing car batteries; the city that wouldn't let him come back to perform until the late 1950s—and then gave him a police escort to the state line right after the show.

Brown still can't find much sympathy down here. Instead, he has seen resentment, even contempt. Many in Augusta believe that, rather than being socked with too harsh a sentence, James Brown had gotten away with too much too long. They see "a genuine abuse of the legal system," said Augusta Mayor Charles DeVaney. "They believe [that] because of his status, he got special treatment."

In the last two years, Brown has seemed to self-destruct in public view. In May, South Carolina officers had to hogtie him when he tried to kick out a squad-car window. He has been charged once with possessing PCP, an illegal drug, and once with using it, although he was never prosecuted and has consistently denied having a drug problem. The Internal Revenue Service has $3.5 million in liens against his property, the result of income-tax problems dating to 1969. His nightmarish third marriage has been fodder for the tabloids; his wife still faces two felony charges for possession of PCP.

Rather than rally around him, some of Brown's oldest and closest friends have kept their distance, angry at how he cheated and hurt them over the years—corrupted, as they see it, by fame and money.

"Where are his friends?" said Bobby Byrd, the musician who had been like a brother to Brown, helped him get his start in the 1950s—and now has given up on him. "They're as far away as they can get."

Would James Brown be a free man today if not for sweet-potato pie? That's what he ate only minutes after leaving an Atlanta hospital where, back in September, his lower jaw was reconstructed in preparation for tooth implants.

James Brown always believed in teeth and hair. "Hair is the first thing," he wrote in his autobiography three years ago. "And teeth are second. A man got those two things, he's got it all."

3 DENTAL OPERATIONS

To that end, he underwent major dental surgery three times. The last was in early September—just two weeks before the arrest that landed him in prison. His dentist, Terry Reynolds, believes there is a connection.

Brown left Emory University's Crawford Long Hospital on Sept. 11 and, on his way back to Augusta, ate a sweet-potato pie. Ten days later, Brown returned to Reynolds with an infected, bloody mouth.

"During eating, he tore the sutures, exposed the bone," Reynolds said. "The surgery is not profoundly traumatic for the patient at all, unless the patient doesn't follow the instructions. There's a strict diet you're supposed to be on, which he ignores. . . . If he goes out and gets food in the wound and it blows up on him, he feels that the medication I prescribe won't do him any good. He must have chosen to deal with it himself—via whatever he was taking on his own."

Brown has denied using any illegal drugs to dull the pain. "He still hasn't 'fessed up," Reynolds said. "He's still trying to say he was on medication from the surgery, which wasn't the case."

At 11 a.m. on Sept. 24, James Brown went to his business office, Top Notch Inc., in a corporate park on the outskirts of Augusta. Geraldine Phillips, an Atlanta businesswoman, was holding an insurance seminar in an adjacent office.

A SHOTGUN

James Brown walked in. He was carrying a shotgun.

"He just said, 'Why are you all using my bathroom?'" recalled Phillips. "He had grass in his hair. He said rats and roaches were running out of his hat."

Brown, said Phillips, began asking nonsensical questions. "If I answer these wrong," she remembered thinking, "he's going to kill me and everybody in there."

According to Brown's South Carolina attorney, Bill Weeks, the shotgun was broken. "It wouldn't fire," he said. "Of course, I'll agree that people in that room didn't know that."

Weeks insisted that the scene in the meeting room was hardly as menacing as Phillips described. Some participants had been tape-recording the seminar and left their machines running during the episode. "He leaned the gun against the wall," said Weeks, who has listened to the tapes. "He wasn't ranting or raving." Brown, in fact, walked into the bathroom at one point—and left his gun behind. "They said, 'Mr. Brown, you forgot your rifle,'" Weeks recounted from the tape, "and he said, 'Oh, thank you.'"

Phillips said a seminar member sneaked out of the room and called the police. "[Brown] left," she said, "when he heard the sirens."

A Georgia sheriff pursued him to the South Carolina state line. Brown didn't stop. South Carolina authorities took up pursuit across the Savannah River, at speeds hitting 80 m.p.h. Defense attorneys said Brown stopped at an intersection, but took off when sheriffs broke the window of his pickup truck.

"I was scared to death," Brown testified at his South Carolina trial. "I went to Vietnam [to perform for U.S. troops] and I wasn't that frightened."

Police saw Brown differently, as reckless, armed and dangerous. Two officers said they had to jump out of his way as he fled the intersection. They tried, Weeks said, to shoot out Brown's tires, firing 17 hollow-point bullets that flattened the front two.

Fourteen police cars followed Brown, driving about 30 m.p.h. on his wheel rims, back into Augusta and arrested him in a friend's yard.

At 7:30 the next morning, less than 10 hours after he was released on bond, James Brown was arrested in Augusta again—this time in his Lincoln Town Car—and charged with driving under the influence of drugs. Tests showed he had PCP in his blood.

In the early 1970s, after a decade in New York, Brown moved back to the South, a superstar coming home. "Everyone that leaves home," said old friend Leon Austin, "one day or another wants to come back if he makes it big."

He first moved into the oldest, wealthiest and whitest of Augusta's neighborhoods, "The Hill." Throngs paraded past his house every Christmas to see the black Santas in the yard. In the late 1970s, he moved 10 miles away to rural Beech Island, S.C., to a 40-acre spread a mile down a dirt road.

IRS SEIZES HOUSE

In 1985, the IRS seized the house. Brown's lawyer bought it at auction and now rents it to him. The dirt road leads to a paved driveway that Brown had dubbed "James Brown Boulevard."

About two years ago, things started to heat up. Brown was married for a third time in September 1984, to Adrienne "Alfie" Rodriguez, a hairdresser he met on the TV show *Solid Gold*. "It wasn't love at first sight, it was recognition at first sight." Brown wrote in his autobiography. "Our souls had met before."

Heaven soon became hell. In April, Mrs. Brown filed for divorce. She said in court records that her husband had abused her "over the years by slapping her around, throwing things at her, shooting at her, knocked her teeth out . . . and on April 3, 1988 cut up her clothes, beat her with his first and an iron pipe, inflicting various injuries requiring hospital treatment."

One close friend described their relationship as "just one of those sort of classic, sado-masochistic, fight-to-the-death marriages."

In the last two years, South Carolina sheriffs were summoned to the Browns' home at least 10 times; they arrested him twice for domestic violence, according to James W. Whitehurst, captain of investigations for the Aiken Country Sheriff's Department. "As far as James is concerned," Whitehurst said, "he just went bad."

"His wife would call and tell us he's beating her," Whitehurst said. "He was shooting at her. She was shooting at him. One time he shot her mink coat full of holes. We were concerned the situation could develop into a homicide."

Often, when deputies arrived, the ruckus already had died down. "A lot of officers would go out," Whitehurst said. "Before they left, they'd have autographed pictures of James."

Then drug allegations entered the picture.

Last summer, while searching Brown after an arrest, Whitehurst found PCP, concealed in a nasal-spray bottle. Although Brown said his wife planted the drugs on him, he pleaded no contest to the possession charge.

Martha High, a singer who has toured with Brown for 20 years and says she loves him dearly, noticed a change after his marriage. She had never known him to miss a show—until last year at the Lone Star in New York.

"The paramedics were there at the hotel before we got there," she said. "He was really sick. His pressure was over 200. He was basically incoherent. He thought he had done the show that night and he hadn't. We told him that we were there with him, and would always be with him, and stayed with him until he started making sense again. It was really scary."

Adrienne Brown knows that many blame her for her husband's problems. "I'm the scapegoat, and I realize that," she said. But she said their marriage problems have been exaggerated. "I'm still his queen. I'm the woman he wants me to be."

The evening after her husband's Georgia court appearance, she sat at his desk at Top Notch. On the wall hung Ronald Reagan's picture and a personal note, along with plaques honoring Brown for years of antidrug work. Her face was flushed. She was exhausted.

The phone rang. It was her husband—"Sugawuga"—who had visited his dentist before returning to prison. "You sound *beautiful*," she gushed. "You got your new teeth in?"

Mrs. Brown said her husband's problem was not drugs, but stress.

"Why can't they look at a man," she said, "and say, 'You know what? You got problems because of stress, because of tension, because of family affairs, because of downfalls, things that happen, IRS, surgeries, having to go to work without healing, a bloody mouth, removing of toenails, and having to work with bloody feet.' I mean, this man has not stopped. And I have not stopped. And they think we're some kind of machine, that we go on day to day and we're just picture-perfect, storybook. We have some problems, too. Everyone has problems, but our problems have to be just a little bit bigger. No one's writing stuff about *you*, that *you* owe the government $9 million. . . . The bigger you are, the bigger the problems, the harder you fall. This is where it's at."

James Brown was born in a shack with no heat or plumbing in Barnwell, S.C. Soon after, his mother left.

As a kid in Augusta, he danced for nickels and dimes on the steps of a radio station he would later own. He picked peanuts and cotton, shined shoes and wore underwear "stitched together from flour sacks."

GOSPEL MUSIC IN PRISON

Caught breaking into cars, he spent three years in the Georgia Juvenile Training Institute in Toccoa, Ga. In prison he was known as "Music Box." Locals would go to gospel concerts by the prison choir. Bobby Byrd, whose family lived in Toccoa, had organized a gospel group of his own and re-members the first time he heard James Brown play. "Man, if we had this fella," he recalls thinking, "could we go!"

With the help of Byrd's mother and some others in Toccoa, Brown was paroled. He went to live with Bobby Byrd. "James became the sixth child in our family," Byrd said. "He was like a brother to me. And we never separated. . . .

"He was a good man, but he was a wild man. You had to really stay on top of him to keep him out of trouble."

The two formed a new group, the Gospel Starlighters. Soon they switched to rhythm-and-blues and traveled the South, sleeping in cars or, when they were lucky, four and five to a bed. "Those days were good days, believe me," said Byrd. "All we wanted was to hear the girls scream. Money didn't matter."

In 1956, they recorded their first hit, "Please, Please, Please," and Brown emerged a star. But many who were with him then—and stayed with him for decades—saw him change. In interviews recently, they said that he cheated them out of royalties and credit for songs they wrote, that he demanded their loyalty and told them they could never make it without him.

Many said they stuck with him because of tremendous pressure not to bring down black America's greatest star. And undeniably, they loved him, and still do. He had taught them so much.

They kept hoping he would change.

"There's been many times I've cried from things he's done," said Martha High. "It's just so ugly. I'm always asking why, for a man to be in such a position he is, why would he deliberately hurt people. And he does."

Many of Brown's longtime singers and musicians have gotten together—led by Byrd—and organized a European tour. All three weeks are already booked.

"We are hoping," said Marva Whitney, who sang for years with Brown and accompanied him to Vietnam, "that all of us can make some kind of last comeback because we feel like we've been robbed. We hope we can get a little respect back in the United States, too. We hope these people will give us a little chance. So we can capture it a little. So we can be at peace. So many of us are not at peace."

Although Byrd has tried to stay away from Brown, he broke down in December and called him, ready to offer support. "I say, 'Well, I'm a little worried about you. I know you're having a lot of problems. I want to know how you feel, is there anything I can do? . . .'

" 'Well, you're worried about a rich man?' " he said Brown had told him. " 'Man, what you sitting up there with? I'm rich, so how can you worry about a rich man? What do you all have? You better be worried about yourselves.' That's how he came off on me."

In prison, James Brown rises at 6 to serve breakfast to his fellow inmates. Most days he talks to his agent, Larry Myers, in New York. His wife drives up on Saturdays, with her blow dryer and relaxers to do his hair. He writes songs. He leads the choir.

Universal Studios has been talking about doing a movie on Brown's life.

"He wants to play himself," said Myers, "but he can't do that. . . . I can't pass him off as 25 years old. He'll come on as a cameo, somewhere near the end. I got to make my star happy."

"Pleas, Pleas, Pleas: The Tribulations and Trials of James Brown"

Ivan Solotaroff
February 21, 1989 • *The Village Voice*

Gus, the pasty-white 300-pound cabbie driving me to the State Park Correctional Center outside Columbia, South Carolina, doesn't need to ask which of the 288 inmates I'm going to see. He just wants to know if I'm a writer or a lawyer. "Reason I ask," he says in his mellifluous, surprisingly feminine drawl, "is if you're a writer, I might just wait around for the return trip. Mr. James Brown don't see no more writers. They were coming down here by the busload till a few weeks ago, fans too, but they all went away empty-handed. That roly-poly preacher from New York seen to that."

I ask Gus if he means the Reverend Al Sharpton, an old friend of Brown's (they cut a gospel single, "God Has Smiled on Me," together in 1981). Sharpton brought the Brawley family to visit Brown after their pilgrimage to the Atlanta Democratic Convention last July, then returned south alone in December to lobby for Brown's release. Gus, who's been fairly taciturn the whole ride up, lets out with a riptide at Sharpton's name. "That loud roun' moun' of soun'! He was standing on the courthouse steps in Aiken the day after the trial, holding onto Adrienne Brown and them ancient photographs of President Bush and Mr. Brown and him, talking racist verdicts, media circuses, and whatnot, making that bogus offer to serve Mr. Brown's time for him. He was *here* on Christmas too, holding his candlelight vigil in front of the prison with that lawyer buddy, Perry Mason, trying to stir up the ministers. They wouldn't give him the time of day. People here say James Brown got his day in court—and more. Got to be every time you turned around him and that wife's acting up. Time and again they let them off, time, time, time and again he's shooting something up. People behaving like that—pistols, drugs, shotguns. Me and you'd have got all 30 years he was looking at, that's for sure."

Gus gets pacified as we coast past the rolling green lawns and maples hedging the State Park driveway and stop in front of what he calls the "nursing home." A jet of steam is coming out of the ventilation duct of a block-long, white-stone hospital to the left; a tacky gift shop on our right is open, even though it's Super Bowl Sunday. Down a series of stone stairways strewn with ivy is the dirty red-brick prison, looking more like a 1940s subway station on the Grand Concourse than a penal institution. "Still, I *feel* for the man," Gus says as I get out, "because it was that wife who drove him to it. Filing them charges for assaulting her, filing them divorce papers, saying his men planted those PCPs they busted her with all them times, setting fire to their hotel room up north. She done him in, that's for sure."

James Brown, probably the most influential black musician of all time, will turn 56 in this prison on May 3—and then 57 and perhaps 58 as well—short of successfully petitioning to have his sentence commuted to time spent in drug rehabilitation, which seems unlikely: Brown resolutely maintains he has no drug problem. On December 17, 1988, an Aiken, South Carolina, judge sentenced Brown to six years for "running a blue light" (failing to stop for an officer's signal) and aggravated assault—reduced from two counts of assault with intent to kill. Brown's targets were two South Carolina police officers who had pulled him over on September 24 during a now-legendary two-state, 80 mph car chase that began after Brown, armed with a shotgun, had berated 40 people at an insurance seminar held in a building adjoining his Augusta, Georgia, offices for using his rest rooms. His trial in Augusta for the Georgia half of the chase and a second arrest the following morning—for nine misdemeanor charges of assault, carrying a deadly weapon to a public gathering, carrying a weapon without a license, driving under the influence (PCP), and related charges—was set for January 23.

The Aiken trial was the fourth time in 12 months Brown had appeared before a South Carolina court on criminal charges, all four, in one way or another, involving cars, two involving PCP and guns. Two '87 arrests resulted in one speeding charge, one count of leaving the scene of an accident, two charges of eluding arrest, and a total of $1460 in fines. On the Monday after Easter, 1988, he was arrested after he'd allegedly emptied his pistol into the trunk of his wife's car as she tried to leave their Beech Island, South Carolina, house and then beaten her with an iron pipe; Adrienne eventually dropped the charges. Five weeks later, on May 17, he spent another night in an Aiken County jail before a $24,218 bond was posted on charges of PCP possession, possession of a pistol, assault and battery (his wife again), failing to stop for blue lights, and resisting arrest; Brown received two and a half years, probated to a concert benefiting local charities.

In the last year, Brown was indicted for more than 45 years worth of felonies and misdemeanors, of which all but 12 and a half were probated or commuted to more than $50,000 in fines, restitution, and public service. The IRS, Brown's 20-year nemesis, is also suing him for $9 million in back taxes, two years after Brown was forced to auction his home in South Carolina (his Georgia lawyer purchased it and now rents it back to Brown as trustee for his two daughters from his second marriage).

Throughout his career, James Brown has remained the same unresolved American paradox that Martin Luther King, if in radically different fashion, represented: a street-smart activist who was clearly motivated by his own, innate sense of the law. At a Black Power conference, Amiri Baraka (then Leroi Jones) dubbed Brown "our No. 1 black poet." At the 1966 Memphis-to-Mississippi march in support of James Meredith, Stokely Carmichael told Brown he was the man "most dangerous" to the Movement. In '68 he alienated the left by touring Vietnam; later that year he terrified the right with "Say It Loud, I'm Black and I'm Proud." After a highly coveted endorsement of Humphrey in '68, he became a more active campaigner for Nixon in '72.

Only the jukebox provided a consensus: James Brown's singles routinely hit the high reaches of the pop charts for 30 years. Though he never tried to cross over into the integrated record-buying market he and Motown helped to create, he consistently outperformed every act that did: Brown hit the charts 114 times, a quantum leap beyond Aretha Franklin's 84, Ray Charles's 83, and the Temptations' 76. Among the handful of performers who arose unfiltered out of what was openly called *race music*, Brown was one of the few to escape death on the road, death by drugs, death in prison, the living death of golden-oldie status, or the retreat into the obscure immortality of gospel. Twenty years before rappers appropriated him, 10 before disco digitalized him, Brown anticipated the future of black music by stripping his sound to pure rhythm, blueprinting Pan-African pop, a worldwide explosion against which the Beatles and Stones are circumscribed, Anglo phenomena. At 53, James Brown, the man who taught us all how to dance, was rocking the pop charts ("Living in America," No. 4), and last year only Sade's "Paradise" stopped Brown from topping the r&b charts for the 18th time.

As the first, relatively minor charges became public, there were predictable, occasional snickers in the national press about James Brown—

high-minded pillar of black capitalism, proud singer of "King Heroin," "America Is My Home," "Don't Be a Dropout," and "Living in America," recipient of numerous citations for public service, 30-year hero to black youth all over the world—having misdemeanor troubles with the local authorities. After the Easter shooting of his wife's car (and the gruesome detail of the iron pipe) launched Brown onto the tabloid headlines, the media began scrupulously detailing an almost unbelievable string of marital incidents:

Adrienne files for divorce in March 1988, citing years of cruel treatment and showing a *National Enquirer* photographer bruises on her face and bullet holes in their Beech Island bedroom. In April Adrienne, arrested at Augusta's small airport with eight grams of PCP, says it was planted by men hired by her husband to pressure her to drop her divorce suit. In early May, Brown tells reporters his wife set fire to some of his clothes in their Sheraton Hotel room in Bedford, New Hampshire, shortly after she is arraigned on charges of arson and PCP possession (seven ounces, this time) early in May. "My wife is a real stinker," he says. "She sets rooms on fire. She's a brat." Four days later, Adrienne calls police claiming that Brown was beating her again and he is captured a mile into a high-speed chase that begins at his driveway. "He was letting that Lincoln sail," says the local police captain. "We thought it was a B-17 coming out of there." Brown claims his wife planted the seven grams of PCP he's caught with. Two days after this, Adrienne, arrested at Augusta's airport for possession of eight ounces of PCP, again says she was set up: "The Godfather of Soul isn't what he pretends to be," she tells deputies. "He warns young people to stay off drugs, but he doesn't practice what he preaches to children. He's high on drugs, PCP, angel dust. . . ."

And on it went: bench warrants, missed court dates, indictments, the now legendary motion filed by one of Adrienne's lawyers to have her September 7, 1987, speeding, DUI, and criminal trespass charges waived on grounds of diplomatic immunity as "the wife of the Ambassador of Soul," a suit filed by that same lawyer for $4500 of Adrienne's legal fees incurred in connection therewith, and the ensuing arrests and convictions for weapons possession, PCP possession, resisting arrest, etc., etc., etc.

The Browns, clearly under the strain of severe financial, domestic, and career problems, were airing too many of them in public, and the media was there waiting, cameras clicking and tape recorders whirring. In a May 13 interview given to the local press, after assuring the reporter, "You know I love my wife. I love you, too, as a brother in friendship," Brown was asked why Adrienne had made "those serious accusations and set fire to the singer's clothes." Never one to waste words, Brown summed it all up in four: "Love's a funny thing."

At the door of the prison, a gangly, red-haired guard in short sleeves and a handlebar mustache wants to know just where the hell I think I'm going. I explain I'm going to see James Brown, and he places a meaty hand around the entirety of my left elbow, saying, "No you ain't neither." As we head back up the ivied stairway, he says, "You look like you're from the *Rolling Stone*. That where you're from?" I mention the paper I'm with, and he gets a big kick out of it, big enough to turn me around and lead us 50 paces to a tiny guardhouse at the edge of the compound. "Here's one at *The Village Voice*," he hollers to four colleagues as we approach; one of them thinks that's just too rich not to share with the lieutenant in the prison office.

Now on my second day in the New South, I'm a bit surprised to see the lieutenant is a black man, and clearly very much in control of this prison, which he's quick to inform me is not a prison but a correctional facility. Stroking his salt-and-pepper mustache, he carefully lists the ordinances I've violated by coming as far as I have, then instructs the red-haired guard to escort me to my vehicle, making sure no one congregates with me in the meantime.

At the top of the stairs I listen while the guard explains the difficulty of maintaining security at such a facility; he also wants me to know he's not a guard, he's a corrections officer, that Mr. Brown is not a prisoner, he's an inmate, and that I will certainly be placed in custody "if apprehended at the facility again." A chunky, raven-haired woman in a thick sable coat, whom I recognize as Adrienne Brown, wants to get past, and I step aside, getting a whiff of cosmetics as she negotiates her way down the steps on her spike heels. In her right hand is a plate of food under Saran Wrap; tucked under her left arm is a huge, salon-style hairdryer.

The cloying odor of Thai stick fills Gus's cab as I climb back in, and he's giggling mischievously, stopping long enough to assure me the guard was just having some fun with me, then lapsing into a fit of chuckling and coughing as we head to the airport; 10 minutes later he's still laughing so hard he can't get the roach of his joint lit. "I was just thinking about the poor man," he apologizes, gunning the cab across a double yellow line onto the airport highway. "Checks into that nursing home for six years, still

can't get away from his wife. Guess that's why they call 'em housekeepers,"
he guffaws, going 20 mph over the highway speed limit. "They always keep
the house."

Whoever gave PCP the nickname *angel dust* was looking at the
ephemera through the wrong end of the telescope. Phencyclidine, an animal tranquilizer, is a diabolic substance, pure and simple, attractive on
a protracted basis only to those interested in testing the extreme limits of
physical and emotional experience—the limits, more specifically, of their
control. Variously mislabeled a narcotic, hallucinogen, or psychotropic,
PCP—even in the smallest doses—is well-documented to produce psy-
chotic reactions in humans, and cases of dust-induced homicide are
legion.

"James Brown certainly never had a drug problem till he remarried,"
says Bob Patton, his tour and booking manager through the '60s and late
'70s, "but he does have one now. He's been smoking a joint or two of PCP
a day, probably for the last year or so." Patton, like everyone I've talked to
who knows Brown well, insists he is not a violent man and does not have a
short fuse. "He is a paranoid person though," says Patton, "even without
the drug. Doubly so with it. It was paranoia that was driving him on the
chase. I think he was terrified. He had a gun, he was being chased by policemen across state lines, he was probably stoned out of his mind, and the
police in South Carolina overreacted. How often does your average South
Carolina policeman get a chance to pull a gun on James Brown, smash in
his windows?"

Anne Weston, who sang for the James Brown Revue from 1977–81,
also attributes the recent arrests "directly to PCP. Since his marriage to
Adrienne, the drugs have been really bad. And I think he's been getting
some awful stuff lately. I can't say when he started smoking, or how often.
It was only onstage that you could tell when he was off, out of *control*,
which is a sure sign with James Brown. Normally he's totally in control, especially onstage. By 1981, when the Revue started heading downhill, it
was clear he was slipping. We'd gone around the world many times, playing to packed stadiums from Australia to Kuwait to Surinam. It was like the
Beatles, only much bigger. When we were landing the plane in Africa,
you'd look down from a mile up and see the runway moving—literally
hundreds of thousands of people waiting. I think his smoking then was
recreational, and he could control it. Not anymore."

In a September 27 interview given in his Executive Park office to Linda Day, a staff writer for the *Augusta Chronicle*, Brown, accompanied by his lawyer, his lower teeth missing and his cheeks Scotch-Taped together under his chin (a home remedy for a slack jaw after reconstructive surgery for a degenerative jaw disease), said he'd begun "substance control" treatment. Two days after twice being arrested DUI, though, he still seemed out of control and under the influence of something. Brown, who has always spoken publicly in purposeful proclamations, was all epiphany on this occasion.

Asked about the shotgun-brandishing incident at the Augusta insurance seminar, for example, Brown replied, "I went to my gospel office, that I have, I own. [Brown actually rents his office space.] Went to the gospel office and it was open, and they were using my rest rooms . . . without saying 'May I use it?' . . . So then I want to know, do I own something, or am I just kidding myself? I mean, what do I own here, or what do I control? I mean do I control anything? Can't accept that. The last name is Brown. . . . Now when I can't do that, never do I want to exist anymore. A problem I have, you have problems. . . . We all have problems. Exactly why the Bible says to take the Sabbath Day to ask God's forgiveness of our problems and our sins, because we're human. We're not God. We're human. And he has saints down here that he designates for different programs. He called John, He called Job, He took Moses out of the — away from his sheep. He said you must go. He said I can't go, I can't speak the language. Your brother can speak the language. I will fix it so you can speak all the languages. But you will go. But the Lord, who controls everything, knowing that He has the final say-so, He has the key to everyone, body, tongue, the devil, everybody, He did not take it upon His almighty power to rule. He called Aaron and the three wise men. Said I need some help here. We have a roundtable discussion, like the United Nations. Now God, who controls nothing before him, don't make the decision, how are you gonna make the decision on me? I need help. I accept that. We all need help. Can we accept the ridiculing or the formalness? Go get you one. When I tell my Daddy I don't disagree he get offended. Why? I'm your father. I have my own mind. When you go to the rest room, I can be seated and you use it by yourself. When I go to the rest room, you can't go in there, so you be seated. When you eat I don't taste it. What you eat don't make me fat or lean. Independence is all I'm asking for. The word is spelled F-R-E-E-D-O-M. Nothing I need to say. I rest my case. . . . I'm not going to say the devil made me do it.

Stress made me do it. s-t-r-e-s-s! Emphasize that three times, s-t-r-e-s-s!, s-t-r-e-s-s!, one more time, s-t-r-e-s-s!"

Asked if he felt he owed the people of Augusta an apology, Brown was more succinct: "I apologize," he said, "for the unawareness of what I was about. I apologize for the discomfort that I caused you. I apologize for saying I simply love you. Just let me pass."

"James will talk stream of consciousness from time to time," said Anne Weston, to whom I showed a transcript of the interview. "It can be brilliant, poetic. You can only sit back and let him flow. But not like *that*. That's a very different James Brown. That's PCP talking."

I asked Bob Patton why a man like James Brown would be attracted to a drug like PCP. "He's not attracted to it," Patton said automatically, "he's addicted to it. He thinks it gives him power."

Augusta is a three-hour drive from Toccoa along the South Carolina–Georgia border on Highway 17, an endless strip of road connecting towns with names testifying to their isolation—Pignail, Black Well, Lost Mountain. The only thing that holds this monotony of farmland and pine forest together is the radio, a veritable House of Music down here, built from the bottom up: gospel, bluegrass, jazz, and Delta blues filling the 80s on the dial, rockabilly, early Stones, and Broadway show tunes in the low 90s, everything from Vanilla Fudge to Simply Red for the rest of the dial, a few staticky black stations playing rap and funk at the top. Dotted throughout, of course, is *country*—the music Brown grew up hating as the sound "playing on the radio of every white man I ever worked for"—everything from Hoyt Axton singing "Work your fingers to the bone / What do you get? / Bony fingers" to Charlie Daniels bragging how country boys survive.

If you drive around long enough, you find your way into the black sections of these pretty, dirt-poor towns, where you'll find the only bar and liquor store open at this time of night, the only signs of life. In the '50s these bars formed the chitlin' circuit, the subject of James Brown's 1962 hit "Night Train": a swath of juke-joints from Washington, D.C., to Macon to Jackson to Miami. In cars like Guy Wilson's station wagon, Brown put in tens of thousands of miles along Highway 17 and other roads during the six years he and his fellow travelers were refining and swapping their various strains of rhythm and blues. There was Little Willie John and fellow Georgians Little Richard and Otis Redding, but James Brown was the greatest of them, with a voice that screamed and crooned in coloratura range through songs like "Try Me," "Don't Let It Happen to Me," and "Lost Someone."

On a line with Greenville, South Carolina, I pick up the legendary Country Earl broadcasting "way past my bedtime," learning the best places to buy boiled peanuts on Highway 25 ("tell 'em Country Earl sent you"), listening to his rare Bob Wills, Shorty Long, and Tennessee Plowboy singles. When I pass the Augusta Corporate Line I start losing him as he reads a letter from a reverend who says he's thinking about marrying after all these years. Earl plays him a warning, Tammy Wynette and George Jones singing about living in the "Two-Story House" they dreamed of when young and poor, Tammy singing, "I've got my story," George responding, "And I've got *mine*," and the two joining for the refrain: "How sad it is we live in a two-story house."

A couple stations up the dial, by way of announcing James Brown's trial tomorrow morning, an Augusta DJ with an overripe sense of humor is playing early singles, all on themes of confinement and bad love. The power of Brown's voice turns the intended irony into pathos:

> *I need no shackles to remind me*
> *I'm just a prisoner*
> *Don't let me be a prisoner*
> *You made me a prisoner*
> *When you made me love you.*

PART IV

1990s

"The Blue Funk of a Soul Man" (excerpts)

David Mills
September 28, 1990 • *The Washington Post*

Music Legend James Brown, Taxed, Jailed and Feeling Harassed.

————————

I n the middle of a moist, hot morning, a silver Lincoln Continental rolls
to a stoplight. A black man at the corner gas station smiles gently, proud
somehow, recognizing one of the passengers. "The Godfather," he says,
pointing casually.

Two young fellows washing a car look over at the Lincoln, their faces
blank. Again the man says simply, "The Godfather."

The light turns green, and all eyes follow the Lincoln as it sails down
the street, on its way to jail.

While imprisoned in Georgia as a teenager—he had made a habit of
breaking into cars—James Brown "always tried to look sharp, which was
one reason I didn't like the baggy pants they gave us," he recalled in his
1986 autobiography, "James Brown: The Godfather of Soul."

"[A] lot of it went back to not having decent clothes as a kid. Really, it
was wanting better clothes that got me into prison in the first place. I'd do
anything to look better," he wrote. "Whenever I worked in the laundry I
pulled out new pants and put my number, 33, on 'em and took the number off the pants I had on and exchanged 'em. I got all the new pants that
way for a long time, then one day they caught me and gave me an old
baggy pair and put me out on the farm.

"Man, I couldn't stand being seen in those things. . . ."

On this day, though he again finds himself imprisoned, James Brown at
least is wearing pants he designed himself—many years ago, it would
seem. They are bell-bottomed with four-inch cuffs, part of a snug gray
three-piece suit with black stripes. He also has on an emerald green shirt,
a necktie a shade darker, burgundy cowboy boots and a pinkie ring.

With all the vanity befitting one of the world's greatest showmen,

Brown demands that a photographer not shoot him sitting down. "It makes me look chubby," he says, even rising from his chair to prove the point.

It's a strange, strange Saturday afternoon in the troubled life of James Brown. He has the weekend off from the minimum-security Lower Savannah Community Work Center, where he's serving a six-year sentence for leading police on a high-speed chase in 1988. Brown and his wife, Adrienne, are at the home of friends, along with a video production crew and, of all people, Dick Cavett.

Cavett is here to conduct a one-hour interview with Brown for his cable television talk show and for a documentary—"James Brown: The Man, the Music & the Message"—that will be shown tonight, tomorrow and Sunday at the American Film Institute Theater at the Kennedy Center.

They trade compliments and wisecracks. Cavett thanks Brown several times for teaching him years ago to do the Funky Chicken. Brown fingers a nearby piano. "Mozart?" Cavett deadpans. " 'Sex Machine,' " says Brown.

That incorrigible quipster Cavett even makes light of Brown's incarceration, suggesting that he take a lesson from Zsa Zsa Gabor and next time *slap* a cop. "That way you only serve three days," Cavett says, immediately adding with embarrassed laughter, "I can't believe I said that." Brown smiles and says nothing.

For much of their conversation, Brown recounts some of the many dramatic episodes that amount to this life, from entertaining troops in Vietnam to helping quell the riots in Boston and in Washington after the assassination of Martin Luther King. But to an observer in the room, the poignancy of these stories is undercut by the sight of Adrienne, a former TV makeup artist, standing just off camera, dutifully flapping her arms, fanning her husband's face with an album cover so he doesn't get too sweaty.

The truly uncomfortable thing about watching James Brown do show biz chitchat—hearing him tell the cameras that his incarceration hasn't soured him—is that you realize, once you get him alone, how profoundly resentful he is. Not just about the incident two years ago that got him jailed, but about a multi-million-dollar debt to the Internal Revenue Service that has withered his fortune.

"It was set that I was going to jail," Brown says, fast and raspy. "Why, I don't know. Is it because I'm successful? I probably went to jail the same reason Joe Louis was put in Arlington Cemetery for his good deeds, [but] remained broke after he quit fighting. Joe Louis. Why do all black people wind up penniless? Why do they come and take tax from me? That case is 25, almost 30 years old, and was never about but $211,000 from the get-go."

For several years before the notorious chase in which Brown and up to 14 cop cars crisscrossed the border between Georgia and South Carolina, the legendary performer was getting into trouble with the law, arrested on charges of drug possession, traffic violations and beating his wife.

About all of this, Brown says: "What about harass? I was harassed [by the police] three years. Three years, Georgia and South Carolina, across the borders."

Why would the police pick on him? "I don't think it's as much South as the fact that I just might be a little too popular for the area," he says. "And I'm news, you know. And being news, things happen bad. It was definitely put together. I mean, well organized. . . ."

THE CHASE

On Sept. 24, 1988, James Brown burst in on an insurance seminar taking place next to his Augusta office. With a shotgun in his hands, he accused the people there of using his private restroom. The police were summoned, and Brown took off in his Ford pickup truck.

There are two versions of what happened after the police cornered Brown in a parking lot. According to police testimony, several officers shot out Brown's front tires when he tried to run them down. But Brown insists his truck was sitting still when the police opened fire, and that's why he drove off again—afraid for his life.

Either way, the wild chase continued, Brown driving on two bare wheel rims. It ended with his truck in a ditch.

On Dec. 15, 1988, in Aiken, Brown was convicted of failing to stop for the police—a felony in South Carolina—and two counts of assault "of a high and aggravated nature" for trying to run down officers. He was acquitted of assault with intent to kill.

To this day, James Brown doesn't acknowledge smoking PCP, though a drug test after his arrest indicates that he had been. "They can say anything they want to say," he declares. "And if I'm guilty of everything I'm supposed to have done—robbery, drugs, murder, whatever you want to say—if you're already under arrest, setting still, should a police shoot your truck up?" He adds, strangely hushed, "I think you understood me, didn't you?

"If you're guilty of all those things, and you come to a sudden stop, and setting there for 10 minutes, is it right for a police to come out from the clear blue—four or five—stand there and shoot up your truck? They're trying to make you antagonize 'em so they can kill you," he says, smiling. "And I set there and let 'em do it." (Brown had his shotgun with him throughout the chase, but the police never accused him of threatening them with it.)

Brown's attorney, Reginald D. Simmons, brought in after the conviction, doesn't care about disputed points of fact, or about Brown's talk of a police setup. "We're just trying to focus on shortening his stay in the system," he says.

Judge Hubert Long sentenced Brown to six years for failure to stop. On the assault counts, Brown was given two concurrent five-year sentences that were suspended to five years of probation, tacked onto the end of his six-year term. For the purposes of calculating parole eligibility, Brown got an 11-year sentence. He would have been up for parole months ago had the judge ordered that all three sentences run concurrently.

For the past five months, Brown has been on a work-release program, speaking to young people and the poor on behalf of the nonprofit Aiken and Barnwell Counties Community Action Commission. As of now, counting work credit he has earned, he will be eligible for parole next March.

"I think the courts wanted to send a message that, despite who the person might be, they want to apply the law evenly across the board," Simmons says. "But it doesn't always happen that way. I don't think it was applied evenly in this case." He says he considers the judge's sentence "extremely harsh, not commensurate at all with the crime."

Still, Simmons isn't optimistic about persuading the state to pardon Brown and wipe out the rest of his sentence. "That's a pretty high hurdle," he says.

To talk to James Brown these days is to struggle to keep up with shifts in his mood and in the topic. He can speak bitterly of being "harassed" by the police, then later seem almost at peace with his circumstances:

"I will come out a winner. But I was confined and it caused my wife to be ill . . . and I can't get to see my father, who has just had a stroke, and I need to be with him. Those are the things that hurt, you know. Other than that, it don't really bother me. I really needed the rest. I really needed the rest.

"I've had a chance to sit and see a lot of things that are wrong that kind of disturb me," he says, turning philosophical. "See, the only thing that bugs me about the country is that it hasn't grown a bit. It went backwards.

"We're fighting for the same things that people fought for 25, 30 years ago. The same people are poor, the same people don't have jobs, and for the ethnic people, education is getting more shoddy. A man has to become a criminal because of survival. The easiest thing, it looks to them, is getting involved in crime. Basically selling drugs. In the '30s, it was selling moonshine liquor. Today it's drugs. So what's changed?

"I saw 'em selling moonshine liquor. I was a little boy, looking in the trapdoor, getting a half a pint for my people. Ain't that the same as a cat selling drugs today?"

MRS. BROWN

This day, Sept. 22, happens to be the wedding anniversary of James Brown and his fourth wife, Adrienne, who is fortyish. They met eight years ago on the TV show "Solid Gold," where she did makeup.

This anniversary Adrienne is sharing with Dick Cavett and a video crew. And she's not exactly overjoyed. She is sunk into a fleshy leather chair, her painted eyes peeping drowsily from under a storm cloud of hair.

"This is actually the first holiday, this is the first time we've been able to . . . well, we haven't celebrated yet, but at least we're together," she says. A cigarette filter absorbs some of the lavender gloss from her plump, pretty lips. "And I really, I love this work. I've been in television for 26 years, you know? And I love this work and I love the business. Today is not the day," she says of the taping. "Today I want to be selfish. I don't know if you can understand that."

Her husband's tribulation has taken a physical toll on her, she says. "I've been in front of the cameras, CNN, I've been fighting all the whole time, and I've made myself sick, believing this attorney could help, and this attorney, and knowing that this was all planned from jump street.

"If they can lock James Brown up, they can lock anybody else up," she says. "It wasn't a racial thing, but that's what they're telling every race: If they can lock Mr. Brown up—a world ambassador like that, who's done everything possible for people—then they can do anything."

Mrs. Brown has written to the governor of South Carolina. "I sent numerous telegrams to President Reagan just before he left. Telegrams and letters to Bush. I handed Mrs. Bush a nine-page letter when I was at the White House. Senator Sam Nunn. I have written [Sen. Strom]

Thurmond. I have pleaded with these people not to read the police reports, but to at least call this man in and listen to his story itself, the way it went down."

She says she has received only a couple of sympathetic responses.

Adrienne is especially disappointed with the show business community for not rallying to her husband's aid. "But you know, what it is, it's like, when you're in trouble or something happens . . . it's like you have a bad disease."

Adrienne herself was convicted of a felony, PCP possession, last year. . . .

"Dances with Nations: James Brown's Star Time Names Names" (excerpts)

Dave Marsh
May 1, 1991 • *Rock & Roll Disc*

"I was marked from the getup. You might say that I've got a mark on my back that I never knew was there. That's because they fixed it where I couldn't see myself," writes James Brown in the opening passage of his autobiography, *The Godfather of Soul* (Thunder's Mouth Press, 1990, $13.95). "I was marked a lot of different ways. With names, for example. I was marked with a lot of different names. And each one has a story behind it." Two hundred fifty pages later, the book rolls to a conclusion with this: "Where I grew up there was no way out, no avenue of escape, so you had to make a way. Mine was to create JAMES BROWN. God made me but . . . I created the myth. I've tried to fulfill it. But I've always tried to remember that there's JAMES BROWN the myth and James Brown the man. The people own JAMES BROWN . . . I'm James Brown."

The people who have the pleasure of living with *Star Time* and *Messing With the Blues*, seven hours of JAMES BROWN music in which the master musician of our lifetimes calls out the names of dozens of dances, cities, sidemen, and loved ones in the course of seeking home and shelter (that is, a repository for his own overwhelming joy and pain) will be pardoned for disagreeing with the man's own interpretation. It is impossible that this music was made by any ordinary mortal; it springs, if not from an extraterrestrial source—a whole planet or perhaps galaxy called JAMES BROWN—then certainly from very near the Godhead of our time, from a king of rhythm, a totemic figure whose many tribulations, from criminal incarceration to artistic neglect, form one of the great mythic sagas of our time, and one with the perfect punchline: It all really happened.

Like thousands of my brothers and sisters I find myself listening more and more obsessively to James Brown records as the years of his megastardom recede into history. The difference is that I know it; most of my countrymen think they're listening to the best and newest hip-hop innovations. And they are. This is what happens when an artist is truly, profoundly, totally ahead of his time. And nevertheless, I submit, we have barely begun to comprehend the true nature of James Brown's music, because it has never been presented to us properly or whole, never been given its authentic historical context, either in terms of roots or in terms of influence.

To hear James Brown recast blues, jazz, and R&B standards on *Messing With the Blues* is to listen to a man reshaping his background in his own image. Brown was never half as talented a singer as Billy Eckstine or Little Willie John (to name two of his greatest influences); he lacked any of their smooth suavity, let alone their range and timbre, but when he propelled himself into their songs, they became so totally different that in many cases, you could say he owned them. Check out Eckstine's "Prisoner of Love" and James' usurpation of its cool distance into music of all-but-unbearable intimacy, listen to Willie John's "Need Your Love So Bad" and James' conversion of what was once sublime into a raspy epiphany and you've heard this material not eclipsed but transformed. (One thing that means is that we need a companion volume of Brown's source material, like the Pea-Vine label Japanese disc that collected the R&B originals covered by the early Stones.)

Through two discs (unfortunately *Messing With the Blues* is not available on a U.S. label, but is worth every penny you have to invest to hear it), compilers Harry Weinger and Cliff White show James Brown (or should that be JAMES BROWN?) transubstantiating songs by Clyde McPhatter, Wynonie Harris, Wilbert Harrison, Guitar Slim, Roy Brown, and Louis Jordan, a virtual roll call of mentors and influences, the kind of sophisticated jazz and blues performers to whom James Brown listened studiously and lovingly in his youth, some of them the very men with whom he was competing when he snarled that first, shattering "Please," into a King Records microphone in 1956.

But as in all true tragedies (which, as a fundamental precondition, must involve characters of highest station), what's past is mere prologue and *Messing With the Blues* is just an addendum here, an embellishment to the main story, which is told on *Star Time*, so far as I'm concerned the greatest-ever reissue box set, outstripping even the Otis Redding and Bob Dylan compilations for comprehensive coverage of its subject, judicious display of rarities, and, above all, breathtaking new discoveries.

To hear the extended, almost eight-minute take of "Papa's Got A Brand New Bag," with its long, elliptical conclusion in which James implores Maceo Parker and the rest of his band to help him make sense of his revolution, invoking their names with all the frenzy with which he'd invoked dance crazes a few minutes earlier on the part of the record we all know, is to know that Brown grasped *even then* all the implications of his music that have been successively mined by Sly and the Family Stone, Earth Wind and Fire, George Clinton's P/Funk mob, and an entire generation or three of powerful funkateers; the disco crowd; and now the hip-hop generation. It's all right there, in five minutes of tag that spells out the possibilities of that "Brand New Bag."

The extended "Papa's Got A Brand New Bag" concludes Disc One of *Star Time*. In 70-plus minutes, we have come from the jarring gospel crudity of "Please Please Please," in which Brown masters the shout, through the magnificence of "It's A Man's World," a ballad whose original master (deployed here for the first time in eons of reissuing) offers a breathtaking climax to old-style (pre–"Brand New Bag") soul balladry. The hits—"I Got You," "Out of Sight," "Night Train," "Lost Someone," "Think," "I'll Go Crazy," even the pseudonymous "(Do The) Mashed Potatoes, Pt. 1"—establish the original James Brown: a vulnerable egomaniac whose obsession with groove is matched by his preoccupation with harmony and lacklove.

"Papa's Got A Brand New Bag" smashed that mold, not just placing the rhythm at the center of the story, but reinventing American popular music as part of a palette in which the tones and textures are entirely composed of beat, and beat almost alone. On Discs Two and Three and Four, melodies and harmonies and lyrics and all else arise out of the necessity of the groove. And when the groove doesn't need 'em, *they aren't there*. It's the difference between "I Got You" and "I Got You (I Feel Good)," one in which the shout is central and the other in which the shout simply serves as stunning downbeat, a way of signifying the true energy that's about to commence.

"That's right, you keep playing, Maceo, because the *groove is there*," James exclaims in the midst of "Get It Together," and he approaches the whole project like that, as if he's teaching not only his audience but even his band a new system of musical priority.

And one of the magnificent things about *Star Time* is the way in which it brings to the fore the considerable achievements of all his bands and sidemen: Maceo Parker, Fred Wesley, St. Clair Pinckney, Pee Wee Ellis, Nat Jones, Jabo Starks, Clyde Stubblefield, Bernard Odum, James Nolen, Bobby Byrd, Nat Kendrick, Melvin Parker, Bernard Purdie, Panama Francis, and of course, the later group, drafted in Cincinnati, led by Bootsy and Catfish Collins, that provided the direct pipeline between JB's funk and the P/Funk clan. As a roll call of drummers and bassists alone, that list is awesome, and it's far from inclusive. Brown's ability to find great musicians, over and over again, remains one of the most remarkable parts of his story.

But it's also true that the one constant through this four-hour extravaganza is no musician but JAMES BROWN. If *Star Time*'s beautiful remastering and us uncovering of such stunning tracks as the live "There Was A Time" forcibly reminds us who really ran the greatest rock and roll band in the 1960s, its vast expanse and the sheer quantity of masterful music it contains forces us to recognize James Brown as the true king of all he surveyed. Anybody could bring him a lick or a groove or, for that matter, a title concept. But what makes "Licking Stick Licking Stick" or "King Heroin," which work changes on sometimes ancient black vernacular, something more than new toys is the sheer force of personality with which Brown approached his music. That's why the level of his achievement remained constant even when there was turmoil among his playing personnel.

It's also why *Star Time* works as a real album—one in which a personality blooms and tells a story. Most boxed sets aren't very listenable for exactly this reason; over their length they lose shape and focus. Since James' music was uniquely tuned into a finite set of concerns—the beat, the beat, the beat, the BEAT—and since his entire lyrical odyssey is a quest to define his name and his nature, you can listen to *Star Time* as obsessively as any great album in rock history.

Much of the story James Brown has to tell involves an increasing awareness not only of his own personal powers but of his blackness, and of the power inherent in acknowledging and reclaiming *that*. Even though there has never been a form of vocal music in which the words were more clearly and totally subordinate to the music, James Brown's songs have words for a purpose.

Even though his pop audience essentially rejected that purpose after he (quite unintentionally) threatened it with "Say It Loud, I'm Black and I'm Proud," James never gave up. Straight through the rumbling funk of Disc Three, which ranges from "Mother Popcorn" to another climax in "King Heroin," James, as much and as clearly as Fela himself, uses his words as a platform for African-American statesmanship. In the mélange of Disc Four, the final act in which James loses and then refinds himself with the help of Afrika Bambaataa on "Unity, Part One" (which blessedly closes the set instead of the lame and halting and jingoistic "Living In America"), the message remains clear. If James really needs a name, he finds it in these passages, often including great records that reached only a relatively tiny audience: "Public Enemy #1," "Get On the Good Foot," "I Got A Bag of My Own," "Super Bad," "Talking Loud and Saying Nothing," "Get Up Get Into It Get Involved," "Funky President," and "Rapp Payback (Where Iz Moses)," all portray James Brown as far more than the dancing fool critics too often make him out to be. He sees himself instead as a kind of rhythmic statesman, not so much the King of Soul as as Prime Minister of the Funk. That is why I believe his true name should be Dances With Nations, for he not only made multitudes dance, he brought them together and, however much evil forces may try to tear them apart, wherever James Brown's music is played, the truth emerges, joyous and undeniable.

PART V

2000-2007

"Gettin' Down with Mr Brown"

David Jenkins
March 3, 2002 • *The Sunday Telegraph Magazine*

James Brown says it loud and says it proud: he's the most influential musician on the planet. He's also attracted more than his share of lawsuits and trouble. He talks to David Jenkins in South Carolina about women, drugs, his new album and the Pope.

James Brown—Godfather of Soul, Hardest-Working Man in Showbusiness and First Minister of the New, Super-Heavy Funk—has never been known for false modesty, and today, as he addresses me in his deep, deep, dark, dark, hyper-gravelly voice, the Southern accent thicker than Mississippi mud, he's staying true to form: 'Boxin'—ah was super-good. Football—ah was super-good. Basketball—ah was super-good. But none was mah callin'. Mah callin' was *music*.'

Brown's verbal style is preacherly, his look relaxed. His thick, blue-black hair is still 'fried and laid to the side'; his implanted teeth gleam out of his broad face. He sits legs wide apart, favouring a slightly bulging stomach, furiously tapping his silver-toed boots on the marble floor of his South Carolina home. His shirt is black, his fringed jacket ornamented with Native American beading—his bloodline, he believes, includes Geronimo, the great Apache chief. But right now he's thinking about his callin', and he's on a roll: 'And God gave me that. Yeah, here ah am in the world with a father and a mother that's got nothin'. And ah was gonna have nothin'—because nothin' from nothin' leave nothin'. But God blessed me: ah had Soul!'

He's right, of course. James Brown was born black and dirt-poor 68 years ago—or 72, according to some sources—in Barnwell, South Carolina. He was, in fact, still-born; his Aunt Minnie breathed life into his body. When he was four his mother left for the north, and Brown didn't see her again until he was a star. He was farmed out to relatives, hustled jobs, directed soldiers to brothels, shone shoes and grew streetwise in the Terry district of Augusta, Georgia. His father did menial work and—to revert to straightforward orthography—'If I'd been an obedient child and done everything my Daddy want, I'd have been a filling station worker. Because that's all he was; he was lined up to be the hoss, not the boss. And I worked with him at the filling station, and he was trying to teach me all the things I need to know. But I was not thinking about cleaning that car: I was thinking about how I could buy a whole fleet of them.'

Today, outside his mansion deep in the South Carolina countryside, ten or so cars—a Mercedes, a Jaguar, a Jeep, Cadillac, a Lincoln and a dark-blue Rolls-Royce among them—offer Soul Brother Number One a choice of transport. Stands of pines stretch into the distance, all on Brown's land; a spring-fed lake spawns freshwater fish; a drive leads to a set of curlicued black and gold gates, flanked by a sentry box. Inside, the living-room, where Brown is talking to me, is the sort of living-room any self-respecting rock star should have—a vast chandelier dangles from the high, high ceiling; in the middle of the room steps descend into what looks as though it should be a Jacuzzi but turns out to be a sunken bar, complete with red leather stools; from beneath a garish 1974 portrait of the great man water pours out of a figurine's mouth into a conch shell and thence into a bubbling pool. Brown's housekeeper, Miss Overton, has bid me and the photographer welcome; a manservant, Mr Washington—with Southern courtesy, everybody in James Brown's orbit is addressed as Mr This and Miss That—has brought a stream of soft drinks and coffee. Life seems pretty plush, though ten years ago James Brown owed the Internal Revenue Service more than $9 million; but when, two years ago, he raised $30 million from Wall Street, secured by future royalties on such songs as 'I Feel Good', 'Sex Machine', 'Papa's Got a Brand New Bag', 'Get on the Good Foot' and 'Cold Sweat', the bond was given an 'A' rating and financiers 'found no liens on his assets'.

That's not, says Brown, necessarily a good thing. 'Havin' that IRS problem kept me from having other problems. Because if they see you owe money, other people don't sue you. So once I paid off the IRS, I got 25 lawsuits for nothing. You don't have to *do* nothin', you just have to be who you are.' This, effectively, was Brown's defence against Lisa Agbalaya, a 36-year-old ex-employee of his who pursued a claim for $2 million off Brown for subjecting her to 'a continued pattern of discrimination and harassment'. Brown, she said, had grabbed her by the hips and boasted he 'had been given powerful testicles by the government'; he also urged her to wear zebra-striped underwear while he rubbed her with oil. Brown denied the claim, and won.

It's not, naturally, that he has anything against sex—'When I first opened my mouth and started singing, and the girls started screaming, I forgot about everything else. I didn't want to do nothing else. Heh! Heh! I didn't want the money so much, I just wanted those girls. *Very* important.' It's merely that he thinks 'they' are out to get him. 'America's a funny place,' he says, sighing. 'They will forgive you anything, except being successful. They did Elvis that way; they do everybody that way.'

But James Brown is a difficult man—even to understand: when, ten minutes into our interview, he suddenly declared, 'This isn't supposed to be about me! This is supposed to be about Lloyd Price [a singer and promoter]!'. The photographer, a Californian, was convinced Brown had said, 'This is supposed to be about the Lord Jesus Christ!' But he's also a genius and, like many geniuses, a monster of ego: 'I've led this thing since 1965— all the music from 1965 to now, 90 per cent of it has been James Brown. You have hip-hop, you have rap, you have disco—that's all James Brown.' He is, he once told a colleague, 'The only man who can do anything I want.' This self-centredness can manifest itself in many ways. On a trivial level I'd flown the Atlantic to meet him on a specific day, and he cancelled—'Well, it's rainin',' explained an aide. On a more important level it gives him the conviction to produce great work. And on a more disturbing level it's contributed to the fact that he's twice been to jail, has been involved in several scrapes involving weapons, and has been accused of both wife-and woman-beating. In fact Brown is on his fourth marriage. His first, to Velma Warren, in 1954, produced three sons. His second, to Deirdre Jenkins, in 1970, produced two daughters. His third, to Adrienne Rodriguez, in 1984, produced no children but a whole heap of trouble. His fourth, to Tomi Rae Hynie, a white 32-year-old Southerner who's the lead backing vocalist of his current band, the Soul Generals, took place just before Christmas 2001; it has already produced one boy, seven-month-old James Joseph Jr. Brown admits to two extramarital children, one of whom, Darryl, now plays rhythm guitar with Brown's band.

But trouble and James Brown have walked hand in hand with success since 1949, when he was jailed for eight to 16 years for stealing from cars. While at the Alto Reform School, near Toccoa, Georgia, he played baseball

against an outside team and met Bobby Byrd, the respectable son of respectable black parents. Byrd's parents vouched for Brown's eagerness to go
straight; on 14 June 1952 he was paroled and, with Bobby, set about making
music. In 1956 James Brown and the Famous Flames had their first hit, that
urgent exercise in soulful eroticism, 'Please, Please, Please'. Brown went on
to develop a stage show that's never been bettered for drama, dynamism
and pyrotechnic dancing—a mesmerising mélange of the slop, the slide,
the mashed potato, the camelwalk, the funky chicken and the splits that
electrified audiences: 'You could,' said Bill Wyman, 'put Little Richard,
Jerry Lee Lewis, Bo Diddley and Chuck Berry on one side of the stage, and
James Brown on the other, and you wouldn't even notice the others were up
there.' Brown would, he tells me, lose 7lb a show, and have to be put on a
saline drip.

In 1967 he played to three million people at 350 gigs and sold more
than 50 million records. He had 500 suits, 300 pairs of shoes and a private
jet; the suitcase he carried gate receipts in was often filled with as much as
$250,000 a night. In 1968, during the riots that followed Dr Martin Luther
King's assassination, he appeared on television, pleading successfully for
calm. In return, President Lyndon Johnson had him to dinner at the
White House and personally wrote on his place-card: 'Thanks much [sic]
for what you're doing for your country.'

But problems were coming. Brown's 'Say It Loud—I'm Black and I'm
Proud' (1969) frightened off white fans, while his endorsement of Richard
Nixon alienated blacks. There were, too, personal travails. In 1973 Brown's
adored eldest son, Teddy, was killed in a car crash; he was 19. And though,
in the 1970s, Brown carried on playing more than 300 gigs a year and
recorded and recorded, he blamed his new label, Polydor, for failing to
translate his success in the R&B charts into mainstream success. (To date,
Brown has had 98 entries in the Billboard Top 40 R&B charts, and 17
Number Ones.) Debts began to mount. Businesses Brown owned began to
fail. His music became less fashionable. And he began to believe that the
FBI and the CIA had him under surveillance.

But it was not until 1988 that James Brown imploded. In March he was
arrested for beating up his wife; as the year went on, he was repeatedly arrested on drugs and weapons charges. Finally, on 24 September, Brown
burst into an insurance seminar being held next to his offices in Augusta,
Georgia, waving a shotgun and demanding to know who had used his personal lavatory. The police were called, and a car chase ensued. Twenty-

three shots were fired into Brown's vehicle, and his two front tyres were shot out; Brown drove on his rims for six miles before stopping in a ditch. When police removed Brown from his vehicle, he began, they reported, to sing 'Georgia' and 'do his "Good Foot" dance'. PCP—a powerful hallucinogenic animal tranquilliser, popularly known as Angel Dust—was found in his bloodstream; Brown claimed it had been planted. Offered just 90 days in jail if he pleaded guilty, he refused and was sentenced to two concurrent six-year terms in prison. He served his time, spiffed up the prison choir and on weekend visits Adrienne fixed his precious hair: 'During the week,' she said, 'the prison barber would put some sponge rollers on for him to sleep in.' On 27 February 1991 he was paroled. Two days later he flew to Los Angeles to get a new set of eyebrows tattooed on by a 'dermapigmentation artist'. (His own, Brown says, fell out because he boxed so much when young.) He continued to tour, record and get into trouble: more marital spats reported to the police in 1994 and 1995, followed by the death in 1996, two days after eight hours of liposuction surgery, of Adrienne; firearms and marijuana charges in January 1998, after being taken to hospital by police as 'a mental transport'.

Today he seems a happier man. the dermapigmentation, he tells me, was no use, but his eyebrows are growing back of their own accord: 'Ain't that somethin'?' His hair is still important, but fortunately his housekeeper is good at dealing with it. 'I used to wear it real, real high,' he says, 'because I wanted them to say not, "Where he is?" but, "There he is!"'

He drags out a well-thumbed copy of Joel Whitburn's *Record Research 1955–1972*, and points to his own name and the hits that accompany it. 'See? See? See? All those songs. I got three times as many now—I got more songs than anybody *born*. And that's by me changing the music from what Mozart, Schubert, Beethoven, Bach and Strauss had. They got what they got and mine—what God gave me—is mine. One's on the to-and-fro, for waltzes, and one's on the one and three, and the one and three is *me*. Which makes it different. I've got a new record, called *The Next Step*. I'll show you.'

He pops a CD on, and out comes the unmistakeable voice of James Brown, singing 'Be natural! . . . Oh, mashed potatoes, collard greens! . . . That's natural . . . that's good advice . . .'

'"Good and Natural,"' Brown declares, a beam on his face. 'Goes with my environment: good and natural. See, I'm not into the drugs. They try to make out I am but I'm not. You can walk around, look at my place—you can tell if people are on drugs by the way they live. I don't knock people that is using drugs but . . . Good and natural. Never use nothin' but marijuana in my life . . .'

There's an interruption as Tomi Rae enters, clutching sweet baby James. She's wearing black trousers, black velvet slippers embossed with gold and a black-and-white top; he's in animal-print pyjamas. He's a bit sick, she tells me, otherwise he rarely cries—only at his circumcision or when I'm a little late with his bottle. He *adores* his Daddy; I have to put his spoon on Daddy's plate before he'll eat.'

'Yeah,' says Brown, 'her mother work is *very* good.' And not just her mother work: 'God gave me a chance to do it all,' Brown goes on, 'and then he brought me another baby, at 67 years old. But I think the biggest thing God did, he brought me a nice, young, experienced lady from show business, somebody who . . .' He pauses. 'Somebody who caught a hard time on themselves. She had a problem—so she understand my problem. And my problem is I proven to be such a genius in this country and instead of them using my ingenious ideas, they steal them. I made so many performers. Who made Michael Jackson?'

Brown still does about a 100 shows a year. Given that he suffers from diabetes and that he is, as he says, '68, goin' on 100,' how much can he dance now? Can he still do the splits?

'He did three at the same show just recently,' cries Tomi Rae. 'I was *very* concerned. But he said, "Baby, baby, don't worry about it. Let me do my thing." But he was fine—he did hurt his knee, though, and I did have to put some alcohol on it . . .'

It's easy to laugh: here's the old crock, still trying to rock, and still uttering bombastic proclamations of his primacy. But Brown is a phenomenon. His music was groundbreaking and his rhythms are still the most sampled of today, ornamenting thousands of rap, hip-hop and DJ-created tunes. It was Brown who created the sound, Brown who, as one writer put it, 'would stand in the studio and tutor each musician, hector him, until he heard the improbable horn patterns, the bruising polyrhythms that danced in his head . . .' Does Brown know where his inspiration comes from?

'They want me to do a lot of seminars,' he says. 'People would like to know what it is I'm doing and if they stay with me a long time, they'll get a sense of that feeling. I'm exact! Bam! But knowing—only God knows and I know. And I'm glad of that.'

God alone knows, too, what makes Brown move in such mysterious ways. One moment we're talking amiably about his time in jail in 1988. 'They' had, he suggests, given him a chance to save himself, 'Because I'd probably have died. They accused me of things I didn't do, just because they wanted me to rest.' He hadn't 'done nothin',' and he'd refused to cop a plea because 'I'd have been no man at all, if they'd deprived me of my liberty when I say I'm innocent.' Then, suddenly, he stops talking. The mood changes. He looks puzzled, worried, agitated.

'I really wasn't ready to do no [interview] . . . ,' he says and trails off. There's tension in the air. 'Let me see your story,' he says, 'your business. You got a magazine or something?'

Not with me, I say.

'Well, let me see something. You got any identification? I'm talking to somebody I don't know.' Anxiously, I hand him the pass that lets me into *The Sunday Telegraph*'s premises in Canary Wharf.

'*Telegraph*, huh,' he says, a semi-smile on his lips (Brown's an anglophile; he loves fish and chips.) 'Jenkins, huh. My second wife named Jenkins.'

It is, I blather, an old Welsh name . . .

'*Way*-uls,' goes Brown, mimicking the accent perfectly, mockingly. '*Way*-uls.'

And, I say in desperation, I'm a minister's son.

The clouds lift. The sun shines. Birds sing. The Godfather of Soul is tickled.

'Oh, that's good, that's good. That's one thing about ministers' sons and ministers' daughters, they're the *funkiest*. Because they're trying to get out from under that thing, you know? And one day I could be a minister—but I wouldn't want to be a minister unless I could not get paid. It's like being a politician, you should already be wealthy. Because you've got too much access to money.'

Speaking of ministers, hadn't Brown met the Pope, back in 1987?

'Oh yes. That . . . that was an important situation.' He pauses, broods. 'Babe,' he calls to Tomi Rae, 'take them right in there and show them the Pope . . .'

He gestures towards a closed door. 'You know, you're the first somebody's been in there?' 'Yeah,' says Tomi Rae. 'We don't normally allow people in our *home* home. We're very private. *He's* very private.'

And here's his privacy: a small, snug room with a bust of Pope John

Paul II—'He told James to keep on singing rather than go into the ministry 'cos he reached more people that way'; a Yamaha piano, with some Burt Bacharach sheet music on it; a semicircular sofa upholstered in sparkling green; photos of Brown's son Teddy and his father, Joe; a James Brown doll, merchandised at Christmas, that sings 'I Feel Good' and apes the maestro's movements; and, through the window, a bleak brick patio with a pile of stones in the middle—Brown's oriental garden, Tomi Rae explains.

Brown's been as close to presidents as he has to the Pope—he's met at least four, including the current one. He thinks they have a terrible job: his 1974 song 'Hell' ruminated on the nightmare of being in the White House. 'Who I am today,' he says, 'I wouldn't want to be president. Because God made me another way. Can you imagine me dropping a bomb on your homeland? Or on China? I couldn't be it. Because I've got to tell the truth and you can't tell the truth about America's business if you're president. But I admire the people who lie. And as long as they're trying to cure something, I'm on their side. But sometimes you have to make a dreadful decision. But it has to be made.'

But wasn't Brown a notoriously ruthless—even tyrannical—band leader? Didn't he levy merciless fines on his band for ill-discipline or poor musicianship?

'Still does,' interjects Tomi Rae. 'I sweat more than anybody on that stage because he's tougher on me than he is on anyone else. Because I should know better. Yes, he still fines us: our shoes gotta be shined, and our coats gotta be pressed and we've gotta be on the note. And we know it.'

Brown listens reflectively. Suddenly he looks tired. As the afternoon has worn on he's complained that 'the kids' don't understand his importance, musically, that 'the kids' have been lied to, that he's produced a song called 'Killing Is Out, School Is In', 'but still you find 200 to 300 people a week get killed. I find myself in a position where I am trying to profess right, and it ain't going that way.' He sounds like a man with a legend to live up to, and trouble on his mind. None the less, he galvanises himself once more to count his blessings and curse his woes.

'You know,' he says, 'this is my fourth wife. And I think this is the first time that I had a spouse, or had a relationship with a woman, as a friend that I can talk to about the situation I'm in. She does a very, very good job. She keep me from being a vegetable, you know? Because you might as well be a vegetable once you wear yourself out. I probably look all right, but I'm not fit now. Lovin' her's not enough—that's not strenuous.'

Not, indeed, as strenuous as separating James Brown the Myth from James Brown the Man. Brown once told a friend that no one could understand James Brown. Does *he* understand James Brown?

'No. Because the things I do—where is the answer coming from? My concept was individual, never been used before. The closest thing to the downbeat was jazz—but I was only listening to it last night, and I said to my wife, "These people are very good, but they've missed everything." And a lot of those people played with me. And when they played gigs with me, they couldn't make the cut. They couldn't give what I wanted. They couldn't get down; they had to stay up! The point is to get to people's heart and people's soul—and the thing about me was all the soul I put in. I had to earn what I got, because I had nothing. N-O-T-H-I-N-G. But I had soul.'

"Mr. Brown"

Philip Gourevitch
July 29, 2002 • *The New Yorker*

On the road with His Bad Self.

Forty-seven years ago, at a radio station in Macon, Georgia, five young men stood around a microphone and sang a song. One played guitar, another played piano, but the station's recording equipment picked up the instruments so faintly that the tape they made that day is often recalled as an a-cappella performance. The lead singer was shorter than the others. He had to stand on an overturned Coca-Cola crate to get his mouth level with the mike. When the tape started rolling, he cried out the word "Please" with an immensity of feeling that might, more conventionally, have been reserved for a song's climax. Then he cried out again, "Please," and again and again, "Please, please," at heartbeat intervals. With each repetition, he invested the monosyllable with a different emotional accent and stress—prayer and pride, impatience and invitation—and although there was ache in his voice, he did not sound like a man pleading so much as commanding what was rightfully his. After his fourth "Please," the rest of the group filled in softly behind him, crooning, "Please, please don't go," until the lead singer's colossal voice surged back over theirs: "Please, please, please." That was the name of the song, the same word thrice, and, like all truly original things, this song had a past to which it simultaneously paid tribute and bid adieu. Its genesis lay in a rearrangement of the standard "Baby Please Don't Go," so that the rhythmic backup line became the lead, and the melodic lead was relegated to the chorus. A simple gimmick; but, as "Please, Please, Please" progressed, the lead singer's initial passion only intensified, and it became clear that the reversal of foreground and background voices reflected a deliberate emotional attitude that brought a bold new energy and freedom to the spirit of black popular music. Instead of describing feelings in the smooth lyrical surface of a tune you could whistle or at least hum, the singer created the impression of sounds rising untamed from the rawness and obscurity of a soul that refused all masks.

The song was over in less than three minutes, but that time had the sense of compressed eternity which one experiences in the memory of dreams. Transcribed as text, the words suggest a man gnawing at the last frayed ends of his tether, yet the febrile repetitions, elongations, and elisions of the singer's phrasing make of these words not a lament but a rhapsody, even an ecstasy:

> Please. Please. Please. Please. Please. Please. Please. Honey, please! Don't. Yeah! Oh, yea-ah. Oh. I love you so. Baby! You did me wrong. Whoa! Whoa-oh. You done me wrong. You know you done! Done me wrong. Whoa. Oh yeah! You took my love. And now you're gone. Please! Please. Please. Please. Please. Please. Please. Please. Please. Please. Honey, please. Don't! Whoah. Oh, yeah. Lord. I love you so. I just want to hear you say, I . . . I . . . I . . . I . . . I . . . I . . . I . . . I . . . I! Honey, please. Don't. Oh! Oh, yeah. Oh. I love you so. Baby! Take my hand. I want to be your lover man. Oh, yes. Good God almighty. Honey, please! Don't. Ohhh. Oh. Yeahh. Lord. I love you so! Pleeeeeeeease. Don't go. Pleeee-ee-ee-ease. Don't go. Honey, please don't go. Oh. I love you so. Please. Please.

The song doesn't tell a story so much as express a condition. The singer might be speaking from the cradle of his lover's arms, or chasing her down a street, or watching the lights of her train diminish in the night; he might

be crouched alone in an alleyway, or wandering an empty house, or smiling for all the world to see while his words rattle, unspoken, inside his
skull. He could be anyone anywhere. His lover might be dying. He might
be dying. He might not even be addressing an actual lover. He could be
speaking of someone or something he's never had. He could be talking to
God, or to the Devil. It doesn't matter. Despite the implication of a story, a
specific predicament, the song is abstract. The words jockey for release
and describe the impossibility of release, yet the singing is pure release, defiant, exultant. Speech is inadequate, so the singer makes music, and music is inadequate, so he makes his music speak. Feeling is stripped to its
essence, and the feeling is the whole story. And, if that feeling seems inel-
egant, the singer's immaculately disciplined performance makes his representation of turmoil unmistakably styled and stylish—the brink of frenzy
as a style unto itself.

A few months after the Macon recording session, Ralph Bass, a talent
scout for King Records, heard a copy of the tape in Atlanta. King was one
of the country's leading independent labels, with a particularly strong catalogue of what was then known as "race music"—the music produced by
black artists for black audiences which, despite its ghettoized marketing
label, was already widely recognized by the mid-fifties as the defining
sound of the twentieth century. In the early postwar years especially, King
played a big part in bringing rhythm and blues to a national audience,
recording and publishing the work of such now largely forgotten acts as
Bull Moose Jackson and Eddie (Cleanhead) Vinson, as well as more enduring names: the Five Royales, Little Willie John, and Hank Ballard and
the Midnighters. So Ralph Bass knew the repertoire; he'd heard more
gravel-voiced shouters, high-pitched keeners, hopped-up rockers, churchy
belters, burlesque barkers, doo-wop crooners, and sweet, soft moaners—
more lovers, leavers, losers, loners, lady-killers, lambasters, lounge lizards,
lemme-show-you men, and lawdy-be boys—than any dozen jukeboxes
could contain. But he had never heard a voice that possessed the essence
of all these styles while moving beyond them toward a sound at once more
feral and more self-assured, until he heard "Please, Please, Please."

The tape identified the singers collectively as the Famous Flames.
That was it: nothing more about them, or where they might be found. The
Flames, however, had been performing nearly constantly around Georgia,
where they were known as "house-wrecking" showmen who danced as
they sang, in paroxysms of astounding acrobatic agility. Bass, a white man

who always stayed in black hotels along with the musicians, promoters, and disk jockeys who best knew his terrain, soon tracked down the group's manager at a barbershop in Macon. He brought two hundred dollars in cash and a contract, and declared, "I want them now." The Flames were summoned, they signed, and left for a gig. "I still didn't know who the lead singer was," Bass later told the writer Geoff Brown, but he figured it out that night when he stopped in at the club where the Flames were billed to play at ten o'clock. Right on time, Bass said, "out comes this guy, crawling on his stomach, going from table to table, wherever a pretty girl was sitting, singing, 'Please, Please, Please.'"

This guy was James Brown. He was twenty-two years old, a lithe, rippling sinew of a man, on parole after three years in the state-penitentiary system. He had been locked up at the age of fifteen for stealing from parked cars in Augusta, where he was raised in a whorehouse run by his Aunt Honey. He was a middle-school dropout, with no formal musical training (he could not read a chart, much less write one), yet from early childhood he had realized in himself an intuitive capacity not only to remember and reproduce any tune or riff he heard but also to hear the underlying structures of music, and to make them his own. He had started singing in church, not long after he began walking, and the hand-clapping, stomp-and-shout, get-all-the-way-down-on-your-knees spirit of the Baptist gospel pulpit formed the bedrock of his musical impulse. But his attunement to the sacred never inhibited his appetite for the profane. He claims to have mastered the harmonica at the age of five, blowing "Lost John," "Oh, Susannah," and "John Henry," and one afternoon, when he was seven, he taught himself to play the organ by working out the fingering of "Coonshine Baby." Before long, he was picking up guitar licks to such songs as "(Honey) It's Tight Like That" from the great bluesman Tampa Red, who was dating one of Aunt Honey's girls. By the time he was twelve, the young prodigy was fronting his own group, the Cremona Trio, and winning talent shows with a romping rendition of Louis Jordan's "Caldonia (What Makes Your Big Head So Hard?)." In reform school in the tiny north Georgia town of Toccoa, his nickname was Music Box, and he returned to singing for the Lord, forming a gospel quartet that made its own instruments: a paper-and-comb harmonica, a drum set of old lard tins, a broomstick-and-washtub bass. The warden was impressed, as was a young gospel singer in Toccoa named Bobby Byrd, who'd heard him sing at the prison gate, and offered to give him a home and find him a job if he could win his release. "I want to get out and sing for the Lord," James Brown wrote to the parole board, and although these words suggest an act of a rather different order than the one he and Byrd eventually put together with the Flames, nobody could deny, as he slithered among the ladies on night-club floors, that he sang as if he'd burn in Hell if he stopped.

In February of 1956, the Famous Flames crossed the Mason-Dixon Line for the first time, and drove into Cincinnati, where King Records had its headquarters in an old ice factory. When they were shown into the studio, King's founder and president, Syd Nathan, was seated in the sound booth—a fat little man with a big cigar, a shouter and a bully, who reminded James Brown of Edward G. Robinson in "Little Caesar." Nathan's first impression of his new talent was equally unflattering: the Flames were barely a minute into "Please, Please, Please" when he exploded from his chair, hollering, "What in hell are they doing? Stop the tape," and "Nobody wants to hear that noise," and "It's a stupid song," and so on, until he stalked out. In his autobiography, the singer recalled protesting to King's music director, "Mr. Nathan doesn't understand it. Everybody's music can't be alike."

The tape got made, and Nathan still hated it. When Ralph Bass heard of the debacle, he was in St. Louis. "I get Syd on the phone," he told Geoff Brown. "He's yelling . . . 'That's the worst piece of shit I've ever heard! He's just singing one word. It sounds like he's stuttering.' . . . Before I could say anything, Syd says, 'You're fired!' But I knew what I had. I had been playing the dub from town to town, in every hotel I stayed. And the women would go crazy. I told Syd, 'Don't fire me. Put it out in Atlanta, test it. You'll see.' He says, 'Fuck it, I'm putting it out cross-country, just to prove what a piece of shit it is.'"

Within a year, the song had climbed to sixth place on the R. & B. charts, and was on its way to selling more than a million records; the band had a new manager, Ben Bart, of Universal Attractions in New York, who began booking the act—and its recording and publishing credits—as James Brown and the Famous Flames. The rest of the group, embittered at being upstaged, quit, leaving James Brown feeling both bereft and liberated. "I was sorry," he wrote. "I was heartbroken. . . . They couldn't see that we were really just getting started. There's not much more I can say about it except that they went home, and when they went home I kept going."

I'M BACK!

Mr. Brown, as he insists on being addressed, has described himself as "the Napoleon of the stage," and, like the French emperor, he has a compact body, with a big head and big hands, and a taste for loud, tightly fitted costumes. One evening not long ago, in a dressing room at the great Art Deco pile of the Paramount Theatre in Oakland, California, as his valet Roosevelt Johnson ironed a gold lamé suit with heavily fringed epaulettes for the night's performance, Mr. Brown sat before a mirror contemplating his reflection. His totemic hair—an inky, blue-black processed pompadour, "fried, dyed, and laid to the side"—was bunched up in curlers, awaiting release. A black silk shirt hung open from his shoulders, baring a boyishly smooth and muscular torso for a man who says he's sixty-nine and is alleged by various old spoilers down South to be as much as five years older. He had just finished refurbishing the thick greasepaint of his eyebrows and, wielding a wedgeshaped sponge, was lightening the upper edges of his high, flat cheekbones with some latte-colored paste. He studied his smile, a wide, gleaming streak of dental implants whose electrifying whiteness might have made Melville blink. In show business, he has said, "Hair is the first thing, and teeth are the second. Hair and teeth. A man got those two things, he's got it all." Still, he looked tired and lonely and even smaller than he is, as old men tend to look when applying their makeup.

In performance, however, he makes the stage look small, and wears his years with a survivor's defiant pride. James Brown is, after all, pretty universally recognized as the dominant song-and-dance man of the past half century in black-American music, perhaps in American popular music as a whole: he is the source of more hits than anyone of any color after Elvis Presley. He stands virtually unrivalled as the preëminent pioneer and practitioner of the essential black musical styles of the sixties and early seventies—soul and funk—and the progenitor of rap and hip-hop. Since 1968, however, he has had only one Top Ten hit, "Living in America," from the 1985 soundtrack to Sylvester Stallone's "Rocky IV," which was followed by a period of seeming ruin, marked by serial scrapes with the law on charges of spousal abuse (later dropped) and drug possession, and a return to jail, from 1988 to 1991, after he led a fleet of police cars on a high-speed chase back and forth across the Georgia-South Carolina border. Yet his iconic stature as an entertainer has steadily increased in the decade since his release, and his return to the stage.

He still performs about fifty concerts a year, and, while his sound and style are always unmistakably his own, he manages in the course of each evening to present a sweeping retrospective not only of his own vast repertoire but of all the musical genres to which his originality pays homage: from the field hollers of slavery, the call-and-response, organ-surging exultation of gospel, the tragicomic clowning of minstrel shows, and the boastful reckonings and imploring incantations of the blues, to the sugary seductions of country balladeers and cosmopolitan crooners, the horns of jazz, the guitars of rock and roll, and the percussive insinuations of a thousand local beats from across America, Africa, and the Caribbean. He has repeatedly revolutionized these traditions, discovering in them previously unexpressed possibilities. In turn, his music and dance moves have been so widely studied, reinterpreted, ripped off, and sampled by so many artists of so many different musical dispositions throughout the world that it has become nearly impossible to say, "This is where James Brown's influence ends and the rest of music begins."

By the time he appears onstage, the show is well under way. If there is a curtain, it has risen (and, if there is none, the lights have done the rising) on his band, the Soul Generals—at last count, fourteen men, ten black, four white—four guitarists, two bassists, two full drum sets, a percussionist, a trumpeter, three saxophonists, and an organist. The players wear uniforms with thigh-length blazers and matching trousers (the color varies from night to night: cherry red or pool-chalk blue), and white shirts with Chippendale collars folded over bow ties, a look that places them about midway on the sartorial trajectory between zoot-suiters and riverboat gamblers. They come on full tilt, cranking a sassy medley of funk hooks for several minutes before a deep, commanding voice with the drawling singsong excitement and syllable-parsing precision of a carnival barker rises over the music: "Ladies and gentlemen, James Brown Enterprises is proud to present the James Brown Show!"

The voice belongs to a diminutive man who stands backstage with a cordless microphone, clad in tails, a high-buttoned vest, a bunched silk cravat, and, on some nights, a cocked fedora. This is Danny Ray, who has been Mr. Brown's master of ceremonies for thirty-eight years. As the band ratchets up to a crescendo, he steps jauntily into view—an astounding apparition, natty as Cab Calloway, with a face as hard-lived and angular as Keith Richards's. "And now," he proclaims, "the Bittersweets." A quartet of lady backup singers saunter onstage, identically and snugly sheathed in black, ankle-length gowns, banded in overlapping, wedding-cake tiers of fringe that ripple to their every twitch and undulation. Two are white (a willowy, porcelain-skinned brunette and a glowing redhead); and two are black (a bouncy, radiant woman with cornrow braids and a massive, heavy-set dame hooded in a processed, pumpkin-colored mane). They assemble downstage left, cock their hips, extend their arms with pointed fingers, and coo, "Ooooh, ahhh, gimme some more."

Danny Ray rocks and grins. "And now," he says, holding the "now" for a full second, "let me tell you this." A beat elapses in silence, and Danny Ray continues, "I want to ask you one thing. Are you ready for some su-per, dy-no-mite soul?" The house answers with a deafening "Yes!" "Thank you," he says. "Because right about now it is star time." The band kicks back in, play-ing canonical riffs from James Brown crowd-pleasers, as each of the Bitter-sweets takes a turn naming the songs in a lilting arpeggio: "I Feel Good" . . . "Papa's Got a Brand New Bag" . . . "Try Me" . . . "Doin' It to Death." Danny Ray picks up where they leave off—" 'Please, Please, Please' . . . 'Sex Machine' . . . 'I Got the Feelin' ' . . . 'Living in America' "— and with that he starts chanting, "James Brown! James Brown!" The house chants back, full-bore, hands clapping, bodies swinging, and, lest anybody out there still be seated, the Bittersweets start a cheer of their own: "James Brown, git up, git up. James Brown, git up."

Mr. Brown has always regarded his public with an attitude akin to that of a politician on the campaign trail: by their adulation, he says, "the peo-ple" made him, and to keep them he must serve them. At the same time, he has the peculiar idiomatic habit of describing himself as a slayer of au-diences. "Normally, I just go out there and kill 'em," he declared in the Oakland dressing room. What he means by such remarks is that, for as long as the price of a ticket brings you to him, he will transport you so to-tally into the grip of his groove that you will forget your mortal coil in ea-ger surrender, and, if he does his job well, he will literally control your breathing as precisely as if he had his hand clenched around your trachea. So the relationship is symbiotic: he gives his all, and asks for nothing less in return. He was in particularly high swagger in Oakland, after leading his band through an afternoon rehearsal of the overture to his entrance. "You gotta hear the new opening," he said. "When I get up there—the au-dience, they already dead. I just stand there and look around."

This is precisely what he does, and the ebullient commotion of singers and musicians onstage is such that it's easy not to notice him strolling on from the wings until, all at once, there he is: arms out from his sides as if to welcome an embrace, dentistry blazing in a beatific grin, head turning slowly from side to side, eyes goggle-wide—looking downright blown away to find himself the focus of such a rite of overwhelming acclamation. He lingers thus for several seconds, then, throwing his head back, he lets out a happy scream and rips into the song "Make It Funky." Within seconds, he has sent his microphone stand toppling toward the first row of orchestra seats, only to snatch the cord and yank it back, while spinning on the ball of one foot in a perfect pirouette, so that his mouth returns to the mike and the mike to his mouth in the same instant. He howls. The crowd howls back. The music is irresistibly danceable; the whole house is churning, and the Bittersweets are setting the pace, pelvises swivelling, arms cycling, chanting, "Make it funky," while Mr. Brown, whose microphone is lashed to its stand with a fat snarl of electrical tape, drags the whole assembly with him like a mannequin dance partner, as he stalks the edge of the stage, barking, "Tell me. Uh! So it is. Ha! Got to do it now. . . . Oh, yes. Take me home. To the bridge. To the bridge." He screams, he spins, he does the mashed potato—gliding several yards on one foot. He starts the second song with his back to the crowd, then wheels to face it, and cries, "I'm back, I'm back, I'm back, I'm back . . . ," and screams again.

James Brown screams in nearly every song he has ever recorded or performed. He also grunts, honks, yowls, and hoots, and there are long stretches in many of his songs where he does little else. When he chooses to, of course, he can also sing melody and enunciate lyrics with a piercing clarity. In the space of a sixteenth note, his voice can shift from a honeyed falsetto to anguished lamentation or bellowing bombast. There is very little, if anything, in the range of vocal emotion that he cannot express, and the same can be said of his almost perpetual motion on a stage: although his dance routines are briefer than they once were, and he no longer does splits, or falls to his knees so hard or so often as to draw blood, as he used to, his energy still seems radically at odds with the conventional limitations of human biology. He is a showman of the old school, equal parts high artist and stuntman, and his boldest moments leave art and stunt indistinguishable.

This is never more evident than at the point in his show—during "Please, Please, Please"—when he cuts from the peak of a feverish vocal and instrumental crescendo and collapses to his knees in stunned silence.

His band simultaneously fades to a worried murmur of pulsing rhythms, while the audience, as he puts it, falls "so quiet you can hear a rat peelin' cotton," and in a high, pleading quaver, he announces, "I feel like I'm gonna scream." The crowd goes silent as he sinks even lower to the floor and lets the beats pass. "You make me feel so good I wanna scre-e-eam," he wails. The crowd roars, he falls still, and when the crowd settles down he wails again, "Can I screeeeam?" And again: "Is it all right if I screeeeeeeeeeeam?" The crowd appears fit to riot. He appears fit to be tied. Then he screams. The scream has a sound of such overwhelming feeling that you cannot believe the man controls it. The impression, to the contrary, is that he is controlled by it, as if out of all the throats in the cosmos it had found his, and rendered him wild: the sound in the wild man's throat from beyond the wild man's consciousness that is the wild man's being.

As he screams, Mr. Brown uncoils and staggers upright, dripping sweat. The band cranks up behind him, he resumes singing, and Danny Ray, who drifted offstage during "Make It Funky," reappears. Under his arm he now carries a bundle, which he unfurls with a swooping snap of both wrists into a wide, floor-length cape of sequinned velvet. The cape's design varies from show to show, and on occasion in the same show from scream to scream; sometimes it is red, sometimes green, sometimes black, sometimes gold, and sometimes the sequins spell out the words "Godfather of Soul" or the acronym "G.O.S." Mr. Brown pays no attention as Danny Ray stalks him with the cape, but when it is flung over his shoulders he bows deeply, soaking up the applause, before taking heavy, tentative, stiff-legged steps. As he starts moving he shrugs the cape off, finally flinging it aside and prancing free. On some nights, Danny Ray will come back at him with the cape, and Mr. Brown will shrug it off once more, or he may drop back to his knees, and work himself up to scream again.

Take this spectacle as you will—as death or birth; conquest or surrender; hellfire or apotheosis; sexual climax or heartbreak's abjection; vaudeville hamming or sublime authenticity—you won't be wrong. James Brown is a master of the simultaneous suggestion of opposing possibilities. He is a shaman as much as a showman; but, while his uncanny melding of church and carnival is akin to the convulsive "speaking in tongues" of gospel congregationists, the impression James Brown creates of a man flying off the handle is just that: an impression.

His performances are, and have always been, orchestrated according to the most rigorous discipline. Although no two nights with him are the same, and much of what you see and hear when he's onstage is truly spontaneous, the dazzle of these unpredictable moments is grounded in his ensemble's equally dazzling tightness. He proceeds without song lists, conducting fiercely drilled sidemen and sidewomen through each split-second transition with an elaborate vocabulary of hand signals. "It's like a quarterback—I call the songs as we go," he says, and players whose attention wanders, who miss a beat, or trip into the wrong key, or who merely show up onstage in rumpled uniforms or scuffed shoes, may be fined on the spot, a punishment that is also communicated with hand signals: five fingers suddenly flashed five times, for instance, means twenty-five dollars' docked pay. "I gotta keep order," he explains. "They don't spank children no more, that's why there's no order."

Even in his earliest, wildest days, when his determination to kill an audience was such that he would swing from the rafters, cut flying splits from atop a grand piano, and even leap from a theatre balcony into the orchestra pit, his outrageousness was carefully calculated to convey that, while he cannot be contained, he is always in control. In contrast to the appearance of effortlessness that so many performers strive for in their quest to exhibit mastery, James Brown makes the display of effort one of the most striking features of his art.

In the greatest of his dance performances to be preserved on film—the made-for-television "T.A.M.I." show, of 1964 (in which he stole the thunder from the headline act, an up-and-coming British band called the Rolling Stones, leaving Mick Jagger to complain that it was his greatest mistake ever to follow James Brown)—he hurls himself about, a frenetic dynamo, feet blurring, sweat flying, arms pumping, hairdo collapsing. He is the image of abandon, yet his precision remains absolute, his equilibrium is never shaken, there is no abandon. Even at his most unleashed, he moves like a captive of his body, frantic to shake free, and coming closer than one might have imagined possible.

"Time made me the Godfather, continuous and continuous doing it," Mr. Brown said one afternoon last summer, as he rode in a chauffeur-driven white stretch limousine through the slums of Augusta, where he spent his boyhood—a neighborhood known as the Terry, short for Negro Territory. Beyond the limo's one-way windows, the season's first tropical storm, Allison, was blowing sea-green clouds and rain across a wide street lined with blighted-looking shops and slum dwellings. The street sign said

James Brown Boulevard, and James Brown said, "But what made me want to do it? My daddy couldn't do it, his daddy couldn't do it, and his daddy better not tried it."

JAMES BROWN BOULEVARD

We have this idea in America that pedigree doesn't matter. Never mind your ma and pa, set your own sights, and you are what you make of what God made you—that's the idea. The ancestors held its truth to be self-evident, but we have come to call it our dream, and it follows that our inclination to be entertained by success, to be inspired by excellence and enterprise, and to heroize genius increases in direct proportion to the inauspiciousness of an achiever's origins. So it should probably come as no surprise that the man who is very likely better known to more of the world by more fabulous titles than any other American—His Bad Self, Mr. Dynamite, Soul Brother No. 1, the Sex Machine, the Hardest-Working Man in Show Business, Mr. Excitement, the Ruler of R. & B., the Godfather of Soul, King of the One-Nighters, the Minister of the New New Super-Heavy Funk, the Forefather of Hip-Hop, Mr. Please Please Please, James (Butane) Brown—was not only born dirt-poor and black (with a heavy dose of American Indian blood) at the height of the Great Depression, in the depths of the Jim Crow South, but also claims to have been born dead.

"I wasn't supposed to be alive," he declares in the first lines of his autobiography. "You see, I was a stillborn kid." One can't start out any worse off than that. In fact, one can't start out that way, period; stillborn means you're finished. ("Compare live-born," Webster's suggests.) Never mind: in dealing with James Brown, we are not operating in the conventional show-business realm of legend but in that zone of mystical, folkloric, and allegorical interpretations of life's molding forces which can only be called myth. So the story goes that he emerged lifeless from the womb, and remained that way, unresponsive to the paddlings and proddings of his mother and a pair of aunts, who had attended at his birth (in his parents' one-room shack, without windows, plumbing, or electricity, in the pinewoods outside Barnwell, South Carolina), until they gave up on him. One aunt told his father, "He never drew a breath, Joe," while his mother wept. But the other aunt, Minnie, was moved to keep at him, lifting him up and blowing into his mouth. In this way he was resurrected, and promptly issued his first scream.

One of his earliest memories is of his mother leaving his father for another man: his mother in the doorway saying goodbye, his father telling her, "Take your child," his mother saying, "You keep him." He was four years old, and he didn't see her again for twenty years. His father was a second-grade dropout who subsisted by tapping the surrounding pines for pitch to sell to turpentine mills, and by brewing moonshine. He was rarely at home, and although as an adult James Brown cannot stand to be without company, in his autobiography he credits the solitude of his earliest years—"Being alone in the woods like that, spending nights in a cabin with nobody else there"—as an enduring source of inner strength. "It gave me my own mind," he says. "No matter what came my way after that— prison, personal problems, government harassment—I had the ability to fall back on myself." Still, he was relieved, in his sixth year, when his father decided to move across the Savannah River to Augusta in search of steadier employment, and deposited him in the care of Aunt Honey.

Thereafter, his father kept in touch, but they never again lived at the same address. Mr. Brown remembers him as an inspiringly tireless worker, but also as a depressingly angry man, particularly when it came to race. "Where white people were concerned, I would say my father threw a rock and hit his hand," he says in his autobiography. "He'd call white people 'crackers,' curse 'em and everything when they weren't around, but when he was in front of them, he'd say, 'Yessir, nawsir.' That's when I lost respect for my father." A frightened man, in his view, is a cowed man, and a cowed man is a frightening man. For his own part, he comes across, offstage and on, as fundamentally fearless. "I fear God," he told me. "I fear a man with a gun. I fear a man with a knife. I fear a fool behind the wheel. That's what I fear. I fear death." Then he remembered that he feared something else even more. "Death may come to me," he said. "I may not run from it like a lot of people if my rights is there. I put my rights first, 'cause if I can't live then I'm already dead . . . If I'm already dead, how can I live? I mean, my daddy was a dead man. He walked around, he gone into the service, he did everything he could. He was the bible of the dead man. He come back, he never said a voice. Dead man."

Race, poverty, and exclusion were the defining features of James Brown's childhood world, and he might easily have seen himself as cursed. Instead, he seems to have understood himself to be a free agent—denied the comforts of a conventional home, but also spared its constraints—with no choice but to fight for emancipation however he could. If anything, he can sound nostalgic for the harsh but tight-knit community of his childhood in the

Terry. "Age mellowed me. Yeah, success mellowed me," he said as we rode around. "'Cause now I look and see people that ain't got nothing, and I got *everything* and a sense of what they got. I say, You know what? You know why I say everything? 'Cause I got bein' poor as well as bein' wealthy. A man who's been always richer than I, he's in worse shape than a cat who never had nothin'. Cat never had nothin' got a dream. Cat richer than you'll say, What can I do now?"

After a while, he said again, "I got everything I could ever have wanted. Well, I thought it was everything I could want. What I wanted was peace and happiness, and a little success. I don't want hell and happiness. I got a hell of a lot of happiness, but I got hell with it, too."

The limousine tour of his childhood turf was Mr. Brown's idea. We set out from his office, from which he also ran a radio station, in a former H. L. Green department store on Augusta's Broad Street, downtown. He was dressed for the occasion in a throbbingly purple training suit, and at first he seemed quite happy to point out landmarks and reminisce. Here was the corner where he used to work a shoeshine box outside a parlor known as the Shoeshine King: "There was a man used to give us fifty cent and one used to give us a dollar. And we used to almost disjoint that man's arm when we see him coming, trying to hold him till he get to our stand. Oh, a dollar was unbelievable. . . . My daddy didn't make but seven dollars a week." Here was the liquor store where he first outearned his father, delivering whiskey ("Can't do that no more, they don't allow it") for nine dollars and ninety cents a week, "and you keep the bicycle—almost like you give me a home." Here was the fairground where he used to sneak into the circus, here was the railroad siding where he learned to roller-skate, and "On this corner was a warehouse, I used to eat food out of there. . . . The can would be old, it would be popped up, broken, I mean, like just about to blow up. We put a hole in it, let the pressure off it, and then take it home and cook it. We ate that. Lord." Here was 944 Twiggs Street, where he lived with Aunt Honey—now abandoned and bristling with weeds. Here, by these train tracks, he buck-danced for the soldiers passing through town at the start of the Second World War, they'd throw him coins, which he took home to Aunt Honey: "Men made thirty cents an hour, twenty cents an hour, fifteen cents an hour. . . . I brought her back five dollars to pay the rent for a month." Here was the narrow canal where he once took refuge from the law: "Police were running me, and I saw 'em coming, and I made a few turns, jumped in the water, and breathed through a cane. I saw it in a movie." He mimicked the police, "Where'd he go? Where he at? Where he at? I know I saw him. I swear I saw that boy—Gawd damn." Then he recalled telling himself, "'Now listen up, it's either jail, either reform school, or you stay in the water,' so I stayed in the water." And here was an oil company that he used to burglarize when he was nine: "That was wrong, but it was survival."

Taken together, these memory vignettes composed a portrait of an artist as a young entrepreneur. The image pleased him. Alongside his career as a performer, James Brown has consistently promoted himself as an exemplary figure of black capitalist self-empowerment, touting a doctrine of enterprise as emancipation; ownership and tycoondom as the ultimate social justice. In Jim Crow days, he says, whites didn't keep blacks down because they disliked them (some of his most enthusiastic, best-paying audiences, in his early days with the Famous Flames, were at the fraternity houses of all-white Southern colleges); rather, whites kept blacks disempowered in order to exploit them in a system of "economic slavery."

He claims that he never stole from blacks, preferring to operate as a sort of freelance Robin Hood, redistributing white wealth, much as he sought to do when he began to command power in the music business. In 1962, when he wanted to make a live record of his act at the Apollo Theatre, Syd Nathan of King Records opposed the idea on the ground that such a disk would get no radio play. Mr. Brown put up the money himself, and the full record went on to become a fixture on the playlist of many stations; it was also a crossover success, substantially bolstering his burgeoning white audience. It has never stopped selling, and remains to this day one of the freshest, most charged, and most satisfying concert recordings available. Soon after its release, Mr. Brown began waging a dogged and ultimately successful campaign to wrest ownership of the royalty-generating master tapes of most of his recordings from the King archives. This was a measure of creative and commercial control that no popular musician, black or white, had quite achieved, and for years afterward he kept the tapes in a bag that was with him at all times. In 1966, he bought his own Learjet, and before long he had established a restaurant franchise and acquired several radio stations. As he flew from gig to gig on a relentless touring schedule, he spoke of himself as a trailblazing "model man"—self-made and self-owned—in whose wake black Americans could no longer be held back.

* * *

At the peak of the civil-rights struggle, Mr. Brown's idiosyncratic rhetoric of business as revolution simultaneously appealed to and appalled ideologues on both the left and the right of the political spectrum, who could never decide whether the man who sang, "You got to live for yourself, yourself and nobody else," was with them or against them. In 1966, the Black Power activist Stokely Carmichael (who became Kwame Ture) called him the man most dangerous to the movement, and two years later, at a Black Power conference, the poet LeRoi Jones (later Amiri Baraka) described him as "our No. 1 black poet." But nobody could question that James Brown's greatest public triumph of the era was a direct consequence of his hard-charging capitalism. On the night following Martin Luther King's assassination, in April of 1968, he was booked to play the fourteen-thousand-seat Boston Garden. Elsewhere, major cities were already aflame. Boston was on the brink, and Mayor Kevin White was under heavy pressure to cancel the concert. Mr. Brown, however, was not prepared to forgo the night's pay. Instead, he persuaded the city to guarantee the money—a staggering sixty thousand dollars—and the show would be televised live, then immediately rebroadcast to keep the city's young blacks in front of their TV screens and out of trouble. Toward the end of the concert, some young fans leaped onto the stage, and cops rushed from the wings to push them off. "Wait a minute," Mr. Brown told the police, his hand raised. The music stopped. "Move on back," he said. "I'll be all right. I'll be fine." The cops shrugged and withdrew, but the fans kept coming, mobbing the singer as he said, "You make me look very bad, 'cause I asked the po-lice to step back and you wouldn't go down. No, that's wrong. You not bein' fair to yourself and me and all your race." When he was alone again in the spotlight, he said, "Now, are we together or are we ain't?" Then he told the drummer, "Hit that thing, man," and he resumed singing: "Can't stand it. Can't stand your love."

The concert worked. The streets of Boston remained mostly quiet, and Mr. Brown was soon summoned to the smoking ruins of Washington, D.C., to spread his message: "Build something, don't burn something." In that same year, 1968, one of his hit songs, "Say It Loud (I'm Black and I'm Proud)," was embraced as an anthem by the Black Power crowd, and decried as incendiary by white conservatives, while another of his hits, "America Is My Home," was denounced by black militants as a jingoist sellout and acclaimed as a message of interracial healing by their opponents. To James Brown, there was no contradiction. He wasn't just unapologetically black; he was the darkest-skinned American performer to achieve such stardom, and his pride in that fact was to him a fulfillment of the American Dream. (Prior to September 11th of last year, a James Brown concert was the rare place where you could count on seeing someone publicly wrapped in the flag.) Unfazed by his critics on the left, he also went to Vietnam that summer to entertain the troops—one of the few times he has performed for free—then returned home and endorsed the Democratic Presidential candidate, Hubert Humphrey, who had befriended him two years earlier after hearing his hit song "Don't Be a Drop Out," which became the theme of a White House–sponsored stay-in-school campaign. When Richard Nixon won, however, Mr. Brown accepted an invitation to play at his Inauguration, where he made his mark by performing "I'm Black and I'm Proud." (In 1972, he endorsed Nixon's successful bid for reëlection, believing that the President would promote minority-enterprise initiatives, but he skipped the Inaugural festivities, because the Nixon people declined to pay for his act.)

"Is he the most important black man in America?" asked the cover line for a profile of James Brown in *Look*, in February of 1969. The article celebrated Mr. Brown's business empire (eighty-five employees; gross annual income, four and a half million dollars) and his populism (travelling a hundred thousand miles a year to reach three million fans where they lived; capping ticket prices at five dollars for adults and ninety-nine cents for children under twelve), and it said, "James Brown is a new important leader. His constituency dwarfs Stokely Carmichael's and the late Dr. Martin Luther King's. . . . He is the black Horatio Alger." Never mind that all of Mr. Brown's early businesses, save for his performing and recording career, failed, or that the Internal Revenue Service discovered by the early seventies that he had never got around to paying more than four million dollars in income tax. (In his autobiography, he proffers the extraordinary argument that the government was to blame for his tax troubles, "because they didn't allow me to go to school." As a result, he says, "they have no legal boundaries over me. . . . You pay tax when you exercise all of your rights. I didn't exercise rights. I didn't have a chance to. I lived with the word can't, so I can't pay taxes.")

As we turned off Twiggs Street onto a narrow and particularly abject strip called Hopkins Street, Mr. Brown's mood turned sombre. The façade of a brick house on the corner was spray-painted with the words "Fuck the world," and farther along the real estate grew more dismal: tottering clap-board bungalows, half of them burned out, and the rest, he said, "probably crack houses now—you come from that, you use crack." In this setting, the limo looked like a spaceship, but none of the street's ragtag residents ex-pressed any surprise. They waved from sidewalks and porches, and al-though they couldn't see through the rain-streaked one-way glass, they called out, "Hello, Mr. Brown," and "God bless, Mr. Brown." The vehicle could belong to nobody else: every Thanksgiving, he comes through pass-ing out turkeys, and at Christmas he brings toys. Now he said, "They want me to help build this place back. What can I do? Get on my knees and pray, and ask, 'Mr. President, come—Mr. Bush, come in here and clean it out and put decent homes in here'?"

He told his driver to stop outside a broken-down shack, where an ema-ciated woman and two young men sat on a porch surrounded by house-hold debris. One of the young men stepped forward in the rain, and Mr. Brown lowered his window and held out a fifty-dollar bill. The man bowed, and withdrew. "Wait a minute," Mr. Brown called after him. "Y'all split that. Give that lady some, too." When he rolled his window up, he told me, "I'm not doin' this because you here. I wasn't gonna do it today. I didn't want you to see me handin' no money out there. I wasn't gonna do it. That's the honest-to-God truth." He sounded embarrassed. "You look at this, it kinda take your breath," he said.

At the end of the block, we reached James Brown Boulevard, and he said, "Out here on these same streets, you may see my daughter, and she has no business out here. She don't have to be there. I give her a home, she got a new Mercedes, and her Mercedes just sitting there. I can't give it to her, 'cause I can't—'cause she shrug off everything I do."

Family life has never been Mr. Brown's strong suit; he has been married four times, divorced twice, and made a widower in 1996 when his third wife died from complications following plastic surgery; he had three chil-dren with his first wife, two with his second, none with his third, and on the day before my visit to Augusta his current wife (then still his fiancée), Tomi Rae Hynie, a thirty-three-year-old singer of Norwegian descent, who has performed and lived with him on and off for the past four years, gave birth to a son, James Joseph Brown II. In addition to these relationships, through-out much of his career he maintained a succession of girlfriends and mis-tresses, with a couple of whom he sired children, including the daughter he was keeping an eye out for on the street named after him. "She's got worse than a habit," he said. "When a person is just spooked, we say she got a monkey on her back. She got a gorilla on her back." He fell silent for a beat, then said it again, "She got a gorilla on her back."

So our journey into his past had brought him hard up against the present, and he did not seem to feel so at home anymore. As he spoke of his helplessness before his daughter's destitution, his earlier discomfort at being seen giving handouts suddenly made sense: he wasn't embarrassed for himself, but for the people who accepted his charity. After all, this was the man whose ultimate civil-rights-era message song was "I Don't Want Nobody to Give Me Nothing (Open Up the Door, I'll Get It Myself)." He had wanted to show me the "nothingness" he'd come from, but that nothingness, which had been created by a sense of exclusion, had been a full and vibrant world to him. Now it was gone—the door had been opened, and those who found a way had moved on through it—and he was at a loss to account for the new nothingness of oblivion that had taken its place, a genuine wasteland without the blatant boot-heel of Jim Crow to blame.

"I don't know whether this freedom is as good as segregation," he said at one point. "I'll let you figure that out." And he said, "I got a street named after me, and I'm still riding around—I can't say not one thing."

BACK TO THE CROSSROAD

Mr. Brown has plenty to say, of course, and he does not hesitate to say much of it. He talked non-stop for more than three hours in Augusta, and once we'd put James Brown Boulevard behind us his mood grew easy again, and his words flowed more freely, in long, looping monologues. In his speech, as in his music and dance, he is at once fiercely controlling and wildly spontaneous, unpredictable even to himself. But, unlike his songs, his conversation can be nearly impossible to follow. The patchwork of his syntax and the guttural slipstream of his diction—a gravelly, half-swallowed slur whose viscosity has increased through the decades, in lock-step with his pursuit of perfect dentistry—are only part of the challenge. After deciphering what he's saying, it frequently remains necessary to determine what he's talking about. And much of the time he appears to be wondering the same thing, because his speech is a form of improvisation. So Mr. Brown speaks with an attentive ear, stringing words and ideas along in contrapuntal themes and variations, at times falling back on reliable old formulations to give the jam shape, until he hears some new riff emerging, at which point he works and worries the key elements, juggling their sequence and refining their emphasis, until they converge in a sudden burst of determined lucidity, or fade out and are forgotten.

In one characteristic outburst, he began by pointing to a block of abandoned buildings that were slated by the city for rehabilitation, and said the only way to go was to tear them down and start over from scratch. "What you see now is a shell of a building," he said. "At least if there was nothing there you could build good. You could imagine. But now you can't imagine—you got to think of how to salvage it and save it." He worked this vein for a while, and it soon broadened out: "America needs an overhaul. Overhaul. Go back. I made a song called 'A Man Has to Go Back to the Crossroad.' So America now needs overhauls. She gotta go back to the crossroad. She gotta go back to the drawing board. 'Cause what is happening to it?" He went on, "I mean, you got to go back to the beginning and rewind yourself. You got to do like a tape deck, you got to rewind and start all over again." He said, "I don't want to tear nothing up, I want to be able to—I want to own part of it. I don't want to tear it up, I want to build it up, and then own part of it. Or I want an opportunity to build one just like it."

He said, "Free enterprise is as good as it can be, but when you start going with one is educated and the other's not, it's not free enterprise no more. When one is educated, and the other don't know A from B, it's not free enterprise no more." He said, "The same intent they showed to keep us separated years ago, they should show that same intent to put us together." He said, "America has committed a lot more crimes on civilization than we committed trying to get into civilization. We was out of civilization. What we was livin' was not civilization, it was uncivil. Our whole thing was uncivil. It wasn't even civilized! The people know that. You gonna let people come in your house and cook for you—Look here, you gonna let people come in your house and cook food and plan for the whole family, little babies come and there'd be a nanny and let the baby suck the titty, and then tell 'em, 'Lady, you can't be eatin' with them'? Come on. It's crazy."

And he went on, "I ask you, let up a little bit. Let's give the small man a little more chance to be human. Let's not dehumanize the man and put him in jail for bein' a criminal. Dehumanize! I mean, you won't put a dog in jail for tryin' to eat out your garbage can or eat out your yard. So why you gonna do that to a poor man that has no guides. More schools. The people in jail need to go to school. Anybody with any less than a ten-year sentence should stay in school all the time. 'Cause you know that's a dumping ground. Even the toilet dumps into a refinery and goes round and back to you as clean. Even a *toilet*. O.K.? It goes to the reservoir and everything before it come back to the people as drinkin' water. But you take a man out of prison, who don't know nothing but killin' and doin' anything wrong, and put him out and expect him to function with people, like he can live with them. He cannot *live* with them. He can't live with nobody. I think of all this stuff, and I see it's cause that's called L-O-S-T, lost—unless you put music back in it. Music right now, whether it's gospel, jazz, you need music. You need to have a music revolution to get these people's mind right."

Once James Brown gets talking, it is not easy to steer him. You may ask a question, you may get an answer—there may or may not be any correlation. I asked if he knew that he was not like other people; that he had a much higher level of energy. "Mmm-hmm," he said. After a moment, he added, "I'm not going to endorse marijuana for sale, but for health I will." He said, "A man should never confess, but I think that anything that's good for people—gotta do." Besides, if the alternative is hard drugs and a person needs something gentler, "you better bring marijuana back so you have some place to get off. You can't jump one-four. You know, one-two. One *and* two. Get 'em on the 'and.' Then we can bring 'em back home."

In the late eighties, Mr. Brown and his third wife were widely reported to have a habit of getting high on angel dust, or PCP, an animal tranquillizer that tends to induce paranoid and often violent psychosis in humans. On September 24, 1988, the singer, dishevelled, enraged, and carrying a shotgun, burst into an office next to his own in Augusta and accused its occupants—forty men and women attending an insurance-licensing seminar—of using his bathroom without permission. After a brief standoff, he retreated. "God said, 'Boy, go home,' " he later told a local reporter. He drove off in his pickup truck; and soon found himself pursued by a police car with flashing lights. He pulled the truck over and stopped, and when the cruiser stopped behind him he peeled back onto the road. The police stayed on his tail for four miles, until he pulled over once more. By now he was heading east on Interstate 20, and this time he waited for the officer to get out of his car before taking off again. He entered South Carolina at eighty miles an hour, shot off the interstate, and almost immediately found himself facing the flashing blue lights of a police car blocking the road, with the lights of another behind him. When he stopped, an officer approached and began questioning him through his window. According to Mr. Brown, another officer appeared at the passenger door and started smashing the window in with his pistol. The singer threw the truck into gear and floored it. By then, there were at least four policemen standing in his dust and they opened fire, striking the truck eighteen times, puncturing the gas tank and all four of the tires. "They act like I done rob ten banks," Mr. Brown said later. "I left to protect my life."

Driving full throttle on his wheel rims, he trundled back to Augusta at thirty miles an hour, and meandered through downtown, trailed by a posse of fourteen cruisers. When he finally lost control of the truck, and ground to a halt in a ditch, he was about a mile from the scene of his first arrest (for larceny), thirty-nine years earlier. This time, he was brought back to South Carolina, where he was convicted of aggravated assault and "failure to stop for a blue light," and sentenced to six years. Once again, he served three.

Mr. Brown keeps the crippled hulk of his truck in a shed at his home, a several-hundred-acre estate in Beech Island, South Carolina. There, behind a wrought-iron replica of the gate at Buckingham Palace, guarded by a bloodhound and a white security guard who addresses him with "Yessir" and "Nawsir," a winding two-lane road leads through a forest of pine and live oak, dipping past a large man-made pond (soon to be banked with "six foot of concrete, so people can stand back off and fish"), to his residence. He has been expanding the building according to his own design in recent years to become "just a monstrosity, it's unbelievable, a pleasure monstrosity—one that's gonna be good for you to show your kids to—and it's gonna be quite a monument, so you'll say, 'You know what, that James Brown got somethin' on his mind.'" He wouldn't allow me inside the house, but he made a point of showing me the truck. He claimed he'd turned down offers of as much as a million dollars for it. "That was the truck that started all my success," he said mysteriously.

"Goin' to jail in the nineties was really a great awakening," he added, "because I didn't know people were still that ignorant." I took him to mean his fellow-inmates, but it turned out he was speaking of the police, who had refused to just let him go home, as God told him to. "I stayed away from the ghetto too long," he said. "You living all this and you think musicians got a umbrella, till they come pick you up. You don't have no rights." He scoffed at allegations that he was high on PCP at the time of his arrest—"Not in my life," he said of hard drugs in general—but then he added, "Well, I wouldn't say as I did buy PCP. It might've been in the marijuana. And, if it was, I sure wish I had some more."

I started to say something, and he cut me off. "I'm'a say that again. Whatever I had, I need some more, 'cause everybody else is insane with them drugs they're using. Now, what was you goin' to ask me?" I no longer remembered, so I said, "How do you account for an insane generation?" He couldn't. He could only describe its insanity. "Black kids shootin' every one of each other, they got a quick temper. . . . But then the white kids, after they go in the service and all this stuff, come back—they shootin' and nobody cutting 'em, they shootin' at a whole room of people, shootin' at the teacher, they doin' everything. You know, whites are extremists, they go all the way with it." And he prescribed a solution: "We need a substance now to make us afraid. A-F-R-A-I-D. That's what we need. We need something—the kids need a pessimistic drug to slow them down, to make them, you know, 'I ain't gonna do that.' Ain't nothin' these kids wanna do today. Ain't nothin' you wanna do. They in a different bag. They need somethin' to make them pessimistic, and make them come out of this craziness so we can go to work and save this country."

There are no computers in the offices of James Brown Enterprises. "He's got this strange notion that they can see back at you," Maria Moon, one of his staffers, explained. "I guess he watched too many Russian-spy movies when he was young or something, but he thinks that they can see you and that they can track everything that you do." Mr. Brown put it slightly differently: "I don't want computers coming feeding direct off of me, 'cause I know what I got to tell a computer that it ain't got in there, and I don't want to. If the government would want me to be heading up the computer people, I would give 'em a basic idea what we should put in a computer— not just basic things, you know, but things that will be helpful in the future. We don't have that, but I could tell 'em a lot of things." He didn't elaborate, but he told me that on several occasions, while watching television news, he had foreseen the deaths of people on the screen. President Anwar Sadat, of Egypt, was one. "I looked at him when he got off the plane. I said, 'Oh, Lord.' I looked at the man's eyes. 'Oh, Lord!' I said. 'He's a dead man.' And he was dead." On an earlier occasion, during the Attica prison riots in 1971, he foresaw that the inmates who had taken over the prison would be slaughtered. "I was getting my hair fixed, and I looked up at the television," he said, and again his reaction was "Oh, Lord." His hairdresser asked, "What'd you see?" Mr. Brown told him, "All those dead men. They didn't even have no face no more, far as I was concerned. I looked at 'em, I didn't want 'em to be there no more."

James Brown is rarely unaccompanied; he employs a large court of attendants, whom he summons at all hours to listen as he speaks, and he told me, "I got all the friends in the world. My friends—that's all that matter to me." But he has the air of a man who is eternally alone. Even those who have spent a great deal of private time with him hesitate to describe themselves as knowing him. The Reverend Al Sharpton says, "I probably would have been as close to him as anybody for the last twenty-some years." But he is quick to add, "Close as he lets people get close. There's a zone nobody goes in. He draws a crowd, but then he's also centered, lonely, in the crowd." At his core—"deep down inside his solitude"—Sharpton believes, Mr. Brown is a mystical man who "probably has more faith than most preachers," and he said, "In the middle of the night, when there's no crowd, no nothing, that's all he talks about."

James Brown was living in New York, in a Victorian mansion in Queens, surrounded by a moat and decorated each Christmas with black Santa Claus lawn sculptures, when he was introduced to Sharpton, in the late sixties. (He liked New York, he said, except for one thing. "No wholesome people," he said, although in those days New York was a better place for interracial romance than the South, where if you met "a brunette, a blonde, a redhead, you can't even write to her—they'd hang the letter when it gets there.") Sharpton was nineteen when they met again, an unknown, aspiring black activist, and Mr. Brown, whose firstborn son, Teddy, had just died in a car crash, took him under his wing. Sharpton, who came from a broken home, and whose strongest memories of his father were "that we used to stand in front of the Apollo and he'd bribe the guys so we could get up on line to see James Brown," said, "I became in effect, over the next decade, his surrogate son, and he was my surrogate father." Sharpton, who eventually married one of Mr. Brown's singers (Kathy Jordan, who was a backup on a recording of "Tennessee Waltz"), in turn introduced the Godfather to his third wife, and for many years the Reverend was a regular member of their entourage.

Politically, James Brown and Al Sharpton make something of an odd couple. Mr. Brown has always defended his support for Richard Nixon, and a few years ago, when *Rolling Stone* asked him to name a hero from the twentieth century, he chose the reactionary senator from his home state, Strom Thurmond. He also performed at Thurmond's daughter's wedding, and sang "God Bless America" at a ceremony marking the ninety-eight-year-old senator's plan to retire. "But his style, his soul force, was very much an influence on me—and his whole thing of defiance and standing up against great odds if he believed in something," Sharpton said. "He's the only man I've ever met that doesn't need the acceptance and certification of the external world. He goes by his beliefs. He could care less about everybody else's."

By way of an example, Sharpton recalled accompanying his friend when he received a Grammy Award for lifetime achievement shortly after he got out of jail. Mr. Brown got a standing ovation, returned to his seat, said, "Let's go. I have my award, I'm not sitting here watching everybody," and they walked out. "And where do we have to go?" Sharpton said. "The Stage Deli, and eat Hungarian goulash." Similarly, in 1974 James Brown went to Zaire to play at the black-music festival that President Mobutu Sese Seko sponsored to coincide with the world heavyweight championship fight between Muhammad Ali and George Foreman, and the day after the concert he went home. Sharpton couldn't imagine skipping the fight, but his mentor told him, "Reverend, I'm going to be over here making my next dollar while Ali's making his."

Sharpton doesn't see much of his mentor these days, and when I asked Mr. Brown whether he would ever endorse Sharpton for elected office he said, "I would endorse his intent." But he said he no longer meddles with political endorsements, and he reminded me that, "being an ex-offender," he has never voted. At this point, he said, black people don't need leaders—"We need jobs"—and he'd told Sharpton as much. "'You don't lead us, we know how to lead.' I said, 'We don't need that no more. That was all right when we didn't have the nerve and the ambition, but now you can be anything you want to be, so you your own leader.'" Besides, he said, "leaders become dictators."

TIME AFTER TIME

In late May of last year, the mayor of Cincinnati, Charlie Luken, asked James Brown for help. Seven weeks earlier, on April 7th, a city policeman had shot and killed an unarmed nineteen-year-old black man named Timothy Thomas, after a foot chase in the ghetto neighborhood of Over-the-Rhine. Thomas was the fifteenth black man to lose his life in a confrontation with Cincinnati police since 1995. His death was followed by several days of protests and rioting. Motorists were dragged from their cars and beaten; stores along a wide swath of the city center were looted; fires were set; a citywide dusk-to-dawn curfew was imposed; and although calm was restored within a week, the city remained deeply riven and on edge. Prominent black churchmen continued to lead protests, and were threatening to disrupt the city's annual Memorial Day outdoor food-and-music festival, Taste of Cincinnati. Mayor Luken wanted the festival to mark a return to normal for the city, and he wanted a musical act to set the tone. That meant he wanted a black act. The rhythm-and-blues band Midnight Star and the Isley Brothers were booked, but local black leaders persuaded them to withdraw. Now, with two days to go, the Mayor asked James Brown to come to town.

As it happened, Mr. Brown had just finished recording a new song, addressed to America's youths, called "Killing Is Out, School Is In," and he thought the message was perfectly suited to Cincinnati's plight. He said he would not get mixed up in local politics, but for fifteen thousand dollars, to cover expenses, he agreed to give a midday press conference and to sing his new song. The news of his intended appearance was not well received at the New Prospect Baptist Church in Over-the-Rhine, the hub of the peaceful-protest movement that had coalesced since the riots. On the morning the Taste was to open, the pews were filled with several hundred men and women (about a quarter of them white) who sang gospel hymns and listened to the pastor, Reverend Damon Lynch III, rally them to stage a boycott of the food fair. In the atrium, a middle-aged black-enterprise activist named Jim Clingman explained the prevailing attitude. "James Brown is being used. He's just window dressing," he said, adding, "I lived by James Brown for a long time. I don't want to hurt the brother, I want to help him."

Pastor Lynch's rhetoric from the pulpit was more high-flown. He spoke of Cincinnati's "economic apartheid," and said, "Every once in a while we got to rise up. . . . What we got now is a Rosa Parks moment in our lives." He spoke the name James Brown, and said the attitude of the city fathers was "If we can just get 'em dancin'—bring in Negro dancers and just get the Negro dancin', he'll forget about his anger, he'll forget about his pain." He explained that he was going to meet the singer before the press conference, and persuade him to join the boycott, because "he is and has been our brother," and "for him now to be drawn into this—we just gotta tap him on the shoulder."

It didn't happen that way. James Brown rode straight from the airport to the press conference, at a downtown hotel. He wore a gunmetal-blue suit and turtleneck, silver-toed black cowboy boots, and, until the Mayor was done introducing him, heavy dark sunglasses. Then he took the podium, with half a dozen of his loyal retainers arrayed behind him, and for the next twenty minutes he held forth in a characteristically kaleidoscopic manner, full of oblique personal references. He called Cincinnati his second home, on account of King Records ("I wouldn't have a career if it wasn't for God, America, and especially Cincinnati"); and he said he was born dead, but didn't elaborate. He said, "I was out there with Dr. King, I was out there with Malcolm, I was out there with Mr. Abernathy, and I knew a lot of people—trying to make it better." And he said, "I didn't come for the Mayor, I didn't come for the police, I didn't come for the people out in the street. I come for the kids." This was his key point: that children were in peril. He criticized TV violence ("You see a show on television today, they done killed twenty people already, and you ain't even got to the show yet"), put in a plug for school prayer, and said we shouldn't be hiring teachers from overseas. He talked briefly about volunteering to entertain the troops in Indochina, and how hot it was there, and about flying around Russia in an old bomber plane, and about going to jail as a teen-ager. He said he'd never met a person he didn't like, and he said that, whatever Cincinnati's current trouble was, "it's going to end in the courthouse, whether you like it or not, it's never going to end in the outhouse." He invoked Rwanda and Bosnia, and asked, "What are we doing killing each other in our community?" He said, "Ants can work together, why can't people work together?" He cited Scripture—John 3:17 ("For God sent not his Son into the world to condemn the world; but that the world through him might be saved")— and said, "God don't want me to quit it, because Papa got a brand new bag."

Jim Clingman, the activist, ventured a question from the floor: "Brother Brown, one of your records that you made had the words 'Let's get together and get some land, raise our food like the man, save our money like the Mob, put up the factory on the job.' Speak on economic empowerment."

"All we got to do is get black Americans to put in one dollar, and from everybody build a company," Mr. Brown said.

"That's what I'm talking about," Clingman agreed.

"All we got to do is build our own stuff," Mr. Brown said.

"That's right."

"Not whether you're black or white."

"Thank you."

"Just have your own. And it's bad, see, if ballplayers, athletes, can't give one dollar apiece a year . . ."

"Thank you."

"It would be that much. They don't give no money."

"Speak."

He went on for a while longer—"We're all in it together, the Italian, the Jew, the German, nobody but all of us. Who am I? I'm 259-32-3801, not black or white, just that Social Security card"—then he rode the elevator down to his limo, and was driven to the festival stage. A thousand people had gathered in the midday sun to see him, most of them white, and around the periphery marched several hundred protesters, chanting, "James Brown sold out." Suddenly, a very loud, thumping beat blared from the sound system, and Mr. Brown appeared onstage, rapping out a karaoke version of his new song, "Killing Is Out, School Is In," with a vocal accompanist, who barked back, "I don't think they heard you, brother. Say it again." Despite the volume, their voices were barely audible over the chants of the protesters. From here and there in the crowd, people began hurling pennies at the stage. Two young black men looked on, discussing James Brown's presence in tones of disgust: "He's done. . . . He's finished. . . . Out the window with all them records—like Frisbees."

All at once, with the song still playing, Mr. Brown spun around and walked offstage. He did not wait for applause, or return for it. One second he was there, and the next he was gone. Protesters surged toward him as he climbed into his limo. Mounted policemen moved to hold them back. An old man screamed, "Bring Elvis back—they both dead now." James Brown got back out of the car to hug a well-wisher. A few protesters rushed forward, and he ducked back inside. With the police cavalry as an escort, the car finally began to move off. A new chant began: "Say it loud, we got him out now."

A few weeks later, in Augusta, Mr. Brown told me that he had just received an invitation to the White House to present President Bush with a CD of his new song. "He called me," he said. "I knew it had to lead to that, because when they saw us stop the riots in Cincinnati—that was a good thing." His manager, Charles Bobbit, sustained this fantasy: "It was a repeat of 1968—Boston, Massachusetts—and both cities, both mayors, called for help 'cause they couldn't do it." Mr. Brown chuckled. "You right," he said.

"That was a repeat. I didn't think about that." He was moved to declare that the new song, with its heavy rap beat, and its obvious reproach to the mayhem-boosting lyrics of so much hip-hop, would be "the biggest thing ever happened in history." He said, "You know, the President didn't call for us to be talkin' jive. He gonna tie it in. And I don't blame him."

Before America was drawn into war last September 11th, James Brown and his handlers had been talking up the release of the new song in the fall, as a sort of back-to-school special. It was an article of faith among the inner circle at James Brown Enterprises that it would be a hit as big as his best civil-rights-era numbers. Members of his band thought otherwise: the words were too blunt, even mildly scolding, lacking the buoyant bravura of his enduring message songs; the arrangement was a bit ham-fisted, and audiences weren't taking to it. The consensus among his sidemen seemed to be that Mr. Brown was wasting his time trying to reach today's kids, and should go back to his roots by recording an album of the music he loves to sing best when he's alone with a few friends: his greatest hits, a little gospel, even some ballads—songs of pure feeling. Mr. Brown himself never seemed quite satisfied with the recorded version of "Killing Is Out," and his producer was constantly reworking the mix, with overdubbed vocals and patched-in instrumentals—a process totally alien to the way the singer has worked for most of his life. "He must've mixed that thing fifty times, trying to come up with something else. I mean, he not really understanding that when it come from me, it's the real thing," he said. "It's God. When I first go in and cut, it's God. If I go back to cut, it's me. You see, God is always right. All the records, I used to always use my first cuts. Bam! Cat say, 'You want to cut it again?' I say, 'For what?'"

I wondered what Syd Nathan, who had so often recoiled from Mr. Brown's best innovations, would think. For all their struggles over the years, it was at King Records that Mr. Brown had done his best work. But Nathan has been dead for more than thirty years, so I went to see Ahmet Ertegun, the Turkish-born éminence grise of record producers, who started Atlantic Records around the time that Nathan started King, and whose backlist of R. & B. and soul classics includes the best of Ray Charles, Otis Redding, Wilson Pickett, and Aretha Franklin. Ertegun never recorded James Brown, but he has known the singer on and off for fifty years, and admires him as "one of the great geniuses of this most important kind of music." Rappers, he said, "are all James Brown freaks." (Indeed,

James Brown earns millions each year on royalties from rap samplings.) "He's got hooks that will outlive most people's compositions," Ertegun said. "Just his little hooks."

Still, the moment Ertegun heard the title "Killing Is Out, School Is In," he shook his head. "Sad thing is those songs are sure to flop," he said. "The public is not looking to take lessons." (After many delays, the song is set to be released in August on Mr. Brown's new album, "The Next Step.") In Ertegun's experience, the black public is especially tough. "A black artist cannot keep a black audience," he said. "I mean, black audiences live this music. I mean, black audiences are the ones that create what black artists do, whereas white people imitate that, and they love it forever. We have white kids imitating Tampa Red, and they're playing Big Bill Broonzy, and they're students, they're scholars, who go back and listen to the old 78-r.p.m. records and get heavily into that, like all the English rock and rollers did in the sixties. They went back to that music. But black people, they don't study that music. That's the music they invented, and they don't give a shit about it, and they don't like what their mothers like. Their mothers like Billy Eckstine; well, they laugh at Billy Eckstine."

It's true that James Brown's audiences are now predominantly white, and that he gets his most avid response in Europe and Japan. "I'm ten times bigger over there than I am over here," he told me. Of course, Ertegun said, "they're the opposite of black audiences, they're just finding out about all of this." But, here in America, "there's the real expression of black people through, you know, all the rappers," he said. "It's dirty, but it's reality. It's reality for those people who live in the condition that we have more or less put them in. They can't write songs like Cole Porter, because they don't come from a Cole Porter background. They come from a rat-infested basement place somewhere in Compton, and you know that's a different life than putting on your white tie and dancing at the Savoy."

It wasn't the Savoy, but late one night in San Francisco, after playing a show, Mr. Brown returned to the Ritz-Carlton on Nob Hill, where he was staying, and stood stock-still in the center of the lobby. By the angle of his head, you could see that he was listening, and, sure enough, in the nearly vacant bar, a trio was playing: a gray-haired man hunched over a string bass, a young goateed fellow at the grand piano, and, on a stool, in a black evening gown, a woman singing "Somewhere Over the Rainbow." "Let's get a juice or something," Mr. Brown said to his entourage, which numbered about ten that night. He led the way, attired in a dusky-maroon three-piece suit, a purple shirt, and a necktie of golden silk with a pattern of blue slashes. The musicians beamed at the sight of him, and the dozen or so remaining patrons, scattered on banquettes around the edge of the room, sat up and began poking one another and pointing. When the singer, blushing, finished her song, Mr. Brown had one of his men give each of the trio a hundred-dollar bill. The singer asked for requests, and Mr. Brown said, "Anybody here mind if I do one?"

There was no objection. He conferred briefly with the musicians, grinning and joking, looking out at the room, where the audience of twenty had now grown to twenty-five, with an additional contingent of bellhops and valet parkers standing against the back wall. "Up-tempo or slow?" he said. "Oh, I'll give it to you on the up." He started snapping his fingers, his body swayed with them, the piano and bass came in softly, and he sang, "Time after time, when we're together . . ." There was sweetness in his voice, and grit, and as always, an ache, but, most of all, pure pleasure. He clipped the phrases, and juggled some words, making the song his: "Time after time, you hear me say that I feel alone tonight . . ."

After a verse, he sidled up behind the pianist and, gently nudging him to keep playing at the low end of the keyboard, reached in to pick out a liltingly funky right-handed solo. Back at the edge of the tiny stage, he crouched into the words until, making an abrupt signal to the musicians to cut, he finished, with a soft whispered "Aowh." Then, equally softly, he spoke the word "Scream."

"Being James Brown"

Jonathan Lethem
June 29, 2006 • *Rolling Stone*

In Augusta, Georgia, in May 2005, they put up a bronze statue of James Brown, the Godfather of Soul, in the middle of Broad Street. During a visit to meet James Brown and observe him recording parts of his new album in an Augusta studio. I went and had a look at it. The James Brown

statue is an odd one in several ways. For one, it is odd to see a statue standing not on a pedestal, flat on its feet on the ground. This was done at
James Brown's request, reportedly. The premise being: man of the people.
The result, however: somewhat fake-looking statue. Another difficulty is
that the statue is grinning. Members of James Brown's band, present
while he was photographed for reference by the statue's sculptor, told me
of their attempts to get James Brown to quit smiling for the photographs.
A statue shouldn't grin, they told him. Yet James Brown refused to do
other than grin. It is the grin of a man who has succeeded, and as the proposed statue struck him as a measure of his success, he determined that it
would measure him grinning. Otherwise, the statue is admirable: flowing
bronze cape, helmetlike bronze hair perhaps not so much harder than
the actual hair it depicts, and vintage bronze microphone with its base
tipped, as if to make a kind of dance partner with James Brown, who is
not shown in a dancing pose but nonetheless appears lithe, pert, ready.
Still, as with postage stamps, statues of the living seem somehow disconcerting. And very few statues are located at quite such weighty symbolic
crossroads as this one. The statue's back is to what was in 1993 renamed
James Brown Boulevard, which cuts from Broad Street for a mile, deep
into the neighborhood where James Brown was raised from age six, by his
aunts, in a Twiggs Street house that was a den of what James Brown himself calls "gambling, moonshine liquor and prostitution." The neighborhood around Twiggs is still devastatingly sunk in poverty's ruin. The
shocking depths of deprivation from which James Brown excavated himself are still intact, frozen in time, almost like a statue. A photographer
would be hard-pressed to snap a view in this neighborhood that couldn't,
apart from the make of the cars, slip neatly into Walker Evans' portfolio of
Appalachian scenes from Let Us Now Praise Famous Men. Except, of
course, that everyone in Augusta's Appalachia is black. So, the James
Brown statue may seem to have walked on its flat bronze feet the mile
from Twiggs to Broad, to which it keeps its back, reserving its grin for the
gentlefolk on and across Broad Street, the side that gives way to the river—
the white neighborhoods to which James Brown, as a shoeshine boy, hustler, juvenile delinquent, possibly even as a teenage pimp, directed his
ambition and guile. Policemen regularly chased James Brown the length
of that mile, back toward Twiggs—he tells stories of diving into a watery
gutter, barely more than a trench, and hiding underwater with an up-
raised reed for breathing while the policemen rumbled past—and, once

the chase was over, he'd creep again toward Broad, where the lights and music were, where the action was, where Augusta's stationed soldiers with their monthly paycheck binges were to be found. Eventually, the city of Augusta jailed the teenager, sentenced him to eight-to-sixteen for four counts of breaking and entering. When he attained an early release, with the support of the family of his friend and future bandmate Bobby Byrd, it was on the condition that he never return to Augusta. Deep into the Sixties, years past "Papa's Got a Brand New Bag." James Brown had to apply for special permits to bring his band to perform in Augusta; he essentially had been exiled from the city for having the audacity to transverse that mile from Twiggs to Broad. Now his statue stands at the end of the mile, facing away. Grinning. Resolving nothing. James Brown, you see, may in fact be less a statue than any human being who ever lived. James Brown is kinetic; an idea, a problem, a genre, a concept, a method—anything, really, but a statue.

This we know: the James Brown Show begins without James Brown. James Brown, a man who is also an idea, a problem, a method, etc., will have to be invoked, summoned from some other place. The rendezvous between James Brown and his audience—you—is not a simple thing. When the opening acts are done and the waiting is over, you will first be in the hands of James Brown's band. It is the band that begins the Show. The band is there to help, to negotiate a space for you to encounter James Brown; it is there, if you will, to take you to the bridge. The band is itself the medium within which James Brown will be summoned, the terms under which he might be enticed into view.

The James Brown Band takes the form, onstage, of an animated frieze or hieroglyphic, timeless in a very slightly seedy, showbiz way but happily so, rows of men in red tuxedos, jitterbugging in lock step even as they miraculously conjure from instruments a perfect hurricane of music: a rumbling, undulating-insinuating (underneath), shimmery-peppery (up on top) braided waveform of groove. The players seem jolly and amazed witnesses to their own virtuosity. They resemble humble, gracious ushers or porters, welcoming you to the enthrallingly physical, jubilant, encompassing groove that pours out of their instruments. It's as if they were merely widening for you a portal offering entry into some new world, a world as much visual and emotional as aural—for, in truth, a first encounter with the James Brown Show can feel like a bodily passage, a deal your mind wasn't sure it was ready for your body to strike with these men and their instruments and the ludicrous, almost cruelly anticipatory drama of their attempt to beckon the star of the show into view. Yes, it's made unmistakable, in case you forgot, that this is merely a prelude, a throat-clearing, though the band has already rollicked through three or four recognizable numbers in succession; we're waiting for something. The name of the something is James Brown. You indeed fear, despite all sense, that something is somehow wrong: Perhaps he's sick or reluctant, or perhaps there's been a mistake. There is no James Brown, it was merely a rumor. Thankfully, someone has told you what to do—you chant, gladly: "James Brown! James Brown!" A natty little man with a pompadour comes onstage and with a booming, familiar voice asks you if you Are Ready for Star Time, and you find yourself confessing that you Are.

To be in the audience when James Brown commences the James Brown Show is to have felt oneself engulfed in a kind of feast of adoration and astonishment, a ritual invocation, one comparable, I'd imagine, to certain ceremonies known to the Mayan peoples, wherein a human person is radiantly costumed and then beheld in lieu of the appearance of a Sun God upon the Earth. For to see James Brown dance and sing, to see him lead his mighty band with the merest glances and tiny flickers of signal from his hands; to see him offer himself to his audience to be adored and enraptured and ravished; to watch him tremble and suffer as he tears his screams and moans of lust, glory and regret from his sweat-drenched body—and is, thereupon, in an act of seeming mercy, draped in the cape of his infirmity; to then see him recover and thrive—shrugging free of the cape—as he basks in the healing regard of an audience now melded into a single passionate body by the stroking and thrumming of his ceaseless cavalcade of impossibly danceable smash Number One hits, is not to see: It is to behold.

The James Brown Show is both an enactment—an unlikely conjuration in the present moment of an alternate reality, one that dissipates into the air and can never be recovered—and at the same time a re-enactment: the ritual celebration of an enshrined historical victory, a battle won long ago, against forces difficult to name—funklessness?—yet whose vanquishing seems to have been so utterly crucial that it requires incessant restaging in a triumphalist ceremony. The show exists on a continnum, the link between ebullient big-band "clown" jazz showmen like Cab Calloway and Louis Jordan and the pornographic parade of a full-bore Prince concert. It is a glimpse of another world, even if only one being routinely dwells there, and his name is James Brown. To have glimpsed him there, dwelling in his world, is a privilege. James Brown is not a statue, no. But the James Brown Show is a monument, one unveiled at select intervals.

James Brown lives just outside of Augusta, so while he is recording an album, he sleeps at home. He frequently exhorts the members of his band to buy homes in Augusta, which they mostly refuse to do. Instead, they stay at the Ramada Inn. James Brown, when he is at home, routinely stays up all night watching the news, and watching old western movies — nothing but westerns. He gets up late. For this reason, a day in the recording studio with James Brown, like the James Brown Show, begins without James Brown.

Instead, I find myself in the company of James Brown's band and his longtime personal manager, Charles Bobbit, approximately fourteen people whom I will soon in varying degrees get to know quite well but whom for now treat me genially, skeptically, shyly but mostly obliviously. They've got work to do. They're working on the new James Brown record. At the moment they're laying down a track without him, because James Brown asked them to, and because since they're waiting around, they might as well do something — though they do this with a degree of helpless certainty that they are wasting their time. It is nearly always a useless occupation, if you are James Brown's band, to lay down a track while he is not present. Yet the band members do it a lot, wasting time in this way, because their time is not their own. So they record. Today's effort is a version of "Hold On, I'm A-Comin'," the classic Sam and Dave song.

The setting is a pleasant modern recording studio in a bland corner of Augusta's suburbs, far from where the statue resides. The band occupies a large room, high-ceilinged, padded in black, with a soundproof-windowed booth for the drummer's kit and folding chairs in a loose circle for the band, plus innumerable microphones and cables and amplifiers and pick-ups running across the floor. On the other side of a large window from this large chamber is a room full of control panels, operated by an incredibly patient man named Howard. It is into this room that James Brown and the band will intermittently retreat in order to listen to playback, to consider what they've recorded. Down the hall from these two rooms is a tiny suite with a kitchen (unused) and a dining room with a table that seats seven or eight at a time (used constantly, for eating takeout).

The band is three guitarists and one bassist and three horn players and two percussionists—a drummer in the soundproof booth and a conga player in the central room. They're led by Hollie Farris, a trim, fiftyish, white trumpeter with a blond mustache and the gentle, acutely Midwestern demeanor of an accountant or middle manager, yet with the enduring humor of a lifelong sideman; a hipster's tolerance. Hollie now pushes the younger guitarists as they hone the changes in "Hold On, I'm A-Comin'." Howard is recording the whole band simultaneously; this method of recording "live in the studio" is no longer how things are generally done. Hollie also sings to mark the vocal line, in a faint but endearing voice.

One of the young guitarists cheating slightly on the "live in the studio" echos, asks to be allowed to punch in his guitar solo. This is Damon Wood: thirtysomething, also blond, with long hair and a neat goatee. Damon, explaining why he screwed up the solo, teases Hollie for his singing: "I can't hear myself with Engelbert Humperdinck over there." Howard rewinds the tape and Damon reworks the solo, then endears himself to me with a fannish quiz for the other guitarists—Keith Jenkins, another white guy, but clean-cut, and Daryl Brown, a light-skinned, roly-poly black man who turns out to be James Brown's son. "What classic funk song am I quoting in this solo?" Damon asks. Nobody can name it, not that they seem to be trying too hard. "'Lady Marmalade.'" Damon says.

"Well," says Hollie, speaking of the track, "we got one for him to come in and say, 'That's terrible.'"

Keith, a young man with a trace of disobedience in his eyes, asks if they're going to put the horns on the track. Hollie shakes his head. "He might be less inclined to throw it out," Keith suggests. "Give it that big sound. If all he hears are those guitars, he'll start picking it apart."

Hollie offers a wry smile. He doesn't want to add the horns. Hollie, I'll learn, has been James Brown's bandleader and arranger on and off since the early Eighties.

It is at that moment that everything changes. Mr. Bobbit explains: "Mr. Brown is here."

When James Brown enters the recording studio, the recording studio becomes a stage. It is not merely that attention quickens in any room this human being inhabits. The phenomenon is more akin to a kind of grade-school physics experiment: Lines of force are suddenly visible in the air, rearranged, oriented. The band, the hangers-on, the very oxygen, every

trace particle is charged in its relation to the gravitational field of James
Brown. We're all waiting for something to happen, and that waiting is itself
a kind of story, an emotional dynamic: We need something from this man,
and he is likely to demand something of us, something we're uncertain we
can fully deliver. The drama here is not, as in the James Brown Show, en-
acted in musical terms. Now it is a psychodrama, a theater of human behavior, one full of Beckett or Pinter pauses.

James Brown is dressed as if for a show, in a purple three-piece suit
and red shirt, highly polished shoes, cuff links and his impeccably coiffed
helmet of hair. When we're introduced, I spend a long moment trying to
conjugate the reality of James Brown's face, one I've contemplated as an
album-cover totem since I was thirteen or fourteen: that impossible slant
of jaw and cheekbone, that Pop Art slash of teeth, the unmistakable rage
of impatience lurking in the eyes. It's a face drawn by Jack Kirby or Mil-
ton Caniff, that's for sure, a visage engineered for maximum impact at
great distances, from back rows of auditoriums. I find it, truthfully, terrifying to have that face examining mine in return, though fear is alleviated
by the rapidity of the process: James Brown seems to have finished de-
vouring the whole prospect of me by the time our brief handshake is concluded.

I'm also struck by the almost extraterrestrial quality of otherness incar-
nated in this human being. James Brown is, by his own count, seventy-two
years old. Biographers have suggested that three or four years ought to be
added to that total. It's also possible that given the circumstances of his
birth, in a shack in the woods outside Barnwell, South Carolina, in an environment of poverty and exile so profound as to be almost unimaginable,
James Brown has no idea how old he is. No matter: He's in his midseventies, yet, encountering him now in person, it occurs to me that James
Brown is kept under wraps for so long at the outset of his own show, and is
viewed primarily at a distance, or mediated through recordings or films, in
order to buffer the unprepared spectator from the awesome strangeness
and intensity of his person. He simply has more energy, is vibrating at a different rate, than anyone I've ever met, young or old. With every preparation I've made, he's still terrifying.

James Brown sits, gesturing with his hand: It's time for playback. Mr.
Brown and Mr. Bobbit sit in the two comfortable leather chairs, while the
band members are bunched around the room, either seated in folding
metal chairs or on their feet.

We listen, twice, to the take of "Hold On, I'm A-Comin'." James Brown lowers his head and closes his eyes. We're all completely silent. At last he mumbles faint praise: "Pretty good. Pretty good." Then, into the recording room. James Brown takes his place behind the mike, facing the band. We dwell now in an atmosphere of immanence, of ceremony, so tangible it's almost oppressive. James Brown is still contained within himself, muttering inaudibly, scratching his chin, barely coming out of himself. Abruptly, he turns to me.

"You're very lucky. Mr. ROLLING STONE. I don't ordinarily let anyone sit in on a session."

"I feel lucky," I say.

Fussing his way into place, James Brown decides he doesn't like the microphone. "I want one with no felt on it. Get me a cheap mike. I made all those hits on a cheap mike." The mike is swapped. He's still irked, turgid, turned inward. "Are we recording this?" he asks. The answer comes back: Yes. "The one we throw out will be the best one," he admonishes, vaguely.

Now he explains to the band that it's not going to bother with the track it recorded before he arrived. Go figure: Hollie was right. "Sounds good," James Brown says, "but it sounds canned. We got to get some James Brown in there." Here it is, the crux of the matter: He wasn't in the room; ipso facto, it isn't James Brown music. The problem is fundamentally one of ontology: In order for James Brown to occur, you need to be James Brown.

He begins reminiscing about a rehearsal they enjoyed the day before, in the practice space at the Ramada. The Ramada's room provided a sound James Brown liked, and he encourages his band to believe they'll recapture it today: "Gonna bring that room in here."

Now that the gears are oiled, a constant stream of remarks and asides flows from James Brown's mouth. Many of these consist of basic statements of policy in regard to the matter of being James Brown, particularly in relationship to his band: "Be mean, but be the best." These statements mingle exhortations to excellence with justifications for his own treatment of the men he calls, alternately, "the cats" and "my family." Though discipline is his law, strife is not only likely but essential: "Any time a cat becomes a nuisance, that's the cat I'm gonna want." The matter of the rejected track is still on his mind: "Don't mean to degrade nobody. People do something they think is good. But you're gonna hear the difference. Get that hard sound." Frequently he dwells on the nature of the sound of which he is forever in pursuit: "Hard. Flat. Flat." One feels James Brown is forever chasing something, a pure hard-flat-jazz-funk he heard once in his dreams, and toward which all subsequent efforts have been pointed. This in turn leads to a reminiscence about Grover Washington Jr., who, apparently, recently presented James Brown with a track James Brown didn't wish to sing on. "He should go play smooth jazz. We got something else going. James Brown jazz. Nothing smooth about it. If it gets smooth, we gonna make it not smooth." Still musing on Grover Washington Jr.'s failings, he blurts, "Just jive." Then corrects himself, looking at me: "Just things. Instead of people. Understand?"

Throughout these ruminations, the members of James Brown's band stand at readiness, their fingers on strings or mouths a few short inches from reeds and mouthpieces, in complete silence, only sometimes nodding to acknowledge a remark of particular emphasis. A given monologue may persist for an hour, no matter: At the slightest drop of a hand signal, these players are expected to be ready. There's nothing new in this. The Hardest-Working Man in Show Business is one of the legendary hard-asses: His bands have always been the Hardest-Worked Men in Show Business, the longest-rehearsed, the most fiercely disciplined, the most worn-out and abused. Fuck-ups, I'll learn, will be cold-shouldered, possibly punished with small monetary fines, occasionally humiliated by a tirade. These men have been systematically indoctrinated into what begins to seem to me less even a military- or cult-style obedience than it is a purely Pavlovian situation, one of reaction and survival, of instincts groomed and curtailed. Their motives for remaining in such a situation? That, I'll need more time to study.

"I'm an old man," James Brown says. "All I can do is love everybody. But I'm still going to be a tough boss. I'm still going to give them hell. I got a family here. I tried to meet everybody's parents." At this, he suddenly squints at Damon, the guitarist, and says, "I don't know your people." Permission has apparently been granted to reply, and Damon corrects him. "Yes, you met them in Las Vegas. Just briefly." Then James Brown points to his son, saying cryptically, "I don't know where this cat's coming from." Daryl dares a joke (which it dimly occurs to me was perhaps the point): "But you do know my people."

"That's what I'm talking about," says James Brown, irritably. "Love." He poses a question, then answers it: "You go to the blood bank, what do you want? Human blood. Not baboon."

Throughout the afternoon, even as the band begins to record, these ruminations will continue, as though James Brown's mind is on perma-nent shuffle. Sometimes the subject is the nature of his art. "Jazz," he states simply at one point. Or he'll segue into a discourse on his relation-ship to hip-hop: "I'm the most sampled and stolen. What's mine is mine, and what's yours is mine, too." At this, the band laughs. "I got a song about that," he tells me. "But I'm never gonna release it. Don't want a war with the rappers. If it wasn't good, they wouldn't steal it." Thinking of his influ-ence on contemporary music, he mentions a song by Alicia Keys with a suspicious riff: "Sometimes you find yourself meeting yourself." Yet he's eager to make me know he's not slagging Keys: "I don't want to scrape no-body." Later, in a moment of seeming insecurity, dissatisfied with some-thing in his own performance, he blurts, "The minute they put up that statue I was in trouble."

Much of the afternoon is spent working on an arrangement of a medley comprising another Sam and Dave song, "Soul Man," and one of James Brown's own most irresistible and enduring classics of the early Seventies, "Soul Power." James Brown tinkers with the guitars, indicating the desired tones by wailing in imitation of a guitar, as well as by issuing what sound like expert commands: "Diminish. Raise nine. Flatten it." Of Damon's solo, he requests, "Go psychedelic." It seems to be the nature of the guitarists—Keith, Damon and Daryl—that they are the center of the band's sound but also the source of considerable problems.

A horn player—a large, slightly hound-doggy saxophonist named Jeff Watkins—interjects. Raising his hand like a schoolboy, he suggests, "They might have it right, sir. They just didn't play it with conviction." To the gui-tarists, Jeff says, ever so gently, "Play it like you mean it."

They do, and James Brown listens, and is persuaded.

"I'm wrong," the Godfather says, marveling. "Play it like you mean it—I like that, Jeff." James Brown's deadpan is perfect: It is as if he's never heard that particular phrase before.

Now he coaches his bass player, an aging, willowy, enigmatically silent black man named Fred Thomas, on the bass line: "Ding-dong, ding-dong." Again, he emphasizes: "Flat. Flat. Hard." Fred Thomas does his best to comply, though I can't hear any difference. James Brown turns to me, urgently, and introduces me to Thomas. "It's all about 'Sex Ma-chine,'" he says. "This man's on more hits than any other bass player in history." I nod. Of course, it will later occur to me that one of the most cel-ebrated partnerships in James Brown's career was with the future

Parliament-Funkadelic bassist Bootsy Collins—and anybody who cares at all about such things can tell you that Bootsy was the bass player on "Sex Machine." Fred Thomas was, in fact, Bootsy's replacement, which is to say he's been in the band since sometime in 1971. Good enough. But in this matter we've at least briefly entered what I will come to call the James Brown Zone of Confusion: James Brown now puts his arm around Fred Thomas. "We're both cancer survivors," he tells me gravely.

Suddenly, James Brown is possessed by an instant of Kabuki insecurity: "I'm recording myself out of a group." This brings a spontaneous response from several players, a collective murmur of sympathy and allegiance, most audibly saxophonist Jeff's "We're not going anywhere, sir." Reassured, James Brown paradoxically regales the band with another example of his imperious command, telling the story of a drummer, a man named Nat Kendrick, who left the room to go to the bathroom during the recording of "Night Train." James Brown, too impatient to wait, played the drum part himself, and the recording was completed by the time Nat Kendrick returned. "Go to the bathroom, you might not have a job."

The two-inch tape is now in place, and James Brown and his band attack "Soul Man / Soul Power" once again. "It's about to be as good as it was yesterday," he says, reminding them again of the Ramada rehearsal. "We're not recording, we're just having fun." Indeed, everything suddenly seems to come together. "Soul Power" is an unbearably funky groove when taken up, as it is now, by a James Brown who sings it as though he's never heard it before, with crazy urgency and rhythmic guile, his voice hopped up on the crest of the music like a surfer riding a curl. In a vocal improvisation, James Brown shouts in Gatling-gun time with the drums: "Food stamps! Welfare!"

This take sounds better by far than anything that's gone before it, and James Brown, seated on his stool at the microphone, looks half a century younger now. At the finish, he rushes from his stool directly to where I sit and slaps me on my knee. "That was deep, Mr. ROLLING STONE!" he exclaims, then dashes from the room. The band exhales a burst of withheld laughter the moment he's through the door. "Food stamps!" several of them cry out. "Never heard that before." His son Daryl says, "Damn, I almost dropped my guitar when he said that." They seem genuinely thrilled and delighted now to have me here as a witness and go rollicking out the door, into the room where James Brown, ever impatient, is already preparing to listen to playback. They've done it, cut a classic James Brown funk jam! Never mind that it is a classic that James Brown already cut in 1971!

The laughter and conversation cease, as Howard is commanded to roll the tape. Midway through the first time he's heard the tape, James Brown's head sinks in weary dissatisfaction: Something's not right. When it ends, after a single beat of total silence, James Brown says soberly, "Let's do it again, a little slower." And so the band trudges back in, in dour, obedient silence.

During the playback session, guitarist Keith leans in and whispers to me, "You've got to tell the truth about what goes on here. Nobody has any idea." I widen my eyes, sympathetic to his request. But what exactly does he mean?

Someday, someone will write a great biography of James Brown. It will, by necessity, though, be more than a biography. It will be a history of a half-century of the contradictions and tragedies embodied in the fate of African-Americans in the New World; it will be a parable, even, of the contradictions of the individual in the capitalist society, portentous as that may sound. For James Brown is both a willing and conscious embodiment of his race, of its strivings toward self-respect in a racist world, and a consummate self-made man, an entrepreneur of the impossible. This is a man who, out of that shack in the woods of South Carolina and that whorehouse on Twiggs, mined for himself a career and a fortune and a legacy and a statue; who owned an airplane; who has employed hundreds; whose band begat many famous and lucrative careers; whose samples provided, truly, the foundation for hip-hop; who had his photograph taken with presidents and whose endorsement was eagerly boasted of, first by Hubert Humphrey, then Richard Nixon; who was credited with single-handedly keeping the city of Boston calm in the twenty-four hours after the assassination of Martin Luther King Jr.; a man who owned radio stations, controlling the very means of control in his industry; and who did all of this despite the fact that no likelihood except desolation, poverty and incarceration may seem to have existed.

He's also a martyr to those contradictions. That James Brown should succeed so absolutely and fail so utterly is the mystery. For no matter his accomplishment and the will that drove it, he has no fortune. No plane. No radio stations. The ranch home that he so proudly bought for himself in a mostly white suburb of Augusta was claimed by the IRS in lieu of back taxes. Unlike those whose fame and money insulate them from scandal, James Brown has been beset: divorces, 911 calls, high-speed road chases ending in ludicrous arrests and jail sentences. This great exponent of black pride, of never dropping out of school, of making something of yourself, found his way, relatively late in life, to the illegal drugs not of glamour and decadence but those of dereliction and street life, like PCP. With their help, he nearly destroyed his reputation.

The shadow of his abuse of musicians and wives, disturbing as it may be, is covered in the larger shadow of his self-abuse, his torment and unrest, little as James Brown would ever admit to anything but the brash and single-minded confidence and pride he wishes to display. It is as though the cape act is a rehearsal onstage of the succor James Brown could never accept in his real life. It is as though, having come from being dressed in potato sacks for grade school and in the drab uniform of a prisoner to being the most spectacularly garbed individual this side of Beau Brummell or Liberace, James Brown found himself compelled also to be the Emperor With No Clothes. What his peculiar nakedness reveals is the full range of the torment of African-American identity. Oblivious to racism, he was also its utter victim; contemptuous of drugs, he was at their mercy. And the exposure of his bullying abuse of women might seem to have made squalid hypocrisy of his calls for universal love and self-respect.

For my part as a witness, if I could convey only one thing about James Brown it would be this: James Brown is, like Billy Pilgrim in Kurt Vonnegut's *Slaughterhouse-Five*, a man unstuck in time. He's a time traveler, but unlike the HG Wells–ian variety, he lacks any control over his migrations in time, which also seem to be circumscribed to the period of his own allotted lifespan. Indeed, it may be the case that James Brown is often confused as to what moment in time he occupies at any given moment.

Practically, this means two things. It means that sometime around 1958—approximately the year he began voyaging in time, if my theory is correct—James Brown began browsing through the decades ahead—Sixties, Seventies, Eighties and perhaps even into the Nineties—and saw, or, more correctly, heard, the future of music. This, if my theory is correct, explains the stubbornly revolutionary cast of his musical efforts from that time on, the way he single-handedly seemed to be trying to impart an epiphany to which only he had easy access, an epiphany to do with rhythm, and with the kinetic possibilities inherent but to that point barely noticed in the R&B and soul music around him. From the moment of "Night Train"—the track, oddly enough, during which Nat Kendrick went to the bathroom and James Brown had to play drums himself—onward, through one radically innovative track after another—"Out of Sight," "I Got You," "Papa's Got a Brand New Bag," "Cold Sweat," etc.—James Brown seemed less a musician with an imperative either to entertain or to express his own emotional reality than one driven to push his musicians and listeners to the verge of a sonic idea, and then past that verge, until the moment when he became, more or less officially, the inventor of an entire genre of music called funk: "Sex Machine," "Super Bad," "Hot Pants," etc. That sonic idea has never been better expressed than by critic Robert Palmer: "The rhythmic elements became the song. . . . Brown and his musicians began to treat every instrument and voice in the group as if it were a drum. The horns played single-note bursts that were often sprung against the downbeats. The bass lines were broken into choppy two- or three-note patterns. . . . Brown's rhythm guitarist choked his guitar strings against the instrument's neck so hard that his playing began to sound like a jagged tin can being scraped with a pocket knife." Another way of thinking about this: James Brown seemed to hear in the interstices of soul and rhythm & blues—in the barked or howled vocal asides, in the brief single-chord jamming on the outros, in the drum breaks and guitar vamps—a potential for discarding the whole of the remainder of the music in favor of a radical expansion of these interstitial moments, these transitional glimpses of rhythm and fervor. James Brown was like a filmmaker who gets interested in the background scenery and fires the screenwriter and actors, except that instead of ending up with experimental films nobody wanted to watch, he forged a style of music so beguilingly futuristic that it made everything else—melody, lyrics, verse-chorus-verse—sound antique.

This time-traveler theory would best explain what is hardest to explain about James Brown, especially to younger listeners who live so entirely in a sonic world of James Brown's creation: that he made it all sound this way. That it sounded different before him. This time-traveler theory would explain, too, how in 1973, right at the moment when it might have seemed that the times had caught up, at last, with James Brown's sonic idea, that the torch of funk had been taken up and his precognitive capacities therefore exhausted, James Brown recorded a song, called "The Payback," that abruptly predicts the aural and social ambience of late-1980s gangsta rap.

My theory also explains the opposite phenomenon, the one I so frequently witnessed in Augusta. If the man was able to see today from the distance of 1958, he's also prone to reliving 1958—and 1967, and 1971, and 1985—now that 2006 has finally come around. We all dwell in the world James Brown saw so completely before we came along into it; James Brown, in turn, hasn't totally joined us here in the future he made. That's why it all remains so startlingly new to him; why, during one playback session, he turned to Mr. Bobbit and said, "Can I scream and moan? I sound so good, I want to kiss myself!" He spoke the phrase as if for the first time, and that may be because for him it was essentially occurring to him for the first time, or, rather, that there is no first time: All his moments are one. James Brown, in this view, is always conceiving the idea of being James Brown, as if nobody, including himself, had thought of it until just now. At any given moment James Brown is presently reinventing funk.

This theory also neatly explains what I call the James Brown Zone of Confusion: Fred Thomas as the bass player on "Sex Machine," and so on. It's hard, for a man of James Brown's helplessly visionary tendencies, to know what happened today, yesterday or, indeed, tomorrow. All accounts are, therefore, highly suspect. Nat Kendrick may in fact have gone to the bathroom during the recording of "Think" or "I'll Go Crazy." Nat Kendrick may not, indeed, have gone to the bathroom yet.

The faster James Brown thinks, the more fiercely his hipster's vernacular impacts upon itself, and the faster he talks, the more his dentures slip. So, though transcribing James Brown's monologues as they occur is my goal, much of what he says is, to my ears, total gibberish. As today's session begins, James Brown is recalling members of his band who've passed. "Jimmy Nolen gone. What about the tall cat?" Hollie, apparently, knows who he means by "the tall cat," and replies, "Coleman? He's alive." This leads James Brown into the subject of health, primarily digestive health. He speaks of dysentery while on tour in third-world countries: "Doing number one and number two at the same time" and exhorts the band: "Maintain yourself." To me: "Olive oil. I always tell them, 'Bring olive oil on the road.'" I don't ask what the olive oil is for. This reminds James Brown of the dangers of the road, generally, especially of exotic locations, which he begins to reel off: "Jakarta. Cameroon. Peru." He recalls, "We were in communist Africa. . . . At the end of the show there were baskets of money . . . protected by machine guns, though. Got confiscated for the government." He recalls the Zairian dictator Mobutu Sese Seko attempting to keep him and his band from departing when George Foreman's injury delayed the Foreman-Ali boxing match: "We got out. We got paid. One hundred grand." James Brown seems torn between bragging of munificence—painting himself an "ambassador to the world" who paid his own way to Vietnam to entertain the troops—and bragging of his shrewdness in always getting paid in cash, even in circumstances of maximum corruption and intrigue: promoters dying mysteriously, funds shifted through Brussels.

Shrewdness wins, for the moment, as he switches to tales of his gambling prowess, though he seems initially most keen on Mr. Bobbit's confirming a time when he came within a digit of winning a million-dollar lottery. "Yes, sir, you almost hit that pot," agrees Bobbit. James Brown then tells of playing craps on the road. "I won enough from the Moonglows to buy myself a Cadillac. Them cats was so mad they stole my shoes. Wilson Pickett, all these guys, I look so clean, they don't think I can play. I was a street man even though I had a suit on." But his stake in being thought of as the luckiest man alive is compromised by an eagerness to divulge his secret: "shaved dice," which always came up the way he wanted them to. Later this day, I ask several members of the band whether James Brown is babbling for my benefit. Not at all, they explain. "He's making us ready for the road," Damon tells me, reminding me that on Monday, James Brown and his band are heading to Europe for a month of shows. "He knows it's going to be hard. He wants us to remember we're a family."

When, what seems hours later, work at last begins for the day, it will be on two different fronts. First, James Brown records a ballad that trumpeter and arranger Hollie has written and arranged in his off-hours. The ballad, it turns out, has been lurking in the background for a while, with Mr. Bobbit and several band members gently inducing James Brown to give it a chance to be heard. Today, James Brown has—impetuously, suddenly—decided to make use of it. Hollie, given this chance, hurriedly transposes the changes for the guitarists and hands out sheet music. The simple ballad is swiftly recorded.

James Brown then goes into a small booth, dons a pair of headphones and, in the space of about fifteen minutes, bashes his way through a vocal track on the second take. Audibly, James Brown is inventing the melody and arriving at decisions about deviations from that melody (syllables to emphasize, words to whisper or moan or shout, vowel sounds to repeat or stretch) simultaneously, as he goes along. With uncanny instincts married to outlandish impatience, he is able to produce a result not wholly unlistenable. Understand: This is a matter of genius but an utterly wasteful sort of genius, and after we listen to the playback, and James Brown is out of range of the band's talk, Hollie and Keith agree that if James Brown were to regard the track he just recorded as a beginning—as a guide vocal to study and refine in some later vocal take—they might really have something. But they also seem resigned to the fact that James Brown considers his work on the track complete.

Next, James Brown writes a lyric, to record over a long, rambling blues-funk track titled "Message to the World." For anyone who has ever wondered how James Brown writes a song, I have a sort of answer for you. First: He borrows Mr. Bobbit's bifocals. James Brown doesn't have glasses of his own, or left them at home, or something. Second: He borrows a pencil. Third: He sits, and writes, for about fifteen minutes. Then he puts himself behind the microphone. The result is a cascading rant not completely unlike his spoken monologues. Impossible to paraphrase, it meanders over subjects as disparate as his four marriages, Charles Barkley, Al Jarreau, a mixture of Georgia and Carolina identities he calls "Georgia-lina," the fact that he still knows Maceo Parker and that Fred Wesley doesn't live very far away, either, Mr. Bobbit's superiority to him as a checkers player, the fact that he believes himself to have both Asian and Native American ancestry, and, most crucially, his appetite for corn on the cob and its role in his health: "I like corn, that's a regular thing with me. Gonna live a long time, live a little longer."

Afterward, we gather in our usual places, for playback. Late in the eleven-minute song, James Brown issues a universal religious salute: "Salaam-aleikum-may-peace-be-unto-you, brother. . . . Believe in the Supreme Being!" As these words resound, James Brown glances at me and then abruptly commands Howard to roll the tape back to that point: There's something he wishes to punch in on the vocal. Hustling into the booth, when the tape arrives at the brief pause between "brother" and "believe," James Brown now wedges in a brief but hearty "shalom!" Re-emerging, he points at me and winks. "Shalom, Mr. ROLLING STONE!" James Brown has pegged me as Jewish. So much for being invisible in this place. He has apparently tampered with the spontaneity of his own vocal, merely in order to appease what he imagines are my religious urgencies.

Indeed, he now fixates on me, for a short while. During this same playback session, while deeply engaged in transcribing what I've heard around me, my head ducked to the screen of my Powerbook, I notice that James Brown has begun singing, a cappella, a portion of the song "Papa Was a Rolling Stone." I continue typing, even transcribing the lyrics of the song

as he sings them: "Papa was a rolling stone / Wherever he laid his hat was
his home. . . ." Odd, I think: This isn't a James Brown song. Then I hear
the band's laughter and look up. James Brown is singing it directly at me,
trying to gain my attention.

"Oh," I say, red-faced, as I look up at him. "Sorry. I forgot my new name."

"That's all right, Mr. ROLLING STONE," says James Brown. "I was just
missing you."

Roosevelt Johnson, known always as R.J., sits with me and explains his
role, a role he's occupied since he was nine, forty-two years ago: "Hold the
coat." Excuse me? "Hold the coat, hold the coat." R.J. expands, then, on
the basic principle of life in the James Brown entourage: You do one thing,
you do it right and you do it forever. It is the nature of traveling with James
Brown that everyone treats him like a god: "The people that show up in
every city, they all fall back into their old jobs, like they never stopped. The
doormen stand by the door, and hairdressers start dressing his hair." R.J. is
being modest, since his responsibilities have grown to a performing role, as
the second voice in a variety of James Brown's call-and-response numbers
("Soul Power," "Make It Funky," "Get Up, Get Into It, Get Involved"), replacing the legendary founding member of the Famous Flames—James
Brown's first band—Bobby Byrd. R.J. sounds uncannily like Byrd when he
sings—or "raps"—Byrd's parts in the classic songs, and in concert R.J.'s
ebullient turns often draw some of the mightiest cheers from the crowd,
who nonetheless can have no idea who he is. Yet for him, his life is defined
by his offstage work: "Someday I'm going to write a book about my life,
called *Holding the Coat*."

(Hearing this, Cynthia Moore, one member of James Brown's backing
singers, the Bitter Sweets, interrupts: "My book's gonna be called *Take
Me to the Bridge, I Want to Jump Off*.")

The greatest exemplar of the Entourage phenomenon is, of course,
Danny Ray, the little man with the pompadour and the voice familiar from
so many decades of live introductions. Danny, from Birmingham, Alabama, joined James Brown in the Fifties, when they met at the Apollo
Theater. He joined as a valet. And, though he has become nearly as recognizable a voice as James Brown himself, he is still a valet; indeed, his concern for the band's clothes obsesses Danny: He is the human incarnation
of James Brown's lifelong concern with being immaculately dressed. Valet,
and master of ceremonies, Danny Ray is also the proprietor of "the cape

routine"—i.e., he comes onstage to settle the cape over James Brown's shoulders when he collapses onstage, and he receives the cape and takes it away when James Brown has shrugged free of it.

R.J. and Danny Ray briefly allude to another responsibility that tends to devolve to valets: wrangling James Brown's irate girlfriends. Danny Ray cites a few vivid episodes: "Candace. Lisa. Heather. The one from Las Vegas that came to his house carrying a .357. She said, 'What is your intention?'" It is R.J. who finishes the story, laughing: "Brown said, 'My intention is for you to get on the plane, go back to Las Vegas. Get out of here.'"

Keith and Damon, the guitarists, ask me if I'd care to join them at a bar. We arrange to meet in Jeff the saxophonist's room at the Ramada. It is here that I learn Jeff's nickname: Sizzler. Sizzler is named for how there's always something aromatic burning in his room—a candle, incense or "something else." And, sure enough, Jeff's room is a haze when I arrive to find Keith and Damon there, along with Hollie, drummer Robert "Mousey" Thompson and George "Spike" Nealy, the second percussionist. Here, safely distant from either James Brown's or Mr. Bobbit's ears, I'm regaled with the affectionate and mocking grievances of a lifer in James Brown's band. I think I'm beginning to understand what story it is Keith feels has never been told: the glorious absurdity of the band's servitude.

"We're supposed to follow these hand signals," Keith explains. "We've got to watch him every minute, you never know when he's going to change something up. But his hand is like an eagle's claw—he'll point with a curved finger, and it's like, 'Do you mean me, or him? Because you're looking at me but you're pointing at him.'"

They take turns imitating James Brown's infuriating mimed commands to them during live shows. "It's like rock-paper-scissors," jokes Damon. Each of the band members, I gradually learn, has a spot-on James Brown impression available. Each has memorized favorite James Brown non sequiturs: "Sixteen of the American presidents were black," or the time he asked an audience for thirty seconds of silence for a fallen celebrity he called "John F.K." To these men, James Brown is both their idol and their jester, their tyrannical father and ludicrous child.

Jeff tells me of going on the *David Letterman* show for a three-minute spot. "We didn't discuss what we were doing until we got out there. Soundchecked a totally different song. I didn't know I was doing a solo on TV until he waved me out front."

Hollie, the longest-enduring among them there, says, "I don't think there's another band on the planet that can do what we do."

Damon adds, "I like to call it Masters of the Impossible."

Yet they hurry to make me understand their vast reverence and devotion—for you see, they're also the luckiest musicians on earth. Keith tells me, "Brown told us, 'You got it made. You cats are lucky, you're made now.' Eleven years later, I get it. The man hasn't had a hit for twenty years, but we'll work forever. We're going to the Hollywood Bowl, Buckingham Palace, the Apollo Theater, it never stops. We could work for a hundred years. You play with someone else, you might have two good years, then sit for two years, wondering if anything's ever going to happen again. With James Brown, you're always working. Because he's James Brown. It's like we're up there with Bugs Bunny, Mickey Mouse. There's no other comparison."

"Listen," says Jeff. "There's something we want you to hear." I've been corralled into Jeff's room for a purpose: the unveiling of the secret recordings of James Brown's band. The frustration these musicians feel at having no voice in composition or arrangement has taken its toll, a certain despair about the prospects for the present recording sessions. James Brown, they complain, just won't let his band help him. Yet these frustrations have, in turn, found an outlet.

Sizzler fires up his iTunes, connected to a fair pair of desktop speakers, and there, seated on a Ramada bedspread, I'm treated to an audio sample of What Could Be, if only James Brown would allow it. The songs are original funk tunes, composed variously by Damon, Mousey, Jeff and Hollie, and recorded, under cover of darkness, in hotel rooms while the band travels, or while they assemble, as now, for official sessions. The songs are tight, catchy, propulsive numbers, each with one foot in Seventies funk and another in a more contemporary style. They have the added benefit of being something new.

No one has dared tell James Brown that this music exists. He might fire them if he knew. In this, the band's wishful thinking tangles with its sense of protectiveness of the boss's feelings. For James Brown, it seems, has had so many important musicians outgrow his band—Bootsy, Maceo, Pee Wee Ellis and Fred Wesley—that his passion for control has outstripped his curiosity about what his present roster might have to offer him. Anyone showing signs of a life of their own, musical or otherwise, tends to be the target of elaborate and vindictive humiliations. "It's abandonment issues," says

Keith. "Has to do with being abandoned by his parents." James Brown will deliberately schedule mandatory rehearsals to clash with weddings or funerals. Keith tells me, "At the Apollo, the first time my wife was going to see me play, he sat me down offstage, didn't let me go on."

The funniest of the secret recordings is a song called "Pimp Danny," which, unlike the others, consists not only of live instruments played directly into laptop computers but of samples of old James Brown records. By pasting together various introductions to shows over the years, the band has created a track where Danny Ray takes the role of lead vocalist, saying things like, "I like to feel dynamite, I like to feel out of sight! I like to feel sexy-sexy-sexy!" "Pimp Danny" also samples the voice of Bobby Byrd and a drumbeat from Clyde Stubblefield, one of the great drummers from James Brown's Sixties band. In this way, "Pimp Danny" is not only a celebration of Danny Ray, who seems in many ways the band's talisman-in-servitude, but a kind of yearning conflation of the legendary past eras of the band with its present incarnation. And there's a plan: Fred Wesley, James Brown's trombonist and bandleader throughout the Sixties and Seventies, has promised to come to the studio tomorrow to record a few trombone solos, for old times' sake. (Everyone comes back.) The band wants to try to sneak Wesley back to the Ramada so he can add his horn to "Pimp Danny."

Many sizzles later, Keith and Damon and I have made it to the Soul Bar, where loud rap is on the soundtrack, which spurs a brief rhapsody from Keith: "You hear a Chuck Berry song, a Jerry Lee Lewis song, it's an oldie. It's got no relevance. James Brown comes on, it's got relevance. Some rapper has a hit, it's got a little piece of him in it. He hears himself everywhere. His relevance sustains him." Keith and Damon go on some more about what they'd do if only they could seize control of the sessions. "James Brown should go out like Johnny Cash did," they say. Keith says, "We're like a blade of grass trying to push up through the concrete."

Now, to note that James Brown is self-centered or egotistical or pleased with himself is hardly an insight worth troubling over. That James "I want to kiss myself" Brown dabbles in self-adulation hardly makes him unique in the history of art. James Brown's subjugation of his various bands' musical ambitions to his own ego, to his all-encompassing need to claim as entirely an extension of his own genius every riff invented by anyone within his orbit, is, needless to say, a cause of much dispute. To put it simply: The

James Brown sound, its historic sequence of innovations, depends on a whole series of collaborators and contributors, none of whom have been adequately acknowledged or compensated. Yet the more I contemplated the band's odd solicitude toward James Brown's ogreish demands, the more completely I became persuaded that James Brown is re-enacting an elemental trauma: the abandonment by his parents into a world of almost feral instability and terror. One doesn't have to look far. His own 1986 autobiography, *James Brown*, bears the dedication "For the child deprived of being able to grow up and say 'Momma' and 'Daddy' and have both of them come put their arms around him."

This is a child who ate "salad we found in the woods" in his first years, a child who was sent home from school—in the rural South—for "insufficient clothes" (i.e., potato sacks). This is a teenager who was nearly electrocuted by a pair of white men who whimsically invited him to touch a car battery they were fooling with. This is a man who, during his incarceration in the 1980s, long after he'd drowned his nightmare of "insufficient clothes" in velvet and fur and leather and jeweled cuff links, was found to be hiding tens of thousands of dollars in cash in his prison cell, an expression of a certainty that society was merely a thin fiction covering a harsh jungle of desolation and violence, and if James Brown wasn't looking out for James Brown, no one was.

His, then, is a solipsism born of necessity. When it most mattered, there was nobody to jump up and kiss James Brown except himself. His "family" is therefore a trickle-down structure, practically a musical Ponzi scheme, and anyone willing to give him his best is going to be taken for as long a ride as he can take him on. Gamble with James Brown, and he will throw the shaved dice, until, like the Moonglows and Wilson Pickett, you are forced to understand that you are dealing with a street man. And much as in the cases of Duke Ellington or Orson Welles, James Brown's ability to catalyze and absorb the efforts of his collaborators is a healthy portion of his genius.

And discipline is good for the child, after all: When James Brown sings, as he does, of corporal punishment: "Mama come here quick / Bring me that lickin' stick" or "Papa didn't cuss, he didn't raise a whole lot of fuss / But when we did wrong, Papa beat the hell out of us," it is with admiration, and pride. Though his band consents to call itself his family, the structure bears at least an equal resemblance to jail—which is where James Brown was more likely to have absorbed his definitive notions of authority. So when his musicians begin to bristle under his hand, they find themselves savaged for their "betrayals",—for daring, that is, to risk subjecting James Brown to further experience of abandonment. This explains what I encountered in Augusta: The band James Brown has gathered in 2005 is the vanishing endpoint of his long struggle with Byrd, Maceo, Bootsy, Pee Wee, Wesley and all the others; a band more inclined to coddle his terror than to attempt to push him to some new musical accomplishment, however tempting it might be.

James Brown is in his mid-seventies, for crying out loud. What more do you want from him? What's really special about James Brown is how undisguised, how ungentrified, he remains, has always remained. Most anyone else from his point of origin would long since be living in Beverly Hills, just as his peers in the R&B and soul genre of the Fifties and Sixties smoothed down their rough edges and negotiated a truce; either went Motown, meeting the needs of a white audience for safe, approachable music, or else went jazzily uptown, like Ray Charles. Whereas James Brown, astonishingly, returned to Augusta, site of his torment, and persistently left the backwoods-shack, backwoods-church, Twiggs Street–whorehouse edges of his music raw and on view. His trauma, his confusion, his desperation; those are worn on the outside of his art, on the outside of his shivering and crawling and pleading onstage. James Brown, you see, is not only the kid from Twiggs Street who wouldn't go away. He's the one who wouldn't pretend he wasn't from Twiggs Street.

Today is Fred Wesley day, and everyone's excited. The studio is more populous than before: For unclear reasons, today is also family day. James Brown's wife, Tommie Rae Brown, a singer who is a part of the band's live act, has brought along their five-year-old son, James Brown II. Then appears James Brown's thirty-one-year-old daughter, Deanna, a local radio talk-show host. Deanna has, variously, sued her father for royalties on songs she claimed to have helped write when she was six years old and attempted to commit her father into a mental institution; lately, they're on better terms. Also on the scene is another son, whose name I don't catch, a shy man who appears to be in his early fifties, and with two sons of his own in attendance—James Brown's grandsons, older than James Brown II.

These different versions of "family," with all their tangible contradictions, mingle politely, deferentially with one another in the overcrowded playback room, where James Brown and Fred Wesley are seated together in the leather chairs. Wesley, his red T-shirt stretched over his full belly, is a figure of doughy charisma and droll warmth, teasing and joshing with the children and with the room full of musicians eager to greet him. His eyes, though, register wariness or confusion, as though he's trying to fathom what is expected of him here, a little as though he fears he may have wandered into a trap.

James Brown, startlingly, has abandoned his three-piece suits today for an entirely different look: black cowboy hat, black sleeveless top, snakeskin boots and wraparound shades. What we have here is the Payback James Brown, a dangerous man to cross. I wonder whether this is for Wesley's benefit, or whether James Brown just woke up on the Miles Davis side of the bed this morning. James Brown is giving Wesley a listen to "Message to the World," plainly hoping to please him. Wesley nods along. The two of them slap hands when the song comes to James Brown's references to Maceo and to Wesley. The smile James Brown shows now is by far the warmest and most genuine I've seen from him.

Next James Brown commands Howard to play an instrumental track for Wesley, a shuffle that James Brown calls "Ancestors." Wesley listens closely to "Ancestors" once through and then says simply, "That makes all the sense in the world, Mr. Brown. Thank you very much." He fetches his trombone, in order to lay a long solo over the shuffle. I gather that, once again, a track is to be unceremoniously slammed together before my eyes.

The entire band, as well as the many family members, lingers to gaze through the sound room's long glass window at Wesley as he plays. Wesley makes a rollicking figure there, his red T-shirt and gleaming trombone spotlit in the otherwise darkened studio. The band members I've come to know seem both exhilarated and tired; these long sequences of not playing are wearing on them, but Wesley is a genuine inspiration. Hollie, meanwhile, is troubling over the track's changes, trying to anticipate the next crisis: "Ask him if he wants me to transpose that keyboard, just so he'll be in D."

Wesley concludes and re-enters the playback room. Next, James Brown enters the studio to lay a "rap" over the top of the track. The moment the boss leaves for the soundproof chamber, the band members laugh with admiring pleasure: "Damn, Fred, you come in here and just start blowing, man!" They're thrilled at his on-the-spot facility. "Just went with those changes, never heard them before. I told him, 'It goes up a half-octave'—*bam*!"

Wesley laughs back: "What could I do—damn! Shuffle in F."

Now we listen as James Brown begins what he calls "rapping," a verbal improv no one seems to want to call a sheer defacement of Wesley's solo. The spontaneous lyrics go more or less like this: "Fred Wesley. Ain't nothing but a blessing. A blessing, doggone it. Get on up. Lean back. Pick it up. Shake it up, yeah. Make your booty jump. Clap your hands. Make your booty jump. Dance. Ra-a-aise your hands. Get funky. Get dirty. Dirty dancin'. Shake your boo-tay. Shake you boo-boo-boo-boo-tay. Plenty *tuchis*. Plenty *tuchis*. Mucho. Mucho grande. Shake your big booty. Mucho grande. Big booty. Cool-a *TUCHIS!*" On delivering this last exclamation, an exhilarated James Brown rushes from behind the glass and, rather horrifyingly, in a whole room full of colleagues and intimates, points directly at me and says *"Tuchis!* You got that, ROLLING STONE?"

I say, "That'll go right into the piece, sir."

James Brown then makes a shape in the air and says, "South American boo-tay." We all laugh, at the helpless insanity of it, at the electricity of his delight. "Jewish boo-tay," he says. "Jewish boys and Latina girls get up to a lot of trouble!"

Unfortunately, James Brown demands that we listen to "Ancestors" five times in a row—which we do, as usual, in a state of silent reverence, heads nodding at each end to the track. James Brown makes a *"tuchis"* joke every time the song resolves on that word, as if surprised to find it there. Then, heart-crushingly, he asks for a playback of "Message to the World"—the eleven-minute rant. A few band members have gradually crept out, but most sit in a trance through all the replays.

Next we listen to Hollie's ballad, recorded the day before. James Brown tells his wife the ballad's lyric is dedicated to her (the innocuous sentiments are along the lines of "If you're not happy, I'm not happy either"). At this, James Brown's wife gets nervous, and in a quiet moment I overhear her asking Damon exactly what it says.

"For me?" she asks again.

In irritation, James Brown says, "For all wives." This seems to put an end to the subject.

Afterward, in front of us all, James Brown's wife urges him to consider breaking from his work for a snack. His blood-sugar level, I learn, has been a problem. "I put a banana in the fridge for you," she says. This information displeases James Brown intensely, and the two begin a brief, awkward verbal tussle.

Mr. Bobbit leans in to me and whispers, "A rolling stone gathers no moss." Taking the hint, I go and join Wesley and the band, most of whom have tiptoed out of the playback room and are hanging out in the kitchen.

There, an ebullient Wesley is teasing a rapt circle of admiring musicians for having the audacity to kvetch about how hard the James Brown of today rehearses his band. "Y'all don't know nothing about no eight-hour rehearsal," he tells them. "Y'all don't got a clue. Y'all don't know about going to Los Angeles, nice bright sunshine, sitting there in a dark little studio for eight hours, all those beautiful women, all the things we could do, stuck rehearsing a song we've been playing for fifty years, going, *'Dun-dun-dun'* instead of *'dun-dun-doo.'*"

Seizing their chance, the cats confide in Wesley about "Pimp Danny" and how they hope Wesley will contribute a solo. "So is that why I'm here?" Wesley replies warily, as if sensing a conspiracy of some kind. "I'll play trombone on anything," he explains to me. "You know the story about the $200 whore? Guy says he's only got fifty dollars, she says, 'That's all right, I'll fuck you anyway.' 'Cause she just likes to fuck. That's me: I like to play."

Suddenly, Mr. Bobbit has arrived with a vast delivery of takeout food: several gallon buckets of Kentucky Fried Chicken, assorted sides and a few boxes of doughnuts, too. These are spread on the table, and James Brown emerges from the playback room and joins us. The blood-sugar issue, it appears, is to be addressed, and not by the banana in the fridge. Mrs. James Brown and James Brown II are now nowhere to be seen.

James Brown, still in his black hat and shades, fills a plate with chicken and plunks himself down between me and Wesley. "You gotta talk to this guy," he says, indicating Wesley. "That's twenty percent of your story, right there."

Wesley demurs: "People always try to tell me that, but I'm always saying, there couldn't be nothing without The Man. It all comes through him. You need someone who thinks unbounded. I used to be contained within the diatonic scale. He'd tell me something and I'd say, 'It can't be written down, so it can't be played.' He'd say, 'Play it, don't write it down.' It took me years to understand. Now I'm a teacher."

James Brown and Keith begin reminiscing, plainly for Wesley's sake, about having to teach the Black Eyed Peas' bass player how to play a James Brown bass line. Usher's people, too, needed a tutorial. James Brown and Keith laugh at how slow others are to get it—the guitarist who said, "That's the wrong chord," and James Brown's reply: "How can it be wrong, when it's never been played before?"

Following this five o'clock lunch break, James Brown leads the Bitter Sweets in some more vocal arrangements, leaving the band and Wesley sitting on their hands. Though James Brown's energy is phenomenal, as the evening drags toward seven the general belief is that nothing further will be accomplished here today. Jeff says, wonderingly, "I never even took my horn out of my case today. Checked my e-mail, smoked a twist, ate some Kentucky Fried Chicken." Yet it is on this cue, seemingly as if he has gleaned the risk of mutiny, that James Brown sends the Bitter Sweets home and calls instead for the band—the whole band.

James Brown's mood has turned again. He's so determined, he's almost enraged. "Got to be ready," he chastises while they assemble. James Brown has decided he wants to play his organ but snaps at Howard and snaps at Jeff as the amplifier cables get tangled and, briefly, unplugged. He also castigates Fred Thomas, who he claims has missed a cue: "You want to play bass? Then play." Next he rages at Mousey, who, trapped in a separate booth, can't watch the hand signals. James Brown actually steps in and briefly plays the drums for Mousey, ostensibly showing him how it's done—shades of Nat Kendrick! The silence in the room, during these attacks, is suffocating. I can't help thinking of the present band's embarrassment in front of Wesley, and of Wesley's embarrassment in front of the present band. Here's living proof of every complaint they've wished to register with me.

The tinkering preparations and ritual outbursts at last conclude. James Brown takes his place behind the keyboards, looking ferocious in his shades and sleeveless top. He leads the band through an endlessly complicated big-band jazz-funk piece, which, after three or four false starts, he runs for a perhaps fifteen-minute take, long enough for him to request, by hand signals, two Fred Wesley trombone solos, a bass solo from Fred Thomas and three organ solos from himself. During his own solos—his famously atonal and abstract keyboard work is truly worthy of Sun Ra or Daniel Johnston—James Brown looks fixated, and again appears to have shed thirty years. At the end of his last solo he directs the horns to finish, and laughs sharply: "Takes a lot of concentration!" He turns to me and slaps me five. Fred Wesley turns to the ashen Fred Thomas and, perhaps trying to put a chipper face on what they've been through, says, "Playing that bebop, damn."

I rendezvous with the band in England ten days later, for a performance in Gateshead. The players are in another kind of survival mode now, keeping themselves healthy under punishing travel conditions, while trying to stay in the mood to put on The Show. Donning their red tuxedos, the guitarists point out details they can guess will amuse me. "Danny Ray had jackets made without pockets," says Damon. "He doesn't want to see any lines. So I don't have any place to put my picks onstage." I obligingly examine his tux—sure enough, no pockets. Damon explains that he has no recourse but to stack a supply of picks on an amp, where they invariably vibrate off, onto the floor.

I ask them how the tour's been to this point. Damon, while not critical of the previous week's shows, says, "He needs to warm up on tour, too. Think of all the bits he has to remember. If he screws up, you notice." Damon recalls for me a night when the floor was slick and James Brown missed his first move, and as a result "lost confidence." Lost confidence? I try not to say, "But he's *James Brown!*" It is somehow true that despite my days in his presence, my tabulation of his foibles, nothing has eroded my certainty that James Brown should be beyond ordinary mortal deficits of confidence. And with this thought I discover that a shift has occurred inside me. I wish for the show tonight to be a triumphant one, not for myself, or even for the sake of the band, but so that James Brown himself will be happy.

I'm wanting to take care of him, too.

It's as if I've joined the family.

Bumbling along with the red-costumed tribe in the tunnel to the stage, I find myself suddenly included in a group prayer—hands held in a circle, heads lowered, hushed words spoken in the spirit of the same wish I've just acknowledged privately to myself: that a generous deity might grant them and Mr. Brown a good night. I still haven't seen Mr. Brown himself. Now I can hear the sound of the crowd stirring, boiling with anticipation at what they are about to see. As the players filter onstage into their accustomed positions, bright and proud in their red tuxes, to an immense roar of acclaim from the Gatesheadians, I settle into a spot beside Danny Ray.

When the band hits its first notes and the room begins to ride the music, a kind of metamorphosis occurs, a sort of transmutation of the air of expectation in this Midlands crowd. They've been relieved of the first layer of their disbelief that James Brown has really come to Gateshead: At the very least, James Brown's Sound has arrived. After the band's long overture, Danny Ray, every impeccable tiny inch of him, pops onstage. He says, "Now comes Star Time!" and the roof comes off. Under Danny Ray's instruction, the crowd rises to its feet and begins to chant its hero's name.

When James Brown is awarded to them, the people of Gateshead are the happiest people on Earth, and I am one of them. Never mind that I now know to watch for the rock-paper-scissors hand signals, I am nevertheless swept up in the deliverance of James Brown to his audience. The Sun God has strode across a new threshold, the alien visitor has unveiled himself to another gathering of humans. I see, too, how James Brown's presence animates his family: Keith, fingers moving automatically on frets, smiling helplessly when James Brown calls out his name. Fred Thomas bopping on a platform with his white beard, an abiding sentinel of funk. Hollie, the invisible man, now stepping up for a trumpet solo. Damon, who during Tommie Rae's rendition of "Hold On, I'm A-Comin'," can be heard to slip a reference to "Lady Marmalade" into his guitar solo.

The show builds to the slow showstopper, "It's a Man's Man's Man's World." The moment when James Brown's voice breaks across those horn riffs is one of the greatest in pop music, and the crowd, already in a fever, further erupts. When they cap the ballad by starting "Sex Machine," it is a climax on top of a climax. The crowd screams in joy when James Brown dances even a little (and these days, it is mostly a little). Perhaps, I think, we are all in his family. We want him to be happy. We want him alive. When the James Brown Show comes to your town—when it comes to Gateshead, U.K., today, as when it came to the Apollo Theater in 1961, as when it came to Atlanta or Oklahoma City or Indianapolis anytime, life has admitted its potential to be astounding, if only for as long as the Show lasts. Now that James Brown is old, we want this to go on occurring for as long as possible. We almost don't wish to allow ourselves to think this, but the James Brown Show is a precious thing that may someday vanish from the Earth.

Now James Brown has paused the Show for a monologue about love. He points into the balconies to the left and right of him. "I love you and you and you up there," he says. "Almost as much as I love myself." He asks the audience to do the corniest thing: to turn and tell the person on your left that you love him. Because it is James Brown who asks, the audience obliges. While he is demonstrating the turn to the left, turning expressively in what is nearly a curtsy to Hollie and the other horns, James Brown spots me there, standing in the wings. The smile he gives me is as natural as the one he gave Fred Wesley, it is nothing like the grin of a statue, and if it is to be my own last moment with James Brown, it is a fine one. I feel good.

"Perry Man Remembers Visit to Graceland After Death of Elvis Presley"

Woody Marshall
August 16, 2007 • *The Macon Telegraph*

For 16 years in the 1960s and '70's, Fred Daviss of Perry was entertainer James Brown's business manager. Daviss remembers visiting Graceland with Brown the day after Elvis Presley died, after Brown said, 'We've got to go see him.'

James Brown couldn't get a flight. The airlines were booked. People were all flying to Memphis to go to Graceland. And James Brown couldn't get a seat on an airline.

We thought about taking a limo but didn't want to ride that far. So I'm talking to Elvis' people, trying to find out when they'd have the body at the house and so forth. Finally I told James Brown, I said, "Mr. Brown, we can go in my plane." I had a twin-engine Comanche.

He said, "Nah, Mr. Daviss, I don't fly on propeller airplanes."

It was getting late in the afternoon, the day after Elvis had died—the day before his funeral—and Brown said, "Mr. Daviss, charter a plane."

I called a couple of guys at Charlie Brown Airport in Atlanta and got a Learjet. We flew to Augusta and picked Mr. Brown up. It was a 55-minute flight to Memphis. I'll never forget it. We got there five minutes before we left. We left at 10 o'clock at night and got there at five minutes to 10 because of the time-zone change.

The police met us at the airport and instead of getting a limo to Graceland, we went in a police car. I'd never been to Graceland. We went in this side gate—after we got through the crowd out on the street—and pulled into the backyard.

There were a few people sitting on the back porch in rocking chairs, people who worked for him, family, cousins, his pilots. But they didn't let them in the house.

I heard that Burt Reynolds and Ann-Margret had just left.

I was kind of in shock. All I could think was, "Man, I can't believe Elvis is dead."

We went in downstairs and went through what was apparently his TV room, that jungle-looking room. But we didn't really pay attention to the room.

It was just me, James Brown and Danny Ray, Brown's emcee, the little guy who looked like Sammy Davis who'd put the cape over him on stage. We just followed this guy who worked for Elvis who'd met us at the door.

In the living room, as you went in, the casket was at the far end of the room. It's really not that big of a house. Elvis was just a good ole boy, an old country boy.

We walked up to the casket just like you'd walk in for visitation at a funeral home.

Brown leaned on the casket and he looked at Elvis and he started crying. He said, "Elvis, you rat. *You* rat."

I looked at Brown like, "What in the hell are you talking about?"

He was talking to Elvis; he said, "You rat."

Brown said, "I'm not No. 2 no more," meaning he'd have to go through all "this mess" that Elvis had to go through as No. 1. James Brown had an ego, you know.

The lower half of Elvis' casket was shut. He had a big old 11-carat ring on. Danny Ray was to my right with his shades on and kind of lifting those shades up, peeking under them, looking around, looking at this huge ring.

Danny said, "Mr. Daviss, that's a heap of ring."

I kidded him, I said, "Danny, you better keep your hands off that ring."

So we're standing there, chit-chatting about supposedly what had happened to Elvis, when it'd happened, just chit-chatting. And Brown's crying.

My mother used to say that if you touch a dead person it won't bother you anymore, that you get closure or something.

Well, Brown tells me, "Mr. Daviss, you need to touch Elvis."

This is an old-folks tale, I guess. But about every five minutes, Brown would reach out and pat him on the chest and then shake his head and turn around and say, "Mr. Daviss, you need to touch him."

I said, "I don't know about that, Mr. Brown."

He said, "Mr. Daviss, you need to touch him. Then it won't bother you no more."

I said, "Mr. Brown, It ain't bothering me now."

But to shut him up, I reached out there and patted Elvis' chest.

Later on, Lisa Marie came down and she sat down at the foot of the stairs. She didn't say much. She was sucking on her finger, real shy.

A maid came in and said they had some cold cuts in the kitchen. So I went in, made myself a ham sandwich.

About 20 minutes after Lisa came down, Priscilla comes in.

We were getting ready to leave and Priscilla says, "Come on, sign the register."

My wrist was in a cast from a minibike accident, so I was telling Priscilla about the wreck and she was saying, "You poor baby," just mothering me like.

Brown was telling her about my accident, too, telling her how I'd been out of my head on pain medication after I wrecked—he was riding with me—and how he'd made the decision for them to operate. He was boasting how "I saved Mr. Daviss' thumb."

Anyway, I was having a hard time writing in the guest register, trying to hold the pen in my fingers. Priscilla takes hold of my hand and says, "Here, let me help you."

You know, it's funny, late last year when Brown died, at the public funeral, I knew that would be the last time I would see him. I knew a guy who'd worked for Brown who was kind of standing guard by his body there at the Civic Center in Augusta.

I said, "You mind if I walk over to the casket?"

He said, "Mr. Daviss, go on over."

I unhooked the velvet rope and walked up to the casket, and I thought about what Brown had said after Elvis died.

I reached down and got his hand.

Now I don't care much about touching dead people, but I had a need to do this.

People were straining to hear me.

A guy I know told me later that people were wondering, "What's that white boy doing up there crying over James Brown?"

But I got his hand and I told him, "Mr. Brown, you remember at Elvis' house that night?"

I said, "Well, you rat. You rat. You've done gone and died on me."

Woody Marshall, "Perry Man Remembers Visit to Graceland After Death of Elvis Presley," *The Telegraph* (Macon), August 16, 2007. Copyright 2007, *The Telegraph*, Macon, Georgia. Reprinted by permission.

"James Brown and His First Family of Soul"

Alan Leeds
February/March 2007 • *Waxpoetics*

We who knew James Brown always thought he'd die on a stage. That his innate sense of showmanship wouldn't miss one last flourish of a bright red cape draped over him. Alas, the closest he'd come would be the foot of a stage in Augusta, Georgia's James Brown Arena where, sure enough, loyal Danny Ray lovingly draped the cape over Brown's coffin. Of course in another sense, what bigger stage is there than Christmas Morn? A Savior born and a Godfather passed. None of us will forget where we were and what day it was when we heard the news.

Everyone asked me if I had known he was sick. I didn't. Turns out he had been ailing for a few weeks but chose to ignore it. Maybe he knew how sick he was and simply preferred spending his last days in gen-pop instead of stuck to a hospital bed.

He loved it in gen-pop—where he could walk like a man, make music from his soul, and make friends from his heart. That's how I met him in 1964—as a teenage disc jockey interviewing him for my radio show in Richmond, Virginia. We stayed in touch. I visited his shows whenever he was within a few hundred miles of Richmond and gradually struck what would prove to be lifelong friendships with guys who rode the JB tour bus—Bobby Byrd, St. Clair Pinckney, Fred Wesley, and the cape crusader, Danny Ray. A week after JB's tour of Vietnam, my brother Eric and I sat up with him into the wee hours listening to his unique viewpoint of the government and the war. After "Say It Loud—I'm Black And Proud" hit the market, he spent hours holding court in a cold arena dressing room, explaining its significance, not just to Blacks but to Whites who needed to "recognize"—explaining that it was up to "liberated" Whites like me to spread the Gospel in the White community, because civil rights was about *White ignorance* more than about hate.

James knew I wanted a career in music. No, not just music, *Black* music. But I couldn't have picked a worse time. In the immediate post–civil rights years, the Black music industry was focused on taking control of itself—erasing decades of institutionalized exploitation by mostly White record companies, managers, agents, and promoters. And every move seemed to be under a microscope.

In that spirit, Brown understandably insisted that job opportunities in his expanding business empire went to the Black community. But, fortunately for me, if someone fit into the family, he wasn't about to disown them because of color. Before hiring me in 1969, he explained, "Of course we gotta control our industry. And a lot of those old-style cats gotta go, both White and Black. But pretty soon we'll have enough control to relax. And then the brothas will recognize we need White cats like you if we're ever gonna get this music of ours outta the ghetto."

Regardless of politics, James wasn't about to fix something that wasn't broken. I joined a company that already included several White "tokens"—production manager Bud Hobgood, recording engineer Ron Lenhoff, and tour director Bob Patton. I only say tokens because the late Hobgood and Lenhoff sometimes behaved as such—distancing themselves from me and Patton as if too many White faces together might provoke a second thought from the boss. But Bud and Ron were pretty much relegated to the Cincinnati studios at King Records—where the only Black faces were staff producers Gene Redd and Henry Glover and the guys who worked in the warehouse.

Within James Brown Enterprises, there were no such distinctions. Patton and I worked for the road show where the bus driver happened to be White and most of the passengers happened to be Black. There were no color lines on that bus—just a group of road rats. The *real* James Brown family. Enough so that one night after a show and a couple of cocktails, James looked at us and laughed. "Look at you and Mr. Patton," he said with affection. "I thought I hired me a couple White boys and I got me two more niggas." (Mind you, this was 1970—several decades before another generation suggested it might be okay to refer to White "insiders" that way. Can I get away with citing this as still another instance of James Brown pre-dating hip-hop?)

James Brown was about a lot of different things to a lot of different people. But to those of us on the inside, he was primarily about discipline and family. He could be a hard-to-please patriarch, so things weren't always warm and fuzzy, but if you ever needed to "come home," the door to Mr. Brown's house was always open.

Mr. Brown. *Mister* Brown. From the day I met him, backstage he was always Mr. Brown—never James. DJs and fans called him James. But one of the initiations into the inner circle was the unequivocal exchange of James for Mister. It was reciprocal. I went from Alan to Mr. Leeds. And it didn't take long to realize how the "mister thing" contributed to the pride we felt in being part of the Brown organization. We were also required to wear dark suits and ties whenever in a business environment—even the band! The show could be in the midst of a string of one-nighters, the band living on the bus for days on end, but they'd be expected to disembark in a suit and tie. A doo rag was never an option. Corny as it sounds today, it really was a respect thing. Imagine the reaction of the motel clerk when they arrived to check in. Imagine the reaction of the sister behind the counter when they invaded the local soul food joint for that rare shot at a real meal. Imagine the effect on the opening acts when the band strutted to their dressing room to change into their uniforms. Elitist? Damn right. Cult-like? Maybe. But it was family. And James Brown was proud of his family.

Brown's reputation as a demanding taskmaster became widely known and, ironically, served me well even after I was off his payroll. In 1983, Prince hired me sight unseen simply because he noticed James Brown Productions on my résumé. "Get that James Brown guy," he ordered manager Steve Fargnoli. Prince had already been through two tour managers, so I suppose his reasoning was that if I could handle JB, I might be up to the challenge. Or maybe he just felt his organization could benefit from some of that old-school James Brown discipline. After two weeks of awkward silence—I had been warned not to approach Prince until he signaled a comfort with me—our first conversation of any substance began with him asking, "Tell me some James Brown stories."

A year later, James played a gig at First Avenue in Minneapolis and afterwards offered to hype Prince's *Purple Rain* tour during his gigs if we'd agree to follow his itinerary by a week or so. I chose not to point out that Prince was already selling out arenas while Brown was then stuck on the rock club circuit. But when MTV asked James how he felt about his protégés outselling him, he boasted that Prince's success might be due to the fact that "he's got some of my old staff over there—namely Alan Leeds." The interview probably didn't play very well with Fargnoli, but far be it from me to deprive a Godfather of his pride.

Truth be told, the idea of James Brown–Prince comparisons struck me funny. So much was different about how artists toured in the 1980s compared to JB in the 1960s. From a production standpoint, 1980s tours were tremendously labor-heavy compared to the standard JB setup that had consisted solely of musical instruments, a few mic stands, a modest audio system, in-house lighting, and two follow spots. We thought it was a huge deal when James added a single strobe light for a special effect.

On the other hand, despite significantly heavier media requirements, a

1980s tour schedule was light action. Prince would do four concerts a week. The occasional after-show could be a bit tiring but still nothing compared to what I witnessed in December 1964, when I followed the James Brown show to three separate gigs on a single Saturday.

He played an early afternoon show at Randolph-Macon University in Ashland, Virginia, an evening set at the University of Richmond, some forty miles to the South, and a late show and dance for the general public that ran from 11:00 P.M. until 3:00 A.M. at the Richmond Arena. I was at the Arena when the show bus pulled in around ten o'clock. The basketball nets were still in place from a high-school game earlier that day, so while the band gear was being loaded in I found myself on the court casually lofting up shots with Famous Flames Bobby Byrd and Bobby Bennett. "Man," I said. "I have no idea how you guys are even standing up."

"It's all right," Byrd shrugged—then laughed. "We do this all the time. We can't sit down, because if we did we might never wake up for the next show."

What's even more staggering is the itinerary that surrounded that busy day in Virginia. This particular run had begun Thanksgiving night with a four-hour dance and show in Raleigh, North Carolina. The next after-noon, they opened a seven-day engagement at the Howard Theatre in Washington, D.C., where they'd perform four shows a day (five on week-ends). The night before leaving D.C. for Virginia, JB called a marathon recording session. As if that's not enough, when the Richmond Arena show ended in the wee hours of the next morning, the group rode 550 miles to Atlanta where they arrived just in time for the first of three shows at the Auburn Avenue Casino. Let's go to the scorecard. That's thirty-seven shows and a recording session spread out over five cities in eleven days. Byrd was right. They didn't have time to be tired.

Obviously, this was an extreme example of what the chitlin circuit could be when a show was in great demand. But the point is that these guys worked their tails off, and it wasn't because any evil managers or agents were cracking the whip. As an artist already pretty much in control of his career, Brown elected to work like that—to leave no stone unturned.

By the time I went to work for him in 1969, James's stardom was secure and his itinerary had settled into something more civil. But the occasional the-atre or club booking still meant several shows per day. And one-nighters were booked as frequently as six nights a week with distances between them of up to five hundred miles. It's no wonder guys from that era, like Bobby Byrd, have a hard time understanding the culture and work habits of today's young artists.

About an hour before the performances at the recent funeral in Augusta, I found myself sitting idly with seventy-two-year-old Bobby Byrd in the band dressing room. Despite the somber occasion, the JB family camaraderie was in full force. Singers and musicians from nearly every era of Brown's career were in the house: original bandleader-saxophonist J.C. Davis, Famous Flames Bobby Bennett and Johnny Terry, 1960s singers Marva Whitney and Vicki Anderson, 1970s stalwarts Fred Wesley, Martha High, and the irrepressible Bootsy Collins. Brown's 1980s sidemen Jerry Poindexter and Ron Laster were running around generously helping the stage manager wherever they could. And, of course, there were the current crop of J.B.'s, aka the Soul Generals.

As Bobby and I sat catching a breath and the Soul Generals dressed for their final performance in James Brown's presence, the other old-timers spread into the audience. Given that most of them never appeared on a James Brown hit record, it's startling to realize that many of the last band had toured with him much longer than the more famous sidemen of the 1960s and 1970s. Bassist Fred Thomas was the senior member, having joined in 1971. Band leader Hollie Farris first came aboard at the end of 1975. Even one of the "youngsters," guitarist Keith Jenkins had been there twelve years. Of course, MC Danny Ray pre-dated everyone, climbing on the bus in 1960.

The atmosphere in the dressing room was fairly casual, although a few musicians seemed to take the loss of their boss harder than others. Hollie looked particularly shell-shocked as he wrote out the *James Brown Show*'s "final" set list. But the most poignant moment of my three funeral days in Augusta came when Byrd turned to me and gestured towards Fred Thomas. "Now I know ol' Fred Thomas," Byrd quietly said in my ear and sighed. "And I known you and Danny Ray. But I don't know nobody else in here."

Poignant because of course Bobby *did* know *everybody* else in there—and they knew him—percussionist Spike Nealy had even come to James via Byrd's own band. As my brother Eric later put it, it was Bobby's *where have all the flowers gone* moment. Maybe it was missing guys like the late St. Clair Pinckney, Jimmy Nolen, Bernard Odum, Baby Lloyd, and Nat Kendrick, who couldn't be there because they were waiting for James at his *next* gig. And maybe it was Byrd's lament that cronies like Maceo and Melvin Parker, Clyde Stubblefield, and Jab'O Starks weren't there— perhaps because they *chose* not to be.

Every generation of James Brown family was equally legit. All enjoyed the cred and camaraderie that touring with Mr. Dynamite earned them. But none of these cats in the dressing room knew what it was like in

Toccoa, Georgia, when Bobby's mother adopted James as a foster son in order to get him out of reform school. Or knew what it sounded like when young James sang gospels with Sarah Byrd while secretly plotting to join her brother's R&B group. Or what *Live at the Apollo really* felt like—back when the Apollo was really *live*. And surely none of them knew anything like those thirty-seven shows in eleven days.

Eventually, it was "show time." Bobby got a sudden burst of energy, the band hit the stage like the dynamite they were taught to be, and soon all 8500 in the James Brown Arena *knew they got soul*. Like Bobby Byrd and the Soul Generals, *if they didn't, they wouldn't be in there*.

I could rag on the absence of some I expected to see at the funerals. But on an individual basis, everyone has their own life, their own commitments, and their own priorities, so who am I to sit in judgment? I do know jazz bassist and JB pal Christian McBride got a sub for his gig with McCoy Tyner in Oakland, California, and flew back and forth across country to see his mentor one last time at the Apollo. As for the hip-hop community, a movement that owes so much to the expansive template James Brown provided, it seemed a travesty that its representation was limited to Chuck D and Hammer. But with further thought, it felt less surprising. James wasn't a particularly social person beyond his immediate orbit. Most of those in the hip-hop culture actually had less in common with their Godfather than one might imagine. He was country and they're largely urban. He was old school and might drive a pickup when home in Georgia. They drive Hummers or use limos. He was about getting paid for the use of his samples and they're often about trying to keep all the paper. The fact is that James Brown's influence goes way beyond the boundaries of any type of music—hip-hop or even his own.

In the past weeks, many have reflected on just how different the world would have been were it not for James Brown. And, like others, I've also recognized just how different I would have been were it not for James Brown. He taught me how to listen to and understand the music I love. He taught me about this country and its many faces. He taught me about race. He taught me how to have hope when there is no hope. He taught me that if you believe in yourself, sooner or later someone else will believe in you too. And he taught me about extended family. He knew a lot about my parents and how supportively and lovingly they raised me and Eric, but he still dedicated a personal note, "To my nephew in blood and adopted son."

I completely recognize that none of this is really about me. James had a lot of "adopted sons"—we're part of a big family. I'm just proud to be one of them.

James Brown Discography

by Alan Leeds

PART I: THE SINGLES

From 1956 to 2006 James Brown released hundreds of singles. A comprehensive discography would be a book unto itself, so we have chosen to list only those singles that achieved success on the national charts. Beginning in 1956 James Brown's singles appeared on the Federal label, a subsidiary of King Records. In 1960 Brown graduated to the parent label. Between 1964 and 1967 some Brown singles appeared on the Smash label, a subsidiary of Mercury Records. In 1971 Brown began his own People Records, which was initially distributed by King. Later, in 1971, James signed with Polydor Records and brought along the People label. After leaving Polydor in 1981, Brown recorded for a variety of companies before signing with Scotti Brothers Records in 1985. Brown also produced countless singles by his bands and protégés. Of those productions, only those titles on which James is featured, vocally or instrumentally, are included in this discography. Each record's original release date follows the titles.

Federal 12258: "Please, Please, Please" / "Why Do You Do Me" (3/56)
Federal 12337: "Try Me" / "Tell Me What I Did Wrong" (10/58)
Federal 12348: "I Want You So Bad" / "There Must Be a Reason" (2/59)
Federal 12361: "Good Good Lovin'" / "Don't Let It Happen to Me" (10/59)
Dade 1804 as "Nat Kendrick & The Swans": "(Do The) Mashed Potatoes," part 1 / "(Do the) Mashed Potatoes," part 2 (12/59)
Federal 12369: "I'll Go Crazy" / "I Know It's True" (1/60)
Federal 12370: "Think" / "You've Got the Power" (4/60)
Federal 12378: "This Old Heart" / "Wonder When You're Coming Home" (8/60)
King 5442: "Bewildered" / "If You Want Me" (1/61)

King 5466: "I Don't Mind" / "Love Don't Love Nobody" (5/61)

King 5524: "Baby, You're Right" / "I'll Never, Never Let You Go" (7/61)

King 5547: "I Love You, Yes I Do" / "Just You and Me, Darling" (8/61)

King 5573: "Lost Someone" / "Cross Firing" (12/61)

King 5614: "Night Train" / "Why Does Everything Happen to Me" (3/62)

King 5657: "Shout and Shimmy" / "Come Over Here" (6/62)

King 5672: "Mashed Potatoes U.S.A." / "You Don't Have to Go . . ." (8/62)

King 5701: "Three Hearts in a Tangle" / "I've Got Money" (11/62)

King 5710: "Like a Baby" / "Every Beat of My Heart" (1/63)

King 5739: "Prisoner of Love" / "Choo-Choo" (3/63)

King 5767: "These Foolish Things" / "(Can You) Feel It, Part 1" (6/63)

King 5803: "Signed, Sealed and Delivered" / "Waiting In Vain" (9/63)

King 5842: "Oh Baby Don't You Weep," part 1 / "Oh Baby Don't You Weep," part 2 (12/63)

King 5853: "Please, Please, Please" / "In the Wee Wee Hours (of the Nite)" (1/64)

Smash 1898: "Caldonia" / "Evil" (4/64)

Smash 1908: "The Things That I Used to Do" / "Out of the Blue" (5/64)

Smash 1919: "Out of Sight" / "Maybe the Last Time" (7/64)

King 5968: "Have Mercy Baby" / "Just Won't Do Right (I Stay in the Chapel Every Night)" (11/64)

King 5999: "Papa's Got a Brand New Bag," part 1 / "Papa's Got a Brand New Bag," part 2 (6/65)

Smash 2008: "Try Me" / "Papa's Got a Brand New Bag" (10/65)

King 6015: "I Got You (I Feel Good)" / "I Can't Help It (I Just Do-Do-Do)" (10/65)

King 6020: "Lost Someone" / "I'll Go Crazy" (12/65)

King 6025: "Ain't That a Groove," part 1 / "Ain't That a Groove," part 2 (2/66)

King 6035: "It's A Man's Man's Man's World" / "Is It Yes or Is It No?" (4/66)

King 6048: "Money Won't Change You," part 1 / "Money Won't Change You," part 2 (7/66)

King 6056: "Don't Be A Drop-Out" / "Tell Me That You Love Me" (9/66)

King 6071: "Bring It Up" / "Nobody Knows" (12/66)

King 6086: "Kansas City" / "Stone Fox" (2/67)

King 6100: "Let Yourself Go" / "Good Rockin' Tonight" (4/67)

King 6110: "Cold Sweat," part 1 / "Cold Sweat," part 2 (6/67)

King 6122: "Get It Together," part 1 / "Get It Together," part 2 (10/67)

King 6144: "I Can't Stand Myself (When You Touch Me)" / "There Was a Time" (11/67)

King 6151 as "Bobby Byrd & James Brown": "You've Got to Change Your Mind" (1/68)

King 6155: "I Got the Feelin'" / "If I Ruled the World" (2/68)

King 6112: "America Is My Home," part 1 / "America Is My Home," part 2 (5/68)

King 6166: "Licking Stick-Licking Stick," part 1 / "Licking Stick-Licking Stick," part 2 (5/68)

King 6141: "I Guess I'll Have to Cry, Cry, Cry" / "Just Plain Funk" (6/68)

King 6187: "Say It Loud—I'm Black and I'm Proud," part 1 / "Say It Loud—I'm Black and I'm Proud," part 2 (8/68)

King 6198: "Goodbye My Love" / "Shades of Brown" (10/68)

King 6203: "Santa Claus Goes Straight to the Ghetto" / "You Know It" (11/68)

King 6213: "Give It Up or Turnit a Loose" / "I'll Lose My Mind" (1/69)

King 6222: "Soul Pride," part 1 / "Soul Pride," part 2 (3/69)

King 6224: "I Don't Want Nobody to Give Me Nothing (Open Up the Door, I'll Get It Myself)," part 1 / "I Don't Want Nobody to Give Me Nothing (Open up the Door, I'll Get It Myself)," part 2 (3/69)

King 6240: "The Popcorn" / "The Chicken" (5/69)

King 6245: "Mother Popcorn (You Got to Have a Mother for Me)," part 1 / "Mother Popcorn (You Got to Have a Mother for Me)," part 2 (5/69)

King 6250: "Lowdown Popcorn" / "Top of the Stack" (7/69)

King 6258: "World," part 1 / "World," part 2 (8/69)

King 6255: "Let a Man Come in and Do the Popcorn, Part 1" / "Sometime" (9/69)

King 6280: "Ain't It Funky Now," part 1 / "Ain't It Funky Now," part 2 (10/69)

King 6275: "Part Two (Let a Man Come in and Do the Popcorn)" / "Gittin' a Little Hipper" (11/69)

King 6292: "It's a New Day," parts 1 and 2 / "Georgia on My Mind" (1/70)

King 6290: "Funky Drummer," part 1 / "Funky Drummer," part 2 (2/70)

King 6310: "Brother Rapp," part 1 / "Bewildered" (4/70)

King 6318: "GET UP I Feel Like Being Like a SEX MACHINE," part 1 / "GET UP I Feel Like Being Like a SEX MACHINE," part 2 (6/70)

King 6329: "Super Bad," parts 1 and 2, / "Super Bad," part 3 (10/70)

King 6347: "Get Up, Get into It, Get Involved," part 1 / "Get Up, Get into It, Get Involved," part 2 (12/70)

King 6363: "I Cried" / "World, Part 2" (1/71)

King 6368: "Soul Power," part 1 / "Soul Power," parts 2 and 3 (2/71)

People 2500: "Escape-ism," part 1 / "Escape-ism," part 2 (5/71)

People 2501: "Hot Pants (She Got to Use What She Got to Get What She Wants)," part 1 / "Hot Pants (She Got to Use What She Got to Get What She Wants)," parts 2 and 3 (6/71)

People 2502 as "The J.B.'s": "My Brother," part 1 / "My Brother," part 2 (6/71)

Polydor 14088: "Make It Funky," part 1 / "Make It Funky," part 2 (8/71)

Polydor 14098: "My Part Make It Funky," part 3 / "My Part Make It Funky," part 4 (10/71)

Polydor 14100: "I'm a Greedy Man," part 1 / "I'm a Greedy Man," part 2 (11/71)

Polydor 14109: "Talking Loud and Saying Nothing," part 1 / "Talking Loud and Saying Nothing," part 2 (1/72)

Polydor 14116: "King Heroin" / "Theme from King Heroin" (2/72)

People 607 as "The J.B.'s": "Pass the Peas" / "Hot Pants Road" (4/72)

Polydor 14125: "There It Is," part 1 / "There It Is," part 2 (4/72)

Polydor 14129 as "James Brown Soul Train": "Honky Tonk," part 1 / "Honky Tonk," part 2 (5/72)

Polydor 14139: "Get on the Good Foot," part 1 / "Get on the Good Foot," part 2 (7/72)

Polydor 14153: "I Got A Bag of My Own" / "Public Enemy #1" (10/72)

Polydor 14162: "I Got Ants in My Pants," part 1 / "I Got Ants in My Pants," parts 15 and 16 (11/72)

Polydor 14157 as "James Brown & Lyn Collins": "What My Baby Needs Now Is a Little More Loving" / "This Guy—This Girl's in Love with You" (12/72)

Polydor 14168: "Down and Out in New York City" / "Mama's Dead" (2/73)

People 621 as "Fred Wesley & The J.B.'s": "Doing It to Death" / "Everybody Got Soul" (3/73)

Polydor 14177: "Think" / "Something" (4/73, withdrawn)

Polydor 14185: "Think" / "Something" (5/73)

People 627 as "Fred Wesley & The J.B.'s": "If You Don't Get It the First Time, Back Up and Try It Again, Party" / "You Can Have Watergate Just Gimme Some Bucks and I'll Be Straight" (8/73)

Polydor 14194: "Sexy Sexy Sexy" / "Slaughter Theme" (8/73)

People 630 as "Lyn Collins": "You Can't Beat Two People in Love" (10/73)

Polydor 14210: "Stoned to the Bone Part 1" / "Stoned to the Bone (Some More)" (11/73)

People 632 as "Fred Wesley & The J.B.'s": "Same Beat," part 1 / "Same Beat," parts 2 and 3 (1/74)

Polydor 14223: "The Payback," part 1 / "The Payback," part 2 (2/74)

People 638 as "Fred Wesley & The J.B.'s": "Damn Right I Am Somebody," part 1 / "Damn Right I Am Somebody," part 2 (5/74)

Polydor 14244: "My Thang" / "Public Enemy #1, Part 1" (6/74)

People 641 as "Lyn Collins": "Rock Me Again & Again & Again & Again & Again & Again (6 Times)" (6/74)

Polydor 14255: "Papa Don't Take No Mess," part 1 / "Papa Don't Take No Mess," part 2 (8/74)

Polydor 14258: "Funky President (People It's Bad)" / "Cold Blooded" (10/74)

Polydor 14268: "Reality" / "Need Your Love So Bad" (1/75)

Polydor 14270: "Sex Machine," part 1 / "Sex Machine," part 2 (2/75)

Polydor 14281: "Hustle!!! (Dead On It)," / "Dead On It Part 2" (6/75)

Polydor 14295: "Superbad, Superslick," part 1 / "Superbad, Superslick," Part 2 (9/75)

Polydor 14301: "Hot (I Need to Be Loved, Loved, Loved, Loved)" / "Superbad, Superslick, Part 1" (11/75)

Polydor 14304: "(I Love You) For Sentimental Reasons" / "Goodnight My Love" (3/76)

Polydor 14326: "Get Up Offa That Thing" / "Release the Pressure" (6/76)

Polydor 14354: "I Refuse to Lose" / "Home Again" (8/76)

Polydor 14360: "Bodyheat," part 1 / "Bodyheat," part 2 (10/76)

Polydor 14388: "Woman" / "Kiss in 77" (1/77)

Polydor 14409: "People Wake Up and Live" / "Give Me Some Skin" (4/77)

Polydor 14438: "If You Don't Give a Doggone about It" / "People Who Criticize" (8/77)

Polydor 14465: "Eyesight" / "I Never, Never, Never Will Forget" (2/78)

Polydor 14487: "The Spank" / "Love Me Tender" (5/78)

Polydor 14522: "For Goodness Sakes, Look at Those Cakes," part 1 / "For Goodness Sakes, Look at Those Cakes," part 2 (10/78)

Polydor 14557: "It's Too Funky in Here" / "Are We Really Dancing" (5/79)

Polydor 2005: "Star Generation" / "Women Are Something Else" (8/79)

Polydor 2054: "Regrets" / "Stone Cold Drag" (1/80)

TK 1039: "Rapp Payback (Where Iz Moses)," / "Rapp Payback Part 2" (11/80)

TK 1042: "Stay with Me" / "Smokin' and Drinkin'" (3/81)

Augusta Sound 94023: "Bring It On . . . Bring It On" / "The Night Time Is the Right Time (To Be with the One You Love)" (4/83)

Tommy Boy 847-7 as "Afrika Bambaataa & James Brown": "Unity," part 1 / "Unity," part 2 (8/84)

Scotti Brothers 05682: "Living in America" (12/85)

Scotti Brothers 06275: "Gravity" / "Gravity (Dub Mix)" (10/86)

Scotti Brothers 06568: "How Do You Stop" / "House of Rock" (1/87)

Scotti Brothers 07783: "I'm Real" / "Tribute" (4/88)

Scotti Brothers 07975: "Static" / "Godfather Runnin' the Joint" (7/88)

Arista 9885 as "Aretha Franklin & James Brown": "Gimme Your Love" (9/89)

Scotti Brothers 75286: "(So Tired of Standing Still We Got to) Move On" / "You Are My Everything" (11/91)

Scotti Brothers 75352: "Can't Get Any Harder" (1/93)

Georgia-Lina 825: "Funk on ahh Roll!" / "Lucky Old Sun" (11/96)

PART II: THE ALBUMS

King Records released the first James Brown album in 1958. With few exceptions, most of the King albums were compilations of varied tracks, many of which had appeared on singles. The albums for Smash Records in the midsixties were more cohesive, and the albums for Polydor in the 1970s tended to be more concept driven, but an overview of Brown's recordings highlights that above all he was a master of the singles format. We have chosen to list Brown's most significant albums, many of which have been reissued on CD.

King 610: *Please Please Please* (12/58) (reissued as King 909 in 1964). The first James Brown album compiles a generous sixteen tracks from his Federal singles. Besides the hit of the same name, the LP includes "Try Me" and several of JB's more interesting early sides.

King 683: *Think* (11/60). A high quality collection of late-Federal and early-King singles including "I'll Go Crazy," "Good Good Lovin'," "Bewildered," and "You've Got the Power." This album sets the table for sixties soul.

King 826: *Live at the Apollo* (5/63). Self-financed when King Records balked at the idea of recording JB's road show, this LP stayed on the charts for over a year. Frequently referred to as the greatest live album of all time, the disc's marathon "Lost Someone" became the prototype performance by which all soul singers were measured.

Smash 67054: *Showtime* (4/64). Capturing JB in fine voice, *Showtime* may be the most effective of his collaborations with ace arranger Sammy Lowe's swinging studio band despite sometimes-annoying fake crowd noise. "Caldonia" and "Ain't Nobody Here but Us Chickens" swing like mad and "Don't Cry Baby" and "Somebody Changed the Lock on My Door" are among Brown's best blues performances ever.

Smash 67057: *Grits and Soul* (3/65). An energetic instrumental sampling of the expanded James Brown band under music director Nat Jones. Highlights include "Grits," the group's moody theme, JB's organ on "Who's Afraid of Virginia Woolf?" and the first recordings of young saxophonist Maceo Parker.

King 1020: *Cold Sweat* (8/67). Ignore all the filler, the seven-minute title song reinvented rhythm and blues. Maceo Parker rewrites the role of saxophone and Clyde Stubblefield does the same when Brown hollers, "Give the drummer some."

King 1030: *I Can't Stand Myself* (2/68). Also riddled with filler but essential just for the title song, "Get It Together" and the single version of "There Was a Time."

King 1022: *Live at the Apollo Volume II* (8/68). Not as raw as volume one, but this two-disc set captures the James Brown Show and the best of his bands at a crest—an opportunity to virtually hear James and his gang inventing funk. While epic versions of "Prisoner of Love" and "It's a Man's Man's Man's World" refine what Brown began on volume one, the side-long "Let Yourself Go" / "There Was a Time" medley is the one recorded performance that best represents all of what made James Brown a genius.

King 1047: *Say It Loud—I'm Black and I'm Proud* (3/69). More filler but what other album can boast an anthem to a social movement? Also includes the funky "Licking Stick" and JB's great farewell to the era of the soul ballad, "Goodbye My Love."

King 1055: *James Brown Plays and Directs the Popcorn* (7/69). Perhaps Brown's best instrumental album, every track is a winner and the arrangements by Alfred "Pee Wee" Ellis dance off the turntable. Maceo Parker is the main soloist ("The Popcorn," "Sudsy"), but "Soul Pride" handsomely features guitar-whiz Jimmy Nolen.

King 1100: *Soul on Top* (2/70). A jazz project that really works—JB backed by the stellar Louis Bellson big band with arrangements by the brilliant Oliver Nelson. Brown's vocals are flying without a net and not every track wins, but "That's My Desire," "I Need Your Key," "The Man in the Glass," "Every Day I Have the Blues," and "For Once in My Life" are well worth the price of admission.

King 1095: *It's a New Day So Let a Man Come In* (4/70). Less filler equals more flavor. Terrific full-length versions of singles hits "It's a New Day," "Give It Up or Turnit a Loose," "Georgia on My Mind," "If I Ruled the World," and "Let a Man Come In and Do the Popcorn."

King 1115: *Sex Machine* (9/70). Two red-hot discs: one live in 1969 with his veteran band and the other in the studio (with fake audience reaction) with his upstart 1970 J.B.'s band including a teenage Bootsy Collins. The bands couldn't be more different, but James and his template funk couldn't be more consistent. The J.B.'s reinvention of "Give It Up or Turnit a Loose" is among Brown's most essential recordings.

Polydor 4054: *Hot Pants* (8/71). Due to contractual restrictions James had to recut "Hot Pants" for his debut Polydor LP, but these "pants," "Escape-ism," and a remake of "I Can't Stand Myself" are on fire.

Polydor 2-3003: *Revolution of the Mind* (12/71). Aka "Live at the Apollo Vol. III," these two red-hot discs capture Fred Wesley's post-Bootsy J.B.'s at their best.

Polydor 5028: *There It Is* (6/72). A better than usual compilation thanks to four full-length hits, including "I'm a Greedy Man," "King Heroin," and the essential "Talkin' Loud and Sayin' Nothing."

Polydor 6014: *Black Caesar* (2/73). JB's soundtrack is as action packed as the Fred Williamson film it accompanied.

Polydor 2-3007: *The Payback* (12/73). The closest thing to a legitimate JB concept album, anchored by the landmark title song, "Stoned to the Bone" and the underappreciated "Mind Power."

Polydor 6042: *Sex Machine Today* (3/75). Underrated. The lively remake of the title tune may fall short of the original, but a clever Latin version of "I Feel Good," jams like "Dead On It," and an overlooked anomaly, the tight three-minute "Problems," make for a more than pleasant LP.

Polydor 6140: *Jam 1980's* (3/78). The credits herald JB's "new disco sound," but lengthy smokers "Jam," "The Spank," and "I Never, Never, Never Will Forget" are pure James Brown funk.

Atlantic SD-16017: *The Blues Brothers* (6/80). Brown only appears on one track of this motion-picture soundtrack, but he credited this rousing gospel performance of "The Old Landmark" as the beginning of his 1980's comeback.

Polydor 829624: *In the Jungle Groove* (1986). Four sides of must-have grade A classics, including full-length versions and remixes of "Funky Drummer," "Soul Power," "It's a New Day," "Give It Up or Turnit a Loose," "Talkin' Loud and Sayin' Nothing," "Hot Pants," "Get Up, Get into It, Get Involved," and the previously unissued "I Got to Move."

Scotti Brothers 40380: *Gravity* (1986). There's surely an irony in this Dan Hartman–produced LP of songs mostly derivative of JB's own. But "Living in America" inexplicably became one of Brown's biggest hits ever, and the album spearheaded the comeback that would return his touring show to premier venues through the rest of his career.

PART III: THE CDS

Polydor Records, now part of Universal Music, should be commended for its ongoing commitment to the rich James Brown catalogue. The first JB compact disc compilation in 1985 began an ambitious series of album reissues, imaginative collections of archive material, and previously unissued gems from the tape vault. *Star Time*, a four-disc, career-retrospective box set earned a 1992 GRAMMY for Brown, producer Harry Weinger, British JB historian Cliff White, and the editors of this book. Since then, Weinger and Universal executive Bill Levenson have continued to pour their time, energy, and resources into the James Brown legacy. We have chosen to list what we feel are the most representative CD issues.

Polydor 422-829417: *James Brown's Funky People* (1986). The best singles from Brown's own People label, including hits by Maceo (Parker) and the Macks, Fred Wesley and the J.B.'s, and Brown protégé Lyn Collins.

Polydor 422-847258: *Messing with the Blues* (1990). A lovingly compiled two-disc set of Brown's many covers of blues songs originally made popular by artists and mentors like Roy Brown, Louis Jordan, Memphis Slim, Little Willie John, and Ivory Joe Hunter. A revealing package aimed at R & B traditionalists, lest they think JB is only about funk.

Polydor 422-849108: *Star Time* (1991). The granddaddy of R & B box sets, all the hits are on these four CDs along with some noteworthy obscurities. That all the Federal, King, Smash, and Polydor masters are housed under one corporate roof is a fortunate coincidence and contributed to making this collection as perfectly definitive as it is. No modern music collection should be without it.

Polydor 314-513389: *Love Power Peace: Live at the Olympia, Paris, 1971* (1992). Proposed as a three-disc album in 1971 but never issued until this CD, this landmark show captures the peak of the original Bootsy Collins / Fred Wesley J.B.'s in action. Want to best show an alien what funk is? Play them "Give It Up or Turnit a Loose" or "Sex Machine."

Polydor 314-517845: *Soul Pride: The Instrumentals, 1960–1969* (1993). The evolution of the great 1960s James Brown band revealed through two discs of exciting tracks that feature all the recognizable sidemen who passed through the band's ranks.

Polydor 314-527094 as "the J.B.'s": *Funky Good Time: The Anthology* (1995). Two blistering instrumental CDs that chronicle the innovative James Brown bands through the 1970s. Fred Wesley and Maceo Parker are the stars of this collection, but JB's influence is in every note.

Polydor 314-531165: *Foundations of Funk* (1996). A detailed two-disc study of JB's most important tracks from 1964 to 1969. Includes full-length versions of the hits and a fascinating alternate take of "Cold Sweat."

Polydor 314-531684: *Funk Power 1970: A Brand New Thang* (1996). The album that never was. King Records never properly compiled the groundbreaking hits JB cut in 1970 with his innovative, young J.B.'s. Includes both 1970 versions of "Sex Machine," as well as "Super Bad," and "Soul Power."

Polydor 314-533052: *Make It Funky* (1996). Starting where *Funk Power* left off, this is a robust two-disc collection of JB's best-known tracks from 1971 to 1975. Hit after hit plus a smoking unissued live "Hot Pants."

Polydor 314-537709: *James Brown's Original Funky Divas* (1998). Two CDs assembling the best sides JB produced for his procession of female vocalists. Includes charming 1960s R & B by Yvonne Fair and the little-known Anna King along with key funk tracks by Marva Whitney, Vicki Anderson, and the late Lyn "Mama Feelgood" Collins.

Polydor 314-537901: *Dead on the Heavy Funk: 1975–1983* (1998). The final installment in the series of two-disc chronological compilations. Not quite as many bona fide hits as the earlier volumes but the continued quality of JB's records is eye-opening.

Polydor 314-557668: *Say It Live And Loud* (1998). A fiery 1968 live recording with Brown fronting one of his best bands in a Dallas auditorium. Includes the debut concert performance of "Say It Loud—I'm Black and I'm Proud," a romping "There Was a Time," and a marathon "Cold Sweat."

Polydor B0008549: *Number Ones* (2007). Lean and mean, part ones only. Nineteen hits on a single CD. Amazing music, but this collection is for the casual fan who wants only one JB CD.

Polydor B0008913: *Gold* (2007). Not as lean—and still no part twos. Two discs with forty hits. For the casual fan with deeper pockets.

Hip-O Select.Com: *James Brown: The Singles*. An ongoing series of two-disc volumes collecting each and every James Brown single, including some that were cancelled or never issued. Detailed liner notes and colorful booklets full of rare images gear these limited editions to the serious collector.

Credits

Grateful acknowledgment is made for permission to reprint the following copyrighted works:

"Apollo NY," *Variety*, December 16, 1959. Reprinted by permission.

"James Brown Boasts New Tune and Dance," *Daily Defender*, September 27, 1960. Used with permission *Chicago Defender*.

"Dick Clark Spotlights James Brown's Flames," *Chicago Defender*, October 29, 1960. Used with permission *Chicago Defender*.

Eva Dolin, "James Brown: Vitality, Humility, Soul, Talent," *Chicago Defender*, June 13, 1964. Used with permission *Chicago Defender*.

"James Brown Just 'Sings His Heart Out'," *Chicago Defender*, September 4, 1965. Used with permission *Chicago Defender*.

Ron Courtney, "James Brown Meets the Nine Nobles," *Goldmine*, May 9, 1986. Goldmine® Magazine (www.goldminemag.com) is published bi-weekly by Krause Publications, a division of F+W Publications, Inc. (www.fwpubs.com). Reprinted by permission.

Doon Arbus, "James Brown Is Out of Sight," *New York Herald Tribune*, March 20, 1966. Copyright © 1966 Doon Arbus. Reprinted by permission.

Jonathan Cott, "James Brown in Paris: Sock It A Moi," *Rolling Stone*, November 23, 1967. © Rolling Stone LLC 1967. All rights reserved. Reprinted by Permission.

Harry Weinger with Alan Leeds, "It's a New Day," James Brown, *Foundations of Funk* (CD), 1996. Courtesy of Universal Music Enterprises, a division of Universal Music Group.

Albert Goldman, "Does He Teach Us the Meaning of 'Black Is Beautiful?'," *The New York Times*, June 9, 1968. Copyright by Albert Goldman. Reprinted by permission of SLL/Sterling Lord Literistic, Inc.

Chuck D, "January, 1968," James Brown, *Funk Power* (CD), 1996. Courtesy of Universal Music Enterprises, a division of Universal Music Group.

Mel Ziegler, "James Brown Sells His Soul," *The Miami Herald*, August 18, 1968. Reprinted by permission of the publisher.

David Brackett, "Super Bad" from *Interpreting Popular Music* by David Brackett. Reprinted by permission of The University of California Press.

Alan Leeds, "From the Inside," James Brown, *Star Time* (CD), 1991. Courtesy of Universal Music Enterprises, a division of Universal Music Group.

Ray Brack, "James Brown: 'The Man' vs. 'Negroes'," *Rolling Stone*, January 21, 1970. © Rolling Stone LLC 1970. All rights reserved. Reprinted by permission.

Alan Leeds, "Take It to the Bridge," James Brown, *Funk Power* (CD), 1996. Courtesy of Universal Music Enterprises, a division of Universal Music Group.

Juan Rodriguez, "I Have Two Selves and One Is Black," *The Montreal Star*, July 18, 1970. © Juan Rodriguez, 1970. By permission of the author.

Philip Norman, "Mister Messiah," *The Sunday Times Magazine* (London), March 7, 1971. Reprinted by permission of the publisher.

About the Authors

Nelson George, author and filmmaker, has written seven previous nonfiction books and five novels, and has received two SCAP-Deems Taylor Awards, a Grammy, and the American Book Award from the Before Columbus Foundation for *Elevating the Game* and *Hip Hop America*. He has also twice been a finalist for the National Book Critics Circle Award.

He is cowriter of the films *Strictly Business*, starring Halle Berry, and *CB4*, with Chris Rock, who also starred. George served as executive producer on HBO Films' *Everyday People* and as a consulting producer on HBO's Emmy-winning *The Chris Rock Show*. He has directed several short films, including *To Be a Black Man*, narrated by Samuel L. Jackson. Most recently he wrote and directed the award-winning HBO film *Life Support* starring Queen Latifah.

Nelson is a lifelong resident of Brooklyn, New York.

Alan Leeds was born in Queens, New York. His early passion for soul music and jazz led to a position as a teenage deejay at WANT Radio in Richmond, Virginia, where Leeds met and befriended such stars as Otis Redding, Curtis Mayfield, and James Brown. After studying journalism at Pittsburgh's Point Park College, Leeds joined James Brown Productions in 1969, first as a publicist and then as Brown's tour director until 1974.

A lengthy career as a tour manager included stints with Kool and the Gang, Bootsy's Rubber Band, Harold Melvin and the Blue Notes, Barry White, Maxwell, and Prince. From 1989 to 1992 Leeds ran Prince's Paisley Park Records, a joint venture with Warner Brothers. From 2000 to 2005 Leeds managed rising soul star D'Angelo, and in 2008 his years on the road continue as production-tour manager for Chris Rock's groundbreaking *No Apologies* world tour.

Since 1992 Leeds has also served as a consultant to Universal Music, coproducing an extensive series of James Brown compilations and reissues, writing liner notes, and contributing images from his vast archive of Brown memorabilia. In 1992 Leeds won a Grammy along with Brown, Nelson George, Universal executive Harry Weinger, and British writer Cliff White for the liner notes to the Brown *Star Time* box set.